ADVANCES IN
CHINESE INDUSTRIAL STUDIES

Volume 5 • 1997

A COMING OF AGE: DEVELOPMENTS IN SINO-FOREIGN JOINT VENTURES

ADVANCES IN CHINESE INDUSTRIAL STUDIES

A COMING OF AGE: DEVELOPMENTS IN SINO-FOREIGN JOINT VENTURES

Series Editor: NIGEL CAMPBELL
China Research Unit
Manchester Business School

Volume Editors: SALLY STEWART
ANNE CARVER
The University of Hong Kong

VOLUME 5 • 1997

JAI PRESS INC.

Greenwich, Connecticut *London, England*

55 Old Post Road No. 2
Greenwich, Connecticut 06830

JAI PRESS LTD.
38 Tavistock Street
Covent Garden
London WC2E 7PB
England

ISBN: 1-55938-961-3

Manufactured in the United States of America

CONTENTS

ACKNOWLEDGMENTS

Support from the Research Grants Council of the Hong Kong University Grants Committee made this volume possible and is most gratefully acknowledged.

The editors are once again indebted to Kathryn Wolfendale for her expert assistance and hard work and to their families for their patience and support.

Sally Stewart
Anne Carver
Volume Editors

PART I

INTRODUCTION

RECENT DEVELOPMENTS IN UNDERSTANDING SINO-FOREIGN JOINT VENTURES

Sally Stewart and Anne Carver

INTRODUCTION

This collection of papers has been designed to build on the findings of Volume 4 in the series *Advances in Chinese Industrial Studies* and to gather together some of the findings of research undertaken since Volume 4 was compiled.

This volume reflects the increasing sophistication of contemporary approaches to the study of joint ventures in the People's Republic of China (PRC) and gathered here are perspectives ranging from the historical to economic, ethical, and sociological approaches. These diverse viewpoints are intended to enhance understanding of the wide range of issues and problems confronting all involved in Sino-foreign joint ventures.

RECENT DEVELOPMENTS IN FOREIGN INVESTMENT

It is now almost 20 years since China made the radical decision to open its doors once again to foreign investment, to invite foreign investment, and to

Advances in Chinese Industrial Studies, Volume 5, pages 3-11.

ISBN: 1-55938-961-3

encourage foreign companies to enter China as partners in China's technical development and managerial reform.

The so-called open-door and reform policies have now been in existence for so long that they are taken for granted, but when they were introduced in 1976 they were so radical as to seem almost counterrevolutionary in nature. The decision to borrow money from capitalist sources was a major reversal of the post-1949 policies which had been based on such ideas as "China will stand up, on its own feet," and the determination that the country should owe nothing to foreigners, but pay its way by trade, and no longer be exploited by foreigners. Moreover, the notion of paying significant interest for deposits was for capitalists, not for good socialists. The whole concept of borrowing had, since the revolution, been anathema, one reeking with overtones of foreign exploitation; it was part of the capitalist system categorized by Marxists as exploitation, profiting from the labor of the people, but additionally in China it was also seen in the context of national humiliation by the West and by Japan since the early nineteenth century.

Thus the decision to couple appeals for foreign investment with appeals for foreign participation in China's industry was extraordinary. This bold unexpected invitation to foreigners to make a profit by investing directly or indirectly in China was a sharp departure from the view, traditionally held by Chinese policymakers throughout the nineteenth century and after, that China should use Western technology (*yong*) but try to prevent Western spirit (*ti*) and philosophy from impinging on Chinese culture.

Thus it seemed to many foreign observers in the 1970s, particularly after the 10-year disaster of the Cultural Revolution, that China's new open-door and reform policies were so radically different from the earlier years of Marxist-Leninist-Maoist policies and from Chinese historical attitudes, that they might be short-lived and indeed might hardly live at all in the bureaucratic soil of a socialist state where profit for many years had been a dirty word. The historical precedents gave little ground for optimism: Japan's rapid full-scale embrace of Western technology in the nineteenth century had enabled her by the end of the century to blow the Russian fleet out of the water. China's embrace, however, had always been halfhearted, and as much time had been spent on worrying about the infiltration of the Western spirit as upon the effective adoption and adaptation of the new technology.

By the mid 1980s, however, only the most cynical observers doubted the seriousness of China's purpose in advocating and implementing these new policies and, had it not been for the tragic events of 1989 (Tian An Men) the development of foreign investment, direct and indirect, into Chinese industry would have been a remarkable continuous upward line. Even 1989 produced little more than a hiccup in the line. Chinese officials had been reeducated to accept that profit was not a dirty word and foreign JVs were actually making profits.

In the aftermath of the events of Tian An Men, the received wisdom in the West, fortified by revulsion for the suppression of the demonstrators, was that little more than a decade after the formal opening and announcement of reform, the Chinese door had closed again. In fact, of course, the door remained open for economic purposes: the doorway had never been intended to be used for the promotion of Western ideas such as political science, human rights, or religion. Although there was a pause in foreign investment figures, this was momentary and caused by Western reaction, whether government, academic, media, or business. Asian governments were less critical of the Chinese government's handling of the demonstration. A tendency in Asia to give priority to order, with law and human rights coming second, and no doubt a feeling of sympathy for a fellow Asian government under severe media assault by the West, muted Asian criticism of the Tian An Men affair. The overseas Chinese investment continued almost unaffected.

Another factor no doubt entered into the Asian decision to continue to invest: their assessments of the risk in China. These were not the same as those of Western analysts. The West swung from optimism to pessimism, with many boards questioning their decision to seek opportunities in China, and calling a halt to expansion or entry into China while the situation was reassessed. Long before the writing of this book and its predecessor, however, Tian An Men had ceased to be a significant factor in Western business plan analyses, and the question of investment is once more subjected to commercial rather than political analysis.

There are three "overseas" Chinese facets of interest in this context. These are the three Little Dragons: Hong Kong, Taiwan, and Singapore. The performance of Hong Kong, populated largely by Hans, Cantonese, and Shanghainese, has led the field and heavy investment continues, particularly in neighboring Guangdong, especially in real estate, manufacturing, and sometimes in BOT (Build-Operate-Transfer) projects, preponderantly in manufacturing. Taiwan, although a late starter, has fed copious investment into the mainland, and not only into Fujian Province, geographically and linguistically its closest provincial partner.

In Singapore, unlike Hong Kong and Taiwan, there is no political overlay and sensitivity about ultimate Chinese sovereignty: Singapore is indubitably an independent sovereign state. Investment in China has been vigorously promoted by the Singapore government, leading, for example, to a major project to build a new city at Suzhou and the constant attendance of senior Singapore Chinese as advisers to the Chinese government.

None of these activities by "overseas" Chinese seems to have been significantly affected by the political crosswinds of the post-1989 period, and private investment continues.

Meanwhile, Western academic studies of joint ventures have, for reasons that are perhaps self-evident, tended to concentrate on reviewing the experience of Sino-foreign joint ventures where the foreign partner has been a non-Han. The partnerships consisting of "overseas" and "compact" Chinese in the three Little Dragons have scarcely been tackled.

In so far as the broader issues, such as confidence in China's political economy and ability to navigate the shoals of *guanxi* (reciprocal connections) are concerned, it has been generally assumed that the overseas Han investor will be on the inside track culturally and linguistically, and will not share the basic cross-cultural problems of the non-Han investor. This has often proved an erroneous assumption, but this aspect of the scene has been little studied in the West, while the Chinese academic world has tended to avoid controversial topics and stick rather to descriptive work and macroeconomic effects.

Today the figures for foreign investment suggest that foreign business people have become used to the possibility of industrial and commercial investment in China, whether through equity joint ventures, contractual joint ventures, wholly foreign-owned ventures, or BOT (Build-Operate-Transfer) and BOO (Build-Operate-Own) projects. It might be said that the JV and its derivatives have come of age in China.

The genre has been the subject of voluminous research both inside and outside China and many of the problems of joint ventures have been aired, but joint ventures continue to merit academic as well as practitioners' attention. The subject continues to be of importance worldwide, if only because the lessons of the past are so often ignored by the practitioners, be they government officials or business people.

OVERVIEW OF CONTENTS

Volume 4 in the series *Advances in Chinese Industrial Studies* (1994) was based on papers prepared for a conference on joint ventures held at the University of Hong Kong in 1992. This volume is based on papers prepared for another conference on the same subject held in 1996 in Hong Kong. As on the previous occasion, the authors represent a wide spectrum: apart from Hong Kong, they come from China, the United States, and Europe. The topics chosen are wide-ranging. There are 18 papers, looking in some detail at developments in JV fields.

The conference, like its predecessor, was fortunate to have the personal encouragement of the then Vice-Chancellor, Professor Wang Gungwu, a renowned historian, and several of the points made in his Preface to the 1994 volume seem worth repeating:

a. Has pragmatism replaced ideology in China?
b. Have the contributions of the JVs to changes in the economy been significant?
c. Will the experience of JV managers rub off on bureaucratic managers?

The present collection, written not by historians but by students of management, does not aspire to answer these questions but throws some shafts of light on the subjects; each demands detailed attention.

Peter Ping Li's paper on the unique nature of international joint ventures in China is as much a commentary on differing Asian-Western cultural perspectives as it is on Chinese-Western differences. The paper revisits the whole topic of different attitudes to business: trust taking priority over legalism, the group over the individual, consensus over confrontation. All these differences, as well as the special environment of the Chinese socialist market economy, can affect the smooth running of a Sino-foreign JV. Dr. Li pleads for a paradigm shift in research on the Sino-foreign JV. He studied eight cases in order to come to a conclusion about the factors and processes of JV formation. He found that foreign partners' main objective was to gain access to the Chinese market, but no clear picture emerged from his study about power sharing.

Judith Hollows's historical essay is a clear and concise account of the relations between Japanese and Chinese cotton textile manufacturers in China between 1912 and 1937. After a chronological narrative she explores the reasons for the domination of the industry by the Japanese and the nature of the Chinese response. The analysis illuminates some of the historical roots of current Chinese reactions to joint ventures. She ascribes Japanese success to superior machinery, information gathering, distribution, and access to capital. She then demonstrates how the varied nature of reorganization in Chinese-owned mills was conditioned by social roles, capital regulations, management practices, and the influence of the states and the treaty ports. The essay suggests that a further historical approach to JVs could be conducive to clarification of management problems in China today.

Elizabeth Li's paper on marital discord gives a lively account of the differences likely to arise between partners, reflecting, less gently, the points made in the Beijing papers. The paper centers on a case study of an alliance in Guangdong between an Asian multinational and a state enterprise: the case illustrates all the basic, expected clashes of culture. Perhaps the most important ingredient of this paper is the personal involvement of the writer, a management consultant, from inception to implementation of the JV. The study provides clear evidence that the Asianness of the foreign partner is no cure-all for the culture clash between capitalist and socialist society. The familiar power struggle dominates the scene, and differing cultures, trust, and organization design have been root problems. The paper rightly concludes that the prospects for success will be significantly enhanced if an understanding of principles is established before the partners contract to "marry."

Zheng and Abeele's examination of cultural problems deals with the cultural divide and concludes, perhaps too optimistically, that the differences are part of the strengths of a joint venture, if both partners can find a common basis for profitable operations, regardless of the policies of distant headquarters. They rightly remark that such a melding of culture requires key skills.

Yuan Lu and his colleagues have produced a useful follow-up on their previous work in the joint venture field. The paper looks at the difficulties and conflicts encountered in 67 sample JVs, and is particularly useful because it covers the views of both expatriate and Chinese managers. It identifies three main causes of difficulty, two of which are internal: inter-partner relations and HR problems such as communication and skill levels. The other main difficulty lies in the Chinese environment. The paper notes such problems as the difficulty of effective market research, and immaturity of marketing concepts. Institutional difficulties are similar to those encountered in the Eastern European environment.

The paper presented by Director Chen of the International Technology and Economy Institute provides a useful official overview of the development of foreign investment in China, and China's policies, past, present, and future. The paper reminds us of the state's priorities and the evolutionary process, moving from a tolerant acceptance of foreign investment in low technology in the early days of "opening," to more stringent and more selective criteria today, and moving from secondary to tertiary industry. His guidelines for the future include clear advice to consider the inland provinces, but give little indication on specific special incentives by way of concessions to investors in order to induce them to enter the less convenient hinterland.

Lindholm addresses, exceptionally and usefully, the specific issue of learning processes. The paper sets out an interesting typology of transfer, transformation, and harvesting. The study notes the problem that if the HR manager in a joint venture comes from the Chinese side there may be serious favoritism, ignoring objective tests and interviews. It also points to the benefit of recruiting youngsters who have not had time to learn bad habits in the old system, and to the danger of employing overseas Chinese, who have a tendency to job hop. Production functions are more easily transferred, but not necessarily without problems, particularly in the context of delegating responsibility. The paper is critical of "old China hands" whose cynicism around the bar is dangerous, and of the lack of training of expatriates before being posted to their joint venture.

Björkman and Lu's paper provides a useful overview of developments and problems in the HR field. The paper notes that the need for training has been addressed by large multinationals by setting up in-house schools, and increasing effort and resource into training, which includes postings to overseas offices. Recruitment poses a general problem and so does "poaching," which cannot be satisfactorily prevented by constraints in contracts, or by increasing salaries. Housing can help. Some Chinese employees now seek faster career progress than is customary in a Western MNC. Tensions continue to exist because parent Chinese organizations will not easily relinquish their grasp over staff recruitment. Many larger MNCs have recognized the central importance of the HR function and are pooling knowledge by bringing together HR managers from all their foreign invested enterprises. The study suggests that the gulf between FIEs in China and foreign headquarters remains difficult to bridge, but exchange of experience and knowledge improves within China itself. The conclusion is that Chinese HR practices are gradually becoming more like HR practices in the West.

In his forceful piece, Orlan Lee questions China's claim to be a social democracy. Exploring many of the facets of apparent exploitation of Chinese labor and corrupt practices by the West, he suggests that focus on the moral responsibility of the multinational has concealed the guilt of South Korean, Hong Kong, and Taiwanese manufacturers. He also argues that corruption in China cannot merely be seen as the result of low official wages, which he sees as comparatively high. He claims, after an examination of what he describes as the "enviable start" of the 1994 Labor Law toward the betterment of workers' conditions, that the law is not being enforced. He concludes that the PRC is far from adhering to the moral or welfare norms of democratic socialism in the West.

Following his seminal article on industrial relations in Volume 4, Dr. Ng Sek-Hong expands on the paradoxes and ambiguities inherent in labor relations in joint ventures. His discussion is placed in the context of historical xenophobia, contemporary legal practice, ethnic differences, issues of class consciousness, and modern human resource theory. From these perspectives he explores both the positive and negative consequences of foreign capital on Chinese labor and the response to these two facets both in Chinese legislation and in the development of the All-China Federation of Trade Unions. The ACFTU, he argues, has evolved into a body with three separate roles: a friendly ambassador to foreign firms, a chairperson of its labor force, and a representative of worker grievances. He concludes that the challenge facing Chinese trade unions is simultaneously to allay the fears of foreign businesses and to improve conditions for Chinese labor, and argues that the AFCTU can best achieve this through adopting an Asian consensual style of negotiation.

Yanni Yan provides a timely paper on the effects of ownership on performance: she pursues the thesis that the configuration of ownership has a significant effect on performance. The validity of the thesis is tested by a study of 67 Sino-foreign JVs, where share of ownership seems to correlate with commitment and therefore with resource input. The paper accepts, however, that a precise measurement of performance is difficult to achieve; to this extent the thesis requires further testing, although it seems entirely reasonable to pinpoint the need for foreign commitment. But many other factors impact on performance.

The paper on joint venture performance in Shanghai by Clement Chow and Michael Fung concludes that the Chinese government policies on joint ventures are "paying off," that Shanghai is successful in attracting important investment, and that the JVs are profitable. The attempt to calculate profitability is laudable, and rare indeed. The paper underlines the impressive performance of JVs when compared with the lamentable record of many state enterprises and concludes, contrary to anecdotal comment, that in Shanghai at least JVs are doing well in terms of profitability, whether technically advanced or not.

C.S. Tseng's paper on retail and distribution channels details how these systems have changed through reform in recent years, and the various opportunities for foreign investment in this sector.

Dr. Danming Lin's paper is a welcome addition to the meager literature on joint ventures with Hong Kong partners and points up differences between these JVs and those with Western partners, which form the bulk of the literature on Sino-foreign JVs, although the majority of Sino-foreign JVs are in fact those with Hong Kong partners. Dr. Lin's hypothesis is important: Hong Kong investors are looking for cheap production and do not have the same priorities as their Chinese counterparts. The list of priorities for each partner is quite different except for "exploring favorable policies." Dr. Lin reminds us how much work is required to research the Sino-foreign JV with Hong Kong partners. The paper finds that Hong Kong partners are looking further for cheap production, but there seems to be no indication that rising costs in China are persuading Hong Kong Chinese to look outside China for cheap labor and land. Not surprisingly, *guanxi* (connections) is for Hong Kong investors an important reason for cooperation in a JV in China. The paper confirms that Chinese partners tend, understandably and predictably, to take a parochial view of the benefits of JVs, rather than a view dominated by central policy objectives. Maximization of dividends does not seem to be a top priority for either partner. The study concludes that in Guangdong local rather than national considerations dominate the agenda of both partners, but these findings may be specific to Guangdong Province.

Zhang Shiquan's paper gives a useful reminder of the problems of the twin partners in the joint venture marriage bed, dreaming different dreams, and answering to parents with different objectives. The foreign partner wants market share and long-term position, the Chinese partner wants socialist system reform, while maintaining allegiance to social obligations. Although his description of different perspectives and priorities is not new, it is useful to have in Western literature the evidence that a Chinese research institute has come to the same conclusion.

Liping Deng's paper on foreign investment contrasts the joint venture with the B-share market as instruments available for the foreign investor. The paper concludes that although the government should continue to encourage the B-share market, and the foreign investor should not ignore it, the market still has many problems and the JV method may for the time being be more reliable than the stock market method.

Yu-min Chou's paper on the conglomeration of Chinese enterprises is not strictly about joint ventures but about China's alternative routes to modernization, and to foreign exposure. These routes include the formation of conglomerates, privatization, and acquisition. In 1991 China's State Council approved the formation of 55 conglomerates, mostly in the field of manufacturing. The transfer of assets has been facilitated by the establishment of Asset Transfer Centers. The paper concludes that privatization will be slow in China because state enterprises are much more than businesses: they are also welfare organizations. Unlike the Japanese *keiretsu* groups, the Chinese conglomerate has room for foreign investment: they are still in a state of flux.

The paper on the consequences of change for joint ventures by de Bruijn and his colleagues makes some interesting points about the evolution of the Sino-foreign joint venture, from relatively primitive beginnings to the sophisticated form it takes today. Quality is overtaking *guanxi* as a major success factor. It also points to the changing climate in China, where some of the participants in the 6.4 event (Tian An Men) are now likely to be successful business people. The paper describes types of fake JVs set up basically to earn tax concessions, and the government's intention to tackle this problem. The paper estimates that in 1993 one-third of JVs were "fake," but now less than 10 percent can be so labeled.

THE UNIQUE NATURE OF INTERNATIONAL JOINT VENTURES IN THE PEOPLE'S REPUBLIC OF CHINA:

IMPLICATIONS FOR THEORY-BUILDING WITH REGARD TO STRATEGIC ALLIANCES

Peter Ping Li

INTRODUCTION

The joint venture, especially in its international form, is an increasingly popular type of strategic alliance that has received rapidly growing attention from scholars of management, but there has been little theory-building of strategic alliances in general and joint ventures in particular (see Borys and Jemison 1989; Contractor and Lorange 1988; Harrigan 1988; Kogut 1988; Lyons 1991; Parkhe 1993; Tallman and Shenkar 1994; Yoshino and Rangan 1995). This problem is clearly reflected in the study of international joint ventures (IJVs) in the People's Republic of China (PRC), known as Sino-foreign joint ventures (SFJVs) (see Beamish 1993; Child 1994; Yan and Gray 1994). In addition to the common problems associated with the study of IJVs in general, there are

Advances in Chinese Industrial Studies, Volume 5, pages 13-34.

ISBN: 1-55938-961-3

specific problems unique to the study of SFJVs, such as the critical linkages between them and economic reform in the PRC as well as the potential gap between the extant theories in the West and the unique practice in China.

The purpose of this paper is twofold: first, it is an effort to expand the research on SFJVs by incorporating the literature of economic reform (i.e., the transition from a centrally planned economy to a market-oriented economy; see, for instance, Walder 1995) with research on IJVs in order to explore the interactive link between IJVs and economic reform in China. Second, this paper is an attempt to facilitate theory-building with regard to strategic alliances and joint ventures by interpreting the evidence of SFJVs within the unique context of the PRC from a Chinese perspective that challenges the Western paradigm (see Biggart and Hamilton 1992; Earley 1993; Li 1996; Oi 1995; Putterman 1995; Whyte 1995).

Following the calls for more case studies on joint ventures (Parkhe 1993) and better theoretical guidance for case studies (Yin 1989), this research began with a theoretical framework integrating the literature of IJVs and economic reform in general and the SFJV and economic reform in China in particular. Comparative induction was used to analyze, largely from the Chinese perspective, eight SFJVs: one with a state-owned partner, three with urban-collective partners, three with rural-collective partners, and one with a private partner. The findings of these case studies were then applied to the development of a conceptual framework of strategic alliances in general and joint ventures in particular to produce a complete and consistent paradigm of organization that bridges the cultures of the West and the East.

LITERATURE REVIEW

In this section an attempt is made to integrate the differing views found in the literature concerning IJVs and economic reform in order to emerge with a process-oriented framework for exploring the linkage between IJVs and economic reform. Against this framework we can examine the SFJV case studies, within the unique context of the PRC from the Chinese perspective.

IJVs in General and IJVs in China in Particular

Despite the growing popularity of research on strategic alliances and joint ventures, there has been little theory-building (see Parkhe 1993; Ring and Van de Ven 1994; Tallman and Shenkar 1994). No strong theoretical justification for strategic alliances and joint ventures has emerged (cf. Harrigan 1988; Hennart 1991; Kogut 1988; Lyons 1991; Yoshino and Rangan 1995; Tallman and Shenkar 1994). There is no accepted conceptualization of strategic alliance or joint venture (cf. Borys and Jemison 1989; Contractor and Lorange 1988;

Lyons 1991; Yoshino and Rangan 1995) nor the linkage between control and performance (cf. Beamish 1988; Geringer and Hebert 1989, 1991; Killing 1983; Shenkar 1990). And there is no integrated theoretical framework for strategic alliances and joint ventures (cf. Parkhe 1993; Ring and Van de Ven 1994; Tallman and Shenkar 1994). Ambiguity, bias, and controversy abound and persist (Parkhe 1993; Tallman and Shenkar 1994). These problems are not confined to the study of strategic alliances and joint ventures nor limited to the issue of research methodology since they are common to the whole field of organization study and are rooted in Western ontology and epistemology of organizations. The bias inherent in the Western approach is rendering it increasingly obsolete (Li 1995, 1996; cf. Child 1994; Parkhe 1993).

These problems are reflected in the study of the SFJV (see Beamish 1993; Child 1994; Yan and Gray 1994). In addition to the problems common to the study of joint ventures in general, there are other problems unique to the study of SFJVs. For instance, though many studies have been done to show how economic reform in China has stimulated a proliferation of IJVs in the past decade, or how foreign investors should take advantage of the opportunities created by reform in China (e.g., Campbell 1988; Luo 1995; Newman 1992; Osland and Cavusgil 1996; Pan, Vanhonacker, and Pitts 1995; Shan 1991; Yan and Gray 1994), there is little research on how joint ventures have in themselves affected economic reform in the PRC.

IJVs were initially experiments with restructuring ownership or property rights in state-owned and collectively owned Chinese firms. They were role models for Chinese firms to emulate. They provided training centers for market-oriented and globally minded managers and they became strong competitors to compel Chinese firms toward reform (cf. Lardy 1995). Little research has been conducted on how to manage SFJVs from the Chinese perspective (for more balanced views, see Child 1994; Pearson 1991; Von Glinow and Teagarden 1988). With the exception of the traditional benefits of IJVs for developing transitional economies in the form of access to capital, technology, export market, and managerial skill (see Beamish 1988; Newman 1992), the study of the SFJV has been silent on the effect of ownership structure by Chinese partners on these enterprises (e.g., Beamish 1993; Child 1994; Pearson 1991). Most scholars focus on those SFJVs whose Chinese partners are state-owned firms. There is virtually no comparative study of joint ventures whose partners are state-owned, collectively owned, privately owned, and mixed-owned Chinese firms. Further, there is no study of the possible effects of different ownership structures by Chinese partners upon SFJVs (cf. Putterman 1995). In summary, the study of SFJVs has not been directly linked to that of economic reform in China, and SFJVs have not been analyzed within the unique context of China's economic reform.

In addition to the unique aspect of China as a transitional economy, it is also an Eastern Asian nation that shares many characteristics of all Eastern

Asian nations that differ fundamentally from those of the West (Biggart and Hamilton 1992; Oi 1995; Putterman 1995; Whitley 1992; Whyte 1995). The cultural aspect of SFJVs has been largely neglected in research (e.g., Beamish 1993; Shenkar 1990; also see Child 1994). The unique culture of Chinese management is most evident in China's pattern of economic reform (see Rawski 1995; Walder 1995). The success of China's economic reform has become an intriguing anomaly (Walder 1995), which challenges the Western paradigm and suggests an Eastern paradigm (e.g., Oi 1995; Putterman 1995; Whyte 1995). Consequently, various aspects of China's economic reform now figure prominently in academic analyses, ranging from theories of the firm and property rights to the political foundations of economic growth (Walder 1995, p. 963). However, the existing study of SFJVs has failed to incorporate this critical aspect into its domain of analysis. The study of the SFJV has not been directly linked with that of the Chinese culture, therefore SFJVs have not been analyzed in the context of Chinese culture.

The Need for a Paradigm Shift

In order to resolve the problems of IJV research we need to do two things. First, we need to expand the research of strategic alliances and SFJVs by integrating IJV literature with economic reform (ER) literature in order to explore the interactive link between IJVs and ER. Two interactions are most salient: (1) the effect of IJVs on the managerial behaviors of firms in ER; and (2) the effect of managerial behaviors of various local partners, with different ownership structures, on the operation of joint ventures in ER. Second, we need to facilitate theory-building with regard to strategic alliances and joint ventures on the basis of a complete and consistent paradigm of organization that bridges the cultures of both West and East. To this end, we need to study SFJVs within the unique context of the PRC from a Chinese perspective that will seriously challenge the Western paradigm. From the Chinese perspective, one can argue that the strategic alliance is a distinct form of organization that defies the extant paradigm of organization and requires a paradigm shift. Since the extant paradigm is embedded in the cultural peculiarities of the West, particularly the United States (Biggart and Hamilton 1992; Hofstede 1993; Lincoln 1990; Redding and Whitley 1990), the Eastern paradigm is essential to facilitate the required paradigm shift (Li 1996).

Two elements constitute a paradigm derived by a particular community of researchers or practitioners: an ontology of the nature of the subject matter and an epistemology of the mode of cognition (Kuhn 1970). The extant paradigm of organization in the West is based on an ethnocentric ontology of human nature whereby humans are homogeneous, simple, individualistic, and evil in nature. The Western epistemology is parochial with regard to cognition mode whereby logical consistency is absolute and sufficient for cognition. The Eastern paradigm of organization is based on a geocentric ontology of human nature whereby humans are diverse, complex, social, and paradoxical in nature. The Eastern epistemology is cosmopolitan with regard to cognition mode whereby logical paradox is essential for cognition (Li 1995 1996). Many Western norms, such as discrete private property rights and impersonal control by rational authority, are under serious challenge by Eastern notions of stakeholders' rights and personal trust in multidimensional social networks (Biggart and Hamilton 1992; Earley 1993; Li 1996; Lincoln 1990; Oi 1995; Redding and Whitley 1990; Sampson 1988; Triandis, Bontempo, Villareal, Asai, and Lucca 1988; Whitley 1992; Whyte 1995). In summary, the applicability of the extant paradigm embedded in Western culture is challenged by the unique context of the PRC as a transitional economy with an Eastern culture.

A Process-Oriented Framework for IJV Study

Having argued for a shift in the Western paradigm of organization, the next issue is where to start such a shift. According to the ancient Chinese art of war, the most vulnerable spot of the enemy is the best target for an attack. The most vulnerable spot of the Western paradigm is its static nature, therefore, the paradigm shift starts by introducing the element of dynamic process into the Western paradigm. Given the ethnocentric ontology and parochial epistemology of the Western paradigm, it is no surprise that little scholarly attention has been devoted to studying the *developmental* processes of strategic alliances and joint ventures despite the centrality of the process to both the study and practice of these enterprises (Ring and Van de Ven 1994, p. 91). There is no widely accepted conceptual framework for studying the process of developing strategic alliances and joint ventures (cf. Harrigan 1988; Larson 1992; Ring and Van de Ven 1994). However, a framework may be constructed by integrating the diverse models from a process perspective.

The development of joint ventures can be modeled as a double-loop process whereby an overall loop of development consists of four phases: initiation (birth), trial (growth), consolidation (maturity), and adjustment (death or rebirth). A specific loop of joint venture development is a repetitive sequence of negotiation and execution in interaction with every other phase across the overall loop. Interrelated and interdependent as they are, the two loops are distinct (cf. Larson 1992; Ring and Van de Ven 1994).

Some preconditions are required for the development of joint ventures. Four preconditions are critical: (1) the existence of a *necessity* for certain transactions; (2) the existence of high *uncertainty* that renders both price and authority ineffective as a mode to coordinate those transactions; (3) the existence of parties with an *ability* to match their different needs with those transactions—a potential shared interest; and (4) the existence of *goodwill* among all the parties to entertain the prospect of cooperation—turning a potential shared interest into a real one (Contractor and Lorange 1988; Harrigan 1988; Kogut 1988; Larson 1992; Mayer, Davis, and Schoorman 1995; Ring and Van de Ven 1994).

Once these preconditions are in place, the process of joint venture development will begin. The first phase of development is *initiation*, in which firms begin to crystallize their strategic objectives, select potential partners based on their estimated ability and integrity, negotiate the terms of cooperation, and establish the joint venture. The second phase is *trial*, in which partners begin to clarify their expectations, adapt to their routines, institutionalize tentative procedures, and build an initial mutual trust. The third phase is *consolidation*, in which partners begin to build up their mutual trust and integrate their operation at strategic levels. The fourth phase is *adjustment*, in which partners begin to reevaluate and, if necessary, reconfigure their relationships in accordance with changes in shared interest and trustworthiness in terms of rational trust, moral trust, and affective trust (Harrigan 1988; Larson 1992; Mayer, Davis, and Schoorman 1995; Ring and Van de Ven 1994).

Applying the above framework to the SFJV we can specify the unique features of these ventures in terms of preconditions and developmental processes, as compared with the norm in the West. It is expected that the process of developing SFJVs will be difficult and different due to the large gap in institutional routines and cultural norms.

CASE STUDIES

Method

Following the development of the above conceptual framework, eight case studies of SFJVs were analyzed. Several factors were considered in selecting the cases: (1) cases were limited to manufacturing ventures because they make up the bulk of SFJVs; (2) ventures had to be considered successful by both foreign and Chinese partners; (3) only those ventures that were the *first* SFJV to both Chinese and foreign partners were included; and (4) in order to have a representative sample, cases were selected from across the spectrums of industrial sector, ownership structure of Chinese partner, ownership structure of joint venture, geographical location of joint venture in China, national origin of foreign partner, size of both partner companies, size of venture, bargaining power of both partners, control structure of joint venture, and age of joint venture (see Table 1).

Information on the ventures was collected from archives; approximately 15 pages of data were collected for each venture, including published case descriptions and newspaper and magazine reports about the venture, and coded

Table 1. Profiles of the Selected Sino-Foreign Joint Ventures

	Venture 1	*Venture 2*	*Venture 3*	*Venture 4*	*Venture 5*	*Venture 6*	*Venture 7*	*Venture 8*
Industry Sector of JV	Food Processing	Computer Peripheral	Electronic Product	Fishing Product	Textile Garment	Electronic Part	Telecom. Product	Plastic Product
Ownership Structure of Chinese Partner	Rural Private	Urban Collective-Private	Rural Collective-Foreign	Rural Collective	Rural Collective	Urban Collective-State	Urban Collective-State	Urban State
Equity Share of Chinese Partner	55%	75%	30%	50%	70%	50%	75%	75%
Location of JV in China	Sichuan	Beijing	Guangdong	Shandong	Shandong	Shanghai	Shanghai	Zhejiang
National Origin of Foreign Partner	U.S.A.	Japan	Italy	South Korea	Hong Hong	Japan	U.S.A.	Taiwan
Size of Foreign Partner	Medium	Large	Medium	Small	Small	Medium	Small	Small
Size of Chinese Partner	Large	Large	Medium	Small	Small	Small	Small	Large
Size of JV	Medium	Large	Medium	Medium	Small	Small	Small	Medium
Bargaining Power of Foreign Partner	Medium	Medium	Medium	Medium	Medium	Medium	Medium	Low
Bargaining Power of Chinese Partner	Medium	Medium	Medium	Medium	Medium	Medium	Medium	High
Control Ocus of JV	Both	Chinese	Foreign	Both	Both	Both	Chinese	Chinese
Year of JV Formation	1993	1987	1994	1991	1989	1987	1991	1992

using typical content analysis procedures (Yin 1989) and analyzed into various categories in accordance with the proposed conceptual framework. The three levels of analysis were: (1) the meta-level: preconditions and the four phases of development process (initiation, trial, consolidation, and adjustment); (2) the sublevel: elements of all the above meta-categories (necessity of transaction; uncertainty of transaction; ability for transaction; goodwill for transaction; objective of cooperation; partner cooperation; negotiation of cooperation; establishment of cooperation; clarification of expectation; development of adaptation; development of routine; development of trust; solidification of trust; integration of strategy; reevaluation of relationship; and reconfiguration of relationship; (3) the base level: fundamental elements of all the above subcategories (negotiation and execution).

The method used in analyzing the cases was analytic induction (e.g., Yan and Gray 1994). One case was analyzed and results compared with the proposed conceptual framework. The framework was then modified in view of the findings from the first case. This comparative process was repeated for each successive case, as called for by some scholars (e.g., Parkhe 1993).

Results

The final revision of the proposed conceptual framework is described below, together with the common characteristics of all eight cases according to the proposed framework (see Table 2). Specific features of certain cases are included because of their relevance to further discussion.

Preconditions of JV Development

In all eight cases the four critical preconditions of the proposed framework mentioned above were identified, and found to be highly significant for the formation of the SFJVs. This finding confirms the theoretical prediction that four preconditions, that is, necessity, uncertainty, ability, and goodwill, are necessary and sufficient to start the process of forming a joint venture, which may or may not result in the actual establishment of a joint venture. Put differently, these four preconditions are necessary but insufficient for the formation of a joint venture; the actual formation of a joint venture will depend on whether parties complete the initiation phase of joint venture development.

Initiation Phase

The data analysis supported the proposition of the conceptual framework that the formation of a joint venture results from a successful initiation phase. This phase contains four major components: (1) definition of strategic objectives; (2) selection of potential partners; (3) negotiation of cooperative

Table 2. The Developmental Process of Sino-Foreign Joint Ventures

	Venture 1	*Venture 2*	*Venture 3*	*Venture 4*	*Venture 5*	*Venture 6*	*Venture 7*	*Venture 8*
Precondition								
Chinese Side								
Necessity	High	High	High	High	High	High	High	High
Uncertainty	High	High	High	High	High	High	High	High
Ability	High	High	High	High	High	High	High	High
Goodwill	High	High	High	High	High	High	High	High
Foreign Side								
Necessity	High	High	High	High	High	High	High	High
Uncertainty	High	High	High	High	High	High	High	High
Ability	High	High	High	High	High	High	High	High
Goodwill	High	High	High	High	High	High	High	High
Initiation								
Objective								
Need of Chinese Side								
Strategic Importance	Medium	High	High	High	High	High	High	Medium
Process Tech.	High	High	High	Low	High	High	Low	High
Product Tech.	High	High	Low	Low	High	Low	High	Low
Export Market	Low	Low	Medium	High	High	High	Low	Low
Local Market	High	High	High	Low	Low	Low	High	High
Capital	Low	Medium	Low	Medium	Low	Medium	Low	Low
Managerial Skill	Medium	Medium	High	Medium	High	High	Low	Medium
Change in Ownership Structure	Low	High	High	Low	Low	High	High	High
Foreign Material	Low	High	High	Low	High	High	Medium	Low
Need of Foreign Side								
Strategic Importance	High	High	High	High	Medium	High	High	High
Product Tech.	High	High	Low	Low	Low	High	Low	Medium
Export Market	Low	Low	Medium	High	High	High	Low	Low
Local Market	High	High	High	Low	Low	Low	High	High
Capital	Low	Low	Low	Low	High	Low	High	Medium
Managerial Skill	Medium	Medium	Low	Medium	Low	Medium	Medium	Low
Local Material	High	Low	Low	Medium	Medium	Low	Medium	High
Local Labor	Medium	High	High	High	High	High	High	

(continued)

Table 2. (Continued)

	Venture 1	*Venture 2*	*Venture 3*	*Venture 4*	*Venture 5*	*Venture 6*	*Venture 7*	*Venture 8*
Initiation (continued)								
Partner								
View of Chinese Side								
Fit of Foreign Partner	High	High	High	High	High	High	High	High
Alternative Availability	Some	Little	Little	Some	Some	Little	Little	Much
View of Foreign Side								
Fit of Chinese Partner	High	High	High	High	High	High	High	
Alternative Availability	Some	Some	Little	Little	Little	Little	Little	Little
Prior Knowledge	Little	Extensive	Some	Little	Some	Little	Some	Little
Negotiation								
Mode of Control								
Equity Share	Unequal	Unequal	Unequal	Equal	Unmequal	Equal	Unequal	Unequal
Board Member	Unequal	Unequal	Unequal	Unequal	Unmequal	Equal	Unequal	Unequal
Board Chairman	Chinese	Chinese	Foreign	Foreign	Chinese	Chinese	Chinese	Chinese
General Manager	Foreign	Chinese	Foreign	Chinese	Foreign	Foreign	Chinese	Chinese
Locus of Control								
Chinese Parent	Low	Medium	Low	High	Medium	Low	Low	Medium
Foreign Parent	Low	Medium	Medium	High	Low	Low	Low	Low
JV Autonomy	High	Medium	Medium	Low	Medium	High	High	Medium
Domain of Control								
Shared Overall	Medium	High	Low	High	Low	Medium	Low	Low
Chinese Domain	Narrow	Overall	Narrow	Overall	Broad	Broad	Broad	Broad
Foreign Domain	Broad	Overall	Broad	Overall	Narrow	Narrow	Narrow	Narrow
Degree of Difficulty	Easy	Medium	Medium	Easy	Easy	Hard	Easy	Easy
Length of Negotiation	Short	Medium	Medium	Short	Short	Long	Short	Short
Establishment	Yes	Yes	Yes	Yes	Yes	Yes	Yes	Yes

Trial								
Clarification	Fast	Fast	Fast	Fast	Fast	Slow	Fast	Fast
Adaptation	Fast	Medium	Medium	Fast	Fast	Slow	Fast	Slow
Routine Building	Fast	Medium	Medium	Fast	Fast	Slow	Fast	Slow
Trust Building	Fast	Fast	Fast	Fast	Fast	Slow	Fast	Fast
Consolidation								
Trust Solidification	Unknown	High	Unknown	High	High	High	High	High
Strategic Integration at JV Level	Unknown	High	Unknown	High	High	High	High	High
Strategic Integration at Parent Level	Unknown	Mediuim	Unknown	Medium	Low	High	High	Low
Adjustment								
Reevaluation								
Change in Objective	Unknown	None	Unknown	None	None	Some	None	None
Change in Balance of Bargaining Power	Unknown	Some	Unknown	Some	Some	Much	Some	None
Reconfiguration								
Change in Control Mode	Unknown	Little	Unknown	Little	Little	Little	Little	None
Change in Control Locus	Unknown	Little	Unknown	Little	Little	Little	Little	None
Change in Control Domain	Unknown	Little	Unknown	Little	Little	Little	Little	None

terms; and (4) establishment of the joint venture. There were several interesting findings with regard to this phase.

First, one of the major motives of the Chinese partners to form an SFJV was to facilitate the needed change in ownership structure of those state-owned and collectively owned firms, and this was a strong indication of the significant contribution of SFJVs to economic reform in the PRC. The finding helps to clarify the prevailing ambiguity of the relationship between ownership, authority, responsibility, and compensation among all the state-owned and collectively owned firms in China as inherited from the formerly planned economy. Prior studies have failed to uncover this motivation as they have been largely biased toward the interests of foreign partners (e.g., Beamish 1993; Campbell 1988; Newman 1992; Pan, Vanhonacker, and Pitts 1995; Shan 1991; Shenkar 1990; for more balanced views, see Child 1994; Osland and Cavusgil 1996; Pearson 1991; Von Glinow and Teagarden 1988; Yan and Gray 1994). In addition to the contribution of SFJVs to economic reform in the PRC, the objective of Chinese partners to absorb managerial skills from foreign partners was also found to be significant.

Second, the analysis revealed that one of the main objectives for some foreign firms to form joint ventures in China was to gain access to the technological capabilities of some Chinese firms in product design in order either to penetrate the local market in China or to export to foreign markets. The technological capabilities of product design and process design were clearly defined by SFJV partners as two distinct types of technological capability. It was found that the objective of foreign partners to benefit from the product design capability of Chinese partners was largely related to their objective of penetrating the local market, especially when the product must be adapted for local use. The exception to this rule was the case of Venture 6 (a Sino-Japanese electronics venture in Shanghai), where the product technology of the Chinese partner was sought by the Japanese partner in order to export the products overseas.

Third, it was found that learning was the major objective of both Chinese and foreign partners in forming a joint venture. The Chinese partners wanted to learn about process and product technology, international marketing, and modern management, whereas foreign partners wanted to learn about local marketing, local management, and product technology in China. Although labor, material, and capital were also important, learning, as a composite category, was by far the most significant. It is worth noting that Chinese partners tended to learn from their foreign partners within the boundaries of a specific joint venture, whereas foreign partners tended to "learn by doing" in the PRC, beyond the boundaries of any particular joint venture. It may be hypothesized that foreign partners have the advantage of learning more than their Chinese counterparts. Chinese partners may have to set up their own foreign ventures overseas to remedy the limitations of their localized learning in SFJVs.

Fourth, the data analysis revealed no obvious patterns in bargaining power and management control, and no clear relationship between the two. This brings into question the validity of the findings of previous studies (e.g., Yan and Gray 1994). However, the analysis of bargaining power can never be conclusive without sufficient information to assess the relative significance of each of the elements that determine the overall level of fit in terms of compatibility and complementarity between partners, the overall level of availability of alternatives to each partner, and the overall level of strategic importance of that venture to each partner. The same is true with regard to analysis of management control and venture performance and the relationships between power, control, and performance in any joint venture.

Finally, it was found that many joint venture partners had some knowledge or experience of each other before they entered the initiation phase. In four of the eight cases, joint ventures were formed as an additional project in a continuing alliance between known business partners. This finding is significant since previous studies have tended to assume that joint ventures are undertaken between strangers who must start from scratch. This finding questions the validity of such an assumption.

Trial Phase

Having been established, a joint venture enters a phase of trial. During this second stage in the development process the partners begin to clarify their expectations, adapt to their routines, institutionalize tentative procedures, and build an initial mutual trust (Larson 1992; Ring and Van de Ven 1994). These four elements were found to be significant in all eight cases.

There were three additional findings. First, it was found that the length and the character of the trial phase would differ from case to case, subject to the gap in management style between partners and their willingness to compromise. When the gap in management style between Chinese and foreign partners was wide, with both sides wanting to maintain their own style of management, the trial phase was longer and more bumpy than normal. Second, the problem of length and difficulty in the trial phase was found to be related to the degree of difficulty and length of negotiation in the initiation phase; perhaps an inheritance from the initiation phase. Third, this problem did not seem to carry over into the consolidation phase. Therefore, it may be argued that the status of a joint venture in the initiation and trial phases cannot be an unbiased indicator of its future success.

Consolidation Phase

In the third phase of development partners begin to build up their mutual trust and integrate their operation at strategic levels (Larson 1992; Ring and

Van de Ven 1994). There were two important findings. First, the status of the joint venture in this phase was a fair indicator of its future success, since trust solidification and strategic integration were themselves most important signs of success as measured by the level of satisfaction among all the partners. Unless certain unexpected major changes in the strategy of the partners or the macro environment occurred, the success of a joint venture in its consolidation phase would indicate its continuation.

The second finding was that strategic integration at joint venture level was different from that of the parent companies separately. It is reasonable to differentiate between these two types of strategic integration at two distinct levels. While strategic integration at the venture level was found to be significantly related to the success of the joint venture, strategic integration at the parent level was not directly related to the success of joint venture. Strategic integration at the parent level was found to be more related to the size, strategic importance, and prior cooperation of both partners. When both partners were relatively small, highly interdependent in their operation, and highly successful in prior joint undertakings, they had a higher level of strategic integration at the parent level. It was also found that a higher level of strategic integration at the parent level could lead to a higher level of strategic integration at the venture level, but not vice versa. The strategic integration at the parent level was reflected in the frequency, scope, and nature of cooperation between the same partners.

Adjustment Phase

During this phase partners begin to reevaluate and, if necessary, reconfigure their relationships in accordance with the changes in shared interest and trustworthiness in terms of rational trust, moral trust, and affective trust between partners (Mayer, Davis, and Schoorman 1995; Ring and Van de Ven 1994). There were three major findings.

First, there was little change in the strategic objectives of both Chinese and foreign partners in these joint ventures except in the case of Venture 6 (although Venture 1 and Venture 3 had not yet finished their consolidation phase due to their young age). Second, some changes in the balance of bargaining power between the Chinese and foreign partners were found (many were found in Venture 6) except in the case of Venture 8. Third, it was found that even major changes in the balance of bargaining power and strategic objectives did not necessarily alter the venture's control structure. In the case of Venture 6 the balance of bargaining power had changed dramatically in favor of the Chinese partners, who had also changed their initial strategic objectives. The Chinese partners chose not to touch the overall control structure, the main reason being that they wanted to build a long-lasting relationship with their foreign partner on a level of high shared interest and trust. As they put it, "We cannot afford to dismantle the bridge after we cross a river because we are most interested in the long-term benefit."

One reason for the lack of changes in strategic objectives and bargaining power may be the young age of these joint ventures (1987-1994), and/or their ability to fine tune their relationship to prevent major imbalance. Reasons for the lack of change in control structure, not in accordance with the shift in strategic objective and balance of bargaining power, may be the long-term tenure of these joint ventures (between 10 and 30 years) or the substitution of trust or informal control for formal control (an area often overlooked in previous studies).

Overall Issues

In addition to the above findings the data analysis revealed several findings relevant to the overall issues surrounding IJV development. First, it was noted that many Chinese and foreign partners established other SFJVs in addition to the cases selected for this study, either with the same partner or other new partners (although these case studies were on their first SFJVs in China). It was found that many Chinese partners had some domestic joint ventures with other Chinese partners. It is possible that foreign partners might also have other international and/or domestic joint ventures. Second, it was found that some Chinese parent companies ceased to exist once the joint venture was formed (i.e., the parent company merged with the joint venture or the foreign partner bought into an existing Chinese firm). Third, parent companies could include a joint venture partner (who could be a subsidiary of a parent company) or the parent company of a joint venture partner (who could be a subsidiary of another parent company). Fourth, little evidence of national effect on control structures was found. Rather, in cases where the foreign partners were overseas Chinese, those joint ventures would display some unexpected characteristics such as unusual control structures (e.g., Venture 5), or little learning about management and indirect control over joint ventures by foreign parent companies (e.g., in Venture 7 and Venture 8).

In summary, the findings of this study generally support the validity of our proposed conceptual framework of IJV developmental process. Further, the data analysis reveals the need to further enrich the framework by providing more detailed and refined elements of those major categories in the framework. In addition to its support for the conceptual framework, it raises several critical questions about the validity of the extant paradigm of organizations in general and strategic alliances or joint ventures in particular. This subject will be the focus of the next section.

DISCUSSION

The findings of this study raise serious doubts about the validity of the ontology and epistemology of the extant paradigm of the organization embedded in the Western culture. Central to the ontology of the Western paradigm are such concepts as self-interest, free market, private ownership, and top-down control. Central to the epistemology of the Western paradigm is the either/or orthodox logic that emphasizes consistency rather than completeness. All of this results in ambiguity and bias in conceptualization and theory-building in the West. Both issues will be discussed in the light of the findings of this study. The results augment the view that the Western paradigm, due to its bias, cannot apply to Eastern phenomena and that the latter requires its own paradigm (Biggart and Hamilton 1992; Earley 1993; Li 1996; Oi 1995; Putterman 1995; Redding and Whitley 1990; Sampson 1988; Triandis et al. 1988; Whyte 1995; cf. Child 1994; Lincoln 1990).

The Ontology of the Extant Paradigm and SFJVs

It is possible that the reason for the lack of theory-building with regard to strategic alliances and joint ventures is that new theory must challenge the basic assumptions of the Western paradigm. The results of this research revealed that IJV partners seeking shared interest via trust were more critical to the success of the joint venture than partners seeking self-interest via bargaining power and control. From this perspective, it can be argued that the strategic alliance is a unique form of organization built on shared interest via trust and that this unique form defies the extant paradigm of organization and points to the necessity for a paradigm shift. Because the extant paradigm is embedded in the cultural peculiarities of the West, particularly the United States (Biggart and Hamilton 1992; Hofstede 1993; Lincoln 1990; Redding and Whitley 1990), the Eastern paradigm is needed to challenge and to facilitate the required paradigm shift. Further research designed in accordance with the Eastern paradigm, especially its perspectives on shared interest and trust, is required to facilitate theory-building with regard to strategic alliances.

For example, the research on individualism and collectivism can be drawn on in order to understand better the linkage between self-interest and shared interest. Natural to the East but logical to the West (Earley 1993), the self-interests of stakeholders are partially intertwined, that is, a group-specific shared interest. The task is to draw the boundaries between self, in-group, and out-group among the stakeholders based on their shared interest and non-shared interest (Sampson 1988). In the West the boundary is sharply drawn between self and nonself (but not between in-group and out-group), so self-interest seeking is a personal affair. In the East the boundary is sharply drawn between in-group and out-group (but not between self and in-group), so self-interest seeking is an in-group affair (Earley 1993; Sampson 1988; Triandis et al. 1988). In the West the self-interests of stakeholders are viewed as either compatible or incompatible: if compatible, cooperation may occur; if incompatible, competition should occur. In the East the self-interests of stakeholders are both compatible and incompatible to different degrees in different aspects at different times, so a game of competition and cooperation in interaction will occur. The reasoning is that human interest should be understood as both economic and noneconomic (i.e., political, moral, and emotional); both exclusive (non-shared self-interest) and inclusive (shared self-interest); and both universal and particular, both stable and flexible, as well as both limited and unlimited, in the sense that not all interests are shared by all people at all times (in contrast to the over-embedded view) while various interests can be shared by various people to various degrees at various times (in contrast to the under-embedded view) (see Granovetter 1985, 1992).

With the notion of shared interest as embedded self-interests as a base, other core constructs, such as trust, can be developed. Trust is one of the most critical but least understood concepts in organizational study (Hosmer 1995; Mayer, Davis, and Schoorman 1995). For the purpose of this study, trust is defined as a special (task-specific and person-specific) relationship between the stakeholders where a broadly defined interest (self-interest and shared interest; economic and noneconomic) is recognized, protected, and enhanced under high uncertainty in which both price and authority fail to function (cf. Granovetter 1985; Hosmer 1995; Mayer, Davis, and Schoorman 1995). The concept of trust contains three major components (Knoke 1990; Lewis and Weigert 1985): (1) a rational recognition that cooperation is the best way to achieve one's own self-interest, thus *rational trust* (Axelrod 1984); (2) a moral obligation to honor everyone's self-interest, thus *moral trust* (Hosmer 1995); and (3) an affective friendship to exceed the other's expectations in maximizing shared interest, thus *affective trust* (McAllister 1995).

Corresponding to the three conditions of trustworthiness (Mayer, Davis, and Schoorman 1995), these three elements of trust function differently under different conditions. Rational trust is related to task-specific ability or competence; moral trust is related to culture-specific integrity or morality; and affective trust is related to person-specific benevolence or friendship (Mayer, Davis, and Schoorman 1995, p. 717). Though ability alone could be sufficient to start a relationship and a combination of ability and integrity would be sufficient to develop the relationship, a trustworthy relationship can be built on only through a combination of all three elements to various degrees at various times (Mayer, Davis, and Schoorman 1995, pp. 720-722). Trust differs from authority in that authority connotes a reactive compliance with an extrinsic requirement to prevent the negative and relieve one's own anxiety, whereas trust connotes a proactive contribution to an intrinsic urge to construct the positive and create mutual satisfaction (Alvesson and Lindkvist 1993).

These theoretical arguments are supported by the findings of this study to varying degrees.

The Epistemology of the Extant Paradigm and SFJVs

As previously argued, the primary reason for the lack of theory-building with regard to strategic alliances and joint ventures is that new theory must challenge not only the ontology but also the epistemology of the Western paradigm. These case studies have revealed that the method of holistic, dynamic, and paradoxical analysis was more appropriate for the study of strategic alliances and joint ventures than the method of fragmented, static, and consistent analysis rooted in orthodox logic. From this perspective, it can be argued that the strategic alliance is a unique form of organization whose holistic, dynamic, and paradoxical features can be explained only by a new analytical method built upon dialectic logic.

Dialectic logic claims that (1) each entity is a system of intrinsically related elements in a larger system; (2) these elements exist in pairs as opposites in unity; and (3) the patterns of interaction between opposite elements, both internal and external to the entity, defines the entity's properties of paradoxical existence and its process of circular change (Li 1995). There are three specific rules in dialectic logic. First, the meaning of each concept must be validated with two opposite meanings in contrast; whichever meaning dominates will define the ultimate meaning of that concept. Second, each argument has to be constructed by a thesis-antithesis-synthesis process. Third, each premise or conclusion must be both true and false to various degrees, in various aspects and at various times (Li 1995). As the opposites, in unity, mutually affirm and mutually negate in a circular process of change, paradox is inevitable, desirable, and resolvable (Li 1995). As a cognitive mode, the dialectic logic is neither reserved for only radical views nor subject to Marxist interpretations (cf. Benson 1977; Zeitz 1980). The classical Chinese idea of yin/yang as Tao in *The Book of Change* (*I Ching*) and many other Chinese classics are salient examples of the dialectic logic in East Asia (see Fung 1970; Graham 1989). The centrality of the yin/yang concept to the Chinese culture suggests that the cognitive mode of the Chinese is predominantly holistic, dynamic, and paradoxical in nature.

The application of dialectic logic to the study of strategic alliances and joint ventures would contribute to a better understanding of the nature of organization, the relationship between self-interest and shared interest and the nature of trust as a mode of coordination in contrast to authority, price, and other modes of coordination. In addition, the development of a theoretical framework that is holistic, dynamic, and paradoxical would perhaps be able to describe, explain, predict, and prescribe strategic alliances and joint ventures. The Eastern view, that a whole cannot be separated from its parts, because they are inherently interrelated, challenges the Western view that a whole is a collection of unrelated parts. Western assumptions are that there is no whole unless there are parts of the whole, that a general theory is a collection of special theories, and therefore no general theory can be built before all necessary special theories are fully developed. It is possible to construct a general theoretical framework of organization first by adopting a process perspective. Using this framework as a guide, it is possible to build a theory of strategic alliances and joint ventures that would further enrich the general framework in an interactive process.

CONCLUSIONS

The findings of this comparative case study provide strong evidence that the extant studies fail to clarify the holistic, dynamic, and paradoxical nature of strategic alliances and SFJVs. The study attempted to find a solution to the problem by integrating the literature on IJVs with that of economic reform to explore the links between the two. The study also attempted to facilitate theory-building on strategic alliances and joint ventures by interpreting the evidence of SFJVs in the unique context of the PRC and from the Chinese perspective that challenges the Western paradigm and supports the Eastern paradigm (cf. Yan and Gray 1994). The findings of this study provide confirmative evidence that a shift in the extant paradigm of organization is needed and is possible by adopting the Eastern ontology of human nature (e.g., shared interest and trust) and the Eastern epistemology of cognitive mode (e.g., dialectic logic).

According to Khin (1988), the boundaries of Asian organizational systems are unclear and undefined and the overlap between organizational systems and other systems such as family, kinship, community, and society is very extensive; the very basis of how we view ourselves might make this difference between the West and the East more pronounced. The epistemology, or the difference in the way we see things, is the essence of the differences between human relations in various cultures. As Maruyama (1984) points out, in the West there must be things before there are relations, whereas in the East there is no pre-relational identity; the identity *is* the relations. While Western scholars tend to misinterpret groupism as submission of the individual to the whole as well as homogenization, groupism in the East is viewed as nonhierarchical and interactive, which utilizes diversity for mutual benefit. The web of relationships in the organization may be seen by Asians either as concentric or overlapping circles, with relationship emanating from the common center.

The notions of organizational efficiency and effectiveness seem to differ between Eastern and Western cultures in terms of value judgments on the ends and also the means (the process of achieving ends). The Eastern culture measures the totality of the whole rather than measuring each part. In the West the outcomes of each individual or unit can be aggregated to obtain the results of the whole organization because order, symmetry, linearity, individuality, and analysis are the bases of the Western epistemological framework. In the East organization is viewed as a symbiotic relationship of heterogeneous parts mutually benefiting all concerned; the precise demarcation of contribution is not possible and would not be attempted. A theoretical framework that incorporates the Eastern paradigm is urgently needed to shift the Western paradigm. This study is among the first to attempt to do just that.

REFERENCES

Alvesson, M., and L. Lindkvist. 1993. "Transaction Costs, Clans and Corporate Culture." *Journal of Management Studies* 30: 427-452.

Axelrod, R. 1984. *The Evolution of Cooperation*. New York: Basic Books.

Beamish, P.W. 1988. *Multinational Joint Ventures in Developing Countries*. New York: Routledge.

Beamish, P.W. 1993. "The Characteristics of Joint Ventures in the People's Republic of China." *Journal of International Marketing* 1: 29-48.

Benson, J.K. 1977. "Organizations: A Dialectic View." *Administrative Science Quarterly* 22: 1-21.

Biggart, N.W., and G.G. Hamilton. 1992. "On the Limit of a Firm-Based Theory to Explain Business Networks: The Western Bias of Neoclassical Economics." Pp. 471-490 in *Networks and Organizations*, edited by N. Nohria and R.G. Eccles. Boston, MA: Harvard Business School Press.

Borys, B. and D.B. Jemison. 1989. "Hybrid Arrangements as Strategic Alliances: Theoretical Issues in Organizational Combinations." *Academy of Management Review* 14: 234-249.

Campbell, N. 1988. *A Strategic Guide to Equity Joint Ventures in China*. New York: Pergamon.

Child, J. 1994. *Management in China during the Age of Reform*. Cambridge, UK: Cambridge University Press.

Contractor, F.J., and P. Lorange (Eds.). 1988. *Cooperative Strategies in International Business*. Lexington, MA: Lexington Books.

Earley, P.C. 1993. "East Meets West Meets Mideast: Further Explorations of Collectivistic and Individualistic Work Groups." *Academy of Management Journal* 36: 319-348.

Fung, Y.L. 1970. *The Spirit of Chinese Philosophy*. Westport, CT: Greenwood Press.

Geringer, J.M., and L. Hebert. 1989. "Control and Performance of International Joint Ventures." *Journal of International Business Studies* 20: 235-254.

Geringer, J.M., and L. Hebert. 1991. "Measuring Performance of International Joint Ventures." *Journal of International Business Studies* 22: 249-263.

Graham, A.C. 1989. *Dispute of the Tao: Philosophical Argument in Ancient China*. La Salle, IL: Open Court.

Granovetter, M. 1985. "Economic Action and Social Structure: The Problem of Embeddedness." *American Journal of Sociology* 91: 481-510.

Granovetter, M. 1992. "Problems of Explanation in Economic Sociology." Pp. 25-56 in *Networks and Organizations*, edited by N. Nohria and R. G. Eccles. Boston, MA: Harvard Business School Press.

Harrigan, K.P. 1988. "Joint Ventures and Competitive Strategies." *Strategic Management Journal* 9: 141-158.

Hennart, J.F. 1991. "The Transaction Cost Theory of Joint Ventures: An Empirical Study of Japanese Subsidiaries in the United States." *Management Science* 37: 483-497.

Hofstede, G. 1993. "Cultural Constraints in Management Theories." *Academy of Management Executive* 7 (1): 81-94.

Hosmer, L.T. 1995. "Trust: The Connecting Link Between Organizational Theory and Philosophical Ethics." *Academy of Management Review* 20: 379-403.

Khin, M.K. 1988. "APJM and Comparative Management in Asia." *Asia-Pacific Journal of Management* 5: 207-224.

Killing, J.P. 1983. *Strategies for Joint Venture Success.* New York: Praeger.

Knoke, D. 1990. *Organizing for Collective Action: The Political Economies of Associations.* New York: De Gruyter.

Kogut, B. 1988. "Joint Ventures: Theoretical and Empirical Perspective." *Strategic Management Journal* 9: 319-332.

Kuhn, T.S. 1970. *The Structure of Scientific Revolution.* Chicago, IL: University of Chicago Press.

Lardy, N.R. 1995. "The Role of Foreign Trade and Investment in China's Economic Transformation." *China Quarterly* 144: 1065-1082.

Larson, A. 1992. "Network Dyads in Entrepreneurial Settings: A Study of the Governance of Exchange Relationships." *Administrative Science Quarterly* 37: 76-104.

Lewis, J.D., and A. Weigert. 1985. "Trust as a Social Reality." *Social Forces* 63: 967-985.

Li, P.P. 1995. "Inevitability, Desirability and Resolvability of Paradox: A Dialectic Approach to Global Strategy." Paper presented at the Annual Meeting of the Academy of Management, Vancouver, Canada, August 5-8.

Li, P.P. 1996. "Toward a Paradigm Shift in Organization Study: The Geographic Ontology and Cosmopolitan Epistemology about Organizational Form." Paper presented at The Annual Meeting of the Academy of International Business, Banff, Canada, September 26-29.

Lincoln, J.R. 1990. "Japanese Organization and Organization Theory." Pp. 255-294 in *Research in Organizational Behavior*, edited by L.L. Cummings and B.M. Staw. Greenwich, CT: JAI Press.

Luo, Y. 1995. "Business Strategy, Market Structure, and Performance of International Joint Ventures: The Case of Joint Ventures in China." *Management International Review* 35: 241-264.

Lyons, M.P. 1991. "Joint-Ventures as Strategic Choice—A Literature Review." *Long Range Planning* 24 (4): 130-144.

McAllister, D.J. 1995. "Affect- and Cognition-Based Trust as Foundations for Interpersonal Cooperation in Organizations." *Academy of Management Journal* 38: 24-59.

Maruyama, M. 1984. "Alternative Concepts of Management." *Asia Pacific Journal of Management* 1 (2): 100-111.

Mayer, R.C., J.H. Davis, and F.D. Schoorman. 1995. "An Integrative Model of Organizational Trust." *Academy of Management Review* 20: 709-734.

Oi, J.C. 1995. "The Role of the Local State in China's Transitional Economy." *China Quarterly* 144: 1132-1149.

Osland, G.E., and S.T. Cavusgil. 1996. "Performance Issues in U.S.-China Joint Ventures." *California Management Review* 38 (2): 106-130.

Pan, Y., W.R. Vanhonacker, and R.E. Pitts. 1995. "International Equity Joint Ventures in China: Operations and Potential Close-Down." *Journal of Global Marketing* 8: 125-148.

Parkhe, A. 1993. "Messy Research, Methodological Predispositions, and Theory Developement in International Joint Ventures." *Academy of Management Review* 18: 227-268.

Pearson, M.M. 1991. *Joint Ventures in the People's Republic of China.* Princeton, NJ: Princeton University Press.

Putterman, L. 1995. "The Role of Ownership and Property Rights in China's Economic Transition." *China Quarterly* 144: 1047-1064.

Rawski, T.G. 1995. "Implications of China's Reform Experience." *China Quarterly* 144: 1150-1173.

Redding, S.G., and R.D. Whitley. 1990. "Beyond Bureaucracy: Towards a Comparative Analysis of Forms of Economic Resource Coordination and Control." Pp. 79-104 in *Capitalism in Contrasting Cultures*, edited by S.T. Clegg, S.G. Redding, and M. Carter. New York: De Gruyter.

Ring, P.S., and A.H. Van de Ven. 1994. "Developmental Process of Cooperative Interorganizational Relationships." *Academy of Management Review* 19: 90-118.

Sampson, E.E. 1988. "The Debate on Individualism: Indigenous Psychologies of the Individual and their Role in Personal and Societal Functioning." *American Psychologist* 43: 15-22.

Shan, W. 1991. "Environmental Risks and Joint Venture Sharing Arrangements." *Journal of International Business Studies* 22: 555-578.

Shenkar, O. 1990. "International Joint Venture Problems in China: Risks and Remedies." *Long Range Planning* 23 (3): 82-90.

Tallman, S.B., and O. Shenkar. 1994. "A Managerial Decision Model of International Cooperative Venture Formation." *Journal of International Business Studies* 25: 91-113.

Triandis, H.C., R. Bontempo, M.J. Villareal, M. Asai, and N. Lucca. 1988. "Individualism and Collectivism: Cross-Cultural Perspectives on Self-Ingroup Relationships." *Journal of Personality and Social Psychology* 54: 323-338.

Von Glinow, M.A., and M.B. Teagarden. 1988. "The Transfer of Human Resource Management Technology in Sino-U.S. Cooperative Ventures: Problems and Solutions." *Human Resource Management* 27: 201-229.

Walder, A.G. 1995. "China's Transitional Economy: Interpreting its Significance." *China Quarterly* 144: 963-998.

Whitley, R.D. 1992. *Business Systems in East Asia: Firms, Markets and Societies*. London: Sage.

Whyte, M.K. 1995. "The Social Roots of China's Economic Development." *China Quarterly* 144: 999-1019.

Yan, A., and B. Gray. 1994. "Bargaining Power, Management Control, and Performance in United States-China Joint Ventures: A Comparative Case Study." *Academy of Management Journal* 37: 1478-1517.

Yin, R.K. 1989. *Case Study Research: Design and Methods*. Newsbury Park, CA: Sage.

Yoshino, M., and U.S. Rangan. 1995. *Strategic Alliances: An Entrepreneurial Approach to Globalization*. Boston, MA: Harvard Business School Press.

Zeitz, G. 1980. "Interorganizational Dialectics." *Administrative Science Quarterly* 25: 72-88.

HISTORICAL PROTOTYPES:

THE INFLUENCE OF JAPANESE COTTON TEXTILE FIRMS DURING THE PRE-1949 PERIOD

Judith Hollows

INTRODUCTION

This paper provides a review of the influence of foreign firms (in particular the Japanese) on the modernization of China in the late Ch'ing (1862-1911), Republican (1912-1928), and Nationalist (1928-1937) periods. The aim of this paper is to provide a historical context for the entry of foreign firms since 1979, which might be termed the second "modernization period."

There are many firms that have returned in the second modernization period, among them the German electrical company, Siemens. It first established a permanent office in Shanghai in 1903, which by 1937 accounted for 21 percent of the company's overseas turnover. By the year 2000 Siemens expects the PRC to account for 50 percent of its 60,000 employees in Asia, at least 25 percent of its investment in Asia, and 10 percent of its global sales. Shanghai is Siemens's largest operational base in China, from which 11 of its 35 joint ventures are managed (*SCMP* 1996b). The Japanese textile company Kanebo (then known as Kanegafuchi) first entered China in 1922 when three cotton

Advances in Chinese Industrial Studies, Volume 5, pages 35-66.

ISBN: 1-55938-961-3

spinning mills were established in Shanghai. It returned in 1978 and by 1994 the company had 14 joint venture companies, all but two in Shanghai. In some of Shanghai's industrial suburbs, factory after factory flies the Japanese flag above its gates (*SCMP* 1996a).

I will start by setting out the policies adopted by the late Ch'ing government to set up modern industry from the latter half of the nineteenth century. These policies were initially characterized by an intention to prevent foreigners from gaining a direct foothold in the economy. The Ch'ing government, however, proved to be incapable of resisting the ambitions of foreign powers to establish themselves in an economy with the potential of "400 million customers,"[1] and of resisting the reforming zeal of the early Republican movement led by Dr. Sun Yat Sen. In 1911 the Ch'ing dynasty was overthrown, and Japanese and European firms accelerated their direct entry to the Chinese market, especially through Shanghai.

Second, I will analyze the ability of the Japanese to gain a controlling influence over the Chinese cotton spinning industry in Shanghai in the Republican and Nationalist periods. Finally, I will identify some of the institutional influences in the Chinese economy, such as the role of the state, the Treaty Ports, problems of capital formation, the role of merchants, and management practices in modern Chinese enterprises, and discuss their influence on the development of modern enterprises in the period 1890 to 1937, that is, from the Self-Strengthening Movement to the outbreak of the Sino-Japanese War.

THE EARLY DEVELOPMENT OF MODERN INDUSTRY IN CHINA

The early development of modern industry in China can be divided into four distinct periods which also reflect the changing nature of the competition between the Chinese and foreign enterprises in the Chinese market (King and Lieu 1930, p. 263):

Phase 1: 1860-1904 Government sponsorship of the first modern enterprises;
Phase 2: 1905-1914 Gradual development of modern industry;
Phase 3: 1915-1922 Rapid growth;
Phase 4: 1922-1937 The assertion of foreign influence.

Government Sponsorship of the First Modern Enterprises: 1860-1904

The first modern enterprises in China were government sponsored, part of a movement to establish modern industrial enterprises that could counteract the growing threat of commercial and military domination of China by Western powers. The leading proponent of modern enterprise was a regional governor, Li Hung-chang (1823-1901). He launched a "Self-Strengthening Movement," which initially concentrated on military industries from 1861, but from 1872 developed profit-oriented enterprises for shipping, railways, mining, and the telegraph (Hsu 1983, p. 284). In 1890 he successfully sponsored the setting up of five cotton spinning mills as *kuan-tu shang-pan* enterprises, that is, "official" sponsored, "merchant" managed and financed enterprises in which there was no participation of foreign capital. These projects were profit-oriented for the benefit of the sponsors, and run as government monopolies. The Self-Strengthening Movement came to an end with the defeat of Li Hung-chang's navy by the Japanese in 1895,[2] and it was not until the 1930s that "bureaucratic capital" again tried to gain control of modern industry.

In the late Ch'ing period innovation and change in the Chinese economy was confined to the competence of a small number of high officials as exemplified by the Self-Strengthening Movement (1861-1895). The officials took advantage of the Chinese merchants' ambitions for "official status," inviting them to join monopolistic enterprises controlled by the officials. The scholar-official gentry class was suspicious of any attempts to destabilize the traditional base of economic and political power in China; there was no framework that would enable capital to be used in new ways, no concept of national need, other than to strengthen the position of the bureaucracy (Le Fevour 1968, p. 133).

The Self-Strengthening Movement adopted an organizational form known as the *kuan-tu shang-pan* system for the arsenals, the steamship company, and later the modern cotton mills. It was based on the salt monopoly system that had government-appointed official overseers, and the production, distribution, and retailing functions were farmed out to different groups of salt merchants. The *kuan-tu shang-pan* were "official" sponsored and "merchant" managed, and financed on a joint stock basis by "bureaucratic capitalists" who were gentry officials and ex-compradors who had purchased official titles (Bush 1982, p. 44).

It was anticipated that capital for the *kuan-tu shang-pan* cotton mills would be raised from Treaty Port merchants, from gentry relatives and friends of the promoters, and from official funds that would be deposited at a high rate of return to match that of the old-style pawnbrokers (Feuerwerker 1958, p. 11). There had been a long tradition in China (since 200 BC) for rich merchants to lend money to regional princes in return for rights to lucrative monopolies (Bedikton 1935, p. 10). In the case of the early cotton mills, it was agreed that as joint stock companies they would guarantee a return of 9.6 percent to shareholders, and enjoy a 10-year monopoly of the manufacture of cotton cloth and yarn. They would be managed by compradors who had experience of working in Western trading companies, and officially supported and supervised by regional governor Li Hung-chang, who would protect the enterprises from exaction and interference from other factions in the bureaucracy. The first mill had a faulty start as the first manager, ex-comprador Cheng Kuan-ying,[3] not only had difficulty raising finance, but that which he did raise he used for his personal gain, and he was dismissed in 1884. During the period 1890-1895 five other subsidiary mills were set up (four in Shanghai). All six *kuan-tu shang-pan* mills faced severe financial problems within a few years of being set up; they did, however, provide a demonstration to would-be cotton textile entrepreneurs of the opportunities offered by private enterprise.

The Gradual Development of Modern Industry: 1905-1914

The second phase of the development of modern industry was promoted by a few Chinese merchants and bureaucrats who took advantage of the break up of the Self-Strengthening monopoly. By 1910 the modern textile industry comprised 19 wholly-owned Chinese mills, and three Chinese/foreign joint venture mills (Feuerwerker 1958, p. 222; the foreign companies were Mitsui Bussan and Jardine Matheson). Twelve of the Chinese mills were established by bureaucratic industrialists, three by compradors, two by a combination of merchants and local officials, and two by unknown founders (Feuerwerker 1958, p. 222; Koh 1966, p. 220). The bureaucratic capitalists continued to dominate mill ownership; 90 percent of the capital for the mills set up between 1905 and 1913 came from bureaucratic sources. Between 1913 and 1922 the increase in the number of mills from 46 to 64 was mainly due to the establishment of branch mills by the bureaucratic industrialists (Koh 1966, p. 220).

Rapid Growth: 1915-1922

The expansion of Chinese private enterprises during the First World War was promoted by the Republican government and by a spirit of nationalism. The end of the First World War stimulated a period of rapid growth, and by 1916 the Chinese mills were producing sufficient coarse yarn to meet domestic needs, and therefore were threatening Japan's exports to its main export market. Between 1918 and 1922 there was another period of rapid expansion in spinning capacity; 33 of the 71 mills in existence in 1929 were established between 1918 and 1922 (Pearse 1929, pp. 154-155). This was the last opportunity for the Chinese mills to dominate their own market. Thereafter the Chinese mills had to face the increasing competition from Japanese mills in China.

THE ASSERTION OF FOREIGN INFLUENCE: 1922-1937

Japanese Firms Gain Control

As the Chinese mills concentrated almost solely on their domestic market, they were subject to the retarding forces in the Chinese economy. Although phenomenal production levels were achieved in the late 1920s and early 1930s, the domestic market was unable to absorb the output, and by the mid-1930s a position of overproduction had been reached, and all mills were selling yarn at a loss (Kraus 1980, p. 152). The declining per capita income and the consequent declining per capita cloth consumption had caught up with the industry (p. 153).

The development of the modern Japanese cotton spinning industry from the 1870s to its peak in the 1930s was remarkable because within this period it was transformed from a craft industry to a major international mass production industry, surpassing the primary position of Great Britain in the export of cotton cloth. Exports had been adopted early on as a means of alleviating the effects of depression in the domestic market. By 1909 yarn exports surpassed imports (Seki 1956, p. 19). Exports to China began in 1890 in response to an overproduction of yarn as a result of a temporary depression. The setting up of spinning mills in China by Japanese firms was pioneered by the trading companies of Mitsui and Nihon Menka through joint ventures from 1902 and 1905, and by Naigai Wata (as wholly-owned enterprises from 1911) as a form of forward integration from their raw cotton and yarn trading (Nishida 1990). The massive investment by Japanese cotton spinning firms in the 1920s was based on the need to seek lower production costs in order to compete in the Chinese market and in new Asian export markets (Howe 1996a, p. 415).

Up until the end of the First World War most of the Japanese mills operating in China (known as *zaikabo*) were in Shanghai, and were owned by Japanese trading companies. After the war the "Big Ten" Japanese spinning companies began to establish their own branches in China, in Shanghai in particular, in order to protect their market and take advantage of lower labor costs. They set up new mills employing the latest spinning techniques and well-trained labor, and with the help of the well-established Japanese cotton trading companies proceeded to establish domination of the industry. Between 1925 and 1930, 31 Chinese mills failed (Takamura 1982, p. 137, based on information from Fong 1932). Many of these mills had been set up or had planned expansions in the postwar boom around 1920, for which they borrowed finance from Japanese trading companies.[4] From 1924 some Chinese owners were forced either to assign the management of their mills to the Japanese or agree to sell to the Japanese; by 1930, 15.4 percent of the Japanese spindles had originally been Chinese (Takamura 1982, p. 129). By this date the Japanese had achieved domination of the Chinese cotton spinning industry, and played a leading role in the growth of the Chinese export trade in textiles. By 1936 Chinese exports were mainly high-count yarns produced by *zaikabo*, shipped to Hong Kong, India, and Southeast Asian countries. The *zaikabo*, rather than their parent mills in Japan, had an important role in dominating the Asian market (Chin 1937, p. 197).

The Chinese mills were not capable of handling the requirements of export markets which demanded consistent standards of quality in large production runs at competitive price levels. Neither was there a marketing mechanism to find and develop overseas markets.[5] The Chinese mills also experienced shortages of capital, poor techniques, relatively high costs of production, and frequent labor troubles. They were unable to withstand the pressure exerted by the Japanese mills in China who were strongly organized and backed by large reserves, and who could afford temporary losses if necessary to gain access to a market (Chin 1937, pp. 157-159). Their strength in capitalization, integration, and equipment made them a greater threat to the Chinese mills than the Japanese mills in Japan. Lieu wrote in 1935, "there is much likelihood that the whole industry will sooner or later pass into the hands of the Japanese unless Chinese industrial leaders take steps to stop it" (Lieu 1935, pp. 1116-1117). Fong, a contemporary writer, also had a pessimistic view of China's potential to develop a modern industrial economy. He wrote in 1937, "The medieval social, political and economic environment will prevent modern industry from developing rapidly, [and]...the family and clan system discourages individual enterprise and initiative" (Fong 1937, p. 261).

Japanese Firms Take Advantage of the Financial Weakness of Chinese Firms

A statistic for 1935 shows that the Chinese mills had a reserves:capital ratio of only 4 percent, in comparison with the Japanese mills whose reserves were 23 percent of capital. In 1932, 80 percent of Chinese spindles were many years old, but 50 percent of the Japanese spindles were new (Chin 1937, pp. 243-244). Lieu (1936, p. 30) observed:

> That was really the cause of much of the trouble with this industry. The mill-owners had been accustomed to huge profits during the post-War boom, and they could not be satisfied with the reasonable earnings of normal years. Hence they speculated in the cotton and yarn markets, and often carried heavy stocks to facilitate such operations. Their interest was no more centered in production. In the case of some mills, speculation became their main business, although there were also some mills which shunned such unsound practices. Since 1932, however, the industry has been hit by the general depression and operation has often been suspended (Chin 1937, p. 243, quoting Lieu 1936, p. 30)
>
> Many of the manufacturers carry on their business on a speculative basis. They expect to make much money in a short period of time; therefore they do not want to invest too much capital in their business. When they have made some money, they are ready to clear

> out at any time. Hence they prefer to rent their factory buildings, machinery, and electric power. Anything that will lower the cost of production and make it unnecessary to invest large sums of money is always welcome to them (Chin 1937, p. 245, quoting Lieu 1936, p. 103-104).

A report produced by the Bank of Shanghai in 1934 following an investigation into the finances of the Shen Xin spinning company, the largest of the Chinese firms, concluded that despite its large scale and a history of more than a decade, the Shen Xin group did not have an appropriate cost accounting system in the mills, nor a sound financial accounting system in the chief company (SASS 1980, p. 291). There was no comprehensive report on the chief company's assets and liabilities, profits and losses at the end of each year. The financial division used the old way of bookkeeping, while the accounts division attempted to adopt a modern accounting method. Different mills had their own policies, costs were estimated, and stock prices increased or decreased according to the volume of business. Modern cost accounting methods were considered as less important than meeting the needs of the banks and Japanese consortia for information on their loan accounts (SASS 1980, p. 291). The lack of a depreciation policy for capital equipment led to a reliance on ageing machinery which increased costs and reduced efficiency, whereas the Japanese were quick to take advantage of new technical developments and scrap outdated machinery on which depreciation charges had already been placed.

The financial weakness of the Chinese mills was not only due to their lack of skill in implementing standardized financial and accounting procedures to assist in the coordination and control of their businesses, they were also reliant on a banking system and other sources of finance which did not recognize the need to support the Chinese mill owners in the development of a modern cotton textile industry. Chin (1937, p. 240) observed that owners were forced to mortgage their fixed capital to find working capital. Mills frequently passed into the hands of banks, and the Japanese were quick to purchase a bankrupt mill at a bargain price, and with efficient management and a heavy outlay of capital reorganize the mill onto a profitable basis.

In comparison, the Japanese mills were supported by a financial network that promoted their interests in the Chinese market. When they had to resort to loans they were able to obtain them from Japanese banks at low interest rates (Takamura 1982, p. 185). The Japanese government provided support to the Yokohama Specie Bank to enable favorable financing to be extended to Japanese businesses. These facilities were not extended to the Chinese mills; not infrequently the Japanese traders and finance houses made loans at higher interest rates to the Chinese mills, and when they defaulted, arranged for the Japanese mills to acquire the mills on a lease basis, or outright purchase. The Japan China Mill group acquired three mills in this manner in 1924.

Thus, Japanese investment in textile mills in China was accompanied by investment in China by other supporting institutions in banking, finance, and trading (Chin 1937, p. 237). Nishikawa (1987, p. 241) asserts that the establishment of the Japanese spinning industry in China was the basis of Japanese economic power in China. Accompanying the investments by cotton traders and mills were investments in transport, power supply, banks, construction, foreign exchange broking, retail stores, and restaurants. These investments, although primarily initiated by the business community, were also encouraged by the Japanese government (Howe 1996b, p. 9). The Japanese mills, therefore, had strong institutional support, especially ready supplies of capital at low rates of interest enabling them to expand the number and size of mills, and to purchase raw cotton in large orders. Chinese informants to an American Economic Mission attributed the greater success of the Japanese-owned mills to "modern and efficient machinery and replacements, adequate capital with limited borrowings and low interest rates, an extensive and efficient sales program" (Chin 1937, p. 241). Most of the Japanese mills were associated with the Big Ten spinning companies in Japan, and were thus able to use their parent company's strong financial standing as collateral against requests for line of credit from the Japanese banks in China. The Japanese cotton trading companies helped in the provision of working capital by offering generous periods for the settlement of purchases of raw cotton. The Japanese mills also adopted the same financial management practices as their parent companies by reinvesting profits in the mills, in particular for the depreciation of fixed capital and the development of reserves (Takamura 1982, p. 185).

The Japanese trading companies, finance houses, and banks not only gave favorable terms to Japanese businesses, but discriminated against the Chinese to further weaken their competitive position. The finance houses targeted the large Chinese spinning mill groups such as Shen Xin, Ta Cheng, and Pao Cheng. The centralized control of these mills made it easier for Japanese capital to gain control (Nishikawa 1987, p. 211). The trading companies, the financial institutions, and the spinning companies coordinated their support for each other to control prices of raw cotton and yarn. The periodic dumping of yarn prices forced the Chinese mills to work hard just to meet bank loan interest payments, or to sell their mills, thus enabling the Japanese mills to strengthen their monopoly (Nishikawa 1987, p. 210). In the period 1921-1931 many Chinese mills went bankrupt, changed ownership, merged, or were taken over by banks.

In conclusion, the Chinese mill owners were seriously handicapped in their abilities to compete with the Japanese mills who, because of their financial strength and continued support from Japanese financial institutions and the trading companies, had the resources to control the Chinese raw cotton and yarn markets to their own advantage. The Chinese mill owners were victims not only of their own weak financial and accounting systems, but also faced largely hostile financial institutions, both Chinese-owned and foreign-owned, and governments too preoccupied by civil war to establish appropriate legal and economic frameworks for the establishment of a sound financial sector which could support the development of an indigenous modern textile industry.

Role of the Japanese Trading Companies

The success of the Japanese spinners in China—the *zaikabo*—was recorded in 1929 by the *Spinning and Weaving Daily*—"Japanese yarn has completely overtaken Chinese yarn which previously dominated the market in various places." The Japanese were at the same time exporting huge quantities of cloth from Japan to China—approximately 20 million yuan's worth of cloth was being imported—matching the figure of the previous boom in 1919. The Japanese cotton traders were able to compete with the Chinese traders in cotton piece goods because they had established direct sales channels to customers (Allen and Donnithorne 1954, p. 92). This growing domination was bitterly resented by the Chinese mill owners who in 1930 suggested that loyal Nationalists should be asked to investigate the places, shops, and persons selling Japanese yarn and cloth to persuade them to use native produce, and if they refused to do so they should be punished (SASS 1980, p. 242).

A key factor in the success of the Japanese textile industry both in China and in Japan was the role of the cotton trading companies in the management and development of the markets for the purchase of raw cotton, and the sale of yarn and cloth. Their strong organization in support of the spinning mills enabled the *zaikabo* to replicate to a high degree the spinning and weaving techniques developed in Japan, and to concentrate on efficient mass production. The trading companies had, after all, pioneered Japanese spinning operations in China; they were in a position to do so because of their familiarity with the Chinese market through their trading operations. They used their spinning activities to complement and strengthen their penetration of the Chinese mercantile structure, enabling them to achieve dominance.

Mitsui Bussan pioneered Japanese cotton trading in China. The company used their shareholding in a joint venture, the Shanghai Cotton Spinning Company, to acquire in 1902 and 1906 two mills which were failed *kuan-tu shang-pan* enterprises. These investments were regarded as favorable to Mitsui because their management of them enabled the Shanghai branch to handle all the raw cotton and yarn business of the two mills. It enabled a stronger relationship with the prominent Chinese cotton brokers who were the partners in the joint venture. The Chinese joint venture partners concentrated on the sale of yarn and on the purchase of raw cotton for both Chinese and Japanese Mitsui clients and of course on favorable terms for the two mills. The improvements in the distribution and production systems of the mills enhanced Mitsui's reputation for good cotton yarn. While the Jardine Matheson mills in China were experiencing a decline in sales, and were stopping night shift work, the Shanghai Cotton Spinning Company had orders large enough to continue 24-hour production. The dividends paid for the three years from 1903 to 1905 were 8, 10, and 20 percent. The productivity per spindle in 1905 was 75 percent of that of Kanegafuchi, a leading spinning company in Japan, compared with the average Chinese mill level of 60 percent (Takamura 1982, p. 80).

After 1910, when the Japanese spinning industry virtually stopped importing Chinese raw cotton, Mitsui Bussan's Shanghai branch was able to replace this lost business by having learned to buy and sell Chinese raw cotton to the Chinese, and to handle Chinese yarn which they handled in the same quantities as Japanese yarn for which they were the principle importers. The other two major cotton brokers, Nihon Menka and Naigai Wata, followed Mitsui's example and set up mills in China through a joint venture with the Chinese in 1905, in the case of the former; in the case of the latter, they built their own mills in 1911, 1912, and 1915.

By participating in spinning operations in China these three Japanese trading companies acquired a very detailed knowledge of the Chinese cotton textile industry. By 1922 they had overcome the fierce competition among traders on the Raw Cotton Exchange in Shanghai. After this the Japanese traders gained control, their international intelligence network working considerably in their favor as well as their close contact with cotton growers. By 1922 they had almost full control of supplies of foreign raw cotton, and about half of the supplies of Chinese raw cotton (Takamura 1982, p. 188). Their dominance in Chinese raw cotton had been achieved by setting up branches in the depots for raw cotton in the cotton growing areas. At planting time they made contracts with the farmers and encouraged the farmers to grow American raw cotton for which they would pay an advance cash payment of 70 percent of the agreed price. They then sold the quality-checked raw cotton directly to the mills, in contrast to the Chinese trading structure which involved a long chain of middlemen between the producer and the ultimate purchaser such that the price to the grower hardly covered the cost of production, and there was a temptation to adulterate the raw cotton with sand and water. The Chinese mills had to wait until the cotton harvest for lack of funds to make cash advances to the farmers, by which time they risked higher prices. It has been suggested that the Japanese traders manipulated the prices at key times to ensure that the Chinese mills had to pay high prices (Takamura 1982, p. 185).

The same Japanese trading companies also gained control of yarn transactions; one of the contributing reasons for this was their substantial bargaining power in relation to the Chinese mills and the monopoly of supply from the *zaikabo*. *Zaikabo* were normally given 30 days in which to pay for raw cotton deliveries, which enabled them to delay the sale of yarn according to the prevailing market price. (During the boycotts they were offered 60 days.)

The Chinese mills were given only 10 days for payment for raw cotton, within which time they had to work day and night in order to produce the yarn and sell it, from which payments they settled their raw cotton accounts. This resulted in a weak negotiating position in relation to the yarn purchaser, for a failure to sell would require the raising of loans to pay for the raw cotton. In this haste to produce yarn its quality inevitably suffered. The Japanese trading companies took advantage of this situation and bought from the Chinese mills enforcing low prices.

In conclusion, the Japanese trading companies operated in China as they did in Japan as the driving force of the Japanese cotton textile industry. They opened and developed markets for raw cotton and manufactured product. They assessed the risks and developed strategies to absorb the risks, thus enabling the spinners to concentrate on increasing their efficiency in spinning and weaving operations. In China the Japanese traders were able to protect the spinners from the trading uncertainties, assist them in riding out the political uncertainties, and to replicate to a significant extent the certainties of supply and sales that they enjoyed in Japan, thus helping to minimize the potentially damaging effects of the Chinese economic and political context. The Chinese spinners had no such support, and as a consequence suffered not only from the weakness of their own government, but also from competition from the presence of foreign mills in their domestic economy.

The Operational Efficiency of Japanese Firms in China

Most of the elite Japanese spinning companies started operations in China en bloc between 1920 and 1922 at a time of rapid growth in yarn and cloth output from Chinese mills. One of the motives of the Japanese mills was to protect their export market shares in China, thus the larger Japanese export spinning companies established larger mills in China than the smaller export companies (Kuwahara 1989, p. 159).

The decision to set up production operations in China was based on factors such as the relatively low wage costs in China, the less stringent labor regulations which allowed night shift working, the probability of the Chinese government raising taxes on the import of foreign yarn, and increasing competition in the Chinese yarn market from the Chinese spinners whose prices were lower and volume of production increasing. The setting up of mills in China would therefore give the Japanese mills access to the same capital goods, labor, and raw cotton markets as the Chinese mills, but in order to retain price competitiveness in the yarn and cloth markets, productivity would have to be higher to offset the higher managerial costs. These were quite considerable as all managerial posts, including frontline managers, were held by Japanese (Kuwahara 1992, p. 151). The Big Ten exporting companies were able to draw on the experiences of the Japanese trading companies already operating mainly in Shanghai; these were the three main cotton trading companies that had started mill operations as early as 1902 (Mitsui Bussan), 1905 (Nihon Menka), and 1911 (Naigai Wata).

Having decided to set up production operations in China, the top-ranking Japanese spinning companies drew on their experience of building new mills and of remodeling old mills acquired during the period of rapid expansion and consolidation of ownership in the Japanese industry prior to and during the First World War. Most of the *zaikabo* mills were new buildings, or substantially modified old ones, equipped with heating and humidity control systems, and installed with the most advanced spinning and weaving machines available in Japan (Toyo Boseki 1986, p. 309). There was a replication of the substantial homogeneity among companies of managerial and technical practice which included sophisticated blending techniques and rigorous repair and maintenance schedules. New managerial and technical innovations that were developed in Japan, in particular after 1926, were transferred rapidly to the mills in China. Hence the Chinese mill owners had in their midst a powerful group of competitors who were operating with the most sophisticated technology of the period.

In conclusion, the Chinese mills were generally less well-organized technically, and produced lower quality products, but a few leading mills were striving toward the standards set by the Japanese; improvements in labor productivity nearly doubled between 1929 and 1935. The Chinese mill owners had an impetus to improve efficiency because of the competition from the *zaikabo*, which were exemplary in their employment of the latest technical and managerial technologies. The diffusion of technical best practice from the *zaikabo* to the Chinese mills in terms of know-how was effected through the employment of technical staff who had been trained in the Japanese mills, through the machine suppliers, through visits by the Chinese mill owners to *zaikabo* mills, and as a result of pressure from banks to improve efficiency. There were, however, severe limitations on the implementation of this know-how arising from the weak financial position of the Chinese mill owners, and their inherent disinterest in the technical aspects of mill management (Takamura 1982, p. 192).

Japanese Labor Management Policies

Japanese managers of the *zaikabo* had good technical and administrative support from home country staff who were appointed on the basis of their skill and knowledge, and who were retained in key positions in the mills to control and coordinate mill operations. The transfer of managers and technicians from parent companies to their China mills and the employment of these well-trained people in key positions enabled the continuation of clear demarcation of accountability, close supervision of operatives, and a strong emphasis on the training of Chinese employees. The organization structure of the parent mills was replicated in China, with engineers and experienced workers as a core group, and a hierarchy based on academic training and service (Kuwahara 1992, p. 151). During their leave trips back to Japan they familiarized themselves with the latest techniques which were then reviewed and implemented in the Chinese mills.

Both the Chinese and the *zaikabo* mills were faced with the same reservoir of abundant cheap labor. This was a very important factor in the Japanese spinning companies' decision to set up mills in China. However, the poorer quality of the Chinese workforce in comparison with the Japanese meant that larger numbers of staff were required per unit of output or machine unit, which offset, to a degree, the advantages of lower wages. Hence there was an additional pressure on the *zaikabo* management to raise the productivity of their workforce. Consequent to Muto Sanji's pioneering methods of improving the quality of Kanegafuchi's workforce through a "humanistic" approach, the Japanese mills in Japan had already by the early 1920s developed comprehensive labor management practices. These were sound training practices, including the special training of the overseers, the grading of jobs, comprehensive welfare facilities (dormitories, baths, schooling, medical facilities, recreational facilities, kindergartens), clean, tidy, well-ventilated and well-lit working and living conditions (Pearse 1929, pp. 91-100). This approach was also applied in China with some minor modifications to take account of the different context. In comparison with the Chinese mills, the *zaikabo* ran on slightly shorter hours, paid slightly higher wages, recruited a better type of labor, from whom on the whole they received more efficient results than did the Chinese mills (Chin 1937, pp. 246-247). Under such conditions the Japanese were successful in speeding up production and increasing the intensity of labor, and the Chinese worker came to be considered as little inferior to the Japanese after comparatively little training (Pearse 1929, p. 149). Utley (1938, p. 242) quotes a Japanese director's estimate that Chinese labor had an efficiency level of 85 percent of the Japanese.

A Chinese economist commented in 1932 that:

> Most Chinese employers believe that cheap labor means economical production and greater profits. They have not yet realized that if they bettered the conditions of their employees they would improve the quality of the work performed, reduce the costs due to sickness and accidents, and ultimately make greater profits. Many employers, of course, are virtually prohibited from attempting any improvements simply because they have not the necessary capital (Lasker 1932, p. 160).

There was, however, a growing realization among the owners of the larger Chinese cotton mills that new labor management policies would increase labor productivity and help alleviate the problems of continued debt (SASS 1980, pp. 163-164). This realization occurred from around 1923, soon after the Big Ten Japanese spinners began to establish mills in Shanghai.

Given the relatively poor levels of education of the Chinese workforce, the *zaikabo* instituted extensive training schemes within their mills. Before opening a mill selected groups of Chinese workers were sent to Japan for training. According to Kuwahara (1989, p. 7), Osaka Godo spinning company sent 30 Chinese girls for a month's training at their Kanzaki Mill in 1922, Kanegafuchi trained 170 Chinese staff for three to four months in 1922/1923, and Fukushima Cotton Spinning Company trained 50 in December 1923. When the mills were fully operational, all newly recruited workers were enrolled on a training program for 30-45 days. Kanegafuchi sent 57 Japanese instructors to assist with these programs.

These training schemes were a very important element in the diffusion of modern technologies. Pearse was very struck by the potential influence of the Japanese mills in China on the Chinese:

> Several Chinese mill-owners have praised to me the superiority of the Japanese system of training the Chinese workpeople by having a comparatively large number of young female overseers and by instituting greater discipline; in fact in several Chinese-managed mills this example was clearly followed, though the female overseers seemed less mobile than their Japanese sisters (Pearse 1929, p. 149).

Allen and Donnithorne (1954, pp. 95-96) describe in some detail the role of the foreign machinery suppliers in training and the diffusion of knowledge. After the First World War, overseas manufacturers arranged for Chinese industrial trainees to gain experience in their factories. In the early 1920s a number of Chinese were sent to England to obtain training in the maintenance of textile machinery; for example, the Jardine Engineering Company sponsored a scheme to send Chinese students for training in British factories. During the 1920s and 1930s, 80 percent of imported machinery went to Chinese concerns, in some of which these trained technicians were in managerial posts. The foreign engineering firms not only sold and arranged the installation of machines and trained staff, but in some cases representatives were assigned to Chinese organizations to supervise the plant. The smaller Chinese firms relied on the machine suppliers for machine maintenance and for information on technical innovations and specialities.

The Chinese government took little initiative in organizing technical education, whether overseas or at home. Most technical education was organized by private concerns. Not until the war period were any major initiatives undertaken by the government. In 1940 technical education began to receive increasing emphasis, and all new private or government educational institutions were required to set up engineering departments in preference to other disciplines (*China Institute Bulletin* 1940). The sending of students abroad was not fully coordinated and controlled by the government. For example, in 1932 it was reported that although 1,400 students were enrolled in Japanese schools, only 800 were actually continuing their education (*China Journal* 1932, p. 256). Also, the numbers sent abroad were small compared to the Japanese experience; the Cotton Industry Commission formed in 1932 to improve and develop the cotton industry sent only two college graduates to the United States for two years' study of the economics of cotton cultivation, and five students to Japan to study the technical processes and gain practical experience in Osaka (Yao 1935, p. 166).

In conclusion to this discussion of Japanese labor management policies, the *zaikabo* management were acutely aware of the need to build a skilled, effective workforce in order to maintain a competitive advantage over the Chinese mills. They employed a rational, thorough approach to achieve this aim. The management of their Chinese labor force (it was 63,500 in 1935) (*China Year Book* 1935, p. 572) was virtually the only direct confrontation they had with their Chinese environment; in respect of purchasing and selling activities, and financing, they dealt with Japanese mediators—the trading companies, the banks, or their own head offices in Japan. The Chinese mill owners were able, therefore, to learn directly about how the Japanese mills were able to achieve higher levels of labor and technical efficiency, primarily through themselves taking up employment in the *zaikabo* before setting up their own mills, or by recruiting those who had, and by arranging visits to the mills. The success of the Japanese in effectively adapting their practices to the Chinese context provided a convincing example to the Chinese of their feasibility; the issue for the Chinese mill owners was primarily one of resources to do so.

The Chinese mill owners gave serious consideration to adopting labor reforms in their mills in order to compete more effectively with the Japanese mills who had a much greater edge in terms of costs, quantity, and quality of production from the same number of spindles. After initial successes the reforms were extended in the Chinese mills. In 1925 there was more recruitment of technicians, and more power was given to the workshop leaders. Coordination between technical and administrative leaders was improved, laboratories and maintenance divisions were established. Greater supervision over workers was instituted; rest times and absences from work were controlled, chairs were removed from the production areas, workers were fined if caught sleeping. Dismissals, beating of workers, and fines were used as disciplinary tools. Initially the workers reacted by striking and were agitated by the foremen. By 1927 many of the Chinese cotton and flour mills had gone over to the "supervisor system" from the "foreman system." The power of the foremen gradually declined, machine speeds increased, production costs per piece reduced, and wastage reduced. In Shen Xin Mill No. 3, where the reforms started in 1923, daily production of pieces per 10,000 spindles increased from 17.90 to 20.48 by 1926, an increase of 14 percent (SASS 1980, p. 164). "The preliminary 'scientific management' system was thus completed" (Memoirs of Lou Zhen-dan, 1959, in SASS 1980, p. 157).

Foreign Influences on the Chinese Entrepreneurial Elite

According to Bergere (1983, p. 745), at the beginning of the 1920s a new generation of businessmen appeared, a new urban elite, who through contact with foreigners were able to grasp the importance of modern technology and management (Bergere 1983, p. 753). Bergere identified them as a modern bourgeoisie who were devoted to the ideology of industrial growth, free enterprise, and economic rationality. They emerged from "a semi-colonial environment dominated by the West. The businessmen of the new generation in whom this modern bourgeoisie was embodied had carried out their studies abroad. They were better informed of the realities of the contemporary world and enjoyed greater freedom from the traditional restraints" (Bergere 1983, p. 755). They felt themselves interdependent with the working class; and advocated reduced working hours, increased wages, and introduced profit sharing for the workers. They believed that education had an important role in developing the working class, in improving living conditions, and in improving the quality of manpower for industry.

This new elite had acquired from their Western or Japanese education[6] and through their commercial and political contacts, a profound influence of Western science, technology, economic concepts, social theories, and ethical standards for modern industry. From the mid-1920s significant improvements in managerial practice were made in the leading Chinese cotton mills. In the 1920s, 73 percent of the spindleage in Shanghai was controlled by these "nonofficial," merchant families, whereas the official gentry group predominated in the interior where they controlled 62 percent of the spindleage (Bush 1982, p. 47). For both groups investment in cotton mills was one of a number of ways in which to achieve wealth, status, and power, and it was often combined with other avenues such as political office at local or national level, intermarriage with other families, investment in land and commerce, and investment in the education of children as a mechanism for ensuring continuing status for the family (Bush 1982, p. 51; Wong 1979, p. 155).

Diversified business interests were typical among the Shanghai entrepreneurs of the 1920s and 1930s (Elvin 1981, p. 272). They played both modern and traditional roles—they led both traditional guilds and the newly created Chambers of Commerce. They appeared to be versatile individualists rather than organization men in comparison with their Japanese counterparts. They were closely connected with foreigners, many of them began as or had been compradors for Western or Japanese firms. The initial transfer of modern business skills to both entrepreneurs and workers took place through prior employment in Western and Japanese firms, through repairs and subcontracting carried out for foreign firms, and through Western education and the study and imitation of foreign operations. For example, the Wing On Mills run by the Kwok family were noted for their centralized control and clear-cut division of labor; a second generation son had been sent to the United States to study textile engineering in Massachusetts, and it was thought that the family's many years of exposure to Western settings led them to put more emphasis on Western training (Bush 1982, p. 62).

In the Rong Enterprise organizational reforms were first introduced in 1919, at a time when there was an emphasis on rational administration in the textile industry, and as a result of the overseas education received by the second generation of mill owners. A unified management body was considered necessary for the Rong Enterprise to keep pace with its rapid development. In 1919 a chief company was set up to unify the operations of the two flour mill companies that had 12 mills, and the cotton mill company that now had four mills. Purchasing and selling divisions were established. On the purchasing side, wheat mills and raw cotton collecting points were set up. On the sales side, flour and yarn wholesaling departments were established. Through these activities, more control over the farmers was exerted, as was control over the markets into which the finished products were sold. In 1924 the Rong brothers decided to introduce Japanese methods of labor management. They moved from the contractual foreman system to one of direct labor control using professional graduates as supervisors. The reforms were pioneered in Shen Xin Mill No. 3, by Rong Zong-jing (SASS 1980, pp. 156-159):

> During the early period of operation, the old-fashioned foreman system was continued....Later, because of the inability to compete with outsiders, and of the fundamental conflicts of interests between foreman and capitalists, we gradually employed professional graduates to manage the workshops, and we abolished the foreman system. In this way production was increased and maintenance of machinery was guaranteed.

In contrast with Japan, where the new business elite shared a unity of interest with the government officials in developing Japan's economic status, the new merchant elite in China inherited a justified mistrust in the power of the state. From 1927 the Kuomintang regime began an offensive to subordinate private merchant organizations, for example, the anti-Japanese boycotts were used to subdue the bourgeoisie to the power of the state. The 1928 boycott was controlled and directed by the government, and in 1932 nonobservation of boycotts led to terrorist attacks by Kuomintang militants and gangsters (Bergere 1983, p. 813). The new business elite of perhaps a few hundred (p. 758) tried to preserve their autonomy, but when the government supported by the powerful network of official banks tried to take over their businesses, it was usually successful (Bergere 1983, p. 818). The Kuomintang government made no attempt to create an institutional framework favorable to private enterprise, as evident from the lack of support to industry during the 1932-1935 industrial depression. When the Kuomintang government regained power immediately after the war it continued to pursue similar policies.

In contrasting the industrial development of China and Japan, Jacobs (1958, p. 52) noted that in China the ruler had the ethical right to control production and distribution if he so wished, thus there was a constant threat of possible arbitrary imposition of monopoly, without any institutional channels for protest. Whereas in Japan, because concentrations of economic power were independent, the ruler had to grant political economic concessions, rights, and privileges in order to obtain the necessary economic cooperation of these independent economic interests. The *zaikabo* were confident of the support of their government whenever they needed it, but the Chinese government did little to protect the Chinese cotton industry from dominance by the *zaikabo*, and when it did so it faced retaliation from the Japanese government. The Chinese government was limited by a number of factors in its dealings with the foreign presence in the Chinese cotton industry. The formal treaty system gave foreigners extraterritorial rights, control of taxation, and the capability to defend their interests militarily. Bush (1982), in his analysis of the politics of cotton textiles in Kuomintang China, highlights the political and economic power of the Japanese in China, and the lack of unity of action between the Chinese mill owners and their government in promoting the development of the Chinese cotton industry.

INSTITUTIONAL INFLUENCES ON THE EARLY DEVELOPMENT OF MODERN INDUSTRY IN CHINA

Having traced briefly the development of modern enterprises in China, and the Japanese influence in the textile industry, I now identify some of the institutional influences on the development of modern industry in the Chinese economy in the Republican and Nationalist periods. These are the role of the state, the Treaty Ports, problems of capital formation, the role of merchants, and the management practices in modern Chinese enterprises.

The Role of the State

A significant factor in China's modern industrial development (since the mid-nineteenth century, late Ch'ing period) has been the subjugation of economic activities to the political structure of state officials. Until the late Ch'ing period merchants had been considered as socially inferior to officials and farmers. They were able to influence bureaucrats in support of their interests, but were not allowed to make an independent stand for their interests. Hence the modern industrial enterprise rose in China either under government ownership, according to earlier institutional values (the salt monopoly provided a model) or under constant threat of government interference. Nongovernment capital for investment was either lacking or unwilling to invest in enterprises sponsored by government as a result of previous government interference and control.

In comparison with Japan, there was no conception among the late nineteenth-century elite of China of economic development, industrial revolution, and modern transformation. Chinese officials continued to disdain merchants, and any private initiative in this direction in the government industries or government supervised merchant undertakings was stifled by bureaucratic inefficiency, nepotism, and corruption. In China's political and social hierarchy, the bureaucracy was the source of prestige and privilege, and those permitted to enter it had the highest social status and enjoyed the most privileges protected by sumptuary laws. Merchants were discriminated against because their economic power was a threat to those privileges (Chu 1957, pp. 248, 250). Consequently, the government and its administration paid very little attention to industrial developments and the genuine economic reconstruction of the country. In 1931 a Bank of China official complained that still "most of the government expenditures are used in wasteful and unproductive ways" (HSBC 1931a).

China also faced the problem of a lack of autonomy in her industrial development as the Treaty Powers controlled her foreign trade and revenues, and prevented China from protecting her developing industries.[7] Moulder (1977) concluded that Japan was more successful in its development because it occupied a more autonomous position vis-à-vis the Western powers, and thus was able to pursue policies to promote and protect the development of modern industry and retain the benefits of these policies for further development of her national economy.

Private enterprise in the early industrial development of China developed as a result of foreign intervention in the "official" power structure of the late Ch'ing period. After the Treaty of Shimonoseki in 1895,[8] which broke the monopoly power of the bureaucratic capitalists, merchants and gentry officials took advantage of the opportunity to set up their own enterprises, each drawing on their sphere of connections and resources. In the textile industry the merchants' previous occupations had been largely connected with the cotton trade, such as yarn and cloth trading, general merchandizing, dyeing, and printing. Textile mills run by merchant families were predominant in Shanghai, and those run by gentry officials were predominant in the interior. The latter could draw on their political connections in their home town, while the former had the security of the International Settlement in Shanghai for the avoidance of official interference.

The Treaty Ports

China's modern industry was centered on Shanghai, a natural development of its status as a major national trading center. The British had recognized the importance of Shanghai's role in the economy when it was included as one of the five Treaty Ports in the Treaty of Nanjing in 1842. After this the center for foreign trade shifted from Canton to Shanghai. It was chosen as the location for the first modern cotton spinning mill by Li Chung-hang, who set up the Shanghai Cotton Cloth Mill in the 1880s, and for four of its five subsidiary mills. By the 1930s the concentration of modern industry in Shanghai was overwhelming. It had about half of all the foreign investment in China (including Manchuria), more than half of the modern textile production, and in 1934 more than half of the factories of China—as defined by Chinese law. It was the sixth ranking port in the world, had a population of over four million, and had become a different economic world from the rest of China (Elvin 1981, p. 260).

Elvin, in his discussion of the interrelationship between Shanghai and its rural hinterland (1981, pp. 254-261), suggests that Shanghai's successful economic development was due to the supply and demand provided by the international market which removed the effects of the "high equilibrium trap" in the rural hinterland which he defined as a technological immobility that made any sustained qualitative economic progress impossible. According to Elvin (1972), in China's interior there was no stimulus for changes in the pattern of demand and supply because of premodern technical ceilings in the productivity of agriculture and water transport.

The Treaty Ports[9] gave facilities for secure investment in industry which other parts of China did not have. The prerequisites for industrial development of good government and a modern outlook were satisfied in the Treaty Ports more closely than elsewhere in China. They were governed by the laws of industrial nations, had good transport and communication facilities; trade, finance, and other institutions to support industrial development; good supplies of cheap labor; and easy recruitment of foreigners with technical skills (Fong 1937, pp. 259-260).

Prerequisites that were not satisfied in the rest of China, and therefore were obstacles to China's industrial development, were, firstly, taxes. In particular, the likin or transit tax, and the treaty protection of foreign manufacturing from Chinese taxes: Chinese textile goods were subject to varying transit taxes, up to 2.5 percent higher than taxation on foreign goods. Second, the lack of uniformity in currency, weights, and measures: the standardization of these is crucial for successful economic development. The failure of the Chinese government to deal with the question of currency was important for it introduced an element of speculation in any development of trade. However, in the Treaty Ports, the foreign banks supervised stable monetary systems, and provided a model for the development of Chinese joint stock banking in these ports. Third, unsettled political conditions together with frequent military action prevented the development of an appropriate infrastructure for economic development (Lieu 1928, p. 407). This essential requirement of stable political conditions was never present in China. A political report for 1933 made by the manager of the Hongkong and Shanghai Bank, Shanghai Branch, to his superior in Hong Kong, describes the situation succinctly.

> An undeclared war with a neighbouring country, civil war in several provinces and a vigorous military campaign against a communist rebellion all going on at the same time....We who have lived in China for some years do not regard these conditions as out of the ordinary. They are endemic and we are able to discount much of the disturbance since we know from experience that trade will go on and that the Chinese have an amazing way of localizing their internal disorders. None of these events have directly affected the great trading centres of Shanghai, Canton and the important Yangtze Valley. This has enabled trade to carry on with some measure of normalcy, but the cumulative effect of the disorders in various parts of China has undoubtedly played its part in reducing the value of China's trade to the low record which it now holds (HSBC 1933).

Problems of Capital Formation

The shortage of bureaucratic capital had been exacerbated by the attempts to repel foreign imperialism in the late Ch'ing period, and the cost of the indemnities when these failed.[10] The limited private capital that was available was subject to government taxes to raise support for the new government undertakings, and was wary of becoming involved with the bureaucracy and its inexperience of merchant enterprise. Capital formation was difficult as profits were distributed to shareholders as dividends rather than reinvested because shareholders were only prepared to invest under conditions of guaranteed returns. In the traditional banking sector they were used to returns as high as 25 percent (Feuerwerker 1958, p. 53). These expectations led to very high financing costs for modern private enterprises and drained them of spare capital for reinvestment.

In his study of the first two modern cotton mills, Morrell (1968, pp. 56-61) found that capital-raising efforts for modern industry had to compete with both the Western trading companies in the Treaty Ports, and the traditional outlets for surplus capital such as land and the native banks. Merchants were willing to invest heavily in many of the foreign companies operating in the Treaty Ports but not to invest in Chinese enterprises in which there was no protection from the arbitrary practices of officials or speculation by the comprador managers. These fears were justified in the case of the first mill, the Shanghai Cotton Cloth Mill (1878-1892): by 1887, 30 percent of its capital had been squandered by a combination of speculation, incompetence, and accumulated interest payments and salaries. In 1890 the mill finally began to produce cloth, but the plant was totally destroyed by fire in 1892.

Capital-raising efforts in the textile industry were exacerbated by the size of the mills being promoted; the first three *kuan-tu shang-pan* cotton mills each had between 35,000 and 65,000 spindles[11] compared to the first Japanese mills, which in the early 1890s had an average of around 10,000 spindles. The first government-sponsored mills in Japan had only 6,000 spindles between the three mills. The aspirations for large mills in these early stages of the development of the Chinese textile industry placed an unnecessary strain on the problems of raising capital. Mills were constructed and run before the full required capital had been raised. The promoters of these mills were motivated by the huge demand for cloth; the projected output of 260,000 pieces of cotton goods for the first year from the Shanghai Cotton Cloth Mill would amount to less than 2 percent of the total annual import figure for cotton goods (Morrell 1968, p. 46). The emphasis on quantity rather than quality of operations provided a weak base for long-term viability. Spare capital was used for expansion rather than for building up reserves and the depreciation of equipment and machinery; or it was used for the purchase of land, political office, and other means of developing power and status. The development of a private modern enterprise was not an end in itself, but a means of achieving power and status for the owner's family in Chinese society.

The six mills set up under the Self-Strengthening Movement all failed financially as *kuan-tu shang-pan* enterprises; three were eventually taken over by Japanese interests, and two were privatized by their official managers (Feuerwerker 1958, pp. 223-224). Financial difficulties continued to plague the modern industry right up to the Communist Revolution in 1949. Financial weakness was a constant problem for the Chinese entrepreneurs. Their attitude toward accumulation of capital and its uses was an underlying cause. In periods of boom they were able to make large profits, which were not used as in the Japanese mills, to strengthen their strategic positions in the marketplace, but to support other business interests.

These difficulties were compounded by weaknesses in the Chinese banking system. The Self-Strengthening Movement had included an attempt to establish modern banking "based on the foreign model in order to facilitate development of foreign commerce" (Wei 1987, p. 162). The Commercial Bank of China was founded in 1897 as a private bank with rights to issue currency, coins, to syndicate and manage government borrowing, and to serve as a depository for government funds. The first official bank was formed in 1904, and eventually became known as the Bank of China. Other banks organized on modern banking principles of secured loans and adequate reserves were: Bank of Communications, Chekiang Industrial Bank, Bank of Ningpo, and The Shanghai and Commercial Savings Bank; by 1926, 390 banking institutions in China were listed in the *Banking Year Book*.

These banks developed without the foundation of a legal framework. A 1908 law regulating the operations of commercial houses was never enforced. The Commercial Bank Law was promulgated in 1931 and the Savings Bank Law in 1934, but enforcement was postponed indefinitely. The banks, anticipating their enforcement, did, however, make adjustments (Young 1935, p. 73). The growth of modern banks was rapid but not without setbacks; they were forced to compromise on the issue of secured loans because of the long-standing practice of the native banks of offering loans on personal credit, without any tangible security. Hence, modern banking instruments were only partially developed. Although the native banks were declining in view of the advances of modern banks, they retained their influence in the special localities in which they had established close personal relationships with local industrialists (Chin 1937, p. 238). There were three types of native banks: the customs banks that were depositories of taxes and government revenue; merchant-owned banks principally owned by merchants who had large business transactions in various parts of the country, which issued paper drafts in return for gold and silver currency; and money shops that lent on an unsecured basis, and received deposits without any notion of credit reliability or the principle of reserves (Wei 1987, pp. 156-158).

The development of modern Chinese banks was greatly influenced by the banking of traditional China, and by the great foreign exchange banks of the Treaty Ports. The Republican government achieved some successes in its institution of banking reforms based on Western principles (Young 1935), although according to Remer (1926, p. 187) little could be achieved without the establishment of a stable government. By 1928 the Central Bank of China had been established, and an organization for the exchange of credit information was set up in 1932. In the same year the Bankers' Institute was set up. In 1933 the tael was abolished as a medium of exchange; there had been hundreds of different taels circulating in different localities with different names, weights, and fineness. According to Remer (HSBC 1931b) the modern banks paid little attention to the financial problems of industrial development. The Bank of China took an insignificant role in the development of modern industries. Its 1932 report stated that only 11.46 percent of loans were to industrial enterprises. The political situation was felt to be responsible for a policy of caution in the granting of credit. Undercapitalization was also blamed for the failure of some and the retardation of other industrial enterprises (Nieh 1933, p. 26).

The foreign banks played a very important role in the development of China's international trade, and a less significant role in the development of her indigenous industries. According to Feuerwerker (1976, pp. 86-87), by the 1920s there were 12 foreign banks operating in China, and all had branches in Shanghai. They were principally engaged in financing the import and export trade of foreign firms, but some advances were also made to Chinese merchants. Their main impact on the Chinese commercial structure was, until the 1911 Revolution, through short-term loans to the native banks. The foreign banks used their extraterritorial position to issue bank notes and they controlled the foreign exchange market in China; the exchange rates offered by the Hongkong Bank were accepted as the official rates by the entire Shanghai market. Wealthy

Chinese in particular preferred to deposit their liquid assets in foreign banks because of their extraterritorial protection from the high-handedness of government officials (Bergere 1983, p. 728).

The Role of Merchants

Chinese merchants were able to control the commercial process for much of the import/export trade with Western countries in the early twentieth century (Feuerwerker 1976, pp. 80-83). The foreign traders invariably did business through compradors, and their role became increasingly that of commission agents in Shanghai and Hong Kong serving the established Chinese commercial network. The exceptions were two British firms—Jardine, Matheson & Co. and Butterfield and Swire—and the German and Japanese trading firms who engaged in direct distribution through local Chinese agents who worked on a commission basis. Also, the German traders had extensive distribution networks of Chinese agents supervised by European inspectors, and direct trading methods were adopted at the insistence of the German manufacturing companies. Manufacturing companies of standardized or proprietary goods such as cigarettes, kerosene, dyes, patent medicines and soap, and sewing machines also adopted direct selling methods to Chinese dealers. Hence even "direct" selling methods relied on Chinese dealers and still depended on China's traditional marketing structure to reach the final consumer.

In cotton textiles, the Chinese merchants were able to acquire control of most aspects of the import of cotton piece goods because the technical skill and commercial knowledge required was lower than, say, for machinery imports. Allen and Donnithorne (1954, pp. 90-91) also noted that they were able to acquire a higher degree of control over the import of British cotton goods than those from Japan, and that by the late 1880s the Western foreign merchants' role was largely reduced to sourcing cotton piece goods on a commission basis for Chinese importers. Feuerwerker (1976, pp. 85-86) states that beyond the commercial structure itself, what fundamentally limited the impact of Western merchants and their goods was the overall poverty of the Chinese economy.

The Chinese commercial organization and its relationship with modern textile mills was protected to a degree by the different markets in which the Chinese mills and foreign mills operated.[12] The Chinese mills produced almost exclusively for the domestic market, and the Japanese dominated the export market. The Chinese mills specialized in manufacturing yarn which was distributed to interior points for handloom weaving by farming women during the winter months (*China Year Book* 1928, p. 854). The Chinese mills disposed of their yarn either by their own selling departments or through the yarn dealers—there were about 50 in Shanghai. The dealer charged a commission on each bale sold, and made payment by a five-day bill drawn on a local native bank (King and Lieu 1930, p. 280).

The export market was of little importance to the Chinese mills as they had "not familiarized themselves with the demands of foreign markets, nor [had] they any mercantile organization to distribute their output to foreign countries" (Moser 1930, p. 67). Allen and Donnithorne (1954, p. 204) noted that the Chinese native mercantile enterprise was handicapped by the weak organization of financial and ancillary services, by the fact that most of the large-scale production was in foreign hands, and by the indifference of the Chinese government.

In their study of the role of the Western enterprise in the development of China's modern economy, Allen and Donnithorne (1954, p. 249) concluded that the contribution of Westerners and Japanese to the development of the modern Chinese economy was technical knowledge, capital, and a legal and political framework for business dealings, while the Chinese supplied labor, natural resources, and a subordinate commercial organization. The successful premodern Chinese commercial organization failed to compete in many respects with the strong organization of the Japanese trading companies, but it did manage to compete successfully with Western trading companies.

Management of Chinese Enterprises

The patterns of ownership of modern Chinese enterprises changed according to principles identified by Wong (1988, pp. 140-142). Businesses were often started with partners who split once one of the entrepreneurs had accumulated enough capital to start on their own. Decision making then became centralized and freedom was attained to use capital in the business or for lateral expansion. For example, the Rong family of father and two sons initially set up in business with compradors and bureaucrats. According to Bush (1982, pp. 47-65), the father had been a tax collector. They first set up a money shop, the profits of which were invested in commercial activities and a cocoon business. The profits from these enabled them to set up flour and textile mills with the cooperation of bureaucrats and compradors in 1902 and 1906. The mills faced frequent financial and operational difficulties until the 1911 Revolution. During the First World War the flour mills expanded rapidly, and the textile mills made good profits. The distribution of the profits caused a dispute between the shareholders of the cotton mill, and the nonfamily members tried to oust one of the Rong brothers from power. So the Rong family withdrew and set up Shen Xin in the form of an unlimited company to ensure control by the Rong family. By 1936 their Shen Xin group of mills was the largest—comprising 11 percent of the total spindleage in cotton mills in China (SASS 1980, p. 549).

Labor turnover was very high in the urban industries of China, as it was in Japan. Much of it was due to social reasons, the feature of a workforce which was not yet fully urbanized. The workers returned to their villages as soon as they had saved some money. Slight illness, indisposition, family councils, religious ceremonies, all resulted in workers returning to their native villages, with new untried, untrained workers having to take their places (Takamura 1982, p. 177). In Shanghai most of the workforce came from the country; they were attracted to Shanghai not because they were starving, but because they could increase their earnings and perhaps their savings. Their labor at the beginning was seasonal. The permanently urbanized laborers principally consisted of workers who came to the large cities under these conditions and remained there. Others were those surplus to village life and would otherwise have gone into the army or become household servants (*China Year Book* 1924, p. 540).

Labor supply for urban industries was organized according to the *patou* system, a contract system which had been common for many decades in the mining and tobacco industries and among dock workers. Under the *patou* system, employers delegated the hiring of labor to middlemen, usually professional agents. In many cases these people were also appointed by mine and factory owners as foremen or supervisors, so that they be held responsible for the workers they had signed up. Factory owners therefore had little responsibility for their workers, except in a limited number of cases where the contractor's function was hiring only. The contractors took their "squeeze" from the workers' wages; 10 percent of the daily wage was the tradition, but sometimes it was as high as 20 percent. The contractor supplied food and lodging, paid by the employer or by deduction from the wages of the worker. This countrywide system had been in existence for generations, and resulted in a class of hire labor agents who by the early 1930s were very powerful. Another common practice in Chinese industry was the sale of jobs. In the Pootung factory of British-American Tobacco company, of 4,000 female workers, over 10 percent were substitutes. Jobs were sold to other workers; the price customarily paid for a B.A.T. job was US$150, which was paid off in monthly installments over many years (*China Forum* 1932, pp. 11-12).

In the textile industry, however, there was dissatisfaction with the *patou* or foreman system, to which was attributed low output and high consumption of raw cotton. The foreman system entailed two systems of worker management in the cotton mills, with unskilled and skilled workers being managed separately. By the mid-1920s all the Japanese mills had abandoned the foreman system, and introduced a comprehensive labor management system which had been developed in Japan. This raised the productivity of the Chinese labor force. Lieu (1928) noted that many Chinese cotton and flour mills had also gone over to the "supervisor system" from the "foreman system."

> When modern factories were established in China, managers did not know how to deal with the workforce who were generally hired through foremen....Now the graduates of

> the middle and vocational schools, who know something about the working of machines, are employed as supervisors, and the hands are hired directly by the management and put under their supervision. Many of these young men are intelligent, understand some English terms for machinery, and know the process. They also treat the labor with more consideration than the foremen (Lieu 1928, p. 400).

CONCLUSION

The Japanese spinners were able to dominate the Chinese cotton spinning industry, not only because of their superior technical and organizational efficiency, but also because of the degree of support from associated institutions—finance, trading, and government in particular. The Japanese mills were successful in replicating in China the structure of their industry in Japan, thus limiting the negative effects of the Chinese societal context. The Chinese cotton textile entrepreneurs sought to imitate the *zaikabo*, particularly in respect of intraorganizational practices. Interorganizational practices were not so easy to imitate because of the different institutional structure of Chinese society.

The *zaikabo* were able to concentrate entirely on the improvement of spinning operations, leaving the broker/trading companies to manage the risks inherent in the volatile cotton markets. The Chinese spinners were unable to gain such a shield; they had to cope with the complexities of setting up modern industrial enterprises and of managing the effects of a nonsupportive, if not hostile domestic marketplace with no benefit of support from trading companies or government.

The Chinese cotton spinning industry did not develop the same degree of homogeneity as did the Japanese. There was a wide range in the standards of practice between the Chinese mills. In the case of the *zaikabo*, the mills were set up with the latest production equipment and environmental control devices (the high humidity of Shanghai summers restricted spinning efficiency). Cost accounting procedures were used to provide control information, standards were worked out for raw cotton and processing costs, and comparative studies of each mill made. Mills with a poor performance were investigated and the faults corrected (Seki 1956, p. 88).

In the Chinese mills, however, the management did not necessarily have any knowledge of costing, finance, sales, or engineering, as they were more likely to be appointed on the basis of a personal relationship with the owner. The job of day-to-day management was in some mills assigned to a foreman. It was a matter of luck as to whether a profit was made. As raw cotton comprises a substantial element in the production cost of yarn, and raw cotton prices and yarn prices are volatile according to national and international supply and demand, mill managers were tempted to speculate on the raw cotton market as a way of making profit. When profit was made, the first priority was to pay dividends to the shareholders who were family or relatives of the owner. The depreciation of fixed assets and payment of debt were secondary. Many Chinese entrepreneurs had no practical commercial knowledge and were unwilling to seek advice or employ technical experts (Chin 1937, p. 217).

By the outbreak of war in 1937 it was apparent that the *zaikabo* mills had provided a model for the development of textile mill management for the Shanghainese. The diffusion of Japanese practices was limited by a number of factors among which were the institutional, cultural, political, and economic conditions in prewar China. Chao (1977, p. 136), in his discussion of the relative strengths of the positive impact of the model effect of the Japanese on the Chinese, and the negative impact of lack of protection for the nascent cotton textile industry, concluded that the model effect should be stronger. The combination of the model effect and the sharpened competition with the presence of the Japanese mills led to the rapid development of better management and adoption of more advanced technology.

In conclusion to this analysis of the influence of Japanese influence on China from the mid-nineteenth century to 1937, I quote from Hsu:

> Modern China represents such a broad spectrum of kaleidoscopic change that...it cannot be satisfactorily explained by the restrictive theories of foreign imperialism, Western impact and feudal exploitation. The dynamics of change suggests that modern Chinese history is not characterized by a passive response to the West, but by an active struggle of the Chinese to meet the foreign and domestic challenges in an effort to regenerate and transform their country from an outdated Confucian universal empire to a modern national state (Hsu 1983, p. 13).

In this review of foreign influence on the early modernization of China, I have briefly examined the failure of the Self-Strengthening Movement (1986-1895) which prevented foreign participation in the setting up of modern enterprises. This movement failed under the pressure of Japan and European powers to gain entry into the vast China market. In 1895 Japan successfully broke the resistance of the Chinese government to the setting up of factories by foreigners. The foreign powers took advantage of their protected status in the Treaty Ports, especially Shanghai, and successfully set up their own spheres of economic influence, including an independent financial sector, which were sheltered from the exigencies of the Chinese state.

NOTES

1. The title of a best-selling book written in 1937 by Carl Crow, an American advertising and merchandizing agent with 25 years' experience of business in China (Crow 1937).

2. According to Hsu (1983, p. 344), the defeat exposed the decadence of the Manchu dynasty and invited foreign powers to engage in a scramble for concessions. The intensification of (foreign) imperialism plunged China into a semicolonial state from which it was not freed until 1943.

3. Cheng Kuan-ying (1842-1922) was Cantonese. He had been a comprador for 30 years with Dent and Company and with Butterfield and Swire, leading English firms in Shanghai. He was associated with the China Merchants' Steam Navigation Company from 1882 to 1921. He was a supporter of Sheng Hsuan-huai in a number of *kuan-tu shang-pan* enterprises headed by Sheng. Cheng was useful to him in raising capital for his projects from investors in Canton Province (Feuerwerker 1958, pp. 116-117).

4. Between 1917 and 1931, 14 Chinese mills had borrowed from Japanese sources (Takamura 1982, p. 129).

5. Pearse (1929, p. 222) observed: "The Chinese wholesale dealer is ready to enter into direct business relations with the cotton manufacturer in Europe, but such a change makes the supervision of the business in Shanghai and at other places in the interior imperative. The training of the necessary staff will take some years, but this evolution of direct trade must eventually take the place of the many intermediaries that operate at present."

6. After the 1870s Western educationalists established schools and colleges in China, and Chinese students began to visit in increasing numbers Japanese, American, and European universities. By 1906, 12,000 were studying in Japan, and 500 in the United States. In 1930, 5,032 students were in foreign universities, the majority in Japan and the United States. A 1930 survey of 566 eminent people in Chinese public life found that 27 percent had been educated in the United States, 16 percent in Japan, and 14 percent in Europe (Tawney 1983, pp. 13-14).

7. The right of Japan and Western powers to establish factories and industries in China, won by the Treaty of Shimonosek (1895), was accompanied by a privileged position in the Treaty Ports—the avoidance of customs duties and reduction of transport costs. With their vast capital and technical know-how, the foreign industrialists had a distinct advantage over Chinese entrepreneurs (Hsu 1983, p. 345).

8. The 1894 Sino-Japan War ended in a humiliating defeat for the Chinese. The treaty recognized the independence of Korea, the cession of Taiwan and the Liaotung peninsula to the Japanese, the opening of four ports, and the right of the Japanese to open factories and engage in industry and manufacturing in China. These rights were extended to all treaty powers through the most-favored nation clause (Hsu 1983, p. 342).

9. The 1842 Treaty of Nanjing with Britain ceded Hong Kong to Britain, and opened up five ports—including Shanghai and Canton—for foreign trade. France and the United States were granted access to the ports in 1844. The 1858 Treaties of Tientsin with Britain, France, Russia, and the United States, included the opening of 10 new ports and lifting of travel restrictions on foreigners (Hsu 1983, p. 209).

10. Examples of foreign imperalism:

- 1874 Japanese invasion of Formosa
- 1879 Japanese annexation of Liu-ch'iu islands
- 1875 British attempt to open Yunnan
- 1884-1885 French seizure of Annam
- 1894-1895 Japanese aggression in Korea

11. The Shanghai Cotton Cloth Mill had 35,000 spindles and 350 looms in operation in 1890. It was rebuilt in 1894 as the Hua-sheng Spinning and Weaving Company with close to 65,000 spindles and 750 looms. The second mill, Hupei Cotton Cloth Mill, started with 30,000 spindles and expanded to 40,500 spindles and 1,000 looms. Subsequent *kuan-tu shang-pan* enterprises were less ambitious—a range of 9,000 to 25,000 spindles (Feuerwerker 1958, p. 222).

12. By 1928 there were 74 Chinese mills, 43 Japanese mills, and three British mills, the latter owned by Jardine Matheson (Pearse 1929, p. 156).

REFERENCES

Allen, G.C., and A.G. Donnithorne. 1954. *Western Enterprise in Far Eastern Economic Development.* New York: Macmillan.

Bedikton. 1935. *Commercial and Industrial Hong Kong: A Record of 94 Years Progress of the Colony in Commerce, Trade, Industry and Shipping 1841-1935.* Bedikton Company.

Bergere, M. 1983. "The Chinese Bourgeoisie, 1911-37." In *The Cambridge History of China, Volume 12*, edited by J.K. Fairbank. Cambridge, UK: Cambridge University Press.

Bush, R.C. 1982. *The Politics of Cotton Textiles in Kuomintang China 1927-1937.* New York: Garland Publishing Inc.

Chao, K. 1977. *The Development of Cotton Textile Production in China.* Cambridge, MA: Harvard University Press.

Chin, R.Q.P. 1937. "Japanese-owned Cotton Mills in China. A Study in International Competition." Ph.D. thesis, Yale University.

The China Forum. 1932. May.

China Institute Bulletin. 1940.

The China Journal. 1932.

The China Year Book. 1924.

The China Year Book. 1928.

The China Year Book. 1935.

Chu, T.T. 1957. "Chinese Class Structure and its Ideology." Pp. 235-250 in *Chinese Thought and Institutions*, edited by J.K. Fairbank. Chicago: University of Chicago Press.

Crow, C. 1937. *Four Hundred Million Customers.* Harper & Brothers: New York.

Elvin, M. 1972. "The High Equilibrium Trap." Pp. 137-172 in *Economic Organization in Chinese Society*, edited by W.E. Wilmott. California: Stanford University Press.

Elvin, M. 1981. "Making Progress Pay—A Basic Problem in China's Early Economic Modernization." Pp. 254-287 in *Symposium on the History of the Republic of China, Volume 3.* Taipei.

Feuerwerker, A. 1958. *China's Early Industrialization: Sheng Hsuan-huai [1844-1916] and Mandarin Enterprise.* Cambridge, MA: Harvard University Press.

Feuerwerker, A. 1976. *The Foreign Establishment in China in the Early Twentieth Century.* Michigan Papers in Chinese Studies, No. 29. University of Michigan.

Fong, H.D. 1932. *Cotton Industry and Trade in China.* Tientsin: Nankai Institute of Economics, Nankai University.

Fong, H.D. 1937. "Industrialization and the Rural Industries in China." *The China Quarterly* (Spring): 259-279.

Hongkong and Shanghai Bank (HSBC). 1931a. "HSBC Political Letters 1929-1934." Address by Pinfang Hsia, Assistant Manager, Trust Department, Bank of China, at the Conference of the Institute of Pacific Relations, October 22. Archive Ref.: SHG 379.1.

Hongkong and Shanghai Bank (HSBC). 1931b. Notes taken by a Hongkong Bank official on a paper presented by C. F. Remer entitled "Interim Report on Foreign Investment in China" to a Conference of the Institute of Pacific Relations. October 22. Archive Ref.: SHG 379.1.

Hongkong and Shanghai Bank (HSBC). 1933. "HSBC Political Letters 1929-1934." Letter to V. M. Grayburn, Hong Kong, from W.C. Cassells, Shanghai, January 6. Archive Ref.: SHG 379.1.

Howe, C. 1996a. *The Origins of Japanese Trade Supremacy.* London: Hurst & Company.

Howe, C. 1996b. "Introduction: The Changing Political Economy of Sino-Japanese Relations: Along Term View." Pp. 1-23 in *China and Japan: History, Trends, and Prospects*, edited by C. Howe. Oxford, UK: Clarendon Press.

Hsu, I.C.Y. 1983. *The Rise of Modern China.* Hong Kong: Oxford University Press.

Jacobs, N. 1958. *The Origin of Modern Capitalism in Eastern Asia.* Hong Kong: University of Hong Kong Press.

King, S.T., and D.K. Lieu. 1930. "China's Cotton Industry: A Statistical Study of Ownership of Capital, Output, and Labor Conditions." In *Problems of the Pacific 1929.* Third Conference Proceedings. Chicago, IL: University of Chicago.

Koh, S.J. 1966. *Stages of Industrial Development in Asia: A Comparative History of the Cotton Industry in Japan, India, China and Korea.* Philadelphia: University of Pennsylvania Press.

Kraus, R. 1980. *Cotton and Cotton Goods in China 1918-1936: The Impact of Modernization on the Traditional Sector.* New York: Garland Publishing Inc.

Kuwahara, T. 1989. "The Japanese Cotton Spinners' Direct Investments into China before the Second World War." In *Historical Studies in International Corporate Business*, edited by A. Teichova, M. Levy-Leboyer, and H. Nussbaum. Cambridge, UK: Cambridge University Press.

Kuwahara, T. 1992. "The Local Competitiveness and Management of Japanese Cotton Spinning Mills in China in the Inter-War Years." In *The Transfer of International Technology: Europe, Japan, and the USA in the Twentieth Century*, edited by D. Jeremy. Aldershot: Edward Elgar.

Lasker, B. (Ed.). 1932. *Problems of the Pacific.* Proceedings of the Fourth Conference of the Institute of Pacific Relations. Chicago, IL: University of Chicago Press.

Le Fevour, E. 1968. *Western Enterprise in Late Ch'ing China: A Selective Survey of Jardine, Matheson & Company's Operations, 1842-1895.* Harvard East Asian Monographs. Cambridge, MA: Harvard University.

Lieu, D.K. 1928. "China's Industrial Development." In *Problems of the Pacific.* Proceedings of the Second Conference of the Institute of Pacific Relations. Chicago, IL: University of Chicago Press.

Lieu, D.K. 1935. "Industry." In *Chinese Year Book 1935-1936.*

Lieu, D.K. 1936. *Growth and Industrialization of Shanghai.* Shanghai: China Institute of Pacific Relations.

Morrell, J. 1968. "Two Early Chinese Cotton Mills." In *Papers on China, Volume 21.* Cambridge, MA: Harvard University.

Moser, C.K. 1930. *The Cotton Textile Industry of Far Eastern Countries.* Boston, MA: Pepperell Manufacturing Company.

Moulder, F. V. 1977. *Japan, China and the Modern World Economy: Towards a Reinterpretation of East Asian Development.* Cambridge, UK: Cambridge University Press.

Nieh, C.L. 1933. "China's Industrial Development: its Problems and Prospects." Pp. 1-44 in *Proceedings of the Fifth Conference of the Institute of Pacific Relations.* Shanghai: China Institute of Pacific Relations.

Nishida, J.M. 1990. *The Japanese Influence on the Shanghainese Textile Industry and Implications for Hong Kong.* MPhil dissertation, Hong Kong University.

Nishikawa H. 1987. *Nihon Teikokushugi To Mengyo* (*Japanese Imperialism and the Cotton Industry*). Kyoto: Minerubia Shobo.

Pearse, A.S. 1929. *The Cotton Industry of Japan and China.* Manchester: International Federation of Master Cotton Spinners' and Manufacturers' Associations.

Remer, C.F. 1926. *The Foreign Trade of China.* Shanghai. Reproduced 1967 by Ch'eng-Wen Publishing Company, Taipei, Taiwan.

Seki, K. 1956. *The Cotton Industry of Japan.* Tokyo: Japan Society for the Promotion of Science.

Shanghai Academy of Social Sciences (SASS) Institute of Economic Research (Ed.). 1980. *Rongjia Qiye Shiliao* (*Source Materials on the Rong Family Enterprises*). Shanghai: Peoples' Press.

South China Morning Post (*SCMP*). 1996a. March 17.

South China Morning Post (*SCMP*). 1996b. April 5.

Takamura, N. 1982. *Kindai Nihon Mengyo to Chugoku* (*The Modern Japanese Cotton Industry and China*). Tokyo: University of Tokyo Press.

Tawney, R. 1932. *A Memorandum on Agriculture and Industry*. Honolulu: Institute of Pacific Relations.

Toyo Boseki Company Ltd. 1986. *Toyobo Hyakunen Shi* (*Jo*) (*The Hundred Year History of Toyobo*). Volume 1. Osaka.

Utley, F. 1938. *Japan's Gamble in China*. London: Secker & Warburg.

Wei, B.P.T. 1987. *Shanghai: Crucible of Modern China*. New York: Oxford University Press.

Wong, S.L. 1979. *Industrial Entrepreneurship and Ethnicity: a Study of the Shanghainese Cotton Spinners in Hong Kong*. Ph.D. thesis, University of Oxford.

Wong, S. L. 1988. "The Applicability of Asian Family Values to Other Sociocultural Settings." In *In Search of an East Asian Development Model*, edited by P.L. Berger and M.H.H. Hsiao. New Brunswick, NJ: Transaction Books.

Yao, C.S. 1935. "An Economic Survey of China for the First Half Year of 1935." *China Quarterly* 1 (September): 165-166.

Young, S.Y.P. 1935. "China's Banking Progress in the Past Decade." *China Quarterly* 1 (September): 65-80.

PART II

CULTURAL ISSUES

MARITAL DISCORD:

A CLASH OF VALUES AND ASSUMPTIONS FOR TRANSFORMING ORGANIZATIONS: IMPLICATIONS FOR SINO-FOREIGN JOINT VENTURES

Elizabeth Li

INTRODUCTION

This chapter is a discussion about how the concept of family, embedded within the fundamental values of Chinese culture, can be used to illustrate Sino-foreign joint ventures. Before a marriage is created by the union of two partners from separate families, the respective parents usually have to givc their consent. A date is chosen, terms and conditions are agreed, a contract is signed, usually at a ceremony. The new union will usually go through a honeymoon stage before reality sets in. Contained within the new reality are unspoken expectations of both partners and their respective parents. As time goes by the extent to which the assumed expectations are met determines the level of cooperation and trust. We are living in a world where divorce is a common

Advances in Chinese Industrial Studies, Volume 5, pages 69-92.

ISBN: 1-55938-961-3

phenomenon. Many young Europeans are discouraged from marriage due to the one in three divorce rate.

If the partners are of different nationalities, the potential misalignment of their expectations will be greater. The cross-cultural issue further complicates the establishment of trust by contributing additional dimensions. For instance, Italians are similar to the Chinese in that they share the value of the importance of family units. The French are similar to the Chinese in the paternalism of the government. The Japanese, Germans, and Americans are similar in that they set out boundaries for practices in their laws (Fukuyama 1995).

In establishing a joint venture the parents of the bride and groom are very concerned that their child should not "lose out" in the transaction. The contract established is often inclusive of clauses each to protect their own side. "Contracts—even at their best—can reflect an understanding of costs and markets and technologies only at the moment companies sign them, when things change, the partners don't really try to compromise and adjust" (Ohame 1992, p. 149). The interventions of in-laws trying to influence the marriage often causes discord, manifesting in control, conflict, and political activities. The gap between the partners widens and the trust level reaches negative. The easiest solution in some situations is divorce—either dissolve the partnership (and get a new one), or fire the managing director and use him as the scapegoat. So another conflict arises and the pattern repeats itself for either side of the partnership—lessons need to be extracted from the past and present, so that a new future can be created.

The aspect of equality plays a fundamental role. If one of the partners perceives itself as superior in any way, it may impose without question its values on the weaker partner. These measurements of superiority can be seen in percentage equity split or technologies and financial contributions. This superimposition of one set of values, often without explicit discussion, onto another causes damage to the recipient's self-esteem. In the Chinese context, this is related to the issue of "face." The overt imposition often stimulates covert activities. Some fundamental development must take place before such marital discord can decrease.

Establishing trust involves: (1) understanding the issues of current identity; (2) understanding the issues of a new identity; and (3) creating a mechanism for the new identity. This paper examines the underlying values and assumptions that affect the transformation of organizations, from a state-owned mentality toward market-driven orientation. Data from field research on Alpha, a Sino-foreign joint venture, is examined, in the light of which guidelines are established for the future transforming of organizations to ease marital discord due to clashes in values and assumptions in the early stages.

The description of values and assumptions from the national level to the organizational level and the description of control, conflict, and politics within state-owned enterprises serve as the context upon which the findings from the Alpha case will be based.

THE CHINESE CONTEXT

Values and Assumptions within the Transforming Economy

The underlying values and assumptions at the national level affect the transforming economy within the PRC. The fundamental value is the dualistic existence innate within the Chinese culture and a short-term view in many interventions. In the need to remain Chinese while learning from other cultures by importing ideologies, a conflict may arise.

Two opposing forces have historically existed within China: first, the conversion and integration of foreign expertise into Chinese practices by maintaining a strong Chineseness despite foreign conquest (Wang 1991, pp. 1-10), and second, the import of technologies, expertise, and ideologies while maintaining the Chinese identity. While some hoped to conquer, others focused on influencing. None was able to shift the fundamental values and assumptions. With regard to the present economic transformation, a delicate balance and sensitivity needs to be established for successful integration.

Cultural understanding of different nationalities has been analyzed in Geert Hofstede's original research, adding a fifth dimension, Confucian dynamism (Hofstede and Bond 1988, pp. 9-21). In general, power distance is strong, uncertainty avoidance is low, and the Chinese society leans toward both the collective and masculine tendency. The fifth dimension, the Confucian dynamism, scored the highest in the PRC; this translates into a preference for a long-term orientation. In translating these dimensions into organizational values, one would need to take into account additional considerations.

The existence of the dual forms during the transformation process is in accordance with the findings of weak uncertainty avoidance dimension within the PRC. However, the second value, where the transformation is taking a short-term view, is in opposition to the long-term findings of the Confucian dynamics.

Distinction between National Culture and Organizational Culture

National culture is defined as the collective programming of the mind which distinguishes the members of one group or category of people from another (Hofstede 1984, pp. 14-18). Corporate or organizational culture is defined in a similar way except for the fact that the collective programming of the minds of original members is based on the values of the founder and significant leader. Therefore, the shared perception of daily practices can be considered to be the core of an organization's culture (Hofstede 1991, p. 180). Within this context, Chinese enterprises can be separated into two types: state-owned and privatized forms.

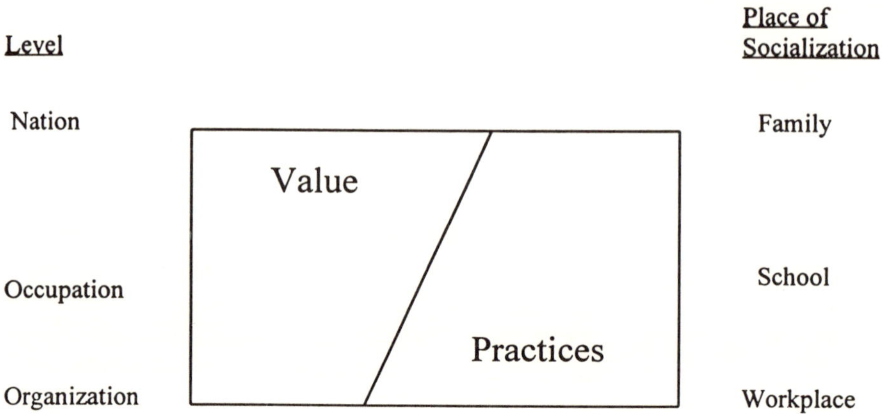

Source: Hofstede (1991, p. 182).

Figure 1. The Nature of Culture Differences: National, Occupational, and Organizational Levels

Many studies on corporate culture (Schein 1985, pp. 49-85; Swieringa and Wierdsma 1992, pp. 10-26; Hofstede 1991, pp. 177-200) discuss the progression toward the embedded values stressed at the deepest level. Hofstede's model is most relevant to this study. He distinguishes between values and practices (see Figure 1).

Values and practices exist in different proportions depending on their level of application. Based on this definition of organization culture, integrating these with the Enterprise Effectiveness Model (Figure 2), we begin to see the complexity of the dynamics between the organizational components of formal and informal structures.

The separation of the formal and informal components of the Enterprise Effectiveness Model is as complex as separating out the values and practices within the organization. The invisible nature of culture or informal structure can in fact be viewed in three-dimensional organic form (Figure 3), where certain activities are the manifestation of cultural influence within the organization, represented by work processes, communication patterns, and integration mechanism. The informal structure with invisible elements can be overlaid in the formal structure of technology, human resources, and structures and systems. This organic entity will interact with the environment (that is, market relationship) to formulate the strategic directions and management goals of the enterprise.

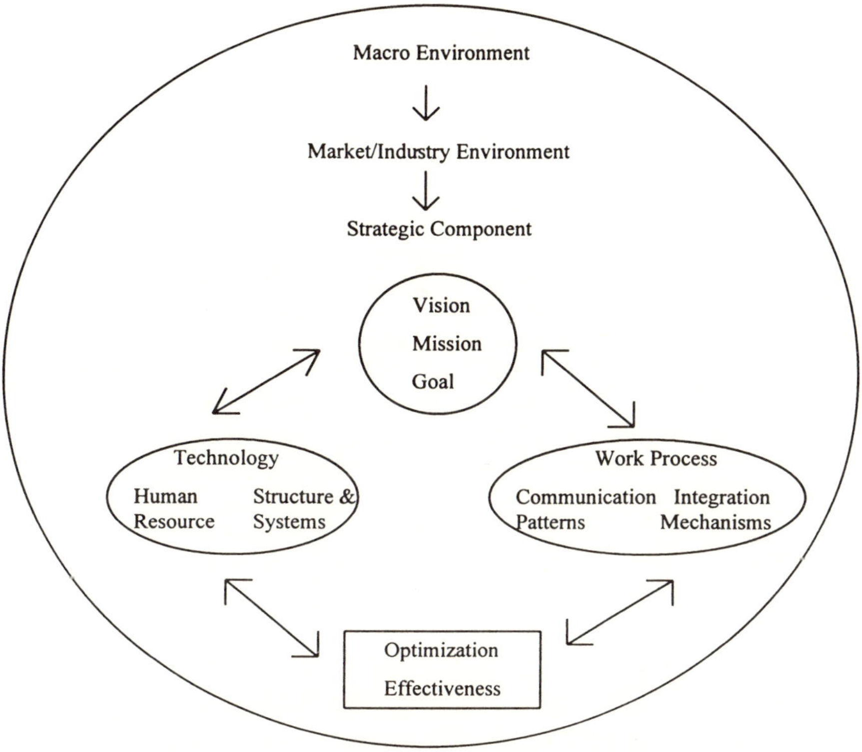

Source: Developed from an unpublished model by Dr. C.G. Worley, Pepperdine University, and used with permission.

Figure 2. Enterprise Effectiveness Model

Therefore, in addition to the distinctions between national and organizational culture, there also needs to be an understanding of the dynamics of formal, informal, and strategic components within the enterprise. The next section analyzes the informal values and assumptions of enterprises moving from a state-owned mentality toward a customer-driven orientation. However, in the context of the PRC, the distinction between national and corporate culture within the state-owned enterprise is questionable. There is a departure from the national culture in the private sector, yet many Sino-foreign joint ventures are created with state-owned entities. Therefore, the development of the eight dimensions analysis (see Table 1) has been focused on state-owned enterprises moving toward market-driven enterprises.

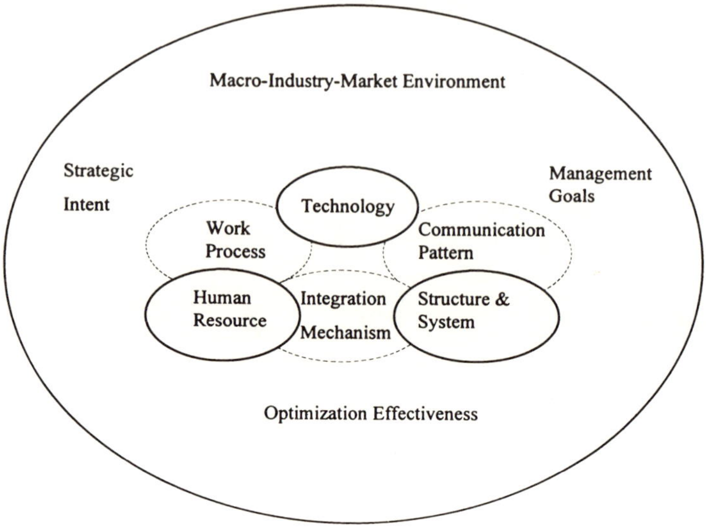

Figure 3. Enterprise Effectiveness Model II

Table 1. Organization Culture within the PRC

	State-owned (Planned) Enterprises	*Private Market-driven Enterprises*
1.	Employee orientation	Job orientation
2.	Closed system	Open system
3.	Process orientation	Result orientation
4.	Parochial	Professional
5.	Loose control	Tight control
6.	Normative	Pragmatic
7.	Entitlement	Accountability
8.	Soft budget	Hard budget

Values and Assumptions within Transforming PRC Enterprises

In an attempt to distinguish between the organization cultures of state-owned and privatized enterprises within the PRC, eight dimensions are used, based on the premise of values and practices discussed earlier. The first six dimensions were defined in a research project involving 20 organizations carried out by the Institute for Research on Intercultural Corporation, at the University of Lumburg at Maastricht. These dimensions can be generalized as follows:

1. Orientation is dependent on historical factors such as the philosophy of the founder and recent situations.
2. Weak uncertainty avoidance would lean toward an open communication climate; strong uncertainty avoidance would lean toward a closed communication system.
3. In the context of PRC organization, process orientation tends to avoid risk taking. The bureaucratic system within the state-owned enterprise tends to reinforce this while the more nimble privatized organization encourages results.
4. Parochial cultures tend to hire employees who have less formal education (Lee 1991, pp. 135-139). Private enterprises have started to use contract laborers.
5. On the surface it seems that state-owned enterprises are tightly controlled while private firms are loosely controlled; often the opposite is true.
6. In state-owned enterprises little pragmatic customer orientation is needed.
7. Employees of the state-owned enterprises believe in their right to be taken care of by the state, while private enterprises are moving toward a pay-by-production approach (Block 1993, pp. 34, 134).
8. The budgeting process in the state-owned sector has been soft; it is struggling to move toward a harder process.

Transforming a state-owned mentality toward that of market-orientation needs constant understanding of where each decision is, in relation to the above mentioned dimensions, in terms of values and assumptions. The marriage of the two perspectives is asking both sides to be sensitive to each other's natural tendencies and habits. Changes in these habits need committed efforts which can be painful. A sense of fear and hopelessness makes it hard to invest in any sense of long-term beliefs. By functional behavior control, conflict and political upheaval will be created by automatic reactions to symptoms without sensibility to the issues involved. Misunderstanding between the two parties will cause further confusion.

The willingness and understanding of individuals within the system undergoing change is crucial; they must believe that change will benefit all before a smooth process can be developed (Beckhard and Harris 1987, pp. 51-59). Consequences of restructuring can cause tremendous damage, as well as extreme apathy among participating individuals. As a result, the demand for immediate benefit overtakes traditional long-term values. This tension creates a loss of control, resulting in conflicts and political activities.

Control, Conflict, and Politics within the Transformation Process

Control, conflict, and politics are three additional dynamics of organizational design. They are manifestations of values and belief systems.

Through observable behaviors in these areas, certain basic assumptions can be made. Control is a system that directs members to achieve organizational goals through strategy and structure, and performance and reward designs (Robey 1991, p. 246). However, it is often important to assess the extent to which control systems are obtaining the results that they are designed to produce. Organizational conflict is often the result of misalignment between interacting parties (Robey 1991, p. 153). The following is a description of the manifested behavior on one side of the marriage.

Control within State-owned Enterprises

Control within state-owned enterprises is confusing. Practices are generally person-centered, with the decisions made by the most senior person in charge. Standards and measurements are often not clearly codified even though the information is disseminated to the whole enterprise and therefore diffused, representing a form of clan management (Boisot 1987, p. 194). Consequently, double standards are created by selective attention and strategic measurement (Robey 1991, p. 251). The rigid bureaucratic form with high control and narrow span encourages entitlement behavior: "do is 36 and don't do is 36" (a phrase commonly used referring to employee morale in state-owned enterprises). That is, the equitable process of distributing rewards and benefits which many state-owned enterprises still practice does not encourage accountable and responsible attitudes. The pay for workers at one time was 36 RMB, whether one worked very hard or did very little. In short, the motivation of the workforce at the local level is a great problem, and it is difficult to direct members of the organization toward enterprise goals.

Conflicts within State-owned Enterprises

Whether conflicts within state-owned enterprises are internal or external, the underlying causes are likely to be related to resource scarcity and information complexity (Lawrence and Dyer 1983, pp. 301-304). The reward system which oils the wheels of the control system is divided into two types: tangible and intangible. It is often the intangible rewards obtained through personal influence that make a substantial difference to the individual. A formal performance appraisal system is in place in many state-owned enterprises; however, a fair degree of personalization and "strategic measurementship" (Robey 1991, p. 251) is exercised via the informal system of influence while still executing the formal structure. Mere individual goals and various subgoals may take priority over the superordinate objectives. Cooperation under these circumstances is difficult where ownership is by "all of the people" and therefore it is difficult to trace accountability and responsibility. These factors contribute to the degree of conflict within the state-owned enterprise which often surpasses the energizing point and creates stress for the system, leading it toward the demotivating side of the conflict curve (Hill and Jones 1992, pp. 406-407).

Dealing with conflict within state-owned enterprises takes three forms. First, conflict is resolved through bargaining and negotiation, where self-interests are protected by the members. Second, collaborative efforts, where members can work rationally toward situations in which everyone wins, are possible when forms of longstanding relationships are present and fundamental trust is strong (Raskin 1991, pp. 179). Third, interpretive efforts, allowing both negotiation and collaborative efforts to coexist and not necessarily taking a right or wrong perspective, are used. This interpretive format seems, however, to be present through continuous forms of negotiation and bargaining (Lee 1991, pp. 35).

Politics within State-owned Enterprises

Politics within state-owned enterprises is an important aspect of their operation. Based on the elements of the political model whereby members focus on subgoals and sub-interests, members may withhold information, or negotiate compromises reached by power balance; winning is possible only when one party has more influence (Robey 1991, pp. 369-371). In a high power distance country such as China (Hofstede 1993, pp. 171-173), the issue of power is particularly important. The categories of power in the individual form include reward, coercive, legitimate, referent, expert, articulate, and self-belief (French and Bentram 1959, pp. 150-167). Negotiations between parties are often by means of exchange and bargain to maximize subgoals rather than the superordinate goals.

ALPHA: THE CASE STUDY

Background and History

At the beginning of the study, Alpha was a two-year-old joint venture between a Chinese state-owned enterprise and a publicly traded Asian multinational. The Asian organization has a strong name, image, and reputation for quality products. It is more than 100 years old and the third-generation owners control a large proportion of its shares. Its headquarters are in a major Asian city. Alpha reports to the Hong Kong Division, which in turn reports through the international holding company (formed in 1992 to manage all the MNE's international actitivies) to headquarters.

The parent company's brand name has been in existence in the Asian region for more than a century, while the Hong Kong Division has a 50-year history. Recent developments in the PRC prompted the Hong Kong Division to establish a subsidiary to penetrate the potential China market. The Hong Kong

Division is publicly listed on the Hong Kong stock exchange, and the majority of its shares are owned by the Asian organization. Alpha was established in 1991 and has a workforce of 1,100. Both partners had had extensive experience in manufacturing this product prior to the joint venture.

The local Chinese partner in Alpha is a state-owned enterprise that has been in the same business as the Asian organization for 50 years. It was previously involved in a similar joint venture that was dissolved. In addition to the Hong Kong Division, Alpha also reports to the Municipal Sub-Bureau, which is supervised by the Central Ministry in Beijing. The cooperation agreement allows the Asian parent to use the land and facilities of the local partner for 30 years.

Formal and Informal Structure

The Asian partner and the Chinese partner each brought their own worldview and ways of operating. Representatives from both parents were sent to monitor their respective interests within Alpha. Employees are divided between manufacturing (65%) and the four support functions of human resources, sales, finance, and marketing (35%).

The Clash of Cultures

Alpha produces two product brands: a local brand developed before the joint venture and an imported brand licensed by the Asian partner. This type of dual system without alignment led to conflict, usually relating to the two separate sets of operating criteria: quality standards, production procedures, operation processes, employee behavior, for instance. Split directives between departments and divisions escalated stress levels to a demotivation point. Due to the intensity of day-to-day operations with its emergencies and on-the-spot decisions, problems were often treated at the symptomatic level, rather than by basic structural and policy change.

The Chinese partner resisted many of the new processes put in place by the senior management team representing the Asian partner at Alpha. This team represented five nationalities and only two of the seven members had spent considerable time in the Hong Kong Division. No experience from the Asian organization's headquarters was represented. The PRC has a strong sense of identity and resisted the haphazard changes put in place by the representatives of its Asian partner.

Credibility was often questioned and higher authority intervention needed. Externally in the hierarchy, and internally within the organization, Alpha's partners were unable to agree on reinvestment approaches, even though the results of the previous two years exceeded expectation. The Asian partner put priority on a high-speed production line while the Chinese partner was looking at property and housing for the employees. Strategic differences could not be agreed on at the highest level.

The communication pattern within Alpha was fragmented and divided both by function and nationality. An "us/them" division existed. Numerous conflicts were mediated and resolved by the managing director and the human resources manager. "Seagull" managers would fly in from supervising bodies and complicate issues with direct reports to the Hong Kong Division, the international holding company, and headquarters or the Municipal Sub-Bureau and Central Ministry. Both the managing director and the human resources director spent more than 50 percent of their time managing these types of situations. Differences in language, values, and assumptions from the different perspectives caused communication problems. There was a constant competition for power and dominance of one over the other. All formal authority was held by representatives from the Asian partner, representing only 5 percent of the total workforce, while the PRC partner, representing the other 95 percent, could only assert its wishes through coercive means, resulting in a series of "win/lose" situations. As one side came off worst, harbored resentments intensified in the next conflicting situation. The managing director and the human resources manager had served as individual mediators since the beginning of the joint venture; however, it became impossible for them to carry out their other responsibilities effectively.

In the same way, many of these activities were reducing the production effectiveness of the enterprise. The formal component of Alpha was not aligned; the technology and human resource structure and systems were not doing what they were designed to do. The formal structure of authority and control was often overruled by higher authority, internal or external, as well as by coercive activities. The informal components represent the culture of Alpha where the communication patterns, work processes, and integration mechanisms were in confusion. The formal and informal components were not being guided by the strategic component with an agreed-upon direction. The misalignment within and between each of the components hindered optimization of organization effectiveness.

Methodology

The study began in April 1993 and continued for three years, in four major stages: (1) organization diagnosis; (2) organization redesign; (3) putting initiatives into operation; (4) sustaining initiatives and repeating in other PRC locations. The first diagnostic stage doubled as an evaluation of the privatization process that had taken place over the previous two years. Exploratory field research involved both qualitative and quantitative methods, so that the two forms of data could serve as different perspectives for interpretation before drawing final conclusions and planning for action.

Table 2. Alpha Stage 1 Diagnostic Phases (1993)

Initiation Phase	April	Contract and briefings by huyman resources manager, Hong Kong Division
	May	Two-day visit to Alpha
	June	Three-day observation diagnosis —management system audit —documentation analysis —process observation and analysis —individual interviews by function and level
Phase 1	July	Three-day managsement workshop Survey questionnaire planning session
Phase 2	August	Quantitative survey of entire workforce
	November	Survey questionnaire feedback
Phase 3	December	Three-day feedback and action plan workshop

Stage 1 comprised four phases (see Table 2), the initiation phase preparing for the design of phases 1-3. The primary emphasis during the three-day observational diagnosis was in-depth interviews which brought to the surface information about functional and inter-functional management systems and the ways in which documentation for in-process work operated within the system. A system audit approach was used in various manufacturing and service departments to check the continuity of the work and task process flow. This provided an opportunity to check the extent to which the processes and approaches used in each area were compatible both internally and externally. Particular emphasis was placed on the purposes of documentation, whether they served an internal (intradepartmental) information flow function or external (interdepartmental) information flow function. The audit process used was spot checking items and tracing and tracking both the origin and the destination of the information documented. Phase 1 involved a three-day management workshop that included all divisional and departmental managers who were of many nationalities. The workshop design focused on the sharing of information and the generation of data. This combination contributed to the organization (group) learning process. Activities emphasized an important consideration that had been revealed in the initial phase: that a safe and protected environment was essential if genuine feelings and authentic information were to be voiced.

The quantitative survey of phase 2 was implemented through an 80-question questionnaire distributed to the entire workforce. The six subjects of the questionnaire were derived from synthesized information gathered from the workshop: communication, performance management, quality management, training and development, reward system, and company image.

Phase 3 was a workshop where management synthesized all the survey data into four types of action plans: divisional or departmental (long term and short term) and organizational (long term and short term). Compared to the characteristics of traditional state-owned enterprises discussed, the conclusions from the survey and diagnosis were expected to provide key insights into the two years of alliance at Alpha and the development of a set of guidelines to be used for other joint ventures.

RESEARCH FINDINGS

It was found that Alpha was in confusion, a discontented, fragmented organization with no direction or identity. It was caught between high market demands for its product and internal conflicts and disputes that hindered effectiveness and efficiency. As a result, production was poorly scheduled and other brand competitors were benefiting these problems.

The research revealed six critical issues arising from Alpha's process of transformation from state-owned to shareholding operating mode: lack of identity, conflicting directions, political activities, unstable systems and structures, demotivated workforce, and general discontent due to lack of mutual trust and respect. The various phases of this research concentrate on these issues. The data from the initial visit and from the survey categories essentially describe the same issues, from a different perspective.

For the purpose of this study, only the first three phases of the organization diagnosis are discussed: the initiation phase, and phases 1 and 2.

Initiation Phase

The purpose of this phase was to establish an agreement to diagnose the organization's current state. The initial contract meeting explored the underlying causes behind the current problems and was attended by two external consultants, and the Hong Kong Division human resources manager and internal consultant. Issues discussed included the negative perception of Alpha's managing director and the unclear relationships and line of authority between the managing directors of the international holding company, the Hong Kong Division, and Alpha.

The first visit to Alpha was made by the international holding company's human resources director, the Hong Kong Division human resources manager, the internal consultant from the Hong Kong Division, and the two external consultants. The purpose of the visit was to resolve differences between the two sides of the joint venture. It was originally intended that both PRC and expatriate representatives would be present to discuss together the planning of future activities. However, when the visiting team arrived, no PRC

Table 3. Alpha Organization Information

Issues	*Data Information*
Organization structure	mechanistic and functional 65 percent of employees based in manufacturing division highly differentiated both vertically and horizontally 7-8 levels intraorganizationally 3 additional levels interorganizationally
Organization systems	unclear perimeter of Human Resources Division unspecified MIS at start-up phase
Roles and responsibilities	confusing decision making centralized overruled by higher authority
Information process flow	highly segregated kept within own territory disjointed process information from one unit not useful to other units
Technology	policy and procedures inconsistent target standards not taken seriously
Sales and marketing	in the process of "professionalization" newly established
Culture	nationality, functionality, hierarchy senior management all foreign nationals superiors and subordinates have different interpretations of task lack of interest in understanding nationality differences lack of understanding of functional requirements lack of mutual respect toward individual competence senior management dining room only for foreign nationals staff functions exist to support manufacturing "us/them" mentality

management was represented. It was deemed impossible to go ahead without the PRC representatives' participation. After an informal discussion and exchange of expectations, the two-day schedule was reorganized, and the visitors divided into two consulting teams, each team interviewing members of Alpha's management team individually. The increase in individual esteem for the PRC managers was so great that many of them were unable to stop talking in the interviews. One critical message gathered from the interviews was the lack of understanding of the foreign partners of how "things" were done. Another was the importance of the different types of *guanxi* needed in their work. After the interviews, the interviewees and other PRC managers from key departments were brought together. The concept of "fit" was presented using the Enterprise Effectiveness Model along with data from the initial interview (see Table 3).

In general, the data suggested that Alpha had unclear organization systems, confusing roles and responsibilities, and segregated information process flow. In addition, the highly interdependent technology created considerable conflict and exacerbated a climate of mistrust. Importantly, a "us/them" mentality between non-PRC managers and the predominantly PRC workforce existed and appeared to be hurting operations. The final contract meeting of this initial phase developed an agreement on how the next phases would proceed.

Phase 1

This phase consisted of the design and implementation of a management workshop. This was designed by a team consisting of Alpha's managing director and two internal and two external consultants. The workshop would run for three days, based on a classical design for intergroup team building: the foreign management workshop would take place on the first day, the local management workshop on the second, and a large community workshop on the third.

In preparation for this workshop, due to the seriousness of the conflicts between the two sides, there was some hesitation regarding the sufficiency of a one-day interaction for the two groups to build trust. It was thought that it would take at least one day for the group members to "warm up" and very little would be accomplished in that time. Therefore, a three-day workshop was held as part of the initiation phase with the entire management group (all divisional and departmental heads) taking part, together with members of supervising bureaus and higher authorities on both sides of the joint venture.

Prior to the workshop questionnaires were sent to all participants. They were asked for a detailed description of each person's role, responsibilities, and daily activities, and to reflect on the changes in their work since the merger. Many elaborate complexities of work relationships surfaced. The meeting represented the first time since the establishment of the joint venture that different levels and nationalities had worked together. The objective was to share information and generate data that would give a clear idea of Alpha's situation at that moment.

Small-group activities included the sharing of personal visions, assessing the changes in the environment that had taken place since the merger, discussions of the strengths and weaknesses of the current organization, and its ideal future. Visions from each group were presented to the community. The community further synthesized the clustered issues via a voting process. Discussion groups were then created to address each issue as an organization improvement project. The five projects were: quality standards, communications, roles and responsibilities, sense of belonging, and interdepartmental cooperation.

The information revealed led to the formation of the "sense of belonging" improvement project. Local employees felt that they were not being valued due to the perceived lack of commitment of the Asian organization to its employees, but an explanation of its corporate policy resulted in a positive change in the PRC managers. They had thought they were being treated as second-class citizens, but accepted that it would take time for them to achieve the same standards as some of the foreign managers. The chairman of Alpha presented a corporate expansion program showing the importance of their management contribution in creating the future together. They were assured by the company's commitment and the vision of a shared ownership and shared context.

This type of "cultural" cleansing began to eliminate some of the covert activities and negative politicking that previously polluted the corporate climate. The transfer of responsibility of the organization improvement issues to self-selected teams resulted in a strong sense of ownership among the participants, who were to work on the tasks. Although it was a struggle to gain agreement from some of the members of the project team, this approach was a welcome change from the normal practice where tasks were usually allocated.

Phase 2

Phase 2 was a survey of the organization. The survey was directed by a committee composed of the managing director, assistant general manager, union chairman, personnel manager, and external consultants (including the author). A Chinese poster was designed to announce the survey, and other internal advertising activities organized to alleviate staff uncertainty. The response rate was 96.6 percent of the total population. The questionnaire was divided into six categories, plus an additional one for general remarks (see Table 4), basically derived from the organization improvement projects synthesized from the first visit and workshop. Great care was given to the the translation of questions, so that precise language accuracy could be obtained in both the Chinese and English versions.

The results indicated that Alpha scored most favorably in the areas of quality management, company image, and training and development. The favorable aspects of quality management referred to the newly developed sales and marketing management with a strong customer focus. While company image scored high on company expansion plans and brand recognition in the market, in both cases there were negative aspects concerning work environment and welfare and development of employees. Training and development was a favorable category in terms of a high demand for more career structure and job variety. In all three cases the issues pointed to an employee orientation where certain ideas of entitlement had not been fulfilled.

Categories that scored low were communication, reward systems, and performance management. These three categories indicate a weak system of

Table 4. Alpha Survey Categories

Categories	*Descriptions*
Communication	sufficient channels that work joint venture has introduced improvement upward channels limited limited information/involvement in changes
Training and development	importance of specific skills need for career development need for job variety insufficient selection/promotion system
Performance managsement	need for supervisor skills lack of job specification fairness and feedback in appraisal work pressure high
Reward system	comprehensive benefit adjustment of annual salary increase competitive to market in pay and benefits
Company image	agreement to expansion plan concern for welfare and personal growth
Quality management	awareness of integration of customer service values acknowledgment of customer groups enhancement of motivation and morale improvement of work environment
General comments	standardization of organizational policies wastage review—work methods, resources, inspection need more specific survey in welfare and commitment

communication patterns and a lack of alignment in expectation. The performance management system was defined by a lack of supervisory skills, unfair treatment, and lack of job specification. Here lie the discrepancies between work processes, structure and systems, communication patterns, and integrating mechanisms. On the one hand, the data point to various specific grievances; but on the other hand, the underlying discontent stems from unfulfilled expectations which had not been clarified at the beginning.

Employees' pay and other important benefits, in comparison with other companies, were not perceived as equitable. Discontent with increased work pressure, an unsatisfactory work environment, and limited involvement in decision making had decreased morale and loyalty. Management needed to address issues such as the improvement of working conditions, the integration of training and development with career and personal development, and a more efficient system to measure and reward successful performance. In addition, dialogue and interaction between staff and functional management needed to be improved.

Table 5. Interpretation of Survey Categories

Author's Interpretation	*Survey Categories*
Lack of identity	Communication
Conflicting directions	Training and development
Political activities	Performance management
Unstable systems and structure	Reward system
General discontent	Company image
Lack of mutual trust	Quality management

These six survey categories were compared with the issues discovered in the initial phase to determine whether important and salient issues for the organization were being raised reliably. The juxtaposition of the two sets of categories, shown in Table 5, one set derived from the survey the other from the researcher's interpretation, demonstrates that the survey subjects were safe and generic on an organizational practice level, while the critical issues uncovered during the initial phase were named at a deeper level. These "names" were never used within Alpha or during the intervention. However, they are used here to give a different perspective for evaluation purposes.

RESEARCH CONCLUSIONS

This section evaluates the Alpha data and creates hypotheses based on the general themes extracted from the information. In addition, a set of guidelines are put forward for possible application by other transforming organizations.

Evaluation of Data from Alpha

The author's interpretation of critical issues from the initial phase at Alpha include lack of identity, conflicting directions, political activities, unstable systems and structure, general discontent, and lack of mutual trust. These issues, when integrated with the survey categories listed in Table 4, produce three broad clusters: trust, culture, and organization design. Common to these three broad areas, for the purpose of evaluating this data, is the fundamental issue of "identity." The failure to establish and agree upon an identity by the parent organizations had caused a lack of trust, resulting in political activities and an "us/them" mentality.

If this evaluation concluded that the fundamental problem was a crisis of identity, it was appropriate to step back from the data and look at the various components of the organization in its relationship to the business environment. Alpha's relationship to the market and its history, values, and formal and informal structures all needed to be taken into consideration. Each of these aspects differs as it relates to state-owned enterprises and shareholding enterprises. In particular, the eight dimensions of organizational culture (see Table 1), have identified contrasting traits and expectations for state-owned enterprises and shareholding enterprises. In the case of Alpha, the two parent organizations brought their own ideals: the Asian parent represented private firm values while the PRC parent espoused state-owned values. The following is an evaluative discussion of the three broad clusters suggested by the data: trust, culture, and organization design.

Trust

In the absence of a solid legal framework within the PRC, the issue of trust within a network is fundamental to interaction. Within a strong clan culture where relationship is more important than law, the fundamental issue of trust cannot be ignored. The data generated from Alpha pointed to the lack of mutual trust among and between all levels, internal and external. The lack of trust resulted in political activities rather than organizational objectives, and mutual respect of subordinate and superior relationships could not be established. Because of the lack of direction and identity, conflicts to protect or further personal or subunit objectives occurred frequently.

This lack of trust proved an obstacle to establishing a mutually accepted identity, as each partner tried to establish its way as the only way, in turn making negotiation and collaboration difficult. The power struggle for control was apparent in interdepartmental conflicts that obstructed maximization of production. The highly segregated information flow contributed to high divisional and departmental conflict within a highly interdependent work flow.

Culture

Cultural elements within Alpha can be understood through the eight dimensions developed to understand the distinct practices between state-owned and shareholding enterprises (Table 1). Alpha had not been able to align its situation according to these dimensions. The following gaps and problems were caused by these differences.

The PRC partner at Alpha had a strong organization culture with communication patterns that had been in operation for 50 years. This can be referred to as a high context culture (Hall 1977, pp. 85-105). The confusion of identity during the transitional period, where Alpha's employees were uncertain about communication patterns, created a low context. Imposing or superimposing sporadic undefined processes on an established system can cause resistance and discontent.

Complex reporting situations, boundaries, relationships, and directions may have been contributory factors to a wavering leadership style. By phase 3 of Alpha's intervention the international holding company had finalized a decision to eliminate the Hong Kong Division level and both Alpha and the Hong Kong Division reported directly to the international holding company. This eliminated one level of the reporting relationship on the Asian side, and thus one layer of confusion.

Enterprises in the PRC are employee oriented by nature, where the entire welfare of the worker, from matchmaking to allocation of baby quotas is part of the responsibility of the paternal enterprise. It is natural, however, for participants in the market-driven economy to be interested in job orientation, where the primary concern is with work. In the same way, the parochial versus professional dimension is based on a similar philosophy with the added element of skill and education. Alpha's mentality was definitely parochial in that many relatives and clans of the same village tended to be drawn to certain industries and enterprises. The needs and wants expressed during the workshops and in the high score of the training and development category reiterate the hope of the Asian partner to lead the workforce toward professionalism. Senior Asian managers who lacked grounding in PRC organization practices created an environment lacking in sensitivity, causing tension. In the same manner, the normative perspective, entitlement concepts, and soft budget mentality caused difficulties in meeting a mutually agreeable standard for working together. The lack of alignment in Alpha's management process meant that managers carried on in whatever way seemed to fit their own needs and history. The performance management category raised the issue of the lack of skills and inconsistency in appraisal and job specification.

Organization Design

The various organizational components within Alpha did not fit on either a philosophical level or an operational level. The previous sections discussed the philosophical levels of values and assumptions; this section will evaluate the operational level where aspects of systems, structures, and technologies surfaced within the study. Referring back to the Enterprise Effectiveness Model (Figure 2), the discussion of trust and culture has mainly focused on informal components; here the focus is on formal components. The data generated in Tables 3 and 4 mostly point to human resources, the structure and the systems of the formal component. The multilevels on both sides of the partners, the unclear roles and responsibilities, the organization systems, and information flow all point to aspects of structure and system within the formal component. It is obvious that each function has designed its own system according to the history and experiences of the manager in charge.

Crisis of Identity

Fundamental to the above three clusters is the crisis of identity. This root cause of the various symptoms generated could be identified as the mismatch of strategic direction. The Asian partner had been operating in a mature market where high production demand had set technology as an organizational competency. However, although the PRC is a growth market, the basic resource available is human; superimposing market strategies from other markets may not take account of local environmental factors. For instance, the two partners at Alpha could not agree upon the reinvestment of profit. The PRC partner wanted to see capital being put into the building of employee accommodation, while the Asian partner preferred to invest in a high-speed production line. This issue touched on all three clusters: trust, culture, and organization design. The Asian partner used its position of being majority shareholder to make the final investment decision, which did not appease the PRC partner; such a use of power to push through decisions violates any trusting relationship that may exist. The cultural conflict is obvious from the basic orientation of each side, where one is more employee focused and parochial and the other is oriented towards results and the job. In the case of organization design, the utilization of a high-speed production line or the development of a system to maximize human resource would both take a very different approach. Therefore, the root cause of identity needs clarification at the strategic level, where there was still a struggle between the partners of Alpha.

Guidelines

Given the above evaluation of the field research data at Alpha, this section examines the fundamental groundrules that were missing during the early processes of privatization, that could have eliminated some of the pain and confusion. The evaluation concluded that lack of trust at all levels of the organization, crisis of identity, struggle for a new identity, and lack of mechanisms, all described Alpha's state. It is necessary to establish trust, understand the issues making up the identity crisis, establish and negotiate the new identity, and create mechanisms that will lead to the formation of the new identity.

Establishing Trust

Trust issues within Alpha surfaced in a number of areas, most often in those of commonality, credibility, and intent. Conflict and politics festered around the issues of foreign nationals not understanding the PRC way, operating just as they would in their own country, with high expectations of work standards, and so forth. Very little time was devoted to understanding the differences and to closing the gaps, resulting in high tension on both sides. Therefore, from the onset of transformation, before moving into activities, it is necessary to manage the trust issue so as to avoid acute dysfunctional symptoms at a later date. The clarification of mutual contributions and benefits by understanding needs, wants, and opportunities could begin the process. Although the process of building trust is not a one-off event, the establishment of a solid foundation is critical to the ongoing process. It is important to be familiar with national values and assumptions so as to understand the interpretation of behavior and intentions, perhaps employing a local "guide" to mediate the process. Due to the issue of face, direct confrontations should be avoided, but discussions could be channelled through a trustworthy mediator.

Understanding the Issues of a Current Identity

As demonstrated with the eight dimensions of organizational culture within a transforming enterprise (Table 1), the need for the establishment of an understanding of each of these dimensions at the beginning is critical. If the present situation is not understood, a forced-fit perception struggles to exist, which leads to conflict and politics, taking away energy that would otherwise be focused on optimizing effectiveness. This was apparent and obvious within the daily activities of Alpha at all internal and external levels. Instructions, directives, and decisions from supervising bodies did not take into consideration the differences in expectations and worldviews. This resulted in resistance in many situations where resolution could only be obtained with intervention from higher authorities. It is necessary for both sides to be aware of the gaps in their expectations and work continuously to evaluate and negotiate where the most appropriate policies and procedures for each dimension would best suit their organization.

Understanding the Issues of a New Identity

In order to agree on a new identity, the conditions of the first two guidelines must be in place. That is, there needs to be a degree of trust and the analysis of issues within the identity crisis should be clarified. However, one of the aids to establishing this guideline would be the alignment of a shared future vision by defining core processes, purpose, objectives, and goals. These activities will assist in assessing the future which would contribute to the present identity. In the case of Alpha, these activities took place only after the company was two years into the transformation process, during the first workshop of the evaluative intervention. The interventions accomplished some of the negotiation of the new identity; however, it would take much longer to sort out differences than if some clarification had taken place at the outset of transformation.

Creating Mechanisms for a New Identity

Once the new identity has been established, organization components must follow. The vision of the future must be established on an organizational level, followed by mission and goals at business and functional levels. At Alpha these activities were carried out at the second workshop, where the individual functions established their unit goals tied into the organizational mission and goals. However, the replacement of the systems and structure that were already in place made it difficult to redesign all the components at the same time. If these issues had been addressed at the beginning, when the enterprise first privatized, the groundwork would have been in place and subsequent building on this foundation would have been more effective.

CONCLUSION

Given the lessons learned at Alpha, some of the activities suggested in the above guidelines would also be useful after the transformation of the enterprise. However, the degree of difficulty and effectiveness would be different if these guidelines were established prior to the start of an alliances/transformation. The basic principles of these guidelines are being applied continuously to Sino-foreign joint ventures of varying size, types, and length of alliance, and have so far demonstrated that the greater the extent to which these issues are clarified at the outset of the alliance, the smoother the operation.

It is fascinating to see the ways in which marriage partners choose each other. Some experience love at first sight, others seize blindly on the first person they meet; some partners maintain the facade of marriage but continue with extracurricular activities. The discovery of "made-in-heaven" marriages among Sino-foreign joint ventures has yet to be made.

REFERENCES

Beckhard, R., and R.T. Harris. 1987. *Organizational Transitions: Managing Complex Change* (2nd ed.). Reading, MA: Addison-Wesley.

Block, P. 1993. *Stewardship.* San Francisco: Berrett-Koehler.

Boisot, M. 1987. *Information and Organizations.* London: Fontana.

French, J.R.D., Jr., and R. Bentram. 1959. "The Bases of Social Power." In *Studies in Social Powers*, edited by D. Cartwright. Ann Arbor, Michigan: University of Michigan Institute of Social Research.

Fukuyama, F. 1995. *Trust: The Social Virtues and the Creation of Prosperity.* New York: The Free Press.

Hall, E.T. 1977. *Beyond Culture.* London: Anchor Press.

Hill and Jones 1992. *Strategic Management Theory* (2nd ed.). Boston, MA: Houghton Mifflin.

Hofstede, G. 1984. *Culture's Consequences: International Differences in Work-Related Values.* Newbury Park, CA: Sage.

Hofstede, G. 1991. *Cultures and Organizations.* Maidenhead, UK: McGraw-Hill.

Hofstede, G. 1993. "Cultural Constraints in Management Theories." *Academy of Management Executive* 7 (1): 81-94.

Hofstede, G., and M. Bond. 1988. "The Confucius Connection: from Cultural Roots to Economic Growth." *Organizational Dynamics* 16 (4): 4-21.

Lawrence, P.R., and D. Dyer. 1983. *Reviewing American Industry*. New York: Free Press.

Lee, K. 1991. *Chinese Firms and the State in Transition.* New York: M.E. Sharpe.

Ohame, K. 1992. *The Borderless World.* London: Fontana.

Raskin, C. 1991. *China's Political Economy*. Oxford, UK: Oxford University Press.

Robey, D. 1991. *Designing Organizations* (3rd ed.). Homewood, IL: Richard D. Irwin.

Schein, E.H. 1985. *Organizational Culture and Leadership.* San Francisco, CA: Jossey-Bass.

Swieringa, J., and A. Wierdsma. 1992. *Becoming a Learning Organization.* Reading, MA: Addison-Wesley.

Wang, G. 1991. *The Chineseness of China.* Hong Kong: Oxford University Press.

Woodward, H. *After Shock: Helping People Through Coporate Changes.* New York: John Wiley.

MANAGING CULTURAL DIFFERENCES AND SYNERGY IN SINO-EUROPEAN JOINT VENTURES

Fan Zheng and Piet Vanden Abeele

INTRODUCTION: CULTURE, MANAGEMENT, AND MANAGEMENT CULTURE

Culture is an enduring concept that has been incorporated into the disciplines of anthropology, sociology, psychology, and economics. In its most general sense, culture refers to a people's way of life. People have always followed certain customary ways of behaving, which give their lives a particular pattern, regularity, and meaning. A more appropriate and potentially useful method for classifying cultures focuses on their value system. The concept of culture is implicitly bound with the concept of values. Kroeber and Parsons (1958, p. 583) arrive at a cross-disciplinary definition of culture as "transmitted and created content and patterns of values, ideas, and other symbolic-meaningful systems as factors in the shaping of human behavior and the artifacts produced through behavior." Geert Hofstede (1980, p. 25) treats culture as "the collective programming of the mind which distinguishes the members of one human

Advances in Chinese Industrial Studies, Volume 5, pages 93-102.

ISBN: 1-55938-961-3

group from another." Culture, in this sense, includes systems of values; and values are among the building blocks of culture.

Management, at the company level, involves the coordination of human effort and material resources toward the achievement of organizational objectives. The basic objectives of industrial organizations in any country are economic in nature and ultimately reflect the desires of society for useful goods and services. The critical productive functions of an enterprise involve marketing, production and procurement, research and development, and finance; the basic functions of management are classified as planning (including decision making and innovation), control, organization, staffing, and direction (including supervision, motivation, and leadership).

By management culture we mean the total of values people in an organization attach to the activities of the management and the way these activities are organized in the organizational structure and in the managerial processes. Culture influences what we want and believe, and how we behave, and the cultural system undoubtedly influences management. Differences in cultural factors are shown to affect all management processes.

The influence of culture on firms is often very important, especially in the case of transnational firms, such as international joint ventures, which are often characterized by problems of misunderstanding and limited effectiveness because of the lack of compatibility of the cultures represented in them. For example, in a seminar on Sino-European cooperation in 1988, both the Chinese and German managers of Shanghai Volkswagen held that the different understanding about management culture was the key problem for their cooperation. The increasing activity between the People's Republic of China (PRC) and Europe provides an interesting opportunity to consider multicultural management in this context.

CHINESE CULTURE AND MANAGEMENT

The culture of traditional China encompasses diverse and competing philosophies, including Taoism, Buddhism, legalism, and a host of local "little traditions." Nevertheless, Confucianism is most clearly defined as the foundation of China's great cultural tradition, and Confucian values still provide the basis for the norms of Chinese interpersonal behavior. The Confucian tradition has a concern for the correct and well-mannered conduct of one's duties, based on a sound respect for the social conventions of a patriarchal system. It stresses order, hierarchy, quality of relationships, and obligation to social collectivities, especially the family. Age is respected, particularly in the case of male heads of family, while education is valued as the means to achieving a better social status, which reflects well on the family.

Various authorities on Chinese culture put forward somewhat differing lists of key elements which are likely to have a particular bearing on management. Four such characteristics can be identified (which are discussed in the Comparison section below), which (1) underlie social interaction within organizations; (2) differ from other cultures, notably Western ones, though the differences are less with respect to Japan and some other Asian societies; (3) have persisted over time; and (4) can be seen in the PRC as well as among Chinese elsewhere.

Given the high rates of economic growth in East Asia over the last decades, cultural explanations of economic success are attractive—and it is reasonable to make the case that culture could be a major factor in this. Here the potential use of lateral relations could fit the model of relationships embodied in Chinese culture. *Group orientation* could make group-based payment and incentive schemes more effective than in other societies, as well as giving greater potential for integration through shared goals. Developing *relationships* can be a basis for effective market operation, as is recognized by Western corporations. And while *face* considerations may inhibit critical discussion of issues, they can also be a powerful force for nonfinancial motivation.

EUROPEAN CULTURE AND MANAGEMENT

Despite the diversity of countries in Europe, the common trunk of European culture developed from the ancient Greek civilization to the Renaissance (which to some extent was inspired by antiquity). The Greek heritage is the first substratum in which European cultures and political systems developed. Five centuries before Christ, the rule of dialectics was established in the Athens agora. According to this principle the dialogue should be maintained between adverse conceptions. Diverse and adverse conceptions should coexist, and no concept should be dictated by force. The Roman domination of Europe contributed to the improvement of communication infrastructures, and to the spread of legal principles and Christianity. Christianity is the second pillar of European culture. Humanism can be considered the third pillar. The basic concepts are that man deserves freedom, and freedom is a condition of the fulfillment of individuals. Humanism broke with both Christianity and Greek philosophy in the sense that it put man at the center of the universe.

When one thinks about management in Europe the image of diversity usually dominates, and the idea of a distinctive European style of management seems like wishful thinking. In fact, practices of management in London, Frankfurt, and Brussels are considered such different realities that some researchers and practitioners have reached the (apparently) paradoxical conclusion that the identity of Europe is to combine diverse cultures. But beneath such differences are there any common characteristics of management across Europe that distinguish it from management in North America, Asia, or elsewhere? Building on shared characteristics would strengthen European integration at the level of the individual, the firm, and the broader society.

A systemic analysis undertaken jointly by the European Round Table of Industrialists and by the Groupe Ecole Superieure de Commerce de Lyon in 1992 (Caland and De Woot 1994) shows that there are four major characteristics (which are discussed below) common to management in Europe in terms of philosophies, structures, and practices. Here, managing international diversity and management through internal negotiation are based on the same ancient principles: the dialectics of Socrates and Plato, Aristotelian logic, and Aristotle's view of the unity and diversity of the universe. The orientation toward people found in European modern enterprises may be related to Christian values. The different aspects of orientation toward people found in modern European enterprises may be rooted in the humanistic tradition.

COMPARISON: EUROPEAN AND CHINESE MANAGEMENT CULTURE

Orientation Toward People Versus Orientation Toward a Group

European firms share a common inclination toward the fulfillment of individual needs, caring about individual people, social responsibility, as well as some perverse aspects of individualism in the workplace.

In the Chinese tradition the extended family is the basic social unit, which encourages the development of a strong collective and group orientation. In such a collectivist society, an honor bestowed upon a family member is shared by the family and beyond, for they have contributed directly or indirectly to their achievement by being members of the kinship unit. The family's moral judgment, especially as expressed by the father, provides the standard for approved behavior. These same features also characterize in a somewhat diluted form the individual's attachment to other groups. They direct people's loyalties toward their family and work groups, and to the specific standards these apply, rather than to broader social entities. A strong orientation toward the group can have further consequences. It tends to unite with the preference for egalitarianism and present difficulties for the development of individual responsibility and for rewarding performance on an individual basis.

Internal Negotiation Versus Internal Hierarchy Respect

In European firms negotiation takes place not only with "external stakeholders," but also inside the firm between different levels of management and the employees, and between the headquarters and the units. The top management has power, but it must consult, discuss, negotiate, convince; there is a need for independence, and authority is questioned. The decisions coming from the top are criticized. People start to involve themselves only after a lot of discussion, dialogue, and information.

It is widely agreed that the Chinese respect age, authority, and hierarchy. This stems from the Confucian concept of *li* (rite, propriety) which plays an important role in maintaining a person's position in the social hierarchy. This ancient concept proved more suitable than any other for the traditional bureaucratic system in Chinese society. The tradition it embodies favors organizational hierarchy and centralized decision making. In China there is a greater distance between ruler and ruled, and the top management heads a strong internal influence coalition comprising all the personnel groups of the firm. Respect for age and hierarchy can inhibit acceptance of younger, more qualified managers, many of whom consequently stay in their positions for a long time.

Managing International Diversity Versus the Importance of Relationship Outside

European managers have an ability to recognize diversity and a particular skill for managing international diversity. To some extent, Europeans like diversity; or, at least, they respect it: "a European without a passport is not a European." In one hour by air, a manager will cross several frontiers in Europe. European firms have been forced to look outside at other different markets, and to develop a culture of working abroad because of the small size of each domestic market.

The importance of *guanxi* (interpersonal relations), which refers to the quality of a personal relationship outside an individual's immediate family, cannot be overestimated in China. Through these networks the Chinese themselves can overcome the hindrances of hierarchical bureaucracy, which often seems for a Westerner an insurmountable barrier in business and in other contacts with the Chinese. When a petitioner asks a resource allocator to disburse a social benefit under his control, the latter will first consider the *guanxi* between them and then adopt appropriate rules of social exchange. In business, relationships are important, as contracts are often not strictly specified in legal terms but rely on trust between the parties.

Managing Between Extremes Versus the Doctrine of Mean

The models of management in the United States and Japan are often considered as two extremes. On the basis of several characteristics, Europe is somewhere inbetween. If there is a European model of management, it is "half-way" between the U.S. and the Japanese styles. This common European characteristic emerges in three dimensions of management: (1) the relationships between the individual and the firm; (2) the time frame (short term versus long term); and (3) the balance between individualism and a sense of collectivism in the workplace.

People live in close relationships with each other in China, and in the long run everybody gains from reciprocal relations. Social harmony can be maintained only if people follow the established rule—the boat must not be rocked, open conflicts must be avoided, and the balance not disturbed. The need for harmony also explains the preference for *zhong yong zhi dao* (the doctrine of mean, a middle path or compromise). This is also related to the need to preserve face both for oneself and for the others. If there is a conflict, it is often solved through cooperation rather than confrontation, since there is a strong uncertainty avoidance in China.

CHINESE-EUROPEAN INTERCULTURAL MANAGEMENT: PRACTICE AND RECOMMENDATIONS

From 1979 to the end of June 1995 the 15 member countries of the European Union had established a total of 5,184 projects in China, with US$4.81 billion already utilized, respectively 2 percent and 4 percent of the national total. Although the EU countries therefore represent only a small percentage of those investing in China, more than 80 percent of Sino-European joint ventures are successful. Both Shanghai Bell (Sino-Belgian) and Shanghai Volkswagen (Sino-German) have been among the 10 best performing joint ventures for several consecutive years.

Cultural differences as a background factor have certainly influenced the cooperating partners to varying degrees. Researchers have found that putting two important factors—investment motives and cooperation skills—together can both affect and intensify the background cultural factor.

Seeking multicultural identity among different cultures is a good way of cross-cultural communication in JVs. Hofstede (1985) hypothesizes that synergy between organizations takes place when cultures are balanced around the masculine and feminine mean and are close on the "organizational" dimensions of power distance and uncertainty avoidance (see Table 1). This may be why Sino-European joint ventures are often successful.

PDI (Power Distance) refers to the degree to which power differences are expected and, indeed, preferred by a society. A high score on this index reflects a societal belief that there should be a well-defined order in which everyone has a rightful place; a low score reflects the belief that all people should have equal rights and the opportunity to change their position in society.

Table 1. Values Comparisons for EU Countries and Various Chinese Subgroups

	General Values Category				
Managers from:	*PDI*	*UAI*	*IDV*	*MAS*	*LTO*
Hong Kong	68	29	25	57	96
Taiwan	58	69	17	45	87
PRC	56	117	36	0	118
Chinese Mean	61	72	26	34	100
Belgium	65	94	75	54	
Denmark	18	23	74	16	
Germany	35	65	67	66	31
Greece	60	112	35	57	
Spain	57	86	51	42	
France	68	86	71	43	
Ireland	28	35	70	68	
Italy	50	75	76	70	
Luxembourg					
Netherlands	38	53	80	14	44
Austria	11	70	55	79	
Portugal	63	104	27	31	
Sweden	31	29	71	5	33
Finland	33	59	63	26	
United Kingdom	35	35	89	6	25
EU Mean	42	66	65	46	33

Source: Hofstede 1980, 1988, 1991; Clegg, Dunphy, and Redding 1986.

UAI (Uncertainty Avoidance) refers to the degree to which the society willingly accepts ambiguity and risk. Nations characterized by high scores are risk averse; they prefer certainty and security. In contrast, nations characterized by low scores are motivated by risk taking and accept ambiguity.

IDV (Individualism) and its opposite, collectivism, refer to the degree to which a society emphasizes the role of the individual versus the role of the group. In nations high on the individualism scale, every person is expected to take care of himself or herself and his or her immediate family. In contrast, nations high on collectivism show an emotional attachment to organizations and institutions. The emphasis is on "we" and the greater good of the group.

MAS (Masculinity) refers to the degree to which a society holds traditional male values, such as competitiveness, assertiveness, ambition, and the acquisition of money and other material possessions. A low masculinity score (or a high feminity score) reflects a more nurturing, caring value orientation, which emphasizes consideration of others.

LTO (Long-Term Orientation) deals with the time perspective in a society for the gratification of people's needs. This runs from long, like a lifetime, to short, focusing on gratifying needs "here and now." Long-term orientation implies a stress on virtuous living in this world, with thrift and persistence as key virtues. Short-term orientation goes together with a stress on finding the Truth with a capital T: Truth rather than Virtue assures salvation. This dimension featured such factors as thrift versus conspicuous expenditure and truth as an absolute versus truth as dependent upon who speaks.

Chinese or European management culture has its own internal coherence, integrity, and logic. No one management culture is inherently better or worse than another. Both Chinese and European management culture systems are equally valid as variations on the human experience. A cooperative relationship, which should be built on the basis of mutual respect, understanding, trust, and equal cooperation, can be realized only with a friendly attitude, frequent exchange of views, and coordinating skills. To learn about likenesses and seek cross-cultural commonalities or identity between two countries or two regions is a good way of improving intercultural communication (Samovar and Porter 1982). The more similar the culture of forming a shared management joint venture (in China, more than 80% of joint ventures are the shared management type), the easier the venture will to be manage (Killing 1983).

The top managers of JVs should be responsible for the interests of the joint venture itself (not for their respective mother company). Results derived from a study in 1990 on managerial effectiveness under cross-cultural situations and the success factors of Sino-European joint ventures show that this is a key success factor. The study using the Delphi method, had a 100 percent response rate from 10 general managers, five professors, and five administrators, and was undertaken jointly by Shanghai Jiao Tong University and Berlin University of Technology involving one author (see Table 2). With a score of 5.7, this success factor comes out on top.

A joint venture is a cultural border region. The culture of the corporate headquarters often influences the subsidiaries located abroad. Similarly, the presence of foreign partners in an international joint venture should influence the functioning of that firm. The establishment of an IJV always results in the crossing or the interaction of parent cultures. When cultures cross, a cultural shock can occur, often accompanied by negative effects on organizational involvement and work climate. Managers of different nationalities may have differing attitudes to such basic things as the importance of material wealth, or on-the-job performance, or change. The larger the cultural distance between partners of the IJV, the more evident the organizational effects of such a shock becomes. It is probably safe to say that if a joint venture is to be successful, its managers will have to develop into an effective, cohesive, operational team. This collective skill, labeled a company's "core skill" (Killing 1983), is less likely

Table 2. Success Factors of Sino-European Joint Ventures

Factor	*Mean*
Top managers should be responsible for the interests of the JV only (not for each mother company)	5.70
Interpersonal relationships between two partners	5.62
High profits	5.42
Clear and coordinated JV objectives	5.42
Full feasibility study	5.20
There is a development plan for the future	5.00
Pay attention to corporate culture	5.00
Foreign exchange equilibrium	4.89
Parent companies do not interfere with the JV	4.65
Autonomy to human resource management	4.30
Managing conflict appropriately	4.00

Note: The maximum score is 6.00.

to develop if the managers in the venture come from both parents rather than just one. Joint ventures will always face significant problems, unless the top managers are responsible for the joint venture itself, not for each parent company.

THE ALCATEL-BELL CHINA EXPERIENCE

Shanghai Bell is a Sino-Belgian joint venture established at the end of 1983 and operational from the end of 1985. The partners are the Post and Telecommunication Industry Corporation of China with 60 percent of the shares, Alcatel Bell from Belgium with 32 percent, and the Belgian Fund for Development Cooperation with 8 percent. With an original input of US$22.8 million capital, a projected annual output capacity of 300,000 lines and sales of US$45 million, Shanghai Bell in the past 10 years has grown to such a size and achieved such returns that could not have been dreamt of in 1983 (it was doubted whether these figures could ever be reached). In 1994 output exceeded 4.5 million lines and sales amounted to US$700 million. The 1993 year-end equity value of the company plus the dividends already distributed to the partners amounted to US$240 million, more than 10 times the primary capital contribution.

The success of the first 10 years of Shanghai Bell is the ultimate and fruitful result of some major factors and unrelenting efforts. As its general manager said in 1993, one of these is cultural differences were overcome in the interests of the common goal.

> Full confidence and sincere collaboration between the Chinese and Belgian partners and the foreign and local staff are a key factor for Shanghai Bell's success. Different cultural backgrounds, different philosophies of value, different social systems and even different fields of interest do not impede such confidence and collaboration as all the parties keep in mind one *common* goal: the success and prosperity of the joint venture. In practice and at the

> different levels, mutual understanding, mutual respect, mutual support and mutual benefits are the acknowledged criteria. The board of directors, the highest authority of the company, sets itself up as a model and so do the different levels of management. Whenever a difference arises in a certain area the Chinese and foreign parties usually make a careful investigation and further discussion trying to find the *common* interest and best solution for the benefit of Shanghai Bell, which is in fact the assurance of the mutual benefits of both parties (Runxing 1993).

Balancing cultures and adapting to the organization are essential features of multicultural management, and are becoming more critical to the success of international joint ventures. World-class companies are developing this approch.

CONCLUSION

The features of European management culture are: (1) orientation toward people; (2) internal negotiation; (3) managing international diversity; and (4) managing between extremes. For the Chinese type the features are: (1) orientation toward group; (2) internal hierarchy respect; (3) the importance of relationship outside; and (4) the doctrine of the mean. Although there are differences and special properties for each, the similarity between them is the exact reason for organization synergy in Sino-European JVs, and the top managers should be responsible for the interests of the joint venture only, not for their respective mother company. This is a key component of cultural compatibility.

REFERENCES

Caland, C., and P. De Woot. 1994. *A European Management Model: Beyond Diversity*. UK: Prentice Hall.

Clegg, S.R., D.C. Dunphy, and S.G. Redding. 1986. *The Enterprise and Management in East Asia.* Hong Kong: University of Hong Kong.

Hofstede, G. 1980. *Culture's Consequence: International Differences in Work-Related Values*. Beverly Hills, CA: Sage Publications.

Hofstede, G. 1985. "The Interaction between National and Organizational Value Systems." *Journal of Management Studies* 22 (4).

Hofstede, G. 1988. "The Confucius Connection: From Cultural Roots to Economic Growth." *Organizational Dynamics* (Spring).

Hofstede, G. 1991. *Cultures and Organizations: Software of the Mind.* London: McGraw-Hill.

Killing, J.P. 1983. *Strategies for Joint Venture Success.* London: Croom Helm.

Kroeber, A.L., and T. Parsons. 1958. "The Concepts of Culture and of Social Systems." *American Sociological Review* 23: 582-583.

Runxing, Gu. 1993. *Shanghai Bell: A Successful Example of Sino-Foreign Joint Ventures.* Report at a Cultural Capital of Europe Conference, Antwerp, December 6-8.

Samovar, L.A., and R.E. Porter. 1982. *Understanding Intercultural Communication.* Belmont, CA: Wadsworth.

ADVENTURING IN NEW TERRAIN: MANAGING INTERNATIONAL JOINT VENTURES IN CHINA

Yuan Lu, John Child, and Yanni Yan

INTRODUCTION

In the late 1970s the People's Republic of China embarked on an open door policy, ending its 30-year history of isolation from the world since the communist party took power in 1949. The PRC passed its first law governing the establishment of Sino-foreign equity joint ventures (referred to in this chapter as international joint ventures or IJVs) on July 1, 1979. In 1980 the first IJV, Beijing Air Catering, was reported (Shenkar 1990) and since then IJVs have been adopted by many international corporations as a central strategy to enter the Chinese market. Between 1979 and the end of 1994 the number of approved foreign invested projects was 221,618 registered in the PRC, contributing a total contractual capital of US$309.437 billion, and of these 63.3 percent of them were international equity joint ventures (State Planning Commission 1996).

The rapid growth of IJVs in China has caught the attention of scholars undertaking academic research, as well as practicing managers, both

Advances in Chinese Industrial Studies, Volume 5, pages 103-123.

ISBN: 1-55938-961-3

attempting to identify factors contributing to successful management. Studies of IJVs in China have benefited from management theories, such as ownership and control (Child, Yan, and Lu 1997; Yan and Gray 1994), negotiation and formation (Gray and Yan 1992; Newman 1992), partner contribution to IJVs (Li and Shenkar 1996), conflict management (Weldon and Jehn 1996), and interaction between Chinese and Western management styles (Beamish and Speiss 1992). Triumphant examples are frequently quoted in the press, such as Coca-Cola, Pepsi-Cola, Procter & Gamble, and Danone. On the other hand, there are plenty of cases indicating that IJV management in the PRC is a painful process in which foreign and local parties clash with each other on every issue ranging from reinvestment to purchasing of materials.

Most studies of IJVs in the PRC appear, however, to limit their focus to the practices of foreign partners, such as their objectives, entry strategies, and conflict with local parties (i.e., local partners and external agencies), or to structural elements such as control mechanisms embedded in IJVs. These accounts contribute to our understanding of the complex relationships involved in IJV management, but they overlook the role of local partners and their behavior patterns. In general, managing IJVs is a difficult task. Some problems are universal, no matter in which country an IJV is located, for instance, hidden agendas or conflicting objectives causing inter-partner conflict. Other problems are more likely to be common to developing countries, such as those caused by uncertainty in the external environment, underdeveloped infrastructure, and government control of foreign ownership.

It is necessary when considering IJVs in the PRC to realize that the country has some distinguishing features. Scholars often simplify the PRC's business environment by limiting their focus to culture, as if difficulties faced by foreign firms all stem from cross-cultural conflicts. Such a view is inadequate and only partially true. In its 40 years of state socialism, the PRC has established a prevailing centrally planned economy and coercive state intervention in enterprises. Prior to the reform of the early 1980s economic activities were profoundly dominated by planning authorities in state commissions, ministries, and bureaus (Lu 1996). In these overcentralized circumstances, managerial behavior differed substantially from that in market economies. First, the market was distorted and underdeveloped; for instance, prices might be artificially set in accordance with state directives, and information communication was usually limited to vertical channels between enterprises and planning agencies such as bureaus, ministries, and commissions. Second, managers usually made their decisions in accordance with state mandatory plans rather than market demand. Third, the state had strong coercive power to influence management issues in enterprises, and thus a firm's activities could be largely restricted by government intervention in the areas where state control was imposed.

These constraints give rise to ambiguity and uncertainty hindering managers from exerting their autonomy in decision making and pursuing strategic objectives. For a foreign firm, particularly one from a country with a market economy, working in China may seem like being an inexperienced explorer creating a new road through strange and difficult terrain.

This chapter attempts to identify factors that lead to problems in managing IJVs in the PRC. Our findings, drawn from a study of 67 Sino-foreign IJVs, suggest that difficulties in management are caused by multiple factors, and that cross-cultural conflicts are only part of the whole story. Problems are caused by inter-partner diversities, conflicts arising from different management approaches, concepts, and styles, behavior patterns of expatriates felt to be unacceptable by Chinese respondents, and external constraints imposed by the environment.

In this chapter we first outline antecedent conceptual backgrounds regarding management of IJVs, and then summarize key points that were identified by managers concerning mutual perceptions and sources of difficulties. Finally, we propose a few practical solutions for improving IJV management.

THE IJV AS A MANAGEMENT SYSTEM

An IJV is created as a new and separate legal entity, jointly invested in by two or more firms from different countries. A distinctive characteristic of IJVs, in comparison with other forms of cooperation in international business, such as the wholly-owned subsidiary (WOS), is their complex organizational arrangements. First, in contrast to the WOS, which is subordinated to one owning company, IJVs may have two or more owning companies that split derived revenue and voting rights according to their proportion of ownership (Kogut 1988). In addition to their ownership control, these owning companies, usually referred to as parent companies, can be stakeholders, provided that they control critical resources as well as knowledge and skills necessary for IJV operation. Given a high enough proportion of ownership plus the control of critical resources, a parent company can exert a substantial influence on the management of the IJV.

Second, parent companies are usually in a paradoxical relationship. On the one hand, they contribute resources and expertise to IJVs and thus establish a cooperative partnership, but, on the other hand, they remain in independent sovereignty from each other with their own self-interests. In most cases, parent companies have different objectives and motives when entering into IJVs (Beamish 1988; Lorange and Roos 1992), and their objectives can conflict with each other. One partner may have a hidden agenda, such as an intention to acquire knowledge and skills from the other partners and eventually become a competitor to the others (Hamel 1991). In order to protect its interests, or to prevent others from manipulating IJVs for their hidden benefits, a partner is bound to introduce control mechanisms. As a result, inter-parent relationship in IJVs is a balance of cooperation versus control.

Third, IJVs usually have managers assigned from the parent companies, and thus become a collection of expatriates and local employees who may have diverse backgrounds, cultures, experiences, and skills. Associated with these diversities, IJV management encounters two kinds of conflicts (Parkhe 1991; Weldon and Jehn 1996): those caused by differences in management styles and approaches, and those that originate from cross-cultural differences. The introduction of management practices based on foreign parent companies requires local managers and staff to change, and, therefore, they have to unlearn their traditional approaches. To expatriates, particularly those in senior positions, working in IJVs means a challenge, too. They have to fit in with local cultures, but also have to create or change management practices within the IJVs if the local approach is thought to be inappropriate for the IJV's performance and development. The greater the differences in management styles and cultures between foreign and local systems, the more easily tensions, conflicts, and resistance arise, and, as a result, the more difficult it becomes to manage the IJV.

Fourth, IJVs involve exchange relations with the external environment. As an independent organization, the IJV competes in the market and interacts with other organizations. One may argue that an IJV's operation might have the minimum relationship with the external environment, if all its inputs/outputs are dependent only on its parent companies. Even so, the IJV remains, to some extent, linked with the local environment because some resources, such as human resources, are likely to be locally dependent.

Moreover, as Lu and Lake (1996) argue, IJVs have to conform with expectations imposed by local institutional authorities such as the state government and professional organizations, as well as social practices and cultures. As at least one parent company is from an alien country, the IJV is seen as a "foreign" affiliate. This "foreignness" may give rise to state measures, which aim to control foreign ownership in strategic industries, or IJVs may be targeted as a threat to national industries and thus be treated differently from indigenous firms. The trend in the 1990s appears to be toward liberalizing national economies, and most governments, particularly those in developing countries, offer positive measures to attract foreign investment, such as the provision of favorable taxation schemes for foreign invested affiliates. However, governmental intervention and external uncertainties embedded in the environment may have significant influences on IJV management.

The above discussion suggests that the managements of IJVs face three types of difficulties. The first kind derives from tension between parent companies. For each parent company the rationale for entering into an IJV is based on both economic and strategic considerations (Tallman and Shenkar 1994), but this does not ensure the goal-congruence of all parent companies in the IJV. A parent company may have hidden objectives, or its purposes may change over time. As the game theory suggests, interfirm partnerships face a dilemma of cheating and cooperation (Parkhe 1993). Mistrust and suspicion between parent companies is likely to extend to IJVs where managers may find it difficult to translate conflicting objectives into a workable task objective.

The second type concerns the IJV-environment relationship. External environments can be grouped into two kinds: institutional and task-related (Scott 1992). The former consists of government agencies and regulatory bodies that exercise various measures to control IJVs (i.e., on ownership limits, location of control, nature of business transacted, and bureaucratic harassment), financial schemes (such as foreign exchange controls, export requirements, and profit repatriation limits), and operational methods (such as interference by government requirements on location, localization of value-added chain activities, and staffing restrictions) (Poynter 1985). The task environment is closely related to the exchange relationship between IJVs and other organizations and conditions such as infrastructure and technology. These include availability of market information, quality of supplies, and efficiency of transactions which IJVs conduct in exchanging resources and outputs with other business units.

The third sort of difficulties arise within the IJV's organization where different management approaches are mingled. For instance, local managers may feel discriminated against if their pay is lower than that of expatriates. As a result, human resource management (HRM) within IJVs encounters motivation problems. Other difficulties include inadequate internal communication, or incompetence of employees and resistance to new management practices.

IJVs IN THE PEOPLE'S REPUBLIC OF CHINA

The trend of increasing foreign direct investment (FDI) in the PRC appears to be consistent with the rapid growth of FDI inflows into most developing countries, where policies have become favorable toward economic liberalization since the early 1990s (United Nations 1994). However, what is regarded as China's miracle is the boom in FDI during the short period since 1992. In 1991 the PRC's FDI inflow ranked only thirteenth in the world and third among developing countries. But the PRC has, since 1993, become the second largest FDI recipient in the world, following the United States, and the single largest host country among developing countries (United Nations 1995). In 1993 the total of dispersed FDI capital reached US$27.5 billion, associated with 83,437 approved projects. Of them, 54,003 were registered IJVs, constituting 64.7 percent of FDI (*Almanac of China's Foreign Economic*

Relations and Trade 1994/1995, p. 706). In 1994 the trend in the FDI boom was sustained, and there were 47,549 FDI projects approved, accounting for US$33.8 billion. Of these, 27,890 were IJVs, about 58.7 percent of the total FDI (*Almanac of China's Foreign Economic Relations and Trade* 1995/1996, p. 757).

A number of factors in combination with one another contributed to the "great leap forward" in FDI in the PRC. These included the rapid expansion of the domestic market (driven by a strong economic performance), the gradual opening of the domestic market and industries to foreign companies, low-cost labor and rich natural resources, the government's efforts to improve the infrastructure and investment environment, as well as other reform measures aimed at transforming a centrally controlled economy to a market-based one, and improvement of the PRC's diplomatic relations with neighboring countries (United Nations 1994, pp. 69-70).

The rapid growth in FDI and the development of IJVs involved an introduction of alien management approaches to the PRC, and this was seen as a way to challenge traditional local management that had been largely established and nurtured by a central planning system before the reform. Prior to 1980 most industrial enterprises were monopolized by state ownership, contributing to more than 75 percent of total industrial output. This figure declined to 43 percent in 1993, but state-owned enterprises still hired 67.88 percent of industrial employees (*China Statistic Yearbook* 1994, pp. 373-374). Most state enterprises suffer from overmanning, low productivity, poor technological capabilities, and government interference in management. About one-third of state enterprises were reported to run at a loss, and it was estimated that more than 70 percent of them had hidden losses, that is, bad credit and wastes of human resources and materials.

As China had been isolated from the international economy before the early 1980s, opportunities for mutual understanding between foreign and local firms were limited, because international business was monopolized by state agencies (Macbean 1996). This is in contrast to an evolutionary process of establishing IJVs, in which partners would start with trading relations, gradually build trust, and eventually enter into IJVs. Although this situation has improved after more than 17 years of reform, as both foreign and local firms have learned from experience, there is still a lack of capable managers with knowledge of both Western management and the Chinese environment.

External environments, both institutional and task, need urgent reform, too. External constraints come from government bureaucracy and frequent changes in policy regarding FDI. For instance, a policy that came into force on July 1, 1995 stipulated that FDI should be guided in accordance with state industrial development strategies. In strategic industries such as the automobile sector, joint ventures are approved with the condition that local partners should constitute a majority of ownership. In other sectors, such as telecommunications, FDI is more restricted or even prohibited. This implies that a local partner in IJVs tends to incorporate government agendas in its objectives, for instance, acquiring knowledge and expertise of foreign technology and management, in addition to seeking foreign capital as additional resources. Regarding task environments, China is in an industrialization process in which most facilities and infrastructure, including the legal framework, quality of supplies, provision of energy, transportation, and communication, are still in underdevelopment.

As discussed previously, difficulties in managing IJVs are embedded in state intervention and distinctive management systems that differ substantially from Western ones based on a market economy. Moreover, traditional Chinese culture adds to the complexity of IJV management. Chinese culture prefers respect for authority and hierarchy, group orientation, the concept of face, and personal relations—*guanxi.* Organizational culture theory suggests that management in such cultural circumstances is characterized by vertical communication, centralized structure and processes, and patronizing behavior. Indeed, previous studies of IJVs in China have noted difficulties caused by local staff behavior, such as poor internal communication, avoidance of risk taking, and reliance on personal relations in problem solving (Child 1994; Bjorkman and Schaap 1995).

THE IJV SURVEY

Research Method

Our data was collected from 67 IJVs in China during the period from March 1994 to April 1995. The purpose of our investigation was to identify ownership structures, organizational arrangements, management processes, and managers' behavior patterns. In order to obtain consistent and comparative data, sample organizations were selected from two industries: industrial electronics and fast-moving consumer goods. The profile of the 67 IJVs is depicted in Table 1.

Of the 67 IJVs, 40 have a foreign ownership of over 50 percent, while 12 have a 50-50 ownership structure. The smallest IJV had only 34 employees, while the largest one had more than 1,700: the majority are of medium size, having between 100 and 500 employees. Nine IJVs have 50-year duration contracts; many of them have fixed duration contracts of between 15 and 30 years.

A team consisting of the three authors, assisted by staff assigned by a Chinese research institute, arranged interviews with both foreign and local managers in the IJVs. In order to avoid subjective biases, the three authors worked together during the first round of interviews and then cross-examined the data.

Table 1. Profile of 67 IJVs

Characteristics	*Range*	*Frequency (N = 67)*
Size: total number employed	< 99	18
	100-299	24
	300-499	6
	500-999	15
	> 1000	4
Share of foreign ownership (%)	25-49	15
	50:50	12
	51-75	33
	> 75	7
Length of IJV contract (years)	< 10	1
	10-15	22
	16-30	35
	> 30	9
National of foreign parent companies	US and UK	17
	Continental Europe	17
	Japanese	16
	Overseas Chinese	17
Industrial sectors	Electronics	33
	Fast-moving consumer goods	34

Later, the fieldwork was led by at least one of the three authors. Where permitted, interviews were taperecorded, and access to documents and statistics was also requested. Eventually, we managed to interview more than 200 expatriates and local managers, including those at the level of general manager (GM), deputy general manager (DGM), and senior executives undertaking such functions as finance, marketing, production, and personnel. Where appropriate, access to documents and statistics was also requested.

In order to understand the difficulties arising in the management of IJVs, each GM and/or DGM was asked to give an open account regarding difficulties they encountered. Qualitative data was collected from a combination of two questions:

- What are the chief difficulties you have encountered in managing this IJV?
- What are the areas where the most conflicts arise?

As the questions were open, the answers depended upon the manager's personal experience and perception. This makes it difficult to compare data because the answers were diverse and inconsistent. Two researchers carefully selected quotations and then categorized each one. During the content analysis we omitted those cases that had no involvement of foreign staff in IJV management and whose data was inadequate for analysis. Finally, there were 51 cases that contained valid data to analyze accounts given by foreign managers, and 56 cases to analyze data from Chinese managers.

After the citation exercise, key phrases and sentences were singled out based on content analysis technique.[1] Both difficulties and suggested improvements were identified and summarized.

Research Findings

Management Structure and Organizational Arrangements

Most IJVs studied had a simple organizational structure, similar to Williamson's U-form (Williamson 1975). This structure contains most basic functions of a business firm, including supply and sales, production, and technology (see Figure 1). Only some had marketing departments and few IJVs had their own research and development units. This means that the IJVs sampled were performing production tasks and sales, but were less likely to be innovative in technology.

A majority of the IJVs studied ($n = 62$) had a deputy general manager (DGM) who assisted the GM. Below the GM and DGM there were several functional departments including operations (taking responsibility for production and manufacturing), marketing and sales, technology, finance, and personnel. Department managers were either selected by the GM or assigned by parent companies. In some cases, the appointment of senior executives, particularly those in charge of finance, needed the board's approval. Table 2 shows the nationalities of the board chairmanship and key management positions.

As Table 2 shows, 48 IJVs (72%) had a Chinese chairman. Of these 48, 23 had foreign majority ownership, including four with 70 percent or more foreign equity ownership. Usually, a Chinese chairman of the board was nominated from those in relevant government agencies, such as industrial bureaus. Unless a foreign firm had a substantial dominance in ownership, IJVs were likely to have a local nominee as chairman of the board. One reason for this was that up until 1990 Chinese law required that IJVs should be chaired by a local. Another reason was that the board chairman was seen as an honorary position (Bjorkman 1995).

In reality, the board chairman usually had little power over the IJV's management. Instead, control was usually in the hands of the GM, and foreign companies were seriously involved in the GM nomination. Table 2 indicates that in 79 percent of the IJVs sampled ($n = 53$) the GM was assigned by the foreign parent company. The dominance of foreign expatriates in the GM position was consistent with policies in many foreign parent companies which

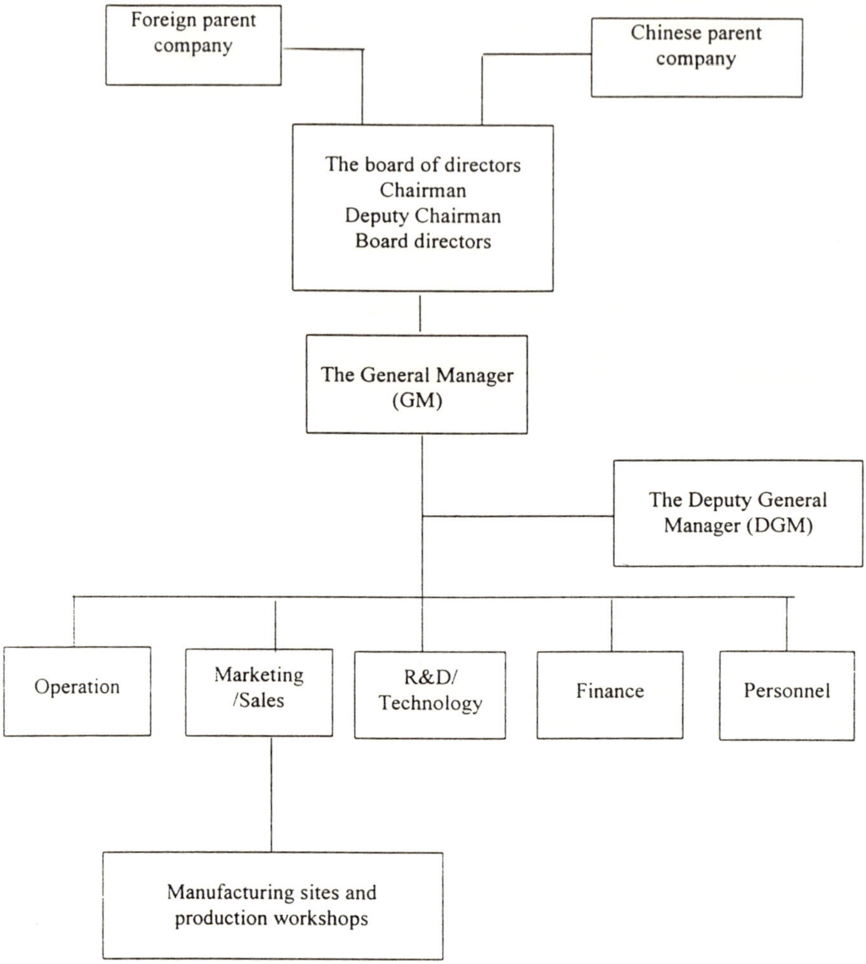

Figure 1. Organizational Chart of an IJV in the PRC

prefer entire control over management systems. This was particularly seen in large international corporations and those of U.S. and British firms. For instance, among seven electronics IJVs with U.S. and British partners, only one IJV had a Chinese GM.

Closely related to foreign parental control over the GM, expatriates were generally assigned to other strategic positions, including operation, marketing, and technology, although these positions were also sometimes occupied by externally recruited managers. Local parent companies usually assigned the

Table 2. Composition of the Board and Management Positions in 67 IJVs

Position	Number of IJVs with Foreign Parent Nomination or Appointment (N = 67)	Number of IJVs with Chinese Parent Nomination or Appointment (N = 67)	Number of IJVs with Executives Recruited from External Sources (N = 67)
Chairman of the IJV board	19 (28%)	48 (72%)	—
IJV General Manager	53 (79%)	14 (20%)	—
IJV Deputy General Manager (N = 62)	12 (19%)	48 (78%)	2 (3%)
Operational manager for manufacturing and production	30 (45%)	23 (34%)	14 (21%)
Marketing manager	34 (51%)	22 (33%)	11 (16%)
Technology or R&D (N = 51)	27 (53%)	13 (25%)	11 (22%)
Finance	25 (37%)	26 (39%)	16 (24%)
Personnel (N = 65)	5 (8%)	47 (72%)	13 (20%)

DGM and personnel functions. Both parent companies had relatively equal nomination of finance managers.

The position of the DGM was the subject of some debate. Although many IJVs had a contract that required the appointment of the DGM as an assistant to the GM, in reality the DGM tended to be marginalized in decision making. Nor did the DGM have much responsibility for the IJV's operation, and most Chinese DGMs were reported to play a coordinating role between the GM and the Chinese parent companies. Many foreign GMs said that they really did not need the DGM. Five IJVs eventually omitted the DGM position, and thus the GM had full authority in management.

The assignment of managers to IJVs is perceived as an exercise of control. We found that assigned managers maintained strong links to their nominee parent companies. Apart from Japanese expatriates, who were encouraged to stay in IJVs long term (five years or longer), expatriates usually signed short-term contracts of about two to three years. Being in China was regarded as a rotation or a step for career development. Foreign companies assessed their assigned staff according to the IJV's performance, such as its profitability. A number of IJVs tied the GM's bonus scheme to the IJV's profitability.

Local managers were either recruited from the external market or assigned by a local parent company. These two groups of managers differed in their loyalty and career development. Externally recruited managers were reported to be capable and competent, with strong loyalty to the IJVs, but their career was largely constrained by intervention from the parent company. In contrast, managers assigned from local parent companies benefited from their closer links with the local parent companies, with secured career development and other benefits such as housing. These managers were assessed by two criteria.

One was set by a GM, who acted as the managerial authority over joint venture managers, the other was in accordance with the authority of the Chinese parent companies. These two criteria sometimes conflicted with each other. In one IJV Chinese managers were required to "stand on the Chinese side" if the two partners were in dispute, and this meant that the Chinese managers were cautious in their communication with the expatriate GM. Internal communication and coordination became problematic.

Difficulties Arising in Managing IJVs

Difficulties in managing IJVs arose from four sources of conflict. Table 3 indicates these sources of conflict which were addressed in interviews.

Difficulties Caused by Inter-partner Relationships

One typical difficulty embedded in inter-partner relationships is that parent companies have different agendas when entering into IJVs. For instance, it was found in several cases that disputes stemmed from conflicting development strategies. A foreign partner might prefer the IJV to distribute imported products with their brand names/trademarks in domestic markets, so that the IJV would be in effect a sales agency. However, the Chinese partner might insist that the IJV should start manufacturing straight away. Many local partners required the IJVs to develop their own brand names and accelerate the pace of export and localization.

Other difficulties included friction between parent companies in decisions concerning profit allocation, the pace of localization and pricing policy of supplies, and lack of trust or coordination between parent companies. For instance, although the pursuit of long-term profitability appeared as one of the strategic objectives for Chinese parent companies, some still preferred quick profit dividends, while foreign partners persisted in reinvestment. One IJV indicated that its Chinese parent companies had established multiple IJVs, which shared information and knowledge with each other, and the foreign partner feared that their product design and technology could be leaked to the other Chinese affiliates. Such suspicious attitudes were certainly likely to cause mistrust between parent companies.

Compared to expatriates, Chinese managers seemed to be more sensitive to inter-partner relationships. The frequency ($f = 16$) of encountering inter-parent difficulties claimed by Chinese managers was much higher than that from foreign expatriates ($f = 9$). One explanation might be a lack of adequate communication between parent companies, leading to misunderstanding and/or mistrust. Indeed, from our observation of communications between IJV managers and parent companies, it became evident that inter-parent communication was largely limited to formal channels, such as board meetings.

Table 3. Main Difficulties Encountered by IJVs in China

Foreign Managers' Accounts	*Frequency of Case (f) (N = 51)*	*Chinese Managers' Accounts*	*Frequency of Cases (f) (N = 56)*
Inter-partner relations		**Inter-partner relations**	
— difficulties caused by different objectives between parent companies	9	**— difficulties caused by different objectives between parent companies**	15
External environments		**External environments**	
Institutional environments (government bureaucracy, ambiguous laws and relagions)	18	Institutional environments (government bureaucracy, ambiguous laws and regulations)	2
Task environments		*Task environments*	
— difficulties caused by underdeveloped infrastructure, poor quality of supplies and a lack of market information	11	— difficulties caused by underdeveloped infrastructure, poor quality of supplies and a lack of market information	4
Internal management systems		**Internal management systems**	
— difficulties caused by different management styles	26	— difficulties caused by different management styles	18
— difficulties caused by human resource management such as payment, welfare, and arrangement of accommodation	18	— difficulties caused by human resource management such as payment, welfare, and arrangement of accommodation	15
— difficulties caused by cross-cultural conflicts such as traditional way of doing business	17	— difficulties caused by cross-cultural conflicts such as foreign way of doing business	6
— difficulties caused by Chinese managers who lack concepts, skills, and behavior	14	— difficulties caused by expatriate managers without knowledge of Chinese environments	29
— difficulties caused by language barriers	14	— difficulties caused by language barriers	13
— difficulties caused by a lack of sufficient communication within IJV organizations	7	— difficulties caused by a lack of sufficient communication within IJV organizations	3

At the same time, foreign managers maintained more frequent communication with their parent company headquarters or regional offices than local managers did with local parent companies. Consequently, Chinese partners tended to feel excluded from the management process.

Difficulties Embedded in External Environments

Institutional environment. The legal environment in the PRC is still underdeveloped, and lawmaking, as well as policy making, remains opaque. A change in the law or government regulations can occur abruptly without much discussion or hearing. For example, in late December 1993 a value-added tax scheme was announced by the PRC government, which came into force on January 1, 1994. Most IJVs had no advance warning of this policy change. China's imperfect legal system and frequent changes in government policies makes it difficult for expatriates to anticipate the environment. As one foreign manager said,

> You have to be extremely well connected in order to get things done here. There is a lack of an independent legal system, and little separation between the monetary policies and fiscal policies of the country. There is no commercial law...and you don't know which one is going to apply.

A firm's long-term plan had to be highly flexible in order to meet the uncertainty and ambiguity embedded in the external environment. This was in contrast to strategic management processes which emphasized long-term objectives. Conflicts arose when two management approaches collided.

Government bureaucracy presented other difficulties; regulatory and functional agencies, such as auditing, taxation, customs, environmental protection, and administration, were slow in dealing with enterprise issues. One IJV found that local government agencies ignored state policies in favor of IJVs in taxation and custom tariffs. In another case, a foreign manager complained that in order to complete one transaction, three or four personal visits to government agencies such as customs or tax offices were necessary. What confused him was that on each visit he received different instructions.

In contrast, Chinese managers appeared to have few difficulties with government behavior, partly because they were accustomed to government practices. Government intervention was mentioned in only two cases. A number of Chinese managers said that in comparison with state enterprises, IJVs enjoyed much more freedom in decision making, and they were quite satisfied with the current situation. For example, IJV managers had the authority to determine the number of employees, which was usually rather difficult for state enterprises. When the Taiwanese GM of one IJV decided not to renew the contracts of 20 workers, some of them complained to the local labor bureau and asked for government arbitration intervention. The bureau replied, however, that it would take no action, and the case was eventually moved to the local industrial tribunal.

Inefficient infrastructure in task environments. As a semi-industrialized country, China has underdeveloped infrastructure and facilities in energy supply, transportation, communication, and the provision of social welfare. IJVs, particularly those that follow international standards, found it difficult to accept local contents, due to their poor quality and unsatisfactory services. Poor quality is not a problem in raw materials, but other supplies, such as packaging materials, had to be imported by some IJVs. This obviously increased costs and eroded profits.

Another difficulty frequently mentioned by managers was a lack of information. Information relating to customers, market development, and labor supplies was either underdeveloped or not available at all. One foreign manager complained that he was unable to conduct strategic planning because "there was little information about the market." In order to obtain information some IJVs formed an association through which they exchanged data and ideas. Human resource managers in 19 large IJVs established regular contact and met together every six months to discuss their policies and circulate data regarding market prices and management practice.

Problems in IJV Internal Management

Perhaps the most frequently occurring difficulties in IJVs are those within the organizations, especially between expatriates and local staff where their backgrounds, experiences, and cultures differ from each other (Weldon and Jehn 1996). In particular, when an IJV is built on the existing site of the Chinese parent company, the introduction of foreign management is immediately likely to trigger anxiety among local staff who, taking traditional approaches for granted, resist enforced change.

In a majority of the IJVs ($f = 26$), foreign managers found it difficult to avoid conflicts with their local colleagues, because of their contrasted management methods. They frequently complained about incompetence of local managers ($f = 14$). As one expatriate said:

> Unfortunately, with management skills, you start to hit the so-called cultural gap between how we think and how the Chinese think. It's my view that this culture gap doesn't exist—it's a myth—because we are all human and we all want basically the same things and we all have the same sort of emotions. It's just that the Chinese, I think because of two things—(1) how they have been educated recently and (2) because they have lived in a tightly controlled society where they have not been given the opportunity to think laterally and have total freedom of thought—they are very reticent to take total responsibility for their own actions. Now it's very difficult to try and make it happen. It's going to be a long and painful process, frankly, before this occurs.

Of the internal management problems referred to by foreign managers, the lack of understanding of marketing concepts, the avoidance of taking responsibility, the preference for centralized decision making, and poor internal communication were top of the list. As one expatriate said:

> There's big differences there. The Westerners feel compulsively that they must be seen to make a decision quickly. The Chinese will talk around a problem from all different angles. One of the descriptions I used to give on the thing is, you know, you're sitting in a group meeting, with a whole table full of people and one person picks up the kitchen knife and sticks it in another person's back. Well, in the West it's very clear, this guy got up and stabbed the other person, so take him off and shoot him. It's a fairly clear thing. In China the discussion immediately starts with who was the manufacturer of the knife, and then works around the thing. It'll end up probably with the same conclusion, but they like to take a lot of time and won't accuse one another directly.

These problems are partly caused by cross-cultural differences. Managers in several IJVs ($f = 16$) insisted that they found it difficult to understand Chinese culture. One of the most serious problems was inadequate internal communication between expatriates and local staff. As one European manager said,

> The thing which surprised me most is the difficulty to really get under the skin of the people [here], to really understand the mind of the people. In the Western world, you can have a very good exchange of ideas with people who can communicate well, which enables both parties to give something to each other. But the Chinese never give anything. What they do is, they give you a very little bit one day, and then they always tell me "you don't understand the Chinese." You have to put the bits and pieces together like a puzzle and then suddenly you have a big picture, and then you go back and check with them, and then you get another piece. At the end of the process, you get a good understanding, but it takes time.

Expatriates also found themselves entangled in a web of complex *guanxi* that played a crucial part in management. Chinese managers were reported as taking a softer approach to deal with workers, tending to avoid direct confrontation, for the purpose of maintaining good *guanxi* among employees. As one European manager said,

> I have found that it has been difficult to try and get Chinese managers to separate the personality from the subject, to deal with the subject not with the particular person. There have been a number of instances where I've had people who got very upset in a meeting, and when I've tried to dig into it afterwards off-line, you'll find them come out with things like "I thought he was my friend"; you know, there's people there and they're arguing from a particular position and I'm well able to separate feelings about the individual at a personal level from what they are saying. But in China, for some reason, that seems to be extremely difficult to do.

A number of IJVs tried to reduce cross-cultural conflicts by employing overseas Chinese as expatriates. This policy proved effective in solving problems caused by language barriers, but seemed to do little to reconcile Western versus Chinese management divergence.

Many Chinese managers agreed that conflicts existed between expatriates and local staff ($f = 22$), but they argued that these problems were caused because expatriates had little knowledge about China ($f = 29$). As one Chinese manager said,

> When dealing with issues relating to domestic systems, for example, how to deal with external institutions and how to understand the government operation, foreign managers lack understanding. These are China-specific issues.

To local employees expatriates were seen as ambassadors representing their national cultures, as well as the foreign parent companies. It became evident that the vastly different work styles and personalities of expatriates, particularly the GM, had substantial influences on organizational processes. The foreign partner of one IJV assigned a total of nine GMs during the first seven years of operation. Chinese managers complained that each GM had a totally different style: "Some preferred formalization, while others were informal. Some required regulatory meetings once a week, while others told us not to see them unless there was an urgent matter."

Regarding managerial functions, both foreign and Chinese managers appeared to be anxious about human resource management ($f = 18$ for foreign managers, $f = 15$ for local ones). One problem that was specified was the high turnover rate and mobility of skilled technicians. "We lose about 11 percent of employees a year. They are always our best technicians," one American manager said. One reason behind such an active labor market was the short supply of capable workers. Foreign companies in particular competed to attract competent technical staff and executives. Salaries and compensation packages were quickly inflated, and many IJVs found that their labor costs had increased dramatically in recent years. The personnel manager in one Japanese JV told us that the traditional Japanese style of management, with lower wages but a corporate family culture, faced rivalry from other companies offering attractive packages of a generous salary and fringe benefits, including substantial allowances for housing and business trips. Under such pressure, his JV had to increase wages in order to keep its best staff.

The language barrier was another difficulty. Non-Chinese foreign managers had to rely on interpreters or secretaries to talk with junior staff or technicians at operational levels. IJVs usually recruited university graduates with English language training, but it took some time to develop their language skills.

Areas for Improvement

We identified four areas for improvement in IJV management: skills, quality of cooperation between parent companies, resource supplies, and market shares. The first is concerned with internal management, the second with inter-parent

Table 4. Areas in Need of Improvement and Scale of Priority

	Foreign Managers' Perception (N = 53)			*Chinese Managers' Perception (N = 67)*		
Areas of Improvement	*Means*	*Std. Dev.*	*Range*	*Means*	*Std. Dev.*	*Range*
Improving internal systems						
Skills (technical and management	3.73	.76	2-5	3.78	.95	2-5
Improving inter-partner relationship						
Quality of cooperation	2.92	1.19	1-5	2.6	1.13	1-5
Improving external environments						
Resource supplies (financing and raw materials)	3.66	1.29	1-5	3.2	1.26	1-5
Improving a competitive position						
Market shares	3.7	1.23	1-5	3.59	1.21	1-5

Note: 1 = less high priority; 2 = priority; 3 = high priority; 4 = fairly high priority; 5 = very high priority.

relations. The third concerns an IJV's expectation to improve external environments, the fourth an IJV's effort to achieve competitive advantages in the marketplace. Table 4 shows the responses of both foreign and local managers.

Improvement of skills. This was singled out as a priority ($m = 3.73$ rated by foreign managers, $m = 3.78$ by local managers), a result consistent with the identification of the difficulties caused by contrasted management approaches. In addition to intensifying training in both technology and management, delegation of decision making to local managers was suggested as another alternative. Our data implies that, as most IJVs were still in an early stage of development, decision making appeared to be highly centralized, with the GM perhaps retaining all decisions in his or her hands. This high degree of centralization hampered local managers by diminishing their learning opportunities.

Market share. Both foreign ($m = 3.7$) and local ($m = 3.59$) managers were aware that market competition was becoming more aggressive. One IJV had enjoyed rapid growth up to 1993 due to its successful commercial campaign and internationally well-known brand names. Then its sales suddenly dropped, as other international corporations started production in China. Managers then began to pay substantial attention to the relationship with customers and new product development.

Resource supplies. Two critical resources were frequently mentioned by managers: financing and materials. Difficulties in gaining access to banks and the poor quality of materials seriously impeded IJV operations. Ways of easing these constraints included relying on foreign partners for the provision of financing resources, as well as strategic materials. Alternatively, IJVs sought material resources from other IJVs.

Cooperation quality. Partner cooperation was undoubtedly the key determinant of IJV success. It was suggested that both partners needed efficient communication and goal congruence. Furthermore, both sides needed to establish a long-term view of IJV development.

CONCLUSION

Despite the difficulties identified earlier, many IJVs were satisfied with their performance, and some were regarded as excellent management models in the PRC. One GM recalled the progress of his IJV as follows:

> The first time I went round (the Chinese parent manufacturing company), when I first came, I was totally appalled. Health and safety conditions in the factory were incredibly bad. The quality systems were a joke, and the product was useless frankly—it was so out of date. I went round [another] factory, one of their joint ventures (with a European partner) and the product is good, the atmosphere is good, controls are very good and the people who were running it were actually the same people who were running the other one [the Chinese parent company]. Again all right, you can say, they are being managed by the Europeans. But effectively it is still the Chinese that are running the factory. The implication I get of this is that the people have the capability all along to do the job and that they were either misdirected or not supported or didn't care. Now it might be that they didn't care because they had no reason to care. But I suspect they were misdirected.

To solve these problems, then, both parent companies should have clear objectives and be able to make complementary contributions in resources and skills. IJVs should develop capable human resources, including a skilled labor force and competent managerial teams. Localization of both resources and management needs to be a top priority. Furthermore, IJVs need to have a stable managerial team, and executives, as well as parent companies, should persist in introducing management concepts and approaches.

ACKNOWLEDGMENT

The authors would like to thank the International Technological Economic Institute for its support for the empirical study in the PRC and the Research Grants Council of the Hong Kong University Grants Council for its financial assistance.

NOTE

1. The following example shows our data analyzing process. The following is a citation from case no. 25:

> Question:
> Do you encounter any difficulties and conflicts (in managing the IJV)?
> Answer:
> We do have, but different kinds. For example, compensation policies. Chinese want to do more automatically. They say Chinese people want that, because, they say, high bonus, high motivation, based on their history and experiences in the past. They want to do things in this way.

This citation suggests that compensation policies are the cause of some difficulties. This is part of the HRM function, thus we codified one case with a difficulty in HRM. Then we calculated the number of cases that shared similar difficulties. Eventually, we found that there were 18 IJVs where foreign managers pointed out difficulties regarding HRM functions.

We then did the same exercise to analyze Chinese managers' interviews. In aspects of HRM, there were 15 IJVs in which local managers outlined similar difficulties to those of foreign managers. As a result, we concluded that the frequency of difficulties in HRM perceived by foreign managers is 18, while that by Chinese managers is 15.

In order to avoid misinterpretation and subjective biases we attempted to focus on specific terms, phrases, and sentences. Key words, such as "training," "welfare facilities," "payment" or "reward policies," obviously suggest HRM functions. When a manager gave further detailed accounts addressing direct difficulties caused by different methods key phrases were usually as follows: "a different way of doing business," "Chinese decision making more centralized," "lack of flexibility in planning."

REFERENCES

Almanac of China's Foreign Economic Relations and Trade. 1994/1995. Beijing: China Resources Advertising Co. Ltd.

Almanac of China's Foreign Economic Relations and Trade. 1995/1996. Beijing: China Resources Advertising Co. Ltd.

Beamish, P.W. 1988. *Multinational Joint Ventures in Developing Countries*. London: Routledge.

Beamish, P.W., and L. Speiss. 1992. "Foreign Direct Investment in China." Pp. 152-171 in *International Business in China*, edited by L. Kelley and O. Shenkar. London: Routledge.

Bjorkman, I. 1995. "The Board of Directors in Sino-Western Joint Ventures." *Corporate Governance* 3 (3): 156-166.

Bjorkman, I., and A. Schaap. 1994. "Outsiders in the Middle Kingdom." *European Management Journal* 12 (2): 147-153.

Child, J. 1994. *Management in China during the Era of Reform*. Cambridge, UK: Cambridge University Press.

Child, J., Y. Yan, and Y. Lu. 1997. "Ownership and Control in Sino-foreign Joint Ventures." In *Co-operative Strategies: Asia-Pacific Perspectives*, edited by P. Beamish and P. Killing. New York: New Lexington Press.

China Statistic Yearbook. 1994. Beijing: China Statistic Press.

Gray, B., and A. Yan. 1992. "Formation and Evolution of International Joint Ventures." Paper presented at the Symposium on the Formation Process of International Co-operative Ventures, the Academy of Management Meeting, Las Vegas, Nevada, August 10.

Hamel, G. 1991. "Competition for Competence and Inter-partner Learning within International Strategic Alliances." *Strategic Management Journal* (12): 83-103.

Kogut, B. 1988. "Joint Ventures: Theoretical and Empirical Perspectives." *Strategic Management Journal* (3): 319-332.

Li, J.T., and O. Shenkar. 1996. "In Search of Complementary Assets: Co-operative Strategies and Knowledge Seeking by Prospective Chinese Partners." Pp. 52-65 in *Management Issues for China: International Enterprises*, edited by J. Child and Y. Lu. London: Routledge.

Lorange, P., and J. Roos. 1992. *Strategic Alliances*. Oxford: Blackwell.

Lu, Y. 1996. *Management Decision-making in Chinese Enterprises*. London: Macmillan.

Lu, Y., and Lake, D. 1996. "Managing International Joint Ventures: An Institutional Approach." Paper presented at Global Perspectives on Co-operative Strategies Conference, Lausanne, Switzerland, March 8-10.

Macbean, A. 1996. "China's Foreign Trade Corporations: Their Role in Economic Reforms and Export Success." Pp. 183-200 in *Management Issues for China: International Enterprises*, edited by J. Child and Y. Lu. London: Routledge.

Newman, W. H. 1992. "Launching a Viable Joint Venture." *California Management Review* (Fall): 68-80.

Parkhe, A. 1991. "Interfirm Diversity, Organisational Learning, and Longevity in Global Strategic alliances." *Journal of International Business Studies* 22 (Fourth Quarter): 579-601.

Parkhe, A. 1993. "Strategic Alliance Structuring: A Game Theoretic and Transaction Cost Examination of Interfirm Co-operation'. *Academy of Management Journal* 36 (4): 794-829.

Poynter, T.A. 1985. *Multinational Enterprises and Government Intervention*. London: Croom Helm.

Scott, W.R. 1992. *Organizations: Rational, Nature, and Open Systems* (3rd ed.). Englewood Cliffs, NJ: Prentice Hall.

Shenkar, O. 1990. "International Joint Ventures' Problems in China: Risks and Remedies." *Long Range Planning* 23 (3): 82-90.

State Planning Commission's Foreign Research Institute. 1996. "Zhongguo liyong waishang zhijie touzi wenti yanjiu." ("A Study of China's Utilization of Foreign Direct Investment"). *Guanli Zhijie (Management World)* 2: 46-54.

Tallman, S., and O. Shenkar. 1994. "A Managerial Decision Model of International Co-operative Venture Formation." *Journal of International Business Studies* 25 (First Quarter): 91-113.

United Nations. 1994. *The World Investment Report*. Geneva: United Nations Conference on Trade and Development.

United Nations. 1995. *The World Investment Report*. Geneva: United Nations Conference on Trade and Development.

Weldon, E., and K. Jehn. 1996. "Conflict Management in US-Chinese Joint Ventures." In *Management Issues for China: International Enterprises*, edited by J. Child and Y. Lu. London: Routledge.

Williamson, O. 1975. *Markets and Hierarchies*. New York: Free Press.

Yan, A., and B. Gray. 1994. "Bargaining Power, Management Control, and Performance in U.S.-China Joint Ventures: A Comparative Case Study." *Academy of Management Journal* 37: 1478-1517.

CHINA'S STRATEGY AND POLICY ON DIRECT FOREIGN INVESTMENT AND ITS CONFIGURATION: PROBLEMS AND PROSPECTS

Chen Lingzhu

INTRODUCTION

China has adopted the opening to the outside world as its basic national policy ever since 1979, deepening reform and opening more widely incessantly. As an important component of reform and opening policy, the attracting of direct foreign investment has had considerable success. This chapter looks in retrospect and prospect at China's strategy and policy for the utilization of direct foreign investment and its configuration.

CHINA'S STRATEGY AND POLICY FOR THE UTILIZATION OF DIRECT FOREIGN INVESTMENT

China's strategy on the attraction of direct foreign investment has been a gradual process. First, in 1979 the country adopted a policy limited

Advances in Chinese Industrial Studies, Volume 5, pages 125-135.

ISBN: 1-55938-961-3

geographically, establishing the four Special Economic Zones of Shenzhen, Zuhai, Shantou, and Xiamen in the provinces of Guangdong and Fujian. They demonstrated their efficiency in attracting direct foreign investment, promoting the local economy and thus justifying the policy for attracting foreign funds. The policy was developed further by the opening up of 14 seacoast cities from Dalian in the east to Beihai in the south, later establishing the Special Economic Zones of the Zhujiang delta, the Yangtze River delta, and the Xiamen-Quanzhou-Zhangzhou delta (southern Fujian). In 1988 the largest Special Economic Zone, Hainan Province, was established. This stage of opening concentrated on the seacoast areas. In the 1990s the Chinese government took the vital decision to develop and open the Pudong New Area in Shanghai and opened 28 cities along the Yangtze River, with Pudong as head of the "Yangtze Dragon." In 1993 China expanded the opening area to include five more coastal cities along the Yangtze River, 19 provincial capitals inland, and 213 cities in the northeast, northwest, and southwest border regions. In these cities favorable tax and other policies, as in the coastal cities, were implemented.

Up to this point China had established 10 types of preferential and open areas for foreign funds, including Special Economic Zones, seacoast open cities (including Economic and Technological Development Zones), river coast open cities, border open cities, inland provincial capital cities, and touring vacation zones.

As well as expanding the open geographical area, China has broadened the industrial scope for foreign investment. Prior to 1992 China emphasized employing foreign capital in processing industries, with export and advanced technology as the objectives. Tertiary industry remained basically closed to foreign investment. After 1992, however, some businesses in the tertiary sector, formerly confined to foreign investment, such as banking, insurance, external trading, real estate, accounting, and consultancy, were opened gradually to foreign investment. The "gradual opening" was conditional and in designated areas only. For example, the geographical area for banking is restricted to seacoast open zones; the operating sphere is limited to the financial business of foreign exchange, and customers are limited to local foreign-funded enterprises. As conditions mature the country will further open up this sphere and joint venture financial firms and exclusively foreign-funded banks will be permitted. After being approved these setups could operate in RMB business in local cities. As for commercial retailing, the country has allowed foreign business people to experiment in running joint ventures or cooperative commercial retailing enterprises in the five Special Economic Zones of Beijing, Tienjing, Guangzhou, Dalian, and Qingdao. In the sphere of external trading foreign business people are permitted to operate in reexport trade in the Free Trade Zone of Pudong New Area of Shanghai, as agents in running importing and exporting business for foreign-funded enterprises within the area.

The types of foreign investment have been diverse. In the initial period of reform and opening the country's main forms of utilization of foreign capital were the joint venture and the cooperative enterprise. After 1986 the country started to permit foreign investors to run wholly foreign-owned enterprises (WFOEs). In recent years the investment forms available to foreign businessmen have notably increased. In Shenzhen and Shanghai there were 20-odd securities exchanges and special stock (B-stock) companies. The country had also ratified selectively a number of investment companies which might partly or even entirely purchase state-operated enterprises. One investment company has invested 330 million RMB yuan in less than two years in the purchase of equity ownership of about 200 state-owned enterprises, and established 35 joint ventures. At the same time, Build-Operate-Transfer (BOT) and various forms of foundations and trust investment have provided new investment channels for outside investors.

In the course of opening China has also paid attention to the improvement of the investing environment. Government at different levels has employed vast manpower, material resources, and financial capacity for the improvement of infrastructural facilities in the fields of energy, traffic, transport, and communication. While improving the hard environment, the soft environment has also undergone change, the most important aspect being the decision to reform the economic system, and to emphasize the establishment of a socialist market economy. Deepening reform and improving the market system created a more normal and sound investing environment for foreign business people. In keeping pace with the establishing of a market economy, the legal system has also been developed. Economic statutes concerning foreign relations, counting only those promulgated by the National People's Congress and the State Council, have numbered over 500; local governments and administrative departments at all levels have also publicized a mass of regulations and rules. Moreover, China has signed investment protection agreements with more than 50 countries and dual tax levy avoidance agreements with almost 30 countries. Meanwhile, laws concerning the protection of intellectual property are being continually refined. Thus the incremental evolution of the opening strategy and policy and the incessant improvement of the investment environment have spurred development on with vigor.

CONFIGURATIONS OF CHINA'S UTILIZATION OF DIRECT FOREIGN INVESTMENT

In the 1980s and early in the 1990s in particular the total amount of direct foreign investment the country had utilized rose at an increasing rate. The negotiated number of foreign invested enterprise projects in 1991 was 12,978, and the negotiated foreign funds was US$11.98 billion. In 1992 the two figures were 48,757 and US$58.08 billion, and 83,625 and US$110.85 billion in 1993. By the end of 1994 the number of foreign invested enterprises was over 220,000, and the negotiated foreign capital to be utilized amounted to over US$300 billion, the actual foreign capital utilized approaching US$100 billion.

The distribution configuration of direct foreign investment in China is affected by the geographical positions and original economic foundation of various localities, and it is linked closely with the regional policy since reform and opening. Between 1979 and 1991 direct foreign investment was concentrated mainly on the seacoast areas, accounting for 89.7 percent of the total number of national foreign-funded enterprises and 81.5 percent of total negotiated capital capacity. Among the provinces in seacoast areas, Guangdong and Fujian constituted the majority. Foreign-funded enterprises and negotiated foreign capital capacity in Guangdong accounted for 44.9 and 43.3 percent, respectively, of the national total, while in Fujian the figures were 12.1 percent and 9.2 percent. In aggregate the two provinces surpassed 50 percent of the total number and volume of the whole nation in the period 1979-1991.

Since 1992 this very uneven configuration has started to change. First, the position of provinces and cities in the northern and middle sectors of seacoast areas, such as Jiangsu, Shanghai, Shandong, and Liaoning improved remarkably. Second, some provinces in the center, such as Hunan, Hubei, and Sichuan, have started to appear in the top 15. Thus, after the development in the early 1990s the position that direct foreign investment was highly concentrated on the two provinces of Guangdong and Fujian has somewhat changed. For example, in 1993 of the total sum of actual foreign investment, Guangdong's share had dropped to 33 percent and its share of the total number of foreign-funded enterprises newly registered in 1993 was down to 29 percent. The configuration of foreign investment has expanded and changed, the trend beginning from south to north, from the east coast to the western hinterland. The businesses relating to foreign-funded enterprises now cover almost all aspects of the national economy. The following are some characteristics in the industrial configuration of foreign investment in the period 1979-1991.

1. The proportion of foreign investment in primary industry, agriculture, forestry, husbandry and fishery, was very small. Up to 1991 the accumulated number of projects and negotiated capital capacity accounted for 3.8 and 2.6 percent, respectively, of the national total.
2. Prior to 1987 the direct foreign investment absorbed by tertiary industry, chiefly resturants and hotels, took up the overwhelming proportion of the national total. Its share of negotiated capital in 1987 accounted for 64.2 percent. This percentage fell year by year to 24.7 percent in 1991.
3. Direct foreign investment in secondary industry, the industrial sector, increased steadily. In 1991 its share of the national total of projects rose to 80.6 percent, and its share of negotiated capital was 63.5 percent.

4. Within secondary industry, most enterprises were labor-intensive and processing assembly types. Although representing 60-70 percent of projects, the share of the capital and technology-intensive types accounted for was not large.

By 1993, owing to the industrial policy guidance of the state and the deregulation of part of the tertiary industry, some changes had occurred in the industrial configuration. After 1991 the changes were as follows.

1. The originally very small share held by primary industry shrank further. The number of foreign invested enterprises in the primary sector approved in 1993 accounted for only 2.5 percent of the total number, down from 3.8 percent in 1979-1991.
2. The share of secondary industry was still quite large. In comparison with 1979-1991 (80.6%), however, the number of direct foreign investment enterprises in secondary industry approved in 1993 was down 13.1 percent, at 67.7 percent of the national total.
3. The number of foreign invested enterprises in the tertiary sector rose from the 15.6 percent share of 1979-1991 to 29.8 percent, up 14.2 percent, the fastest growing business being in commerce and real estate. Direct investment in financial and insurance services also increased. In 1993 the negotiated foreign investment in 12 provinces and cities along the seacoast and in Beijing accounted for 53.7 percent of the national total negotiated foreign funds.

As for sources of direct foreign investment, the countries (regions) in the top 10 during the 1979-1991 period were Hong Kong, Taiwan, the United States, Japan, Macao, Singapore, South Korea, Canada, Thailand, and Australia. Investment from Hong Kong and Taiwan accounted for the overwhelming majority. Hong Kong- and Taiwan-funded enterprises inland comprised 76.1 percent of the national total, while their registered capital accounted for 82 percent of the national total capacity. Western European countries were not among the top 10 investors. The momentum of Japanese direct investment was very vigorous in the 1980s, but its investment in China was only 5 percent of Hong Kong's and 38 percent of Taiwan's. Direct foreign investment has also shown a different regional inclination. The United States preferred to invest in Shanghai, Japan invested more in Dalian, Taiwan invested intensively in Fujian, and South Korea concentrated on the areas around Shandong and Liaoning.

Prior to 1992 there were three modes for direct foreign investment in China: cooperative enterprises, joint venture (JV) enterprises, and wholly foreign-owned enterprises. In the first half of the 1980s the cooperative enterprise constituted the majority, with joint ventures coming second, while the WFOE was still in experimentation. Between 1979 and 1985 the country had approved, accumulatively, 6,316 foreign-funded enterprises, of which cooperative enterprises accounted for 59 percent, joint ventures for 29 percent, and the WFOEs 2 percent. After 1986 JVs began to surpass cooperative enterprises to become an important mode of foreign investment in China. Of the total number of foreign invested enterprises of 1986, joint ventures accounted for 67 percent, cooperative enterprises 22 percent, and WFOEs 1 percent. After 1988 the WFOE expanded swiftly, its share surpassing the cooperative enterprise. Taking 1993 as an example, JVs accounted for 65 percent of the total number of foreign-funded enterprises, WFOEs 27 percent, and cooperative enterprises 12 percent.

To sum up, the changes in the development of various modes of foreign-funded enterprises are:

1. The proportion of cooperative enterprises shrank gradually, the joint venture share kept growing steadily, while the share of the WFOE increased dramatically.
2. The average scale of WFOEs was greater than that of the cooperative enterprises and joint ventures; they were, in general, relatively large projects.
3. In the last two years investing modes appear to have diversified. The most notable development has been that of (outside) companies purchasing the country's state-owned enterprises. One Hong Kong investment company bought the equity ownership of more than 200 state-owned enterprises in less than two years.
4. On average, of the total number of foreign invested enterprises, and the total capital actually used in 1979-1993, the share of JVs accounted for 64.9 and 51.07 percent, respectively, cooperative enterprises accounted for 16 and 21 percent, and WFOEs 9 and 19 percent.

PROBLEMS AND PROSPECTS

Direct foreign investment in China has recorded a swift increase. According to World Bank statistics for 1993, the direct foreign investment absorbed by China accounted for 40 percent of the total direct foreign investment absorbed by the world's developing countries. The *World Investment Report* of 1994 stated that the capital absorbed by China in 1993 ranked second in the world, next to the United States.

The swift rise of the foreign-funded enterprise has actively affected the country's economic construction and system reform. The utilization of foreign investment not only attracts foreign funds, making up for domestic financial inadequacy, but also introduces advanced technology, operational methods, management expertise, and competition mechanism, expands export, and increases tax revenue. In 1993 the industry production value created by foreign-funded enterprises accounted for 11 percent of the gross national industry production, and exports accounted for 27.5 percent of the national total. The tax revenue (including tariff) has surpassed 20 billion RMB yuan and employees exceeded 12 million.

Admittedly, several problems have occurred in the course of using direct foreign investment, and some of them have yet to be solved. While the current problems are being solved new ones and new conditions appear. China is devoting itself to solving such problems so as to create a better investment environment for foreign investment in order to serve China's economic growth. In looking to the future of China's utilization of foreign capital, the following subjects will be on the agenda.

Uneven Rates of Development

First, since reform and opening, owing to the regional policy favoring southern and eastern seacoast areas and the Special Economic Zones in particular, and in parallel with the restraints of objective features such as geographical position and economic foundation, the central and western areas have developed sluggishly in the utilization of foreign funds, compared with the southern and eastern areas where foreign investment has been concentrated. The hinterland was also, in fact, scrambling to transfer funds and skills to the south and east, rendering the already existing regional economy gap wider still, and the already irrational regional industrial structure even more irrational.

Looking ahead, the cost of essential production elements, such as the price of land and labor in the seacoast areas, will increase. Comparatively, the hinterland areas possess certain advantages. There are abundant diverse natural, material, and labor resources with low costs. The Yangtze River valley in particular is an important industrial and agricultural base of China. There are a great number of large, key state-owned industrial enterprises in the hinterland, and technological and production strength is ample with vast development potential. Furthermore, according to the national development plan, a considerable portion of projects will be constructed, expanded, and reconstructed in the hinterland, thus expanding investment opportunity for foreign investors.

From the point of view of national strategy and priorities for the use of foreign funds in emphasizing the development of the coastal areas, the country wants concurrently to accelerate the pace of foreign funds absorption in the central and western areas, so as to promote economic progress there and gradually narrow the growth gap with the coastal areas. The central and western areas will be the key development areas in the next century. A number of development zones have been established in the cities of provincial capitals in the hinterland, and they are key areas for attracting foreign funds. In the future, measures for attracting foreign funds in the central and western areas will be studied further. For example, the proportion of products manufactured by foreign-funded enterprises for sale in the home market could be adjusted; projects for exploiting local resources and improving infrastructural facilities could be given more preferential treatment and flexibility; foreign firms investing in the central and western areas could be permitted to set up "umbrella companies"; foreign-funded enterprises in the coastal areas could be encouraged to go to central and western areas for reinvestment, cooperating with local enterprises for establishing new ventures.

The Industrial Pattern of Foreign Investment

In the 1980s the investment orientation of foreign funds chiefly centered on manufacturing with a large portion in the ordinary processing industry. At present the investment philosophy is still steered by a foreign-fund investment guide dating from 1987-1989. A new version is urgently needed. Moreover, some localities do not abide by the national industrial policy in attracting foreign funds, and foreign funds have not been skilfully guided into tertiary industry. The role of industrial policy must be strengthened: foreign funds must be channelled chiefly into infrastructure, basic industry, technological transformation, and to capital and technology intensive industry, and, moderately, to tertiary services such as finance, commerce, tourism, and real estate.

Accordingly, foreign investment will be encouraged in:

- New agricultural technology and comprehensive development items.
- Industrial projects of energy, traffic, and the production of raw materials which are badly required.
- Advanced technological projects, or projects to introduce advanced technological equipment, to improve product performance, save energy and materials, promote techology advancement and economic efficiency of enterprise, and produce new equipment and new materials to meet the demands of the market.
- Projects for expanding export and increasing foreign exchange earnings, or projects that can meet the demands of internal and external markets, raise the quality of products, expand exports, and increase foreign exchange.
- New technology and equipment projects for the comprehensive exploitation and recycling of resources.

The country will restrict investment of items for which the technology has already been developed and repeatedly introduced, or the production capacity has already met domestic needs while most of the products cannot be exported. Items that are disadvantageous to national security and harmful to the national economic development and social public interests, or that pollute the environment and damage natural resources, will be banned, as well as investment in post and telecommunications services. As for banking, insurance, securities and commercial retailing, establishing external trading organizations, producing audiovisual programs, publishing and printing, and so on, these areas will need to be sanctioned by the state departments concerned.

In attracting foreign funds, hereafter, all localities should integrate with local features, promote regional advantages, and avoid similarities of business and product. Specifically, after more than 10 years of opening and development, the coastal areas should exert themselves to upgrade and readjust the industrial structure, emphasizing high value-added, profitable, and high-tech industries, and develop an export-oriented economy for taking part in international competition and exchange. They should introduce foreign funds selectively for developing the tertiary industry of financial, trading, and retailing businesses, so as to shape up the centers of finance, commerce, and science and technology in some coastal cities. As for the typical processing and labor-intensive industries, they might be transferred gradually to the hinterland. The central and western areas should promote their resource and labor advantages and numerous old industry bases, science and technology strengths, and proximity to bordering countries; they should take the road of utilization of foreign funds exploiting the particular strengths of each locality.

Establishing the Socialist Market System

If the core strategy relating to foreign funding in the 1980s was simply to attract it, then in the 1990s and thereafter emphasis should be given to the economic system reform establishing a socialist market economic system, promoting economic legislation, so as to provide a normal investment environment for foreign funds in accordance with international practice. In the light of targets set forth at the Fourteenth Communist Party Congress for the socialist market economy system, on the basis of the deepening reform and according to the thinking of advancing on the whole front, while breaking through on key points in the reform, we have initiated several major reforming measures of significance relating to treasury, tax revenue, banking, investment, pricing, foreign exchange, foreign funds, and enterprise management systems. The tax system has been unified, and the exchange rate integrated. Integration is only an interim step, as the ultimate goal is the free exchange of RMB.

Accompanying the reform of the economic system, various legislation has been introduced. Intellectual property rights will be increasingly protected by law, and the newly promulgated Labour Law is both the laborer's talisman and investor's and operator's magic weapon that protects their legal rights and interests. In addition, a law of countering unfair competition has also been made public. In the future, all vital economic activities will be brought within the orbit of the legal system in order to realize the condition of having laws and acting by them.

The Chinese government will aim to create a stable macroeconomy for investors. In the last three years the country's economy has developed at an impressive speed, reaching or approaching a 13 percent annual growth rate in consecutive years. But this rapid growth has also brought inflation. In the light of the national economic conditions, since the latter half of 1994, we have started to enhance the macro readjustment and regulations. The aim was that the high growth in the economy be readjusted and regulated in successive years to a rational and moderate rate, while avoiding overall restraints and "slamming on the brakes." The two main regulators of money input and credit scale have been securely kept, the growth of fixed assets have been controlled, economic profit has been further raised, and the total economic volume maintained in balance. These measures have had their effect, as shown by the fact that the financial order has stepped into a normal orbit, the growth rate of fixed assets has started to fall, and the various relations of supply and demand in economic life are relatively coordinated. The situation provides a better external condition for production and operation of foreign-funded enterprises.

COMMITMENTS FOR THE FUTURE

The country is committed to perfecting investment conditions progressively, so that foreign business people can compete in an equitable environment and the establishment, production, and operation of foreign-funded enterprises can proceed in the light of international practice and the rules of a market economy.

The market for technology exchange will be carried through as usual, according to our strategy on absorbing and employing direct foreign investment. As for investment in China from some large transnational companies possessing advanced technology and high-level management expertise, we may offer a part of the market on the basis of adopting the attitude of long-term and strategic cooperation. They would be allowed to set up holding companies to manage and coordinate their various activities in China.

In creating a good operating environment the country will emphasize the management of foreign-funded enterprises according to laws. Now there are more than 90,000 foreign-funded enterprises in operation. Most of them comply with the legal provisions, but there remain some problems. Some take advantage of international selling channels for internal trading by means of purchasing and selling within their own companies and evade tax by using price manipulation. Some foreign business people have adopted the practice of overestimating imported equipment prices by taking advantage of the Chinese side's ignorance of world market prices. Henceforth, the country will improve the supervision of contract fulfillment and production operations of foreign-funded enterprises, urging them to observe state laws, regulations and policies, and protecting employees' legal rights and interests. The country will crack down on unlawful practices of smuggling and tax evasion.

In summary, in the course of comprehensive promotion of the country's socialist modernization construction, the persistence of opening is a firm and unshakable national policy, and the absorption of foreign funds is a vital content of it. We will deepen the reform, accelerate the rate of change in the market system, so as to welcome investment into China from foreign friends with a more standardized and better investment environment.

PART III

HUMAN RESOURCE MANAGEMENT

LEARNING PROCESSES IN INTERNATIONAL JOINT VENTURES IN CHINA

Niklas Lindholm

INTRODUCTION

International joint ventures (IJVs) have proliferated in China since the issue of the Open Door Policy in 1978. For China, IJVs represent opportunities of foreign capital and technology transfer. For foreign investors, IJVs have become a viable way of investing in the Chinese market, perceived as less risky than wholly-owned subsidiaries (Westwood and Leung 1993). IJVs in China are frequently managed jointly by foreign investors and local partners, with management responsibilities shared in organizational functions. The blend of expatriates and local employees brings together individuals who differ in national origin, cultural values, and social norms with the attendant political, economic, and legal system differences (Shenkar and Zeira 1987). The mixture of managers and employees may lead to some controversy regarding how different organizational functions need to be managed and which managerial routines, practices, and policies should be employed.

Advances in Chinese Industrial Studies, Volume 5, pages 139-154.

ISBN: 1-55938-961-3

Foreign expatriate managers often feel forced to incorporate their own way of managing in the IJVs, although a great deal of cross-cultural management and expatriation literature suggests that foreign companies and expatriate managers should adjust their policies and practices to fit the local environment (Brewster 1993). It has been found that the transfer of foreign managerial routines and practices have contributed to problems that have impeded the running of IJVs in China (Campbell 1988; Newman 1992; Child 1991; Björkman and Schaap 1994; Von Glinow and Teagarden 1988; Fan 1993). In line with this, many local managers and employees are frustrated over the demands placed on them by foreign managers who are ignorant of the local context and customs in China (Björkman 1994). Although actors in IJV functions may adopt practices and policies from either partner, influences are usually stronger from the managing partner firm (foreign partner) (Cyr 1995). However, one could also assume that completely new routines, practices, and policies are developed and learned in organizational functions in IJVs.

It would seem that IJVs are likely to pass through noteworthy learning processes (Child 1994) by giving actors access to the skills and capabilities of each other (Inkpen and Crossan 1995; Hamel 1991; Kogut 1988; Lyles 1988). The optimal learning process would require an effective transfer of knowledge to various IJV functions, also an adaptation by the functions to the local conditions, and, moreover, the learning of the complementary strengths of the local organization (Child and Rodrigues 1994). This learning process is most certainly both company and function specific but has been neglected in research on IJVs (Tiemessen, Lane, Crossan, and Inkpen 1996)

The objectives of this paper are twofold. First, it aims to describe what kind of learning processes have taken place in different organizational functions in two IJVs in China. Second, it aims to offer a few tentative explanations for these learning processes. The paper hopes to contribute to an understanding of learning processes in IJV functions in China through examples of case studies.

LEARNING PROCESSES

Learning in this paper is defined as encoding past experiences into organizational routines that are interpreted by organizational members (March and Levitt 1988). As a result of learning, organizations may attain a higher level of efficiency in carrying out their routines but at the same time they build competence barriers against adopting new routines (March and Olsen 1975). To overcome this inertia organizations must also be able to unlearn old routines (Nystrom and Starbuck 1984). This learning process has been neglected in research on IJVs (Tiemessen, Lane, Crossan, and Inkpen 1996).

Learning can occur through three different processes in an IJV: (1) through the transfer of knowledge; (2) through the transformation of knowledge; and (3) through the harvesting of knowledge (Tiemessen, Lane, Crossan, and Inkpen 1996). It should be pointed out that the different processes are very interrelated and used for illustrative purposes.

Transfer

Learning can take place by transfer from the partners to the IJV. The process through which this occurs is usually called technology transfer and has received a lot of attention in research (Tung 1994; Kedia and Bhagat 1988). Transfer is the movement of existing technology, knowledge, or managerial practices between partners and IJVs (Tiemessen, Lane, Crossan, and Inkpen 1996). Learning through transfer in IJVs in China usually means that the local managers and employees are subject to the learning of new technical skills and procedures. It does not entail actual learning for the expatriates.

Transformation

The second learning process is concerned with the transformation of transferred knowledge and the creation of new knowledge within the IJV. Casson (1993) has noted that this may require an adaptation of technology and managerial practices to the local environment, especially in line with cultural and institutional differences. Transformation in IJVs in China would imply that a process of mutual learning occurs (Child and Rodrigues 1994), hence both expatriates and locals in the IJV organization are subject to learning.

Harvesting

Harvesting, the third process of learning, involves retrieving the knowledge that has been created in an IJV and then internalizing this knowledge in the parent firms or other IJVs so that it can be used in other applications. Although harvesting may sound similar to transfer, it is a different process (Tiemessen, Lane, Crossan, and Inkpen 1996). Related to harvesting is the learning that occurs when firms imitate best practice.

METHODOLOGY

This paper employs an exploratory research approach. This type of approach is warranted when relevant variables in certain settings are unknown and dynamic processes are studied. The paper presents some preliminary qualitative data from two ongoing case studies of IJVs in China. The studies were conducted in a European MNC's joint venture operations in China. The study relies to a great extent on the reports of the actors but it has been possible to cross-check statements by interviewing multiple individuals in the organizations. Thirty-five interviews were carried out in Europe and in a major Chinese city. Interviews were conducted relying on relatively open-ended questions. Respondents were mostly in middle or senior management positions, however, some operative and office employees were also interviewed. Interviews lasted between 45 minutes and four-and-a-half hours and were taperecorded if permission was given. The respondent was typically asked to elaborate on their experiences on transfer and learning within their function/department in the joint venture organization, which difficulties they had been confronted with, and how they had tried to alleviate these difficulties. In all, the case studies involved four weeks of participant observation in the MNC's headquarters and the joint ventures. Participation in this sense means that the researcher was given a desk in the office, had the opportunity to take part in organizational activities, and could also partake in social activities after work. In the analysis of interviews and other data it was of interest to identify learning processes and what seemed to influence learning in the organizational functions.

CASE STUDIES

The European MNC has been present in the Chinese market since the beginning of the 1980s. To date it has seven joint venture operations in China, mostly along the coastal regions. The case companies in this paper are referred to as JV1 and JV2. JV1 was founded in 1994, is owned 55/45 by the MNC and Beijing Ministry I, and has a workforce of 91. JV2 was founded in 1995, is owned 50/50 by the MNC and Beijing Ministry II, and has a workforce of 102.

Joint Venture 1

Human Resource Function (HR)

In the HR function of JV1 the MNC's human resource practices and policies were supposed to be transferred. However, the HR function had been assigned to a Chinese personnel manager from the partner organization and severe conflicts emerged when the MNC attempted the transfer. For instance, the local manager resisted the introduction of employee selection practices, such as multiple interviews, psychological tests, and objective selection criteria, which were put forward by the expatriates. Instead, a huge number of employees from the partner were transferred to the IJV, to the expatriates' astonishment. These employees, according to a majority of the respondents, were poorly motivated and bad performers. Later on the screening of new applicants was also done by the local personnel manager and the expatriates never found out on what grounds a shortlist was selected. This incident also caused conflicts. As one expatriate manager put it:

> I demanded to see all the resumes and was able to receive them after several weeks of persuasion. I then found out that he (the personnel manager) was trying to favor partner candidates...I had to put a stop to it...he didn't say hello to me for six months.

Training had been arranged for JV1 employees jointly with the MNC's training center in China. At start-up training was delivered with the same training methods as in other parts of the MNC's operations. This led to difficulties in getting the message through to the trainees. The MNC and the JV started to give training both in Chinese and English by first training some locals to become trainers. Some experiments were conducted with smaller groups and new training methods. Attempts have also been made to identify and test the knowledge of trainees, that is, to see whether they have the right prerequisite skills and whether they have learned anything after completing the training. Frequently, Hong Kong-based consultancy firms and independent consultants are hired for tailor-made management training. JV1 started to send local employees to their headquarters in Europe in order for them to learn and then have them teach their local colleagues when back in China.

Production Function

In the production function of JV1 actual product technology transfer is taking place. The function is managed by an expatriate with the majority of his employees originating from the partner.

The MNC's production techniques and processes have been transferred to the function. The techniques range from purchasing, quality control, production planning, to the assembly processes. The assimilation and learning of these techniques and processes have occurred without major difficulties, although the local Chinese partner's knowledge of technology was, according to the expatriate, lower than expected. At the beginning of the operations employees exhibited the behavior and attitudes apparent in local companies: the expatriate mentioned problems with motivation, communication, responsibility taking, and initiative. The expatriate suggested that time and patience is the real prerequisite for learning in China.

Attempts have been made to localize the function and a localization committee appointed to oversee the localization process. The committee meets from time to time to establish what can be done in terms of localization. The function has also harvested experiences from another European MNC's IJVs in Beijing. However, no harvesting has been taking place between production in JV1 and JV2.

Joint Venture 2

Human Resource Function

The human resource function in JV2 is managed by a Chinese personnel manager appointed by the partner. The transfer of the MNC's HR procedures and practices has gone ahead without problems, although the manager has had difficulties understanding the new techniques. The expatriates are constantly stressing the need to recruit external people for the venture and are scared of getting too many partner employees. They are looking for young people with English skills and a university degree; previous work experience is not considered as important. JV2 has lately been able to participate in job fairs where they have found good candidates. Only a few employees from the partner have been able to join the joint venture organization after passing interviews and psychological tests. One JV2 expatriate manager maintained:

> The major advantage of recruiting young locals is that they are not "caught in the system" and have not adopted certain ways to work that are quite apparent in Chinese state-owned organizations. They are therefore not forced to "unlearn" these behaviors like older Chinese are required to do.

However, there seems to be a flip side to the coin. The young recruits do not have much experience and lack good contacts which are definitely needed in front positions such as sales and customer service. Another problem has been lack of loyalty among young recruits. In JV2 some overseas Chinese have been recruited for key management positions. They have overseas experience, the same cultural heritage, and speak Mandarin fairly well, but also have little sense of loyalty and some have soon left for other firms. One manager referred to the "THS syndrome," implying that overseas Chinese from Taiwan, Hong Kong, and Singapore have a tendency to change jobs regularly, and argued that it would be better to try to develop local managerial competence.

In the field of training JV2 has started to put more effort into management training than JV1. Independent consultants as well as consultancy firms have been called in to give tailor-made training to both expatriate and Chinese managers.

In JV2 some expatriate managers have recently been putting effort into developing a career development system. The development of a career plan for locals has proved to be a good way to increase motivation and loyalty and retain local employees. The career development system means that expatriate managers sit down and talk about career prospects with employees, explaining what kind of training would be provided if they attain another skill level. In JV2 they are also currently trying to implement the MNC's performance management system but it seems to take a great deal of time.

Production Function

The production function in JV2 is represented by two different divisions of the MNC. The function is where the actual product technology transfer takes place in JV2, ranging from storage to assembly processes. In the first part of the function the manager recruited people outside the organization to facilitate the transfer process and put a lot of effort into training. After massive training efforts the young employees have been able to learn the new technology well but language difficulties are still apparent in general communication and in meetings, and on the conceptual/terminology level.

The other part of the production function, representing the other division, is run by an expatriate, and his employees all originate from the local partner. In this function transfer, transformation, and harvesting processes are all apparent. This production department is also making great efforts in trying to utilize local knowledge and initiative. The function seems to have been able also to harvest some experiences to the regional headquarters in Hong Kong.

POTENTIAL INFLUENCES ON LEARNING

Previous research on factors that influence learning has often been broad and general. Some have been concerned with contextual factors, such as structure, strategy, environments, and culture (Fiol and Lyles 1985). These factors are too general to explain differences in learning processes within two case studies belonging to the same MNC. As pointed out by Dogson (1993), learning in organizations is influenced by the contextual environment and internal issues in a complex and iterative manner. It should be kept in mind that learning activities are carried out by individuals (Levitt and March 1988), in this paper by IJV actors. Due to the diversity of actors in IJVs in China the learning processes apparent in IJVs are most certainly affected by the interactions between actors and their relationships. The capacity to learn is conditioned by the attitudes that predominate among members in an organization or a function (Galbraith 1990) and also what motivates people in an organization (Poole, Gray, and Gioia 1990). Previous experience and exposure, previous skills, also the number of expatriates (Björkman 1994) are additional factors. However, there may be different issues that influence the three learning processes transfer, transformation, and harvesting.

In the analysis of the case studies it became apparent that learning had taken place mainly through transfer from the MNC to the IJV. This is natural in the case of IJVs in China since MNCs are often responsible for technology transfer in these ventures. The responsibility of technology transfer usually gives them the management contract, that is, to manage the company according to their standards (Cyr 1995).

In the transfer process the content of the transfer seems to be important. It has been argued that transfer is easiest when the knowledge is easily transported, easily interpreted, and easily absorbed (Tiemessen, Lane, Crossan, and Inkpen 1996; Tung 1994). In the case studies the content of transfer naturally varied in different organizational functions. For instance, in the production function, transfer entailed a great deal of technical knowledge in comparison to the human resources function, where more behaviorally oriented practices were transferred. These functions will be dealt with separately below.

In all organizational functions the MNC also attempted to transfer communication, meeting, and decision-making practices. Interestingly, difficulties were reported with the transfer of these practices on many occasions. One explanation may be that some functions and types of practices are under more direct influence of the cultural and institutional environment. In the case studies it is possible to trace behavior typical of the features of Chinese culture (Lockett 1988). Culture will have the greatest impact on communication patterns, decision-making structures, and also on human resource related practices (Child 1994). Nonetheless, it seems that these are also other influences on the learning process.

HUMAN RESOURCE FUNCTIONS

JV1. In the HR function of JV1 the MNC strived to transfer HR practices and policies to the IJV. Selection practices caused a great amount of conflict with the local side. An explanation for this may be that the HR manager was appointed by the partner and this manager did not understand the concepts behind objective employee selection and subsequently resisted the implementation of these practices. The manager was most likely trapped in his previous ways of working and was unable to unlearn his previous behavior. The fact that the MNC did not provide the manager with training in these issues certainly added to the problem. The learning process that has taken place in this area could be characterized as a forced transfer process. However, in the area of training some transformation of the training practices usually employed by the MNC has been done. The transformation seems to have been triggered by the quite different learning styles of Chinese employees.

JV2. In the HR function in JV2 the transfer of policies and practices was smoother. The MNC had already made it clear in the negotiation stage with the local partner that a minimal number of partner employees would be able to join the IJV. The HR function in JV2 is managed by a Chinese personnel manager who has had difficulties in learning the new policies and procedures but has been given a greater amount of support from the MNC's central HR function than his opposite number in JV1. It seems like the experience of acquiring too many partner employees has been harvested by the MNC's representative office, which has the task of overseeing the policies and practices of the IJVs. In JV2 the MNC put forward the issue of recruiting mainly from external sources such as local employment agencies, universities, and job fairs. This practice has been successful in the sense that very young and motivated people with good English skills have been found, but many of them lack experience and good connections (*guanxi*). The interesting fact is that the harvesting has not taken place between the IJVs directly, although they are situated in the same city.

PRODUCTION FUNCTIONS

In the area of production the MNC aimed to transfer the product technology to the IJVs. The learning processes in the three different functions (three MNC divisions) have been quite different, although the IJVs belong to the same MNC. In conjunction with Child (1995) it seems that techniques related to production generally have been easier to transfer than those related to HR in these cases. An explanation for this could be the greater emphasis on technical skills and production orientation in Chinese management education (Boisot 1988).

JV1. In the production function in JV1 learning has taken place through a received transfer process (Child 1994). The expatriate has been able successfully to transfer the technology to his local employees by committing himself to the transfer process. He maintained:

> You can only create responsibility and initiative among them if you delegate and allow mistakes...you have to gradually extend the task of the employees...I was out there on the factory floor sweeping floors, packing up equipment...it took me seven months before I could get them to take any kind of responsibility and I didn't go home in six months...but it was worth it.

The question of expatriate management style seems to be an important determinant governing the learning processes in this function. The expatriate had a very firm but supportive and participative management style that seems to have fostered trust among local employees. He liked to spend time and solve problems together with his employees. In other interviews several expatriates maintained that their local employees did not take responsibility and show initiative within their tasks. However, in both JV1 and JV2 there seems to be some resistance to delegating to locals and letting them in on decision making.

As one expatriate put it: "Well, I try to delegate the best I can...but it is quite annoying when they don't get anything done...and I stand there to be blamed." The issues of delegation and social interaction seem of great importance in the transfer process.

The production function has harvested experiences with another European MNC's joint venture operations in the same city. The exchange of information, related to day-to-day problems in IJVs in China, has taken place through regular meetings between the companies. The expatriate manager of JV1 has offered to share his experiences with JV2 but until now this has not taken place. Rather, harvesting across JV1 and JV2 seems to have taken place through informal networks, through managers that have known each other previously. The three different divisions that are represented in the joint ventures seem to be competing with each other from time to time.

JV2. In the production function of JV2 a forced transfer process (Child 1994) has taken place. The expatriate preferred to recruit only young people and put a lot of effort into training them technically both in China and in Europe. In this function it seemed that the expatriate did not want to learn from the local organization's knowledge and instead increase the influence of the MNC. According to the expatriate: "... if *I* have learnt something...no, I mean *we* are the ones supplying the technology and the level of their technology is from the sixties."

The lack of a harvesting process in this function seems to be a conscious choice by the expatriate. The expatriate manager describes his approach to working in China:

> I just don't want to listen to some of the old ones (expatriates)...there are so many stories and rumours going round that are just not true...I want to form my own opinion about things and not get caught in all these prejudices.

In the analysis of this function the role of *attitudes* seemed to influence the learning process. Attitudes are evaluative statements, either favorable or unfavorable, concerning objects, people, or events. In organizations attitudes are important because they affect job behavior (Robbins 1993). The case studies revealed several interesting points on the issue of attitudes of expatriates. Many local respondents were under the impression that expatriates did not have a thorough understanding of China. Especially in JV2, some expatriates saw the venture merely as an extension of the MNC, an approach which would be unlikely to entertain any possibility of having anything to learn from the local organization's knowledge in finding the best way of doing things, that is, engage in a transformation process. Both JV1 and JV2 seemed to have problems with expatriates with poor attitudes. One expatriate manager maintained:

> Sometimes they sit in the bars all night complaining about how difficult it is to work with the Chinese...the next day they don't try to do anything about it but continue to work on their own and not trying to solve the problem....

It is possible that the poor attitudes of some expatriates could be accounted for by lack of pre-departure and cross-cultural training. Many MNCs arrange for pre-departure training for their expatriates going on overseas assignments. It is logical to assume that this would facilitate the adjustment to a new culture and context (Black, Mendenhall, and Oddou 1991). In both JV1 and JV2 only a few of the expatriates had received some sort of training prior to or shortly after coming to China. The MNC does arrange training on cross-cultural issues but it seems more or less ad hoc and not really China specific. Several expatriate managers maintained that some sort of cultural and language training would have speeded up the learning process immensely. However, other viewpoints were also offered.

One expatriate manager maintained: "It is useless to provide cross-cultural training before the assignment...it is better to provide that after a short period of stay in China so that people have 'seen' and can therefore understand and reflect." Another expatriate described it like this: "Sure I could have used some training...the first year I was just so amazed by everything, the second I started to understand and learn, and the third I was actually able to accomplish something."

Some expatriates noted that there are no formal support systems for expatriates on arrival in China. Local managers also raised the issue of training for expatriates. A few were under the impression that some expatriates were very badly prepared to work in China.

In the other part of the production function in JV2 learning has taken place through both transfer, transformation, and harvesting. In the case studies it became apparent that some expatriates seemed to be poorly prepared for their assignments, while others seemed to be more open to learn from the local organization's knowledge. The level of previous international experience, for instance, especially in the same country to which a person is assigned, is likely to affect the learning process. Expatriate managers' prior exposure to Asian cultures and environments seemed to lend a degree of openness and flexibility in listening to, and considering, the local perspective (Cyr and Schneider 1994). The experience and exposure argument is logical and has received support in empirical research (Black, Mendenhall, and Oddou 1991). As the expatriate put it, "I always try to stress the fact that if they can think of a better way of doing things we will go for that...you have to treat them as equals...I mean come on, we are in China now."

The harvesting that has taken place in this function can be explained by the fact that the division has had operations in Hong Kong where a bank of knowledge has been built up over the years. The division seemed to have been

Table 1. Summary Functions/Learning Processes

	HR Function	*Production Function*
JV1	Learning through transfer and transformation modes. Forced transfer of HR practices which led to severe conflicts between expatriates failed to provide appropriate *management training* for the local HR manager and locals kept on working with old practices. Transformation has occurred mainly in the area of technical training. Training adapted to the Chinese learning styles.	Learning through transfer and harvesting processes. Expatriate with firm but *participative* management style committed to transfer and was able to build trust with local employees. Harvesting taken place with other European MNC in the same city. No harvesting with JV2.
JV2	Learning through transfer and harvesting mode. Successful transfer has taken place with *support* from the MNC's representative office overseeing IJV policies. Harvesting of experiences from JV.1 mainly in the area of employee selection and training. The IJV is putting much more effort into management training.	Department 1: Learning mainly through the transfer mode by recruiting young locals with no experience. Severe difficulties with communication, meetings, and decision making. A lack of understanding by the expatriates to engage in both a transformation and harvesting process mainly due to *poor attitudes* and *lack of pre-departure* and *cross-cultural training.* Department 2: Learning through all learning modes. Expatriate with *international experience* and able to utilize local knowledge to his advantage. Transformation mainly in the area of meeting practices. Able to harvest and receive support from regional office in Hong Kong.

able to harvest the experiences from Hong Kong to the mainland. As the expatriate maintained, "I think we were more scared about how to co-operate with the other division in the MNC when we got into this project, than with the Chinese...the Chinese we know better than them."

FURTHER EXPLANATIONS

A few further issues that influence the learning process can be identified in the analysis of the data. It could be argued that a certain type of inertia exists and that the MNC wishes to transfer as much as possible of its routines, practices, and procedures to the IJVs' functions to make them resemble the MNC. MNCs generally have standardized policies and practices around the world, and tend to a certain extent to want to transfer these practices to their IJV functions for control purposes (Jaeger 1983). The pressure from the MNC was described clearly by the production manager in JV1.

> My biggest is concern is the lack of support and too many directives from the project organization in headquarters supporting this function...being alone on the field trying to build a plant is hard work and when you need help with technical expertise the MNC sends you some young manager who wants to have a look around and take a tour to the Great Wall....I just don't have time for that anymore.

The number of expatriates in the case companies is likely to affect the learning process. If too many expatriates are employed, it can result in their interfering with the development and learning of local managers. Stressing the use of expatriates in management positions can reflect a lack of trust in local employees. It has been argued that local knowledge is necessary and one should therefore use a large proportion of local managers to ensure this (Beamish 1985).

In JV2 there has been an attempt to increase the number of expatriates in order to speed up the learning process, that is, the transfer process. The MNC does not have any plans to start localization in this joint venture, at least not in the near future. However, the local partner is under the impression that local managers should take over the expatriate positions as soon as possible due to the huge costs of expatriates. Two Chinese top managers maintained that they were not very pleased with the way the expatriates were teaching and training the local employees and wanted to speed up the localization process. However, interviews with expatriates revealed that local successors were not yet even identified and that localization could not begin in the near future.

The case studies disclosed the severe problem of language and communication. In both JV1 and JV2 management meetings are performed with interpreters and so extremely time consuming. Many expatriates and locals complained about the drawback of using interpreters and apparently this had gone so far that people were not prepared to hear the interpreter out. In JV2 they were trying to improve the efficiency of the meetings by having discussions in small groups. However, communication was not just strained between the expatriates and locals: there were also communication problems between different expatriate nationalities. Many of the third country nationals maintained that the MNC's old boy network was impossible to enter and they simply could not understand it.

One expatriate manager argued: "The management meetings are totally inefficient and pure information sharing. I am seriously contemplating staying away from the meetings in the future since all decisions are still done in the corridors afterwards." The expatriate sales manager in JV1 described one misunderstanding:

> I announced to my team that we were going to have a brainstorming session during the next meeting. I was slightly surprised when one of my employees came up to me a couple of hours later with a dictionary and a worried look on his face. He thought that "brainstorming" meant a mental disease and was seriously worried about me.

In the case studies it became apparent that harvesting from previous IJVs that the MNC had been involved with in China has been limited. It seems that both JV1 and JV2 expatriates have been forced to learn from scratch in China. Several expatriates raised this issue during the interviews and referred to learning by trial and error. The MNC's problem seems to be the fact that when an expatriate's contract expires the experiences that they have gathered during their years in China also vanish. Systems for harvesting and documenting their experiences or having returning expatriates teach new expatriates do not exist.

CONCLUSION

This paper has described learning processes in two IJVs in China, belonging to the same MNC. It has identified different learning processes in organizational functions, and a few tentative explanations related to the learning processes have been offered. This paper has been a report of ongoing research. Further research will aim to focus on changes in functional practices in more detail, analyzed from a longitudinal point of view. Empirical studies that examine learning processes in IJVs longitudinally are sparse (Arias and Guillen 1993; Fan 1993), and the subject requires alternative methodologies such as qualitative in-depth case studies.

REFERENCES

Arias E.M., and M.F. Guillen. 1993. *The Transfer of Organizational Management Techniques Across Borders: Combining Neo-Institutional and Comparative Perspectives.* Fontainebleau: INSEAD.

Beamish, P.W. 1985. "The Characteristics of Joint Ventures in Developed and Developing Countries." *Columbia Journal of World Business* (Winter).

Björkman, I. 1994. "Role Perceptions and Behavior among Chinese Managers in Sino-Western Joint Ventures." In *Joint Ventures in the People's Republic of China: Advances in Chinese Industrial Studies, Volume 4*, edited by S. Stewart. Greenwich, CT: JAI Press.

Björkman, I., and A. Schaap. 1994. "Human Resource Management Practices in Sino-Western Joint Ventures." *The Finnish Journal of Business Economics* (2).

Black, J.S., M. Mendenhall, and G. Oddou. 1991. "Toward a Comprehensive Model of International Adjustment: An Integration of Multiple Theoretical Perspectives." *Academy of Management Review* 16 (2): 291-317.

Boisot, M. 1988. "Management Training in the PRC: The Task Ahead." *Euro-Asia Business Review* 6 (2).

Brewster, C. 1993. "The Paradox of Adjustment: UK and Swedish Expatriates in Sweden and the UK." *International Journal of Human Resource Management* 4.

Campbell, N. 1988. *A Strategic Guide to Equity Joint Ventures in China.* Oxford: Pergamon Press.

Casson, M. 1993. "Contractual Arrangements For Technology Transfer: New Evidence from Business History." In *Coalitions and Collaboration in International Business*, edited by G. Jones. Cheltenham: Edward Elgar.

Child, J. 1991. "A Foreign Perspective on the Management of People in China." *International Journal of Human Resource Management* 2.

Child, J. 1994. *Managing in China During the Age of Reform.* Cambridge, UK: Cambridge University Press.

Child, J., and S. Rodrigues. 1994. "The Role of Social Identity in the International Transfer of Knowledge through Joint Ventures." Working Paper Series No. 25, Judge Institute of Management Studies, Cambridge University.

Cyr, D.J. 1995. *The Human Resource Challenge of International Joint Ventures.* Westport, CT: Quorum Books.

Cyr, D.J., and S. Schneider. 1994. "Organizational Learning in East-West Joint Ventures: The Role of HRM." Working paper. Fontainebleau: INSEAD.

Dogson, M. 1993. "Organizational Learning: A Review of some Literatures." *Organization Studies* 14.

Fan, Y. 1992. "Blending East and West: How can Western Management Know-how be Transferred to China's Socialist Economy." Working Paper. Durham University Business School.

Fiol, C.M., and M.A. Lyles. 1985. "Organizational Learning." *Academy of Management Review* 10 (4).

Galbraith, C.S. 1990. "Transferring Core Manufacturing Technologies in High-Technology Firms." *California Management Review* 32 (4).

Hamel, G. 1991. "Competition for Competence and Inter-Partner Learning within International Strategic Alliances." *Strategic Management Journal* 12.

Inkpen, A.C., and M.M. Crossan. 1995. "Believing in Seeing: Joint Ventures and Organization Learning." *Journal of Management Studies* 32 (5).

Jaeger, A.M. 1983. "The Transfer of Organizational Culture Overseas: An Approach to Control in the Multinational Corporation." *Journal of International Business Studies* 14.

Kedia, B.L., and R.S. Bhagat. 1988. "Cultural Constraints on Transfer of Technology across Nations: Implications for Research in International and Comparative Management." *Academy of Management Review* 13 (4).

Kogut, B. 1988. "Joint Ventures: Theoretical and Empirical Perspectives." *Strategic Management Journal* 9.

Levitt, B., and J.G. March. 1988. "Organizational Learning." *Annual Review of Sociology* 14: 319-340.

Lockett, M. 1988. "Culture and the Problems of Chinese Management." *Organization Studies* 9.

Lyles, M.A. 1988. "Learning Among Joint Venture Sophisticated Firms." *Management International Review* 28: 85-98.

March, J.G., and J.P. Olsen. 1975. "The Uncertainty of the Past: Organizational Learning Under Ambiguity." *European Journal of Political Research* 3: 147-171.

Newman, W.H. 1992. "'Focused Joint Ventures' in Transforming Economies." *Academy of Management Executive* 6 (1).

Nystrom, P.C., and W.H. Starbuck. 1984. "To Avoid Organizational Crises, Unlearn." *Organizational Dynamics* 13.

Poole, P., B. Gray, and D.A. Gioia. 1990. "Organizational Script Development Through Interactive Accommodation." *Group and Organization Studies* 15 (22) (June).

Robbins, S.P. 1993. *Organizational Behavior.* Englewood Cliffs, NJ: Prentice Hall International Editions.

Shenkar, O., and Y. Zeira. 1987. "Human Resources Management in International Joint Ventures: Directions for Research." *Academy of Management Review* 12 (3).

Tiemessen I., H.W. Lane, M.M. Crossan, and A.C. Inkpen. 1996. "Knowledge Management in International Joint Ventures." Paper presented at the North American Conference on Global Perspectives on Cooperative Strategies, March 1-3, Ontario, Canada.

Tung, R.L. 1994. "Human Resource Issue and Technology Transfer." *International Journal of Human Resource Management* 5 (4).

Von Glinow, M.A., and M.B. Teagarden. 1988. "The Transfer of Human Resource Management Technology in Sino-US Cooperative Ventures: Problems and Solutions." *Human Resource Management* 27.

Westwood R.I., and S.M. Leung. 1993. "Embracing Mammon: The Acculturation of PRC Trainee Managers to U.S. Business Culture." Paper presented at a Conference on Managing East-West Business in Turbulent Times, June 3-6, Turku, Finland.

HUMAN RESOURCE MANAGEMENT PRACTICES IN FOREIGN INVESTED ENTERPRISES IN CHINA:

WHAT HAS BEEN LEARNED?

Ingmar Björkman and Yuan Lu

INTRODUCTION

It is widely recognized today that the recruitment, development, and retention of competent and high-performing Chinese professionals and managers is a challenge and a problem for foreign firms operating in the People's Republic of China (PRC) (Child 1991 1994; Osland and Cavusgil 1996; Verburg 1996). In fact, recent surveys (Southworth 1996) indicate that the management of human resources tends to be the single biggest challenge for Western companies in the PRC. Although several studies have augmented our understanding of the human resource management (HRM) practices found in foreign invested enterprises (FIEs) in China (Warner 1993; Child 1994), little effort has been made to analyze the learning concerning HRM practices that has taken place among Western-owned FIEs and their parent organizations in China.

Advances in Chinese Industrial Studies, Volume 5, pages 155-172.

ISBN: 1-55938-961-3

The aim of this chapter is to describe the HRM practices observed in Western FIEs in the PRC and, in particular, to discuss the learning that has occurred concerning the effectiveness of different HRM practices. The analysis is confined to the HRM of local managers and professionals working in FIEs with Western parent organizations. The term "learning" as used here refers to the interpretation by corporate managers concerning the kind of practices that are seen to produce favorable organizational outcomes. Managers may learn both from their own experience and from that of others (Levitt and March 1988). The outcome of the learning process is likely to be manifested in changes in HRM policies and practices. An analysis of what business executives with hands-on experience of the phenomenon have learned has the potential to augment both researchers' and practitioners' understanding of the kind of HRM practices that may be successful in the Chinese context.[1] Although the focus of this paper is on *what* managers have learned concerning HRM, we will also discuss *how* learning takes place.

After an introduction to HRM in Chinese state-owned companies and a discussion on "organizational learning," the main part of the chapter concentrates on a description of the HRM practices seen as successful in FIEs. The subsequent section deals with the the question of how learning occurs, and the role of the China headquarters of Western multinational corporations (MNCs) with multiple FIEs in China, followed by a final summary and implications for future research.

HRM IN CHINESE STATE-OWNED ENTERPRISES

Chinese management of human resources differs in many respects from practices found in Western countries (Easterby-Smith, Mulina, and Lu 1995; Warner 1993, 1995). Officially there are two kinds of systems in China, one for workers, the other for technicians, party cadres, administrative clerks and managers. We are concerned with the latter system, for the so-called "personnel." It should be noted that Chinese HRM practices and policies are undergoing considerable change and that there are substantial differences in practices within China itself (Brown and Branine 1995; Warner 1996). The following is intended to provide a general overview of the situation in Chinese state-owned enterprises.

Until relatively recently, graduates were assigned to a certain job, subsequently enjoying the so-called "iron rice-bowl" policy of job security and cradle-to-grave welfare system (Child 1994). Today, recruitment of personnel to state-owned companies is only partly under state control. Most university graduates are allowed to seek their own jobs, but enterprises still need a planning quota from the governmental personnel bureau if the job candidate is recruited as "personnel." These employees are still in the state system as permanent staff. This is, however, mostly limited to government agencies and government-related agencies as many enterprises fail to adhere to the regulations. State-owned enterprises typically sign labor contracts for between one and five years also with university graduates. In spite of the enterprise reforms in the 1990s, state-owned companies appear still to prefer to recruit graduates rather than people with experience from other companies, and managers and professionals enjoy a high degree of job security. Interviews or informal discussions constitute the usual selection methods (Lu 1996), and nepotism seems to be relatively common in the selection of new employees (Warner 1993).

Training has been expanded for employees in state-owned enterprises, but is still rather limited (Warner 1993). Both in-house and external training is provided (Warner 1996). The emphasis of training is on technological skills rather than on "soft" management skills (Child 1994). In China modern management has been understood more as a body of quantitative techniques than as a way of thinking and acting, and an engineering approach to management still seems to be encouraged in China's educational system (Borgonjon and Vanhonacker 1992).

In Western companies performance appraisals (assessments) are typically viewed as top-down processes focused around an annual interview between the individual and his or her superior, sometimes with HRM people taking part (Sparrow and Hiltrop 1994; Easterby-Smith, Mulina, and Lu 1995). In Chinese enterprises the employee typically does an annual written self-assessment. The opinions of colleagues, subordinates, and the superior are seen as extremely important. One-to-one interviews with the boss are relatively uncommon (Easterby-Smith, Mulina, and Lu 1995).

The importance of individual performance and educational level as indicators of career development have increased significantly since the beginning of the Chinese enterprise reforms. Promotion also depends on good personal relationships and "correct political attitude" (Child 1994), the former reflecting the Chinese emphasis on personal relationship (*guanxi*), the latter reflecting the socialist ideology.

Until the mid-1980s wages were determined by government bodies. The salary system has undergone significant change during the last decade: while in 1985 age was by far the most important factor in determining an employee's salary in state-owned enterprises, by 1990 it was job position in the company, and more advanced education and training had begun to make a difference to pay levels (Child 1995). Income differences are still relatively small (Child 1995), although internal differentials have apparently been increasing in the 1990s (Easterby-Smith, Mulina, and Lu 1995). Material bonuses are widespread, but now "many enterprises have begun to pay equal (or almost equal) bonuses to all employees" (Warner 1995, p. 244), and "although there is evidence of individualized payment being discussed in China there is still

Table 1. HRM Practices in Chinese State-owned Enterprises, Western Companies, and FIEs in China

	Chinese	*Western*	*FIEs in China*
Sources of recruitment	Often directly from school	All sources	Often directly from school, other FIEs and representative offices, less from local partner
Selection methods	No references or tests; interview/informal talk	Often references, extensive interviews	Extensive interviews
Selection criteria	Nepotism/contacts common, sometimes tests	Impersonal relationships; prefer experience	No relationships; prefer no experience in foreign company
Training and development	Relatively limited; mostly technical	Rather extensive; technical and general management	Mostly technical, increasingly general management
	in-house and external	(increasingly) in-house and external	mostly in-house, in China, and also abroad
Assessment	By colleagues and subordinates; written self-appraisal important	Mostly by superiors, often personal discussions between superior and subordinate	Relatively uncommon, but increasing; mostly by superiors
Promotion criteria	Performance, personal relationships, political attitude	Predominately performance	Performance; affiliation
Compensation	Small salary differences; bonus important part of salary; limited individual incentives	Considerable salary differences; often individual financial incentives	Increasing differences; experimentation with individual performance incentives
Retention	Limited job mobility	Competitive salaries; career planning and development	Competitive salaries; career planning, housing schemes

much resistance to its implementation—and the preference remains for group incentive schemes" (Easterby-Smith, Mulina, and Lu 1995, p. 49).

Table 1 summarizes some typical features of HRM in Chinese state-owned enterprises and compares them with general characteristics in Western companies, and also includes features of the HRM practices observed in FIEs in China, which will be discussed later in the chapter.

ORGANIZATIONAL LEARNING

This chapter analyzes what FIEs and Western parent companies in the PRC have learned concerning successful HRM practices. But why have we chosen to use an organizational learning perspective for this analysis? Organizations learn from experience, and "organizational learning" has been offered as a crucial way in which companies can improve their operations (Senge 1990). "When learning is defined as a process involving experimentation, monitoring of results, and modifying future behavior on the basis of those results, there is considerable evidence indicating that organizations can improve through learning" (March 1994, p. 28). This chapter takes this assertion seriously, and reports on the learning concerning HRM practices and policies that has taken place within FIEs and MNCs in China. The research interest within the organizational learning perspective covers both the process of learning and its outcome. While our primary focus is on the latter, we will also discuss how learning takes place.

Organizations learn in different ways. In addition to experiential company-internal learning, the entrance of new members is an important way in which organizations learn (Levinthal and March 1993). Furthermore, organizations can learn from the experience of other organizations, including joint venture partners, suppliers and customers, and competitors. Consultancy firms and professional organizations may be instrumental in developing and diffusing knowledge among corporations (DiMaggio and Powell 1983; March 1994). International joint ventures may also learn through the transfer of knowledge from their parent organizations (Inkpen 1997). Lessons from history can subsequently be coded into organizational routines which may survive even if the original "learner" has left the organization (Levitt and March 1988).

However, while organizations learn from their own and others' experience, experience is sometimes a poor teacher. The linkage between cause and effect is often extremely complex, and the difficulties in making inferences can sometimes be insurmountable (Levitt and March 1988). Another problem is that organizations are often forced to draw inferences from small samples of experience (March, Sproull, and Tamuz 1991); for instance, a JV is unlikely to be able to experiment with a number of different compensation systems for their employees. Furthermore, people tend to be resistant to change concerning, for example, the appropriateness of a certain HRM policy. As a general rule, people are more inclined to view their own actions as successful. Consequently, there may be a systematic basis among JV managers toward viewing their own company's HRM practices as successful. Finally, a number of factors may lead to restrictions in terms of the experiments with HRM policies and practices that can be carried out; these include, among others, strong organizational and societal norms, and formal regulations (Westney 1993; Rosenzweig and Nohria 1994).

The problems inherent in organizational learning need to be borne in mind when analyzing what managers have learned in terms of HRM practices in FIEs in China.

THE STUDY

Method

The observations reported here are based on semi-structured interviews carried out during the first half of 1996 with expatriate and local managers in 27 Western production units in different parts of China. The sample consisted of 27 joint ventures (JVs) and three wholly-owned subsidiaries. In 26 of the FIEs the main Western partner was a European company; four had North American parent organizations. A large majority of the companies had a Western general manager, but only one had a Western expatriate manager responsible for HRM. Data was also collected from between one and three representatives for four MNC China headquarters.

In most FIEs one manager was interviewed, in the others discussions were undertaken with two or three managers. The interviewee was usually the general manager and/or the human resource manager. Although a majority of the interviewees had been recruited from the Western company, some had been transferred from the local partner, and others had been externally recruited in China or elsewhere.

The respondents were asked to describe the HRM practices in their companies and to elaborate on what they had learned concerning the types of practices that they considered successful. They were also encouraged to discuss the interaction between the FIE managers and (1) their parent organizations, (2) executives from other FIEs in China, and (3) representatives from other organizations in China. Our intention with the latter questions was to investigate the extent to which FIE managers engage in discussions on HRM issues, and how FIE managers learn from others' experiences. All but a handful of the interviews were taperecorded.

Results

Recruitment and Selection

In a recent round-table discussion with the government of the PRC no less than 59 percent of participants concluded that recruiting and retaining managers was the most significant problem facing FIEs in China. This was twice the number that considered Chinese bureaucracy to be the major issue (Southworth 1996). While it is often possible to find people with good technical education, the lack of qualified and experienced Chinese managers is particularly acute in the areas of financial management and HRM. Consequently there is a great need for the training and development of employees in this area, an issue we will discuss in a later section.

Many of the first joint ventures to be established in China recruited managers and professionals almost exclusively from the local JV partner. They were forced to take over (too) many employees from the Chinese partner's organization. In some JVs local and foreign partners (and JV managers) are still engaged in discussions about whether to recruit local employees from the Chinese partner company or from external sources. Some of the Chinese respondents in our study viewed people transferred from the local partner's organization as more loyal. The term "loyal" seemed to carry two meanings: first, people from the Chinese parent organization are more loyal to that organization than those recruited externally, and, second, they are easier to retain in the JV.

However, according to most expatriate respondents there are several potential problems with direct recruitment from the local partner. First, the employees transferred to the joint venture often lack the skills and knowledge expected by the foreign investor. To further aggravate this problem, many Chinese companies have suffered a serious brain-drain to foreign firms (and to local private and collective firms), and they may therefore be reluctant to transfer high performers to an FIE. Some foreign managers reported that the local partner's personnel department had put forward particularly poor performers to their joint venture, but some Chinese respondents disputed this. It appears that at least some of these perceptual differences are due to differences in terms of the skills, preferences, and attitudes preferred by foreign and Chinese managers. Many foreign managers emphasized professional training, language skills, and adaptability, whereas local managers thought work experience and personal relationships (*guanxi*) more important.

Second, by recruiting large groups of employees from the Chinese partner, the FIE starts with an organizational culture which is embedded in that of the Chinese company. This culture is difficult to change, because of the strong power structures and interpersonal (*guanxi*) networks within the organization. Externally recruited Chinese employees may also have serious problems in integrating themselves into an existing organization.

Today a majority of FIEs, in particular those with a "dominant" foreign partner (Killing 1983), rely extensively on external recruitment, both from domestic Chinese companies, other FIEs, and directly from university/school. Many large companies have developed close ties with Chinese universities as well as with China's only international business school, the China Europe International Business School (CEIBS) in Shanghai. Even though university graduates lack practical work experience, the future development potential of people who, in the words of a Western respondent, "have not been spoilt in state-owned companies," is generally perceived as more than outweighing this disadvantage. The interviewees showed a clear and consistent preference for candidates with experience from other FIEs or the representative offices of foreign companies.

For professional positions, several managers stated that in their experience young females outperformed other groups of people. Among the Chinese females are, generally speaking, thought less highly of than males (Bond 1991) and, according to several respondents, are subject to severe discrimination in the Chinese labor market. Some interviewees preferred females with the appropriate education, whom they found on average to be more intelligent and more hard-working than males.

So far, it seems that Western MNCs in China have learned not to recruit the bulk of managers and professionals from the local JV partner. This issue is now often stressed by MNCs during JV negotiations. Most Western companies pursue a formal agreement stating that the foreign and the local partner organizations will supply only a specified number of "their" people—most commonly in management positions—and that the rest of the JV employees can be recruited from other sources. Some JV contracts also stipulate that successful applicants must fulfill certain criteria and/or must undergo certain tests (Stevenson-Yang 1995).

The most common recruitment method is the use of personal contacts. Our findings are in line with recent survey results: of the JVs situated in Beijing that were surveyed by the American Chamber of Commerce in August 1995, 52 percent used contacts and relationships, compared to 20 percent using newspaper advertisements (Southworth 1996). Employees recruited through personal contacts are considered likely to be more loyal to the organization. Through personal interaction with the applicant it is also easier to convince the person in question about the attractiveness of the company.

Unknown foreign companies generally have experienced problems in attracting high-quality applicants through newspaper advertisements. Another drawback with this method is that dealing with the resulting large numbers of applications and interviews can make the whole process time consuming and inefficient. This problem is aggravated by the fact that many foreign managers play a central role in the recruitment process, sometimes even in the initial screening process, partly to make sure that candidate selection is based on the applicant's professional qualifications rather than personal relationships with those carrying out the screening process. Nepotism (*guanxi*-recruitment) has been a serious problem in many companies (Sensenbrenner and Sensenbrenner 1994). External pressures on local employees to select certain people can be dealt with more easily when a foreign manager takes the formal responsibility for the selection process.

A relatively limited number of companies use recruitment consultants, or headhunters, both domestic Chinese and international ones. Some reported a high success rate with this method, while others have been less satisfied. Within the sampled FIEs no clear pattern could be identified in terms of the companies' experiences. Many firms utilize the job fairs arranged by the governmental labor and personnel bureaus.

Competition for able candidates is fierce, and in order to attract good applicants companies find that they are forced to offer attractive compensation packages. Incentives include so-called "golden handshakes" (a sum of money paid in, say, three instalments, i.e., when the person joins the firm, after the first year, and perhaps when certain targets have been reached) and company-sponsored housing. The practice of offering golden handshakes seems particularly prevalent in Shanghai where the competition for competent candidates is extremely fierce.

In some instances it is difficult to get previous employers to release personal files (*dang'an*) of applicants, and companies can be forced to pay a (negotiable) "transfer" fee. In the sampled FIEs this fee varied during the first half of 1996 between 2,000 and 20,000 Yuan. However, it appears that it is more common for the applicants themselves to arrange for the release of personal files.

Recruitment is obviously one of the first processes undertaken by a newly established FIE, and the human resource manager/officer should, according to several respondents, be one of the first persons to be recruited by the company. Several "old China hands" advised against transferring the HR manager from the partner's organization; they are more likely to maintain their loyalties to that organization (and may, in fact, be one of the managers assigned by the partner, and thus still employed by the partner rather than the JV), and may therefore be severely restricted in their operating flexibility. The HR manager should preferably have been with the FIE for some time before most employees are recruited. This is important in order to give the HR manager enough time to become acquainted with the company and to receive the necessary training, preferably also in other units owned by the Western company.

Training and Development

There are obviously huge training and development needs in China today. Cost reasons alone present significant incentives to reduce the number of expatriate (foreign) managers stationed in China, and to try to implement localization at the managerial level. However, many Chinese employees lack the technical knowledge and skills needed to perform their assignments successfully, and most FIEs focus primarily on technical training. In addition, many expatriates emphasize more than ever the need to install a new way of thinking among their local employees (Melvin 1996). Localization of the management group puts strong demands on the general management development of local managers and professionals, and, consequently, general management training is receiving growing attention.

FIEs appear recently to have begun to allocate more resources to the training and development of their employees. Although a significant number of local JV partners resist the idea of spending much money on training, their attitude seems to be changing gradually as well. A few very large MNCs, for example, Motorola, have even started their own internal "universities" or "business schools" in China. Others are currently in the process of establishing joint training and development programs with other foreign companies.

Many companies send their employees on short external training courses and seminars run by universities and business schools in China, such as CEIBS. This is particularly the case concerning the development of functional specialists, such as HRM and financial managers and professionals, for which knowledge about local conditions is crucial. Some companies invite international management training companies as well as the company's own staff to run company-internal sessions. According to the experience of several companies, a viable and cost-effective solution is to out-source to local educational institutions the task of teaching basic knowledge and skills; subsequently it is easier for employees to utilize fully the training provided by expensive expatriate trainers.

A widely used solution is to send staff overseas for formal and/or on-the-job training. Although very expensive it offers a number of advantages. Employees are exposed to the foreign company's international business practices, and subsequently may be able to introduce these practices into the Chinese operations. A couple of respondents stressed the need to send people not only to units in Europe and North America, but also to use successful operations in other Asian countries as role models for Chinese employees (Melvin 1996). Some companies have experienced a need to set specific goals that the employees should achieve during their stay overseas. They now require that the receiving units tailor a program that fits the needs of the particular trainee, and that the trainees themselves report on their learning experience. In one company the trainees are also asked to specify how they are going to utilize their experience on their return to China. Sometimes overseas training has been used as a way to convince high-level local managers to accept certain organizational changes advocated by foreign executives. Training abroad also constitutes a significant reward for employees, and some even regard it as the single most important incentive at their disposal, the chance to travel abroad perhaps being a unique opportunity not to be missed if at all possible. The daily allowances paid overseas constitutes an additional incentive.

Leading on from this, the poaching of employees who have received foreign training is a serious problem. Companies are trying to alleviate the situation by requiring their employees to sign a contract stating that they will stay with the company for a certain period of time after their return to China. The ability and willingness to enforce such contracts is, however, questioned by many expatriates. A more viable solution is apparently to split overseas training into shorter periods, so that future training periods constitute an incentive for the employees to remain with the company. A visit overseas should thus be seen as an integrated part of the employee's career development, and the employee must be aware of this.

"Shadowing" systems and teamwork with expatriate professionals and managers may constitute important development strategies, although only a limited number of companies report that they are successful in this respect. Foreigners working in China are under constant pressure to succeed, and they often find it difficult to spend enough time developing the performance of their Chinese colleagues who may lack the knowledge and skills needed to learn the issues in question. The tendency on the part of many Chinese employees to transfer responsibility to their foreign superiors (Child 1991; Björkman 1994) may also aggravate the learning problem. Some large Western companies have therefore made it a top priority that their expatriate managers in China should develop their own successors, but it remains a challenge as to how to motivate the overseas managers to concentrate sufficiently on this task.

Assessment and Promotion

Some FIEs have introduced periodic assessment (appraisal) systems, but these systems are often more used as control devices than as the basis for analyzing training and development needs. Although this analysis is sometimes done informally as part of the company's ongoing operations, many FIEs would probably benefit from a better system. Nonetheless, a system whereby specific group and individual goals are set and subsequently followed up can be seen as a part of a development process. Many foreign managers complain that there is a reluctance to take responsibility on the part of local managers (Child 1991); the operation of a planning/appraisal system may enable the organization gradually to be instilled with the value of people taking personal responsibility for the success of their own, their department's, and their company's operations.

During our interviews it was frequently stated that the promotion of local middle managers to senior positions is an important step toward localization of an FIE's operations. Virtually all respondents stated that the performance (and, related to this, the perceived future development potential) of a particular person is the most important promotion criterion. However, while foreign partners in JVs are sometimes reluctant to promote middle managers who have been recruited from the local partner, the Chinese tend to be unwilling to accept externally recruited persons in top positions. In several cases, the choice of people for managerial positions has to be approved by the board of directors, where even the promotion to relatively junior positions has been the source of disagreements and long discussions (Björkman 1995). To avoid situations of this kind, recently several MNCs have insisted that the JV contract specifies that the general manager has full autonomy in promotion decisions.

Localization of top management positions in JVs is thus an issue that is determined not only by the development of competent Chinese managers, but also by the struggle among parent companies to control the JV's operations. For instance, in one FIE the local employees had been told explicitly that they were assessed according to the Chinese parent company's standard performance criteria and by their loyalty to this firm rather than to the FIE. Although this appears to be relatively uncommon in FIEs in China today, apparently many Chinese employees still feel that the way they are evaluated by people in the Chinese parent organization is more important than the way they are assessed by their superiors in the FIE (or the Western MNC) (Björkman 1994). In other words, their main concern is to show their loyalty to the Chinese organization and to develop and maintain *guanxi* with its top managers. An important task for Western MNCs is thus to influence what the FIE employees perceive as key assessment criteria, and the beliefs they hold about the personal consequences of their actions.

Compensation

Few themes are more frequently discussed among Western managers in China than the salaries of their employees. During 1995 the salaries of top performing Chinese managers in FIEs in cities like Beijing and Shanghai appeared to have increased by nearly 50 percent and companies still have serious problems retaining their key employees. Many companies provide their employees with a number of fringe benefits, ranging from housing, pensions, insurance, company cars, and overseas training.

A growing number of Western companies have introduced performance-related compensation schemes in their China operations. Such schemes are today quite widespread among sales people, and in some companies are also found within other functions. Outside the marketing function it is more difficult to establish clear-cut criteria that can be used as the basis for performance evaluation, and many companies have experienced significant problems when introducing a performance-related compensation system based on more or less subjective performance evaluation (Björkman and Schaap 1994). One lesson learned by many executives is that much effort must be spent on a detailed specification of employees' objectives over a certain period of time. Such objectives can then be used both for calculating financial bonuses and for supervising the work performed.

Because of the problems in developing well-functioning incentive systems, several FIEs use salary increases rather than periodic bonuses as a way to motivate their employees. Partly as a consequence of this, the salary differences in FIEs have increased considerably.

Retention

Until recently retention was not an issue in Chinese state-owned enterprises as employees were seldom granted permission to leave a company. In FIEs today it tends to be a major problem, especially in companies situated in large developed cities like Beijing, Shanghai, and Guangzhou. An increase in salary is but one way to try to retain people. According to several respondents, this may work in the short term, but it is unlikely to be the long-term answer. One relatively new solution is the use of housing schemes, where a company may invest in some apartments for key employees. After a certain number of years the apartment will become the property of the employee, who is therefore committed to remaining in the organization for that length of time.

The Chinese interviewees in our study in particular stressed the need to pay attention to career planning. Currently there are plenty of opportunities for well-educated ambitious Chinese employees, and foreign companies and JVs need to be able to convince people about the future development opportunities within their companies. The clear communication of the possibilities for future training, development, and career progress is a crucial part of a successful retention strategy, and these expectations must, obviously, be seen to be fulfilled. Young local employees expect considerably faster career progress than only a few years ago, faster than is customary in Western MNCs.

In the PRC, as elsewhere, the creation of a positive and exciting job environment is contributing to a low personnel turnover.

Mechanisms of Learning

Several large companies with multiple FIEs in China have established "China headquarters." The trend in these companies is quite clearly toward the development of a centralized HRM function, with one China human resources manager responsible for the development of HRM policies and practices. There are clear-scale advantages in this solution, which enables the company to draw on the skills and knowledge of one key HRM manager in all the MNC's China operations. This person may be able to take a leading role in the development of HRM policies for China, participate in the selection of key people for the positions within the units in China, work on the development of the people working with HRM issues, and help each unit carry out training and development needs analyses. The MNCs in our sample had filled the China HR manager position with a Western manager, a local Chinese who had studied abroad, or with a Chinese employee with many years' experience in another Western company. The person chosen as HR manager should preferably be familiar with the MNC's HRM practices, and with the local conditions in China.

Several large MNCs have established China HRM groups, headed by one HR manager from the China headquarters. HR managers from the FIEs are members of these groups, which typically meet several times per year. MNC executives have found several advantages with this system, such as knowledge creation through sharing experiences among the FIEs in terms of HRM practices, and spread of knowledge about efficacious HRM policies and practices to the MNC's units in China. In other words, the groups provide a larger sample from which inferences concerning the success of different practices can be drawn. The MNC, therefore, has the opportunity to engage in more extensive experiental learning than they might otherwise be able to do, and support from other MNC units has also been found to be valuable, for instance when an FIE is trying to introduce new HRM practices.

Respondents frequently stressed that their China headquarters had, during the previous couple of years, begun to pay increasing attention to HRM issues. HRM has been transformed from a neglected area to one that attracts the attention of the top executives. Several of the managers interviewed noted that the MNC's executives had recently become aware of the major HRM issues that the company was facing in China, and that developing central HRM functions was seen as a feasible strategy. It is clear that the role taken by the MNC China headquarters has already influenced, and will increasingly influence in the future, HRM practice in FIEs in the PRC (Meier, Perez, and Woetzel 1995).

Our data suggests that while several FIEs have learned significantly from the MNC headquarters in China, there seems to be more limited interaction between individual FIEs in China and the HRM departments at the corporate headquarters in Europe or North America. This concerns both those FIEs which report to a China headquarters and those that work directly to corporate headquarters. There are few visits by HRM people to China, and even fewer trips by HRM managers in FIEs to the MNCs' organizations outside China. The limited language skills of many HR managers in fact restricts the possibility of international interaction and exposure on their part. The influence of the MNC parent organizations appears more often to occur through FIE managers who are not formally responsible for HRM issues. In particular expatriate general managers, who have brought with them to China their experiences from other locations, seem to have transferred some of that experience to their units in China.

Some MNCs have regional organizations in Asia (typically located in Singapore or Hong Kong), but the role of this organization for FIE organizational learning in terms of HRM appears to be limited. In a relatively small number of MNCs the regional headquarters is instrumental in organizing training for their units in China.

The influence from other FIEs and MNCs in China seems to be stronger. Extensive professional networks apparently play important roles in producing "mimetic behavior" (DiMaggio and Powell 1983). In all locations included in the study there are networks, or "clubs," of expatriate employees who meet to discuss professional issues. HRM issues are reportedly among those discussed most frequently. In locations with a limited number of expatriates the networks are open to everyone, in big cities country-specific organizations have emerged. In several locations, such as Tianjin, Beijing, and Guangzhou, there are also networks consisting of HRM professionals only. In contrast to the expatriate clubs, the working language of the HRM networks is usually Chinese. Some of the networks are closed to outsiders (membership depends on recommendation from an existing member), others are open to all foreign invested enterprises. The HRM groups typically meet once every two months to discuss issues of mutual concern, such as the development of "gentlemen's agreements" concerning recruitment from other members of the network, the structure and level of compensation packages, schemes to retain employees, and how to respond to rules and regulations issued by the governmental labor bureaus. Several respondents said that the discussions in such networks have influenced their HRM practices, as they provide good opportunities for comparing notes with other organizations.

CONCLUSIONS AND DISCUSSION

The aim of the study reported here has been to describe the HRM practices observed in Western FIEs in China and, in particular, to discuss the learning that has taken place concerning the effectiveness of different HRM practices. The analysis has been confined to the HRM of local managers and professionals working in FIEs with Western parent organizations. One of the aims of this chapter has been to describe what managers have learned concerning effective HRM practices, thus providing some suggestions for future investors in China. Some general features that were found in many of the 30 FIEs included in our study can be seen in Table 1.

Overall, the HRM practices found in FIEs in China seem to be becoming more similar to those in Western companies. This trend is quite conspicuous when comparing data gathered in 1992 (Björkman and Schaap 1994) with data gathered in 1996. Several factors may have contributed to this change. First, the learning that takes place across FIEs through the interaction of business executives who participate in different kinds of networks seems to be an important vehicle for spreading HRM practices. Second, Western MNCs are putting more emphasis on HRM issues than only a few years ago, and most of them try to introduce at least some of their international practices in their Chinese operations. Third, while personnel issues in many of the early JVs in China were controlled by the Chinese parent company (Child, Boisot, Ireland, Li, and Watts 1990; Child 1994), the Western parent organization has dominant control in many of the more recent FIEs; hence today MNCs are often in a position to decide on their own HRM policies in FIEs. Fourth, recent enterprise reforms in the PRC have introduced employment contracts of limited duration. There are also reports of more emphasis on training and new wage systems that stress material benefits (Warner 1996). It is likely that these changes have had some effect on the Chinese parent companies' attitudes toward HRM practices in FIEs. While there may be some inertia in old FIEs (Gray and Yan 1997), the Chinese reforms are likely to influence HRM practices in newly established FIEs.

The HRM practices outlined in Table 1 obviously constitute a simplification of what in reality is a wide variety of practices. Wholly-owned enterprises and JVs with a dominant Western partner seem to differ from JVs with shared or split parent company control; FIEs situated in different regions within China exhibit some variations; and FIEs established to continue the ongoing operations of an existing Chinese company often have little in common with those established as greenfield operations. Future research is needed to establish factors able to explain the variance that can be observed among FIEs in China.

ACKNOWLEDGMENT

Funding from the Academy of Finland is gratefully acknowledged.

NOTE

1. The learning is obviously restricted to a certain context. Thus, there may be considerable variations between different situations due to the differences within China itself (Child and Stewart 1996).

REFERENCES

Björkman, I. 1994. "Role Perception and Behavior among Chinese Managers in Sino-western Joint Ventures." In *Joint Ventures in the People's Republic of China: Advances in Chinese Industrial Studies, Volume 4*, edited by S. Stewart. Greenwich, CT: JAI Press.

Björkman, I. 1995. "The Board of Directors in Sino-western Joint Ventures." *Corporate Governance* (3): 156-166.

Björkman, I., and A. Schaap. 1994. "Human Resource Management Practices in Sino-western Joint Ventures." *The Finnish Journal of Business Economics* 43: 111-125.

Bond, M.H. 1991. *Beyond the Chinese Face.* Hong Kong: Oxford University Press.

Borgonjon, J., and W.R. Vanhonacker. 1992. "Modernizing China's Mmanagers." *China Business Review* 19 (5): 12-18.

Brown, D.H., and M. Branine. 1995. "Managing People in China's Foreign Trade Corporations." *International Journal of Human Resource Management* 6: 159-175.

Child, J. 1991. "A Foreign Perspective on the Management of People in China." *International Journal of Human Resource Management* 2: 93-107.

Child, J. 1994. *Management in China during the Age of Reform*. Cambridge, UK: Cambridge University Press.

Child, J. 1995. "Changes in the Structure and Prediction of Earnings in Chinese State Enterprises during the Economic Reform." *International Journal of Human Resource Management* 6: 1-30.

Child, J., M. Boisot, J. Ireland, Z. Li, and J. Watts. 1990. *The Management of Equity Joint Ventures in China*. Beijing: China-Europe Management Institute.

Child, J., and S. Stewart. 1996. "Regional Differences in China and their Implications for Sino-foreign Joint Ventures." Paper presented at the Conference on Managing Joint Ventures in the PRC, University of Hong Kong, April 9-11.

DiMaggio, P.J., and W.W. Powell. 1983. "The Iron Cage Revisited: Institutional Isomorphism and Collective Rationality in Organizational Fields." *American Sociological Review* 48: 147-160.

Easterby-Smith, M., D. Mulina, and Y. Lu. 1995. "How Culture-Sensitive is HRM? A Comparative Analysis of Practice in Chinese and UK Companies." *International Journal of Human Resource Management* 6: 31-59.

Gray, B., and A. Yan. 1997. "Formation and Evolution of International Joint Ventures: Examples from U.S.-Chinese Partnerships." In *Cooperative Strategies: Asian Perspectives*, edited by P.W. Beamish and J.P. Killing. San Francisco, CA: The New Lexington Press.

Inkpen, A. 1997. "An Examination of Knowledge Management in International Joint Ventures. In *Cooperative Strategies: North American Perspectives*, edited by P.W. Beamish and J.P. Killing. San Francisco, CA. The New Lexington Press.

Killing, J.P. 1983. *Strategies for Joint Venture Success*. London: Croom Helm.

Levinthal, D.A., and J.G. March. 1993. "The Myopia of Learning." *Strategic Management Journal* 14 (Special Winter Issue): 95-112.

Levitt, B., and J.G. March. 1988. "Organizational Learning." *Annual Review of Sociology* 14: 319-340.

Lu, Y. 1996. *Management Decision-making in Chinese Enterprises*. London: Macmillan.

March, J.G. 1994. *Three Lectures on Efficiency and Adaptiveness in Organizations*. Helsinki: Swedish School of Economics.

March, J.G., L.S. Sproull, and M. Tamuz. 1991. "Learning from Samples of One and Fewer." *Organization Science* 2: 1-13.

Meier, J., J. Perez, and J.R. Woetzel. 1995. "Solving the Puzzle: MNCs in China." *The McKinsey Quarterly* 2: 20-33.

Melvin, S. 1996. "Training the Troops." *China Business Review* 23 (2): 22-28.

Osland, G.E., and S.T. Cavusgil. 1996. "Performance Issues in U.S.-China Joint Ventures." *California Management Review* 38 (2): 106-130.

Rosenzweig, P.M., and N. Nohria. 1994. "Influences on Human Resource Management Practices in Multinational Corporations." *Journal of International Business Studies* 25: 229-251.

Senge, P.M. 1990. *The Fifth Discipline: The Arts and Practice of the Learning Organization*. New York: Doubleday Currancy.

Sensenbrenner, J.S., and J. Sensenbrenner. 1994. "Personnel Priorities." *China Business Review* 21 (6): 40-45.

Southworth, D.B. 1996. "FIEs in China: Finding Qualified Personnel in China." *GBAktuell*.

Sparrow , P., and J-M. Hiltrop. 1994. *European Human Resource Management in Transition*. New York: Prentice Hall.

Stevenson-Yang, A. 1995. "Making your China Investment Work." *China Business Review* 22 (3): 34-38.

Verburg, R.M. 1996. "Developing HRM in Foreign Chinese Joint Ventures." Unpublished paper for the Department of Work and Organizational Psychology, Vrije Universiteit Amsterdam.

Warner, M. 1993. "Human Resource Management 'with Chinese characteristics'." *International Journal of Human Resource Management* 4: 45-65.

Warner, M. 1995. "Managing China's Human Resources." *Human Systems Management* 14: 239-248.

Warner, M. 1996. "Managing China's Enterprise Reforms: A New Agenda for the 1990s." *Journal of General Management* 21 (3): 1-18.

Westney, E. 1993. "Institutionalization Theory and the Multinational Corporation." In *Organization Theory and the Multinational Corporation*, edited by S. Ghoshal and E. Westney. New York: St. Martin's Press.

WHATEVER BECAME OF SOCIALIST LAW?

BACK TO THE INDUSTRIAL REVOLUTION IN CHINA'S JOINT VENTURES

Orlan Lee

INTRODUCTION

It is 30 years now since the heyday of the Cultural Revolution in the People's Republic of China (PRC). In those days idealist admirers of Mao in the West echoed the cries of the Red Guard vanguard, with their little red books, that we had seen the dawning of the day of the "New Man," and that "selfish" individualistic liberalism was a thing of the past.[1] "Participatory democracy,"[2] they said, had arisen in Asia, and only die-hard capitalist exploitationists believed in individualistic liberalism any more. In China, on the other hand, socialist man looked out for his neighbor.

Today, however, we are told that "building socialism with Chinese characteristics" (Deng 1994, p. 72)[3] means "egalitarianism will not work" (Deng 1984, p. 27), that "it is only fair that people become prosperous through their own hard work," and that "it is good for some people and some regions to be prosperous first" (p. 12).

Advances in Chinese Industrial Studies, Volume 5, pages 173-189.

ISBN: 1-55938-961-3

Since former President Jimmy Carter's decision to normalize U.S. diplomatic relations with the PRC in 1978, there has been practically a generation of new business contacts between China and Western countries. In that time a whole new variety of business joint ventures has been created in China in order to bridge the gap between Western business organizations and state-owned enterprises in China.

The Western business community and news media had been fascinated for years with the prospect of the vast potential of an opening in the China trade. The Chinese themselves were also eager to utilize the capital and technology of Western firms both for economic development projects in the PRC and for expansion of their international trade. Therefore, by July 1979 the Fifth National People's Congress had already adopted a law governing prospective new joint ventures between Western and Chinese enterprises.[4]

Many of the cited authorities were persuaded that, because of the adoption of laws governing this new international business enterprise, China was on its way to becoming a society of law. However, the expansion of laws and regulations in this area must be seen against the background of earlier experience in Chinese trade negotiation and political ideology.[5] The agreement to be bound by certain definite laws and regulations must, of necessity, involve acknowledgment of constraints on absolute power. Moreover, when a people sees the example of constraints on power legislated for the convenience of foreign trading partners, they will begin to see advantages in enjoying the advantages of protection of the laws for themselves.[6] However, in the case of China this should not be seen as commitment to political liberalization. As Deng Xiaoping himself observed about the students' protest in 1989:

> The turmoil that arose in China this year also had to come about sooner or later. We ourselves were partly to blame. As you know, two of our General Secretaries fell because of their failure to deal with the problem of bourgeois liberalization. If China allowed bourgeois liberalization, there would inevitably be turmoil (Deng 1994, p. 333).

The key to understanding this ideological dilemma lies in the Marxist belief that capitalism inevitably involves the exploitation of the working class and class struggle, and that introduction of liberal democratic political institutions entails loss of dictatorship of the proletariat and leadership of the communist party. For this reason, Deng Xiaoping advocates only a limited role for market economics within socialism with no contemplation of development of a capitalist society or of bourgeois liberalism:

> We permit some people and some regions to become prosperous first, for the purpose of achieving common prosperity faster. That is why our policy will not lead to polarization, to a situation where the rich get richer while the poor get poorer. To be frank, we shall not permit the emergence of a new bourgeoisie (Deng 1994, pp. 170, 174).

HARD TIMES: BACK TO THE INDUSTRIAL REVOLUTION IN CHINA'S JOINT VENTURES

For the ideologically trained intelligentsia, exploitation of the working class is already observable in the practices of the joint ventures (JVs) and other foreign invested enterprises (FIEs). This is clearly expressed in the distinctions made between the "strategic intentions" of the foreign JV partners and those of state-owned enterprises as characterized by Professor Zhang Shi Quan in his chapter in this volume (Zhang 1997) where it is presumed that the state-owned enterprise pursues social goals, whereas the foreign JV partner pursues only profit and protection of property.

Actually, incidents cited by Professor Zhang and the press on the China mainland, in Hong Kong, and elsewhere give a very somber picture of conditions in some of the so-called FIEs in China. Reports that have appeared of conditions in these FIEs are indeed reminiscent of working and living conditions unheard of in the Western world since the Industrial Revolution.

In a general report in a Hong Kong China affairs magazine summarizing labor conditions in China's FIEs, we read of a number of common abuses (*Dong Dui Yue Han* 1994). In a Taiwan FIE in the Nanhai District it was reported as an example of strict regulations that workers who violate the rule on silence during working hours are punished by having to stand at the factory entrance for several days holding up a school slate with a chalk message accusing themselves of their crime. A South Korean FIE in Tianjian District has a factory employing 1,300 female staff with only 10 in-the-floor toilets available to them. And workers are allowed only one minute to go to the toilet, or they are fined a dollar for every minute more. In a Shanghai jewelery-making factory supervisors forced 19 employees to strip and submit to body searches when one worker dropped a gold ring and could not find it. In November 1993 at an FIE in Shenzhen, across the border from Hong Kong, an electric motor overheated because of long working hours and poor installation. Sixteen workers, who slept in a loft suspended one meter from the ceiling in a corner of the 1,600 meter-square workshop, were unable to get out and were seriously burned. Another source reported that in a South Korean FIE in Zhuhai District the Korean employers have maintained discipline in their factory when work disputes arise by obliging Chinese workers to kneel down before their Korean supervisors (*Ya Chou Chou Han* 1995).

In preparation for the UN Fourth Women's Conference held in Beijing in 1995 the PRC government issued a "white paper" entitled *On the Situation of Women in China* (PRC 1994), which concludes that Chinese women secured a "historic liberation" in 1949, and claims that in the economic reforms since 1979 equality with men in wages and working conditions has been particularly marked. The China Labour Education and Information Centre in Hong Kong prepared their own study in reply (CLEIC 1995), including many reports with lurid details on the treatment of women in FIEs. In one incident, also reported in the Hong Kong press, a security guard at a shoe factory in Fujian Province was jailed for a year and the Taiwanese manager is said to have fled back to Taiwan to escape prosecution for ordering the guard to beat a woman who had stolen two pairs of shoes and then put her into a cage with two large dogs (*Hsien Tai* 1994).

The practice of housing workers in overcrowded dormitories on factory premises where they are locked in at night has led to a number of disasters. In March 1994 fumes from a solvent used to clean workroom floors caused an explosion, killing 10 people and injuring a number of others who were caught in a locked dormitory above the workrooms; the electric door lock would not open and windows were barred and covered with wire so that no one could get out (*Ya Chou Chan Kan* 1994).

Many similar fires and cases of asphyxiation have been reported in the substandard workplaces tolerated on the mainland. But so far these incidents have been dwarfed into insignificance by a fire in a Hong Kong-owned FIE, a textile JV in Zhuhai in June 1994, where 76 people were killed and 160 injured. In fact, when the fire first broke out apparently no one was injured and everyone escaped; the tragedy occurred later when the six-story building collapsed on 200 workers who had been sent back into the burning building to save the cotton bales left behind when they had fled.[7]

These stories are typical of many that have appeared both in the mainland and Hong Kong press. It is reported that workers are frequently paid less than the legal wage, that they are forced to work four to six hours overtime a day without pay (also a violation of PRC labor law), and/or that their pay is months in arrears. There is widespread criticism of the practice of hiring primarily teenage girls, who are employed only until the age of about 26, and of the refusal to hire older workers or men. Abuse of the child labor laws is also common.

NOMENCLATURE IN THE FIEs

Sooner or later it will dawn on the Western reader that the appalling abuses in the foregoing reports all seem to have occurred in FIEs in the PRC owned by Hong Kong, Taiwan, and Korean investors. While Western readers might not expect the most ideal conditions in what most agree are operations which have gone overseas looking specifically for cheap labor, these are not the kinds of conditions they would expect in reputable multinational corporations.

FIEs in China have taken many forms. The Joint Venture Law of 1979 made it possible for cooperative or equity joint ventures (CJVs and EJVs) to be set up in China, whereas previously all the means of industrial production were expected to be owned by state enterprises. However, in the meantime a number of other variants of foreign invested enterprises have arisen, including wholly foreign-owned enterprises (WFOEs) (see Wang 1994; Campbell and Zhang 1994).

Many WFOEs depart sharply from the model of the vehicle for "transfer of technology" or of "capital investment from abroad" foreseen in the original planning. It appears that many are little more than makeshift sweatshops set up to farm out a particular job or to take advantage of cheap labor, and ready to close at short notice, and/or relocate to more economically depressed areas where their practices are unlikely to be questioned.[8]

The low wages and poor labor conditions that existed in Hong Kong, Taiwan, and South Korea 20 years ago have become largely a thing of the past in their home territories. However, the mentality of small enterprise owners who fulfill offshore contracts of Western manufacturers and department stores has not changed. They have not forgotten the frugal, labor-intensive operations that made them rich. They have merely shifted their sweatshop production facilities offshore to lower-wage labor markets in Mainland China and Southeast Asia (*FEER* 1992a).

The case of athletic shoe production is very instructive in this regard. Nike shoes, for example, are produced in South Korea, Taiwan, China, and other Southeast Asian countries. In the early 1980s Nike attempted its own JVs with PRC state enterprises, but gave up because of its inability to deal with the Chinese partners. Nike retells its bad experiences and the reasons for its subsequent shift to Taiwan-based suppliers in China:

> The inventory problem was overwhelming and threatened to take the company down the tubes....We were making shoes to build up [China's] manufacturing capabilities [rather than to sell under Nike's own brand name]....The state factories couldn't comprehend what we wanted in terms of price, quality, and delivery....We tried to make white shoes, but we couldn't do it. There was too much dirt (*FEER* 1992, p. 60).

The authors of the cited article are obviously duly impressed by the entrepreneurial spirit of the small Taiwan manufacturers and their agility in detecting a current niche in the Western marketplace and producing for that sector:

> James Liao typifies Taiwan's entrepreneurial agility. Once a leather-coat manufacturer, Liao's ADI Corporation now makes computer monitors for IBM....This year ADI will also make more than seven million pairs of Nike shoes. Now, Liao is one of those Taiwan-based businessmen who have made China into Nike's fastest growing production source, eclipsing South Korea and Taiwan (*FEER* 1992, p. 60).

The large multinational corporations that subcontract their job requirements to FIEs of this kind may not have a local presence in China themselves. However, a few reformist Hong Kong public interest groups like the Hong

Kong Christian Industrial Committee (HKCIC) are seeking to target them for abandoning their "ethical responsibilities" in buying blindly from China's FIE sweatshops. Writing about just such entrepreneurial FIE shoe factories in China as those described in the above extracts, the executive secretary of HKCIC cites reports of industrial poisoning on the production line, and numerous other breaches of China's new labor code:

> Since 1984, large numbers of joint venture enterprises, mostly shoe factories, have been rushing to Futian Municipality of Fujian Province. At present in Futian, more than 100 million pairs of shoes are produced every year. There are more than 150 shoe factories whose annual production value is more than RMB 3.5 billion [about US$422 million] and the total production value reaches about RMB 6 billion [about US$723 million]. Most of the shoe factories in Futian have four production lines, each with an annual production value of RMB 25 million [about US$3 million]. These shoe factories generally use a kind of highly volatile adhesive agent which consists of benzene, methylbenzene, and dimethylbenzene....High concentrations of the three benzenes are extremely dangerous to people's health. They directly damage the blood and the nervous system. Some people even suffer cancer or bear deformed babies (Shek 1996b, p. 1).

Two months previously, Mr. Shek had detailed the consequences of such poisoning:

> It was reported last month that more than 70,000 (230,000 reported by *Ming Pao* and *Agence France Presse*) women working in mostly Taiwan-owned shoe factories in southeastern Fujian could have been exposed to benzene poisoning five times the legal maximum (*Ming Pao* claims ten times). At least three deaths were reported. Numerous women workers suffer from severe diseases caused by poisoning, and many are in a critical condition (Shek 1996a, p. 1).

Appalling though these figures and labor conditions are, we have to consider that HKCIC has an audience for their crusade largely because Western buyers and subcontractors are involved. According to the *International Labour Review*, "Official statistics on occupational safety, released for the first time at the end of April 1993, show that more than 15,000 workers were killed in industrial accidents in China last year—a 3 percent increase on 1991."[9] Unfortunately, industrial fatalities and illnesses in the PRC—or in other developing countries—do not raise an eyebrow in the Western press, unless they are somehow attributed to *foreign* negligence.

While Western buyers may not have concerned themselves with anything more than quality control in their offshore contract lots in the past, this, too seems to be changing, at least in the case of high profile subcontractors and buyers. The *Far Eastern Economic Review* reports that as the result of some of the abovementioned incidents reaching the eyes and ears of TV viewers in America and Europe, some companies, for example, Wal-Mart, Dayton Hudson, Walt Disney, and Levi Strauss, have adopted "global sourcing guidelines" (*FEER* 1994a) that would presumably prevent such egregious abuses in fulfilling their purchasing contracts.

The managing director of Levi-Strauss's sourcing company in the Asian region claims: "We have people in these factories, merchandisers, quality-assurance people, finishing people on almost a daily basis" (*FEER* 1994b). So it is at least possible for the home company to keep itself relatively well informed. But others who do not have such close contacts with their sources will have trouble verifying or implementing enforcement of their house codes of conduct. On the other hand, there appear to be critics in the region who consider that "tying trade to social or labour issues is a disguised form of protectionism" or as simply a means of making foreign goods less competitive and, therefore, a threat to less developed countries' exports (*FEER* 1994a, p. 57).

Doubtless there are some in the U.S. labor movement, for example, who are so opposed to loss of jobs to overseas producers that they would even demand equal pay with U.S. workers for equal work in order to discourage out-sourcing altogether. However, the real danger of exclusion from American and Western countries' markets does not arise so much from protectionism or inability to police the Western multinationals' house codes of conduct, as it is confusing political and foreign policy issues for whether or not workers in China have protective gear to prevent injuries, or can escape from burning buildings or noxious fumes.

Nevertheless, there is something cleverly disingenuous in the sympathetic offshore labor organizations and social and ideological critics' protests. First, they do not appeal to the PRC authorities to enforce existing Chinese labor laws, because they recognize the conflict of interest of both local and central government bodies in China, concerned to attract offshore investment and to provide jobs. Neither do they appeal to Chinese official labor unions, because they recognize the PRC's official unions' conflict of interest with their official duty to contribute to maintaining labor peace in the FIEs and to upholding government policy.[10] Sympathetic offshore public interest labor organizations do not even appeal to Chinese labor itself for mass action. For in the most appalling conditions, where FIE factory owners have dismissed the entire workforce for protesting about conditions, a whole new set of workers could be hired the same day.[11]

In other words, where none of the traditional labor appeals will work, the offshore public interest group labor organizers seek to embarrass the foreign buyers, because they are the only ones either sensitive to, or concerned by, public opinion and goodwill in their own markets half-way around the world. In a recent address, Shek Ping-kwan, the Executive Secretary of HKCIC, related:

> In early 1995, Mattel Toys, the famous multinational company, asked its suppliers to abide by decent standards of production safety and working conditions. The company announced it would break all relations with supplying companies that failed to abide by the standards.

> The Hong Kong Coalition on the Safe Production of Toys recently studied the health and safety and working conditions in nine factories in China which supply toys to Mattel....
> Based on interviews with workers in those factories, the Coalition found that the standards were not being consistently met in several areas. Some workers were not given adequate protective gear (dust masks) or were exposed to fumes without proper ventilation. Others were receiving pay that was below minimum wage and some were not getting adequate rest days.[12]

Mr Shek also pointed out that at five Reebok suppliers in the Pearl River delta: "we found workers [who] suffered from skin disease and dizziness and other health problems caused by poor ventilation facilities." He also charged the suppliers with violations of Reebok's standards on child labor, freedom of organization, fair wages, and long working hours.

CORRUPTION

In a chapter dealing with corruption in an earlier volume in this series, Brewer Stone remarks on the "extraordinary transaction costs" of getting initial government approvals for setting up a JV, especially in the Special Economic Zones (SEZs), where he finds that officials and others who deal with foreign investors have become more experienced in exacting their rewards. He cites one investor in Shenzhen who "described how he had bribed his way through what he thought were the five approvals needed to start his venture [an engineering plant], only to be presented with a list of ten more." But it is the investor's judgment on his overall experience that is most illuminating for us when we consider the attitude of the small entrepreneurs who invest and do business in China: "he calculated that he had paid more in bribes than for land, labor during construction, and materials combined" (Stone 1994, p. 36).

The point is that investors in small FIEs, especially the ventures of Taiwan, Hong Kong, and South Korea, are mostly small businesspeople who consider what they pay in gifts, bribes, and graft is just part of the cost of doing business. It is understood that they are expanding into the PRC and Southeast Asia because of the availability of cheap labor. Whenever the added cost of the minimum wage, regulated working hours, mandatory leave and rest days, unemployment insurance, social security tax, medical insurance, and workers compensation, are brought into question, the issue becomes one of labor in that country pricing itself out of the market.

> In general the reaction of foreign investors is that from now on the cost of investment in China will be greatly increased because of a variety of labor regulations. Whether or not it is still profitable to invest in China or one should consider changing to other places such as Indonesia, Vietnam....Once the (new) labor law was announced many foreign investors feared that the cost of their investments in China would increase...small and medium-sized investors from Taiwan, Hong Kong, and Macau especially believed it would.

> According to Taiwan estimates, the cost of their investments in China would increase by between 9 per cent and 13 per cent. If the scheduled labor law rights and responsibilities are implemented, they believe the cost to (other) foreign investors will increase at a rate of at least 20 per cent....
>
> Not only will the costs to foreign investors increase, but also the enterprises in China and joint venture partners will have increased costs because, under the labor regulations, enterprises, whether invested in from inside China or from abroad, big, medium-sized, or small, all will increase their costs. The direct and indirect reasons for these increases are as follows...the eight-hour day, the average 44-hour week...compared with common practices of 8-10 hour day, the six-day week, at least...48 working hours a week. Shortened working hours will require employing more workers and increased labor costs.[13]

Unfortunately, many Asian businesspeople do not have the same sense of horror in dealing with those individuals who merely sell access, information, or government approvals. Nor do PRC critics of foreign investors' selfish "strategic intentions" in China reproach themselves because some of their compatriots suffer from the faults of an avaricious "human nature." One may add, by the way, that it does not appear that PRC officials are necessarily underpaid—the common excuse for bribe-taking in developing countries. We are told that "the Ministry of Personnel would like civil servants to receive pay comparable to that earned elsewhere, specifically in state enterprises" (Chew 1990, p. 781). The overall plan for civil service pay seems to correspond roughly to Western standards. Neither the civil service nor the state enterprise sector could be said to be unduly highly compensated by world standards, but either one would appear to offer a reasonable living in local circumstances. Therefore, pay scale alone should not require the taking of bribes merely to keep up with the living standards of one's peers or the local elite.

This does not mean that the PRC government is not aware of the abuses that are taking place in the course of development toward a market economy. According to a *Xinhua* news agency report, 733,543 cadres were punished for engaging in corruption in 1992, the year the 14th Party Congress met to solemnize the theoretical basis of "Socialism with Chinese characteristics"[14], and government officials have been quoted as recognizing the problem, with incidents reported prominently. An article in *Beijing Review* cites figures from a 1995 report of the PRC's senior procurator to the National People's Congress:

> China's top procurator, Zhang Siqing, said that combating rising violent crime and corruption will remain China's priority. While delivering a report to the annual session of the National People's Congress...Zhang noted that the country has been on a campaign against corruption, aimed at eliminating graft, bribery and embezzlement. Last year the courts sentenced 20,186 such culprits, including a vice minister, 28 bureau directors and 202 branch directors. Zhang said a growing number of corruption and bribery cases had involved law enforcement, economic administration and senior government officials. He disclosed that last year's anti-corruption drive found the biggest number of offenders from judicial and law enforcement bodies since the founding of the People's Republic in 1949 (*Beijing Review* 1995a).

CHINA'S NEW LABOR LAWS

The new codified Labor Law of the PRC was enacted by the National People's Congress in July 1994, and came into effect on January 1, 1995.[15] There are some notable changes in the law as codified. However, the code is largely drawn from the separate laws, rules, and decisions applicable up to then variously to state-owned, collective, private, and foreign invested enterprises. The codification of the Labor Law follows similar codification of the Trade Union Law which was adopted in April 1992, and came into effect at the same time.[16]

The Labor Law prominently enunciates the workers' "right to choose a job," a significant change from the assigned placement of the planned economy. However, this choice does not carry with it anything like the "right to work," or the assurance of a job for one's working life upon assignment, the so-called "iron rice-bowl" assumed in the old system.

There are many other "rights" and protections under the Labor Law, for instance, the right to be paid, to have rest days and holidays, to protective measures in the workplace, to training to improve skills, to guarantees against discrimination on the basis of race, nationality, sex, or religion, to a minimum wage set by the local government, to a contract setting out work and pay conditions, to a working week limited to 44 hours and six days, and to an eight-hour working day, to overtime that is limited and compensated at a set rate. There are also special provisions to prohibit child labor below the age of 16, and for the protection of women, including pregnancy leave and 90 days leave after childbirth. Dispute committees are to be set up in the workplace to include both employers and workers. And there are provisions covering social security, health insurance, workers' compensation, and pensions.

The promulgation of the Labor Law shows that the government has not simply been sitting idly by in the face of deteriorating labor conditions in China. But the official view of what is accomplished here is sometimes a little rosier than practical experience warrants. In a review of the new situation, especially with regard to the FIEs, the *Beijing Review* informs us:

> According to an official in the Labor Relations Bureau of the Labor Ministry, the Chinese labor force is now split into two groups because of their job selection priorities—those who value higher pay go into foreign or private businesses, whereas those who place importance on welfare (including housing, health care, and pension) stay in the public sector. He said, "This is sometimes a dilemma since most wish they could have the best of both" (*Beijing Review* 1995b, p. 19).

In reality, of course, most workers have no such choice. True, there are now private and foreign invested enterprises. But the former are often the last resort: small vendor stands run by workers who have lost all else, are retired or unemployed,[17] and the latter are often the abusive sweatshops described earlier, often long distances from workers' home villages, and many preferring to offer places to pliant teenage girls, not to heads of families seeking steady and reliable sources of family income.

However, corruption appears not to be confined to the squeeze that local officials can put on entrepreneurs in the coastal FIEs. Reports tell us that it may also reach down to the level of heartland villages where migrant peasant workers who make the "choice" to find work in FIEs are under pressure to buy off their own local cadres with an advance share of the riches they aspire to earn for the privilege of relocating to the coastal enterprise zones: "After paying local cadres as much as a year's salary for permission to travel, off they go to the coastal areas where the factory jobs are" (*FEER* 1994c, p. 35). Yet once they reach the SEZs there may be another payoff required by the local labor bureau for permission to take a job there.

If, however, workers stay just beyond the limits of the SEZs—as, for example, in Baoan County in Guangdong Province, which lies just outside the Shenzhen SEZ across the border from Hong Kong—there is theoretically no legal barrier to relocating to the area, but here wages are substantially lower (recently wage levels in Shenzhen were two to five times higher than in Baoan), and work safety standards and labor law protections may be ignored by the local authorities.[18]

IS THIS "SOCIAL MARKET ECONOMY"?

From the above description of the codification of the new Labor Law we can see that this is no mean accomplishment for a country with virtually no civil law only 20 years ago. Significantly, this law is not intended to apply only to foreign invested enterprises, as has been the case with much of the law enacted since 1979. Moreover, we hear that the courts—and that there are courts for this purpose—are beginning to enforce the Labor Law, at least in the case of the worst abuses. In the case of the woman beaten and locked into a dog cage for stealing two pairs of athletic shoes, we read that the court jailed her assailant and would have arrested her employer had he not fled the country (*Hsien Tai* 1994). There have been no reports, so far, of proceedings against those who expose workers to dangerous chemicals and fumes, such as those reported earlier. Officials have been reluctant to bring cases for environmental health reasons against FIEs for fear of alarming them about the potential rising costs of doing business. On the other hand, there have been arrests and trials in cases where disasters with considerable loss of life have occurred as the result of FIE negligence. In 1993 six people were arrested after a fire in a Hong Kong-owned toy factory in Zhili where 84 workers were killed and 40 more injured; these six included the managing director, the owner, and two fire officials accused of bribery and misconduct. Investigators found that overloaded electrical wiring and improper storage of inflammable materials had led to the fire.

In this context, the Ministry of Labor revealed the extent of the problem requiring safety regulations enforcement: 28,200 cases of industrial fires in the first 10 months of 1993, causing 1,480 deaths and 51,340 injuries. Yet bad as this situation is, only 10 percent of the 146 factory fires occurred in FIEs. In other words, it appears that there is a similar problem of enforcement of the safety regulations in state-owned enterprises (see *China Labour Bulletin* 1994).

Where are we, then, on the road to "socialism with Chinese characteristics"? If legislation is the measure, then surely the Labor Law has made an enviable start. How many countries can boast a contract system for all employed labor, a full panoply of social insurance measures, and limits on working hours and holiday provision to compare with those of the most advanced democratic socialist regimes in the West?[19]

The enforcement mechanism is, however, still plainly wanting. Safety and environmental and working conditions in FIEs are recognized to be atrocious. A standard complaint of all—the authorities, the press, and the workers—is that there is practically no evidence so far of the contract system in practice. Workers in Hong Kong, Taiwan, and Korea-owned FIEs are known to be working well beyond the legal hours. In addition, in a system based on the appeal of higher wages than in the state-owned enterprises there is widespread complaint of wage arrears. With all of these social and worker complaints, how can a state with the most dedicated social conscience call this "socialism"?

The ideologists, who dare, like to blame the "market" side of this "socialist market system." But what about the label of "socialist market system" itself? True, there seems to be a wide open attitude of welcome for the most self-seeking elements of small business Asian entrepreneurialism. But are these Asian businesspeople exploitative because they are "capitalists"? Some of them seem to have amassed a certain amount of personal wealth. But there is not really much "capital" invested in either their FIEs or in their overall business structure.

Actually, development in Taiwan and Hong Kong was largely labor-intensive itself. There was perhaps not so much capital as leveraged capital involved. Especially in Taiwan, foreign or overseas Chinese loans were often secured with government guarantees, enabling the developing country to import technology, which they paid for by creating exports. Does that make these newly wealthy entrepreneurs "capitalists"? Or just ingenious at putting to good use the capital of other investors? And are they unfeeling because they are "capitalists"? Or because they also grew up in the school of hard knocks and have no special compassion for those in their former situation?

But what about the rubric "socialist market system" itself? Siegfried Karsten has written two learned articles describing the "social market economy," the economic system developed in West Germany in the years of the so-called "economic miracle," the recovery and development in the years following the Second World War (Karsten 1985, 1988). In the latter article he writes:

"*Socialism* with *Chinese* characteristics resembles a modified version of Eucken's paradigm of a social market economy" (Karsten 1988, p. 129).

Surely this can be true only on paper, and only with regard to such model examples as the Labor Code. Otherwise the concept of the "social market economy" is completely misplaced for the PRC. Not because China does not aspire to make its attempts at market economics serve social goals—after first serving the purpose of national development—but because Eucken, and all those around him, as Karsten himself describes, and especially those involved in the writing of the new West German federal constitution, were committed to the creation of the paradigm liberal democracy.

As we have seen from the outset, "individualistic liberalism" and "bourgeois liberalization" are not among the approved goals of the authors of "socialism with Chinese characteristics." Peter Nolan has successfully captured the spirit of the current social philosophy in China when he compares it to the "NEP," the New Economic Policy, the easing of economic policy in the Soviet Union in the 1920s:

> "Market socialism" was the overarching philosophy of the economic system in the 1980s, albeit that the term "socialist market economy" was not formally enunciated as the guiding principle of economic organisation until as late as 1992. The overall framework strongly resembled that of NEP (New Economic Policy) in the Soviet Union in the mid-1920s and in China itself in the early 1950s. The old Stalinist system of direct administrative planning was rejected decisively in favour of one in which markets and their related incentives were viewed as necessary to effective functioning of the economy. In the 1980s public enterprises were given greatly increased independence in production, marketing, and the disposal of their income. However, since then key party documents have consistently spoken of the economy as one in which public ownership, planning, and "socialist" values are central to socio-economic life (Nolan 1994, p. 5).

Yet, ideology will not do it alone either. When it comes to the nature of the social abuses occurring every day in FIEs—and to a lesser degree perhaps in state-owned enterprises—of the PRC, "socialist law" and practical "social" concerns will have to manifest themselves in much more tangible ways, before China today can compare itself with the democratic socialist countries of the West in caring for the needs of its citizens.

ACKNOWLEDGMENTS

This paper was prepared in part with research and production support of a Direct Allocation Grant from the Research Grants Council of the Hong Kong University Grants Committee. The author would also like to thank Mr. Lee Sheung-wah for his assistance and those students of the School of Business and Management of the Hong Kong University of Science and Technology who helped in collecting material.

NOTES

1. Mao (1967) taught that "liberalism rejects ideological struggle and stands for unprincipled peace" and that therefore "liberalism is extremely harmful in a revolutionary collective." But his admirers went much further in the conviction that Mao's thought had provided the inspiration for a "New Man."

2. Intellectually, there should be no way to connect the Cultural Revolution and the call for "participatory democracy," though some adherents of the latter seem to have drawn reinforcement of their beliefs from the political action of the former. The desire for "participatory democracy" appears to have arisen as nostalgia for times when the New England town meeting played a more vital role involving local citizens in the issues of their small communities, and from American populist drives for a public voice in such measures as recall, referendum, and initiative. The call for a new populism combined with a critique on representative democracy is examined by Pateman (1970).

Despite this "critique," the movement seemed ultimately to belong to more collectivist "progressive" liberal thought. For Mao, deference to public opinion must not lead to "abdication of leadership" of the party, or the error known as the "tail principle" (Mao 1954, p. 44). Moreover, Mao himself warns of the dangers of "ultra-democracy" and of "absolute equalitarianism" (Mao 1968).

3. It should be pointed out that "building socialism with Chinese characteristics" has now been raised to a fundamental, constitutional principle of the PRC, alongside adherence to Marxism-Leninism and the thought of Mao Tse-tung (CCH International 1994, pp. 5, 303; *China Law for Foreign Business,* Vol. 1, Constitution, "Preamble").

4. For a survey of the literature on these developments, see, for example, Rich 1981; Wang 1981; Holtzmann and Surrey 1980; Cohen 1983.

The intervening years have also seen a multitude of individual and group efforts to update studies of ongoing developments in business practice in China. For a summary of developments in law and taxation in China, see Edwards and Ringleb 1990; Buckley and Jehle 1990). Among the more innovative of the recent commercial studies of business organizations in China today is Freeman (1994).

5. See Weggel (1976). This includes an extensive bibliography of earlier major works in this area (pp. 479-482). For this reader, Weggel's contribution is fundamental to a systematic approach to understanding the conceptual framework of law in China and of trade with the PRC, and should not be overlooked in the pressure to be current.

6. The author is also persuaded that legal protections for foreign investors must lead in time to a call for legal protections for ordinary workers and individuals (see Lee 1983, p. 257). To some extent this has already happened in the introduction of laws to permit private enterprise and laws to protect labor. But this is not to say that certain limited legal protections by themselves are tantamount to satisfying all the expectations of liberal democracy.

7. "Zhuhai tragedy firm locks fire exits during protest." *South China Morning Post* (Hong Kong), July 5, 1994. This report occurred when the Hong Kong partner company locked fire exits to prevent protesters from the labor movement in Hong Kong from entering the plant, but was forced to unlock them by the Hong Kong Fire Services Department; see also "Zhuhai lesson ignored." *South China Morning Post*, June 28, 1994, p. 2.

8. See Asia Monitor Resources Center for Coalition for the Charter on the Safe Production of Toys (1995, 1996a, 1996b); also *Toronto Star* (1995); *Sunday Morning Post* (1993). See also China Labour Education and Information Centre (1996).

9. They (*International Labour Review* 1994) cite as sources *China Daily* (Beijing), June 23 and September 12, 1992, and *Financial Times*, April 24-25, 1993.

10. In November 1995, the *China Labour Bulletin* (Hong Kong) reported that since the late 1980s there had been "a growing number of labour protests such as wild-cat strikes and independent labour organizing" in Guangdong province, where the majority of export-processing ventures are located. They continue that: "Alarmed by the growing militancy of the workers, the authorities

set up work committees in the 'problem plants' comprising officials from local ACFTU [All China Federation of Trade Unions] branches, labour bureaux and the PSB [Public Security Bureau] whose jobs are to monitor and pre-empt any independent labour organizing initiatives." Special Issue, November, 1995, p. 10.

11. One of the incidents described in the cited reply to the PRC 1994 White Paper, *On the Situation of Women in China*, is a 1993 report of several hundred workers at a toy factory in Zhuhai SEZ who were dismissed when they went on strike and refused a company offer (CLEIC 1995).

12. From a speech by Shek Ping-kwan, Executive Secretary of the Hong Kong Christian Industrial Committee, April 30, 1996, seeking to promote a Hong Kong coalition *Charter on the Safe Production of Toys* and criticizing the multinationals' reliance on their own independent codes of conduct.

13. See, for example, Wang You-chin (Consultant, Dunstan Styles & Co., Hong Kong, and Law Consultant, Shenzhen District People's Government), and Xiamen District People's Government. 1995. "Difficulties with the Implementation of the Labor Law" (in Chinese). *Hua Nan Ching Chi Hsin Wen* (*South China Economic News*) (Hong Kong), January 26: p. 12.

14. Saitch (1993) cites a *Xinhua* report that appeared in *Japan Economic Newswire*, October 22, 1992, pp. 177-192.

15. The text as published in *Renmin Ribao* was translated and included with a summary as Appendix 2 in Warner (1995). The codified labor law is also to be used as a model for six additional laws covering social insurance, work safety, and labor supervision (see *Beijing Review* 1995c).

16. A translation is included as Appendix 1 in Warner (1995, pp. 167-175).

17. Since the early 1980s regulations have been relaxed allowing individuals to go into business for themselves. However, such persons, and their employees, were also required to leave the work unit and relinquish attendant claims on housing, health insurance, and pensions. Susan McEwen (1994, p. 36) summarizes the steps necessary to register as a small business entrepreneur: "Once these preliminary steps are completed [i.e., police, health, safety, and licensing checks] the *geti bu* or *siying qiye* [i.e., businesses limited to seven employees or eight or more] must register with the local bureau of industry and commerce. Entrepreneurs must submit proof of residence, a declaration of the scope and location of the business, a description of the equipment to be used, and proof of sufficient capital. Depending on the specific industry sector, *siying qiye* must also fulfil certain capital requirements. All private enterprise owners must prove their work status when registering. To do this, the owner must present a former identification card, unemployment or retirement certification, or a certificate of approval from his former *danwei* [work unit]."

18. See *Far Eastern Economic Review* (1992b) The situation may have improved in Baoan itself since this report was written in 1992. At that time, it was expected that the Shenzhen SEZ might be expanded to include Baoan, which would have the initial effect of depressing wages in the SEZ by doubling the size of the labor pool. It would also have applied the labor protection rules in force in Shenzhen to Baoan. However, the codification of the Labor Law in January 1995 has done that in any case, whether or not there is the will or local capability to enforce it.

19. For shortcomings of the new Labor Law—absence of "right to strike," "right to organize independent trade unions," "freedom of political belief," and "employment security" see *China Labour Bulletin* No. 6, August, 1994, p. 7; see also No. 7, September, 1994, pp. 1-4.

REFERENCES

Asia Monitor Resource Center (Ed.). 1995. *Conditions of Workers in the Shoe Industry of China*. Hong Kong.

Asia Monitor Resources Center for Coalition for the Charter on the Safe Production of Toys (Ed.). 1996a. *Labour Rights Report on Hong Kong-Invested Toy Factories in China*. Hong Kong.

Asia Monitor Resource Center (Ed.). 1996b. *Pearl River Delta Labour Rights Report.* Hong Kong.

Beijing Review. 1995a. "China Keeps Crackdown on Corruption" (March 27-April 2): 6.

Beijing Review. 1995b. "A New Problem—Labor Relations in Foreign Enterprises" (May 15-21): 17-19.

Beijing Review. 1995c. "New Laws Gear Up Legislative Procession" (January 16-22): 6.

Buckley, P.J., and E. Jehle. 1990. "Forms of Entrepreneurial Cooperation between Chinese and Foreign Enterprises: Taxation Implications." In *Joint Ventures and Industrial Change in China: Advances in Chinese Industrial Studies, Volume 1* [*Part B*], edited by N. Campbell and J.S. Henley. Greenwich, CT: JAI Press.

Campbell, N., and J. Zhang. 1994. "The Pattern of EJVs in China, 1979-1989." Pp. 3-12 in *Joint Ventures in the People's Republic of China: Advances in Chinese Industrial Studies, Volume 4*, edited by S. Stewart. Greenwich CT: JAI Press.

CCH International. 1994. *China Law for Foreign Business, Volume 1.* #4 Constitution. N. Ryde, N.S.W.: CCH Australia, Ltd.

Chew, D.C.E. 1990. "Recent Developments in Civil Service Pay in China." *International Labour Review* 129.6: 773-782.

China Labour Education and Information Centre. 1996. *The Flip-side of Success: The Situation of Workers and Organising in Foreign-invested Electronics Enterprises in Guangdong.* Hong Kong.

China Labour Bulletin. 1994. "Employers Arrested and Worker Executed for Factory Fires" (March): 11.

China Labour Education and Information Centre (CLEIC). 1995. *The UN Official Report: Women Workers in China.* Hong Kong.

Cohen, J. 1983. *Legal Aspects of Doing Business in China.* New York: PLI.

Deng Xiaoping. 1984. *Build Socialism with Chinese Characteristics.* Beijing: Foreign Languages Press.

Deng Xiaoping. 1994. *Selected Works of Deng Xiaoping, Volume III (1982-1992).* Beijing: Foreign Languages Press.

Dong Dui Yue Han (*Contemporary Monthly*). 1994. "Unspeakable Working Conditions in Three FIEs" (May 15): 42-45 (In Chinese).

Edwards, F.L., and A.H. Ringleb. 1990. "Joint Ventures in China: the Impact of the Legal Environment in Attracting Technology Transfers." In *Joint Ventures and Industrial Change in China: Advances in Chinese Industrial Studies,* Volume 1 (Part B), edited by N. Campbell and J.S. Henley. Greenwich, CT: JAI Press.

Far Eastern Economic Review (*FEER*). 1992a. "The China Connection: Nike is making the most of all that cheap labour" (November 5): 60.

Far Eastern Economic Review (*FEER*). 1992b. "The Sweat Shops Nearby" (May 14): 28-29.

Far Eastern Economic Review (*FEER*). 1994a. "Social Engineers" (April 14): 56-60.

Far Eastern Economic Review (*FEER*). 1994b. "Levi's Law" (April 14): 60.

Far Eastern Economic Review (*FEER*). 1994c. "No Workers' Paradise: Labour activists make little headway in Shenzhen" (June 14): 35-36.

Freeman, D. (Ed.). 1994. *The Life and Death of a Joint Venture in China.* Hong Kong: Asia Law & Practice.

Holtzmann, H.M., and W.S. Surrey (Eds.). 1980. *A New Look at Legal Aspects of Doing Business with China.* New York: PLI.

Hsien Tai (*Modern Daily*). 1994. "Jailed for a Year for Putting Woman Worker into a Dog Cage" (November 4) (In Chinese).

International Labour Review. 1994. "China: Industrial Fatalities Grow Alongside Economic Activity," p. 128.

Karsten, S. 1985. "'Social Market Economy' and its Test in Post-War West Germany: The Economist as Social Philosopher Developed Ideas that Paralleled Progressive Thought in America." *American Journal of Economics and Sociology* 44 (2): 169-183.

Karsten, S. 1988. "China's Approach to Social Market Economics: The Chinese Variant of Market Socialism Seeks to Escape from the Difficulties of Central Command Planning." *American Journal of Economics and Sociology* 47 (2): 129-148.

Lee, O. 1983. "Formation of Contract and Contract Law through Multinational Joint Ventures: Indonesia, China, and the Third World." *The International Lawyer* 17: 257.

Mao Tse-tung. 1954. *Selected Works. Volume 1, 1926-1936.* New York: International Publishers.

Mao Tse-tung. 1968. "On Correcting Mistaken Ideas in the Party." In *Five Articles by Chairman Mao Tse-tung*. Beijing: Foreign Languages Press.

Mao Tse-Tung 1967. *Combat Liberalism*. Beijing: Foreign Languages Press.

McEwen, S. 1994. "New Kids on the Block." *China Business Review* (May-June): 36.

Nolan, P. 1994. "Introduction: The Chinese Puzzle." In *China's Economic Reforms: The Costs and Benefits of Incrementalism*, edited by Q. Fan and P. Nolan. London: Macmillan; New York: St Martin's Press.

Pateman, C. 1970. *Participation and Democratic Theory*. Cambridge, UK: Cambridge University Press.

PRC Government. 1994. *On the Situation of Women in China.* White Paper. Beijing, June 2.

Rich, F.C. 1981. "Joint Ventures in China: The Legal Challenge." *The International Lawyer* 15: 181.

Saitch, T. 1993. "The Fourteenth Party Congress: A Programme for Authoritarian Rule." *The China Quarterly* 132 (December): 1136-1160.

Shek P-K. 1996a. *Reebok, Don't do empty talks with Human Rights.* A flier in the series *Change*. Hong Kong: Hong Kong Christian Industrial Committee (February).

Shek P-K. 1996b. *Mourn for the Deaths. Fight for the Lives!* A flier in the series *Change*. Hong Kong: Hong Kong Christian Industrial Committee (April).

Stone, B.S. 1994. "Sino-Foreign Joint Ventures and Governmental Corruption." Pp. 29-48 in *Joint Ventures in the People's Republic of China: Advances in Chinese Industrial Studies, Volume 4*, edited by S. Stewart. Greenwich, CT: JAI Press.

Sunday Morning Post (Hong Kong). 1993. "Hong Kong Firms Rapped Over Safety" (November 21): 3.

Toronto Star. 1995. "There's no Joy for Workers at China's Toy Sweatshops" (December 17): A24.

Wang, G. 1994. "Introduction and Overview." Pp. xi-xiv in *Joint Ventures in the People's Republic of China: Advances in Chinese Industrial Studies, Volume 4*, edited by S. Stewart. Greenwich CT: JAI Press.

Wang, N.T. 1981. "New Forms of Business Cooperation Between China and International Enterprises." *China International Business* 11.

Warner, M. 1995. *The Management of Human Resources in Chinese Industry*. London: Macmillan; New York: St Martin's Press.

Weggel, O. 1976. *Das Aussenhandelsrecht der Volksrepublik China* (*The Foreign Trade Law of the People's Republic of China*). Baden-Baden: Nomos.

Ya Chou Chan Kan (*Asia Weekly Magazine*). 1994. "A lesson in blood and fire." Hong Kong, June 26 (In Chinese).

Ya Chou Chou Han (*Asia Weekly*). 1995. "Zhuhai Korean FIE punishes [Workers] for dispute by making them kneel down." Hong Kong, April 9, p. 64 (In Chinese).

Zhang, S. Q. 1997. "Strategic Intentions of Parent Companies and Intellectual Property Rights in Joint Ventures." In *A Coming of Age: Developments in Sino-Foreign Joint Ventures: Advances in Chinese Industrial Studies, Volume 5*, edited by S. Stewart and A. Carver. Greenwich, CT: JAI Press.

INDUSTRIAL RELATIONS IN JOINT VENTURES IN CHINA: A REVISIT

Ng Sek-Hong

INTRODUCTION

Foreign capital has been welcomed in the People's Republic of China (PRC) for almost 20 years, since it was readmitted in the mid-1970s when the ambitious "Four Modernizations" were launched and the economy opened up to capital invested by sources from outside the country. In retrospect the foreign-funded enterprises, including joint ventures, have been a pioneering force not only on the frontier of productivity and technological innovation, but also in managerial and labor market reforms for a nation in search for a new realm of "market socialism."

The question worth investigating—after these years of experiments to advance "socialism with Chinese characteristics"—is whether the once "enclaved" practices adopted in these foreign-owned enterprises will be increasingly emulated by their native counterparts in the state-owned sector, now in a vigorous process of restructuring and rationalization, as suggested

Advances in Chinese Industrial Studies, Volume 5, pages 191-216.

ISBN: 1-55938-961-3

by the theory of "institutional convergence" brought about by the unifying imperative of "industrialism" (having its inner logic) (Kerr, Dunlop, Harbison, and Myers 1973). Also, inasmuch as a divide is still ascertainable between state-owned enterprises (SOEs) and foreign-invested enterprises (FIEs) in areas such as workplace industrial relations and human resources practices, is it legitimate to interpret the diversities in terms of a new state of "dualism"—which can appear to coalesce with the imaginative concept which China has recently canvassed in the "one country, two systems" formula as the blueprint to integrate and unify China across the Mainland, Taiwan, and Hong Kong (Deng 1985, p. 31).[1] It is around the theme of these two alternative perspectives that this paper intends to review the situation of workplace industrial relations in joint ventures and other foreign-funded enterprises in the PRC.

IS THE FOREIGN-INVESTED ENTERPRISE SECTOR A "PRIMARY" ENCLAVE IN THE LABOR MARKET?

The general impression has been that foreign-funded businesses have, since their reentry into China, enjoyed a substantial latitude of autonomy in personnel decision making. Joint ventures are heralded as the trendsetters, pioneering the flow of nationwide managerial reforms and innovations. Those in Guangdong Province, for instance, have been distinctive in their ability to attract "personnel of senior secondary graduates and above" by paying attractively high wages (Sit and Wong 1990, pp. 224-225, also pp. 222-223 and 158). The autonomy hitherto extended by the state to these foreign enterprises, enabling them to organize their wage and personnel activities almost independently, is hardly distinguishable from the logic of the free labor market of capitalist societies. Since the beginning of the 1990s their manpower utilization has become even more market responsive because of such newly sanctioned personnel practices as contract worker hiring, practices which were quickly emulated in state enterprises and other domestic collectives. Apparently, the enhanced flexibilities experienced in these labor market practices have displaced and helped break down the socialist system of central manpower allocation, now rejected for its widespread rigidities and lack of human incentives and initiatives. These reforms have far-reaching implications not only for human resource management in both foreign-funded and state enterprises, but also for the work agenda of Chinese trade unions.

In this connection, the paradoxical mix of hospitality and apprehension toward foreign guest capital (which dates back to the imperial Manchu reign, the 1911 Revolution, and the Nationalist-led Republic in the earlier decades of this century, epitomized in such anachronistic institutions as the "unequal treaties" and "foreign settlements" and the instigation of large-scale industrial upheavals like the Canton-Hong Kong Strike-Boycott of 1925-1926) has created a mood of national ambivalence. This attitude can be seen in the complicated legislative code that the state evolved in the 1980s for governing the activities of foreign capital in China. These legal prescriptions, intended to enshrine the special privileges extended to foreign businesses as incentives, and induced by a historic anxiety to hold the "aliens" under rein, have, inter alia, sanctioned the strategic role of the Chinese trade union to act both as ambassador, in bridging links with foreign employers, and as protector of Chinese workers hired in FIEs—a dualistic set of "agency" roles that are, however, not always compatible.

State Law: Regulation, Concession, and the Role of the Union

The principal legal instrument governing labor-management relations in the foreign business sector is the *Regulations for the Implementation of the Law of the People's Republic of China on Joint Ventures Using Chinese and Foreign Investment*, promulgated by the state council in September 1983. It was preceded by the *Regulations of the People's Republic of China for Labour-Management in Chinese Foreign Joint Ventures* of July 1980. By virtue of these provisions, the foreign employer is legally obliged to recognize a workplace union organization, part of the national labor movement under the All-China Federation of Trade Unions (ACFTU). Chapter 13 of the *Regulations for the Implementation of the Law in Joint Ventures* is devoted to the subject of recognition and functions of grass-roots unions inside these enterprises. Article 95 guarantees to the workforce of a joint venture enterprise the basic right to "set up grass-roots trade unions and carry out trade union activities" in the same fashion as governed by China's Trade Union Law and the Articles of Association of Chinese Trade Unions. Yet, Article 39 of the same set of regulations explicitly acknowledges and supports the prerogative of the foreign enterprise management by confirming their autonomy. It is hence reminiscent of the legal status of the employment contract (and relationship) in Western capitalist society that the regulations of 1983 declare that "the general manager shall...empowered...by the board, have the right to appoint and dismiss his subordinates, and exercise other responsibilities and rights as authorized by the board within the joint venture" (Article 39).

The union, however, enjoys a legal right under the regulations to arrange labor contracts on behalf of individual workers and is responsible for their enforcement (Article 99). The union is also the means by which the welfare and bonus funds held by the enterprise are regulated, jointly with management (Article 97), the provision of which is sanctioned by Article 10 of the ancillary *Regulations for Labour-Management in Chinese-Foreign Joint Ventures*. Where the foreign-funded enterprise is exempted from an obligation to establish a workplace union organ, the union is to act, ipso facto, as the sole agent to act on behalf of the entire workforce. These measures seem to suggest an official anxiety to prescribe an obligation in foreign businesses to recognize and to deal with Chinese trade unions at the enterprise level, as the representative organ acting on behalf the Chinese workers in their employ.

The 1983 Regulations also make the provision of specified facilities for the workplace union organization obligatory for foreign enterprises. The foreign employer is required to furnish the union with space to house the union's office and its meetings, and back-up for it to organize welfare, cultural, and sports activities. As in the case of the state-owned enterprise, a fund amounting to a standard 2 percent equivalent of the enterprise's payroll must be subscribed by the foreign employer to support the house union and its activities.

However, in spite of these legal arrangements of the state for the ACFTU to organize FIEs, the national trade union center has always reckoned as problematic the regulation of industrial relations and laboring standards in these workplaces. The explanation of these problems is complex, but in many instances it reflects the lingering psychology of Chinese ambivalence, rooted in history, toward foreigners and the hegemony of their capitalist penetration into the country. The dualistic dictum of having to welcome as well as to "tame" alien investors probably helps shape and sustain the ACFTU's neurosis harbored about FIEs. In addition, it has resulted in a new field of workplace industrial relations which, although still distinctive because of the variety of officially sanctioned concessions extended to the foreign-funded sector, is likely to be replicated, at least in part, in state-owned enterprises, which are going through a vigorous process of renewal. However, is it legitimate to look upon FIEs in China as the standard-bearers of advances and innovations in labor market reforms and labor-management restructuring in order to achieve the enshrined ideal of market socialism? To answer this question, a review of the development of the joint venture approach and practice of human resource management since the early 1980s among FIEs may provide a glimpse of the shifting industrial relations situation in this sector.

Human Resources in Joint Ventures and China's Labor Market Reforms

It appears that labor market reforms in China began with the foreign-invested sector as the standard-bearer, piloting innovations which were later emulated by the SOEs. In the Shenzhen Special Economic Zone, for example, all foreign-funded enterprises have, since 1983, substituted the recruitment of workers by the centrally allocated system with contract labor arrangements. All foreign enterprises have, since the early 1980s, enjoyed a latitude of freedom in their wage and personnel activities that approximates to the free labor market of capitalist societies. Joint ventures in Guangdong Province have "demonstrated a high degree of flexibility in the most critical aspects of operation," notably in paying high wages to "provide sufficient incentive" to the workforce and "attracting personnel of senior secondary graduates and above" (Sit and Wong 1990, pp. 224-225; also pp. 222-223 and 158). This flexibility has been increased by the practice of hiring contract workers, the system of labor hiring ratified by the PRC government in 1986, by virtue of a body of regulations reforming the nationwide system of permanent lifelong employment which was the mainstream practice prior to the labor market reforms.

Dualism in Human Resource Management and Implications for Joint Venture Partnership

In spite of the advances that joint ventures represented in their labor market freedom and flexibilities, FIEs still appeared to be subject to considerable restrictive constraints due to pre-reform practices and institutional controls. One major source of these institutional limits, at least before the resumption and enhancement of the reform policies heralded by Deng Xiaoping's Southern Tour to the coastal provinces, was the unwritten rule that personnel administration be placed under the jurisdiction of the Chinese partner, preserving an implicit "home versus alien" divide, in spite of their business collaboration. The internal demarcation of spheres of influence is vividly narrated in Pearson's report:

> The personnel manager uniformly came from the Chinese side. Chinese personnel managers and Chinese deputy general managers in most cases had final authority over disciplinary actions taken against workers....Indeed, many foreign managers reported strong and successful resistance from the Chinese partner or from local labour authorities to their efforts to fire workers.... Moreover, in labour decisions that required negotiations between partners (such as increasing or decreasing wages), the Chinese deputy general manager sometimes claimed to represent the workers against management (Pearson 1991, p. 173)

Thus it could be said that the Chinese partner or manager became a de facto agency or labor service subcontractor acting on behalf of the foreign partner, especially in the early days of joint ventures. This was vaguely reminiscent of the "comprador" role performed by the Hong Kong staff of British trading houses dealing with China in the last century, because of a mutuality of alienness between the visitors' and the hosts' culture and interests. However, the negative implications of such jurisdictional demarcations were obvious in that they upheld an overtly bureaucratic and parochial "us-and-them" divide which not only kept the foreign and Chinese sides at managerial level separate, but also insulated foreign capital from any direct dialogue, haggling, and control vis-à-vis the laboring masses. What emanated in some joint ventures could therefore be a false situation of labor-management relations which gave the foreign managing partner the impression that the joint venture was tantamount to a labor or service subcontracting shop, where industrial relations either were irrelevant or could be conveniently ignored because of the Chinese intermediary "buffer." Given that such a delegated jurisdiction would suggest an almost laissez-faire detachment of the foreign partner toward any in-house human resource issues, it was logical to suspect that the latitude of autonomy granted to foreign-funded business could be more apparent then real in the joint ventures. What existed in some JV enterprises could be such practices as disclosed by Pearson: "It was possible, for instance, that wages paid in joint ventures to Chinese workers did not go directly to the individual worker but, rather, were distributed through the local labour bureau, to the Chinese partner's 'danwei', or to the labour organizations" (Pearson 1991, p. 173).

Divisions in the Overseas Funded Sector

Within the FIE sector a heterogeneity of arrangements actually proliferated, rather than a uniform pattern of human resources pervading across the diversity of overseas business and investments belonging to different industries and ethnic ownership. Child has added to this spectrum of diversified practice by making explicit the role of such variables as the centralization of control on strategic decisions desired by the foreign partner; as well as the rationale of the overseas participation as whether it was basically to search for a production base or to secure an inroad into, and consolidate a share in, the lucrative market of the mainland. In the former case, human resource organization tended to remain more indigenous with the Chinese partner or deputy manager acting as a labor subcontractor or agent, subject to loose control from the foreign partner. Personnel management practices in this type of joint venture situation hardly represented the innovative characteristics accorded to the stereotyped image of the foreign-funded sector as primary trendsetting employers, but instead could be potential grounds for depressant labor conditions, and this has worried ACFTU. Child summarized a characteristic profile:

> These are low technology products requiring relatively simple production processes. Both the level of investment and time-scale of the foreign partner tended to be limited. The foreign partner has therefore generally not felt the need to intervene a great deal in the Chinese management process, except to ensure productivity and quality standards. The Chinese operation is primarily a sub-contracting one, with wider commercial, financial and product development matters being retained by the foreign company (Child 1994, p. 253).

Labor Market Segmentation and the Vicissitudes of Foreign Capital in the "Secondary" Sector

The "secondary" sector of joint venture business was and is still vulnerable to the notorious sweatshop style of hiring Chinese labor at the whim of capital drawn "by the attraction of low cost labour as a manufacturing base and export platform for products" (Child 1994, p. 253). At this lower end of the overseas investment sector, which includes a sizable contingent of cross-border capital transfer and migration from Hong Kong, Macau, and Taiwan, the wage factor is the nexus of incentive in attracting Chinese workers (which has in turn helped sustain the stampede of the mobile rural labor to the cities). However, it is apparent that the vicissitudes of industrial capital are most conspicuous in this type of workplace: overcrowding, substandard and insanitary conditions of shopfloors and dormitories, and a sequence of factory fires and other industrial hazards and accidents are widely reported in the press. These propensities toward industrial impoverishments (in work and working conditions) suggest a lower or "secondary" tier in the labor market of the joint venture sector which has been isolated, raising the basic issue of work humanization and labor protection under the squeeze of unscrupulous outside investors. That the aristocratic image of employment in the foreign capital sector can be highly illusory is demonstrated graphically in the following commentary:

> Since the late 1970s, foreign capital has been introduced into China in a greater and greater scale....Chinese workers' "fifteen years" of experience in this sector has shattered many of their illusions about foreign capital. These workers' own experience furnishes a stark contrast to the frequently made claim that foreign firms or joint ventures scrupulously abide by international laws and conventions. The behaviour of many such firms is in reality a fairly dramatic departure from the image of themselves they like to project. In Guangdong, for instance, firms with foreign capital always elaborate on the responsibilities and liabilities of the workers in the labour contract....Many of the firms set extraordinarily high task quotas of workers, in some cases 50-60 percent higher than that set for workers in the country providing the capital. Overtime is always adopted as an effective way to extract extra profit from the workers. Some firms force their workers to work as much as 134 hours' overtime per month, severely violating the limit of 48 hours per week set by the Chinese government. Many workers become so exhausted by overtime that they faint in the shopfloor....Compulsory overtime is also used by many foreign firms or joint ventures in other parts of the country (Feng 1996, pp. 26-27).

A host of such complaints presented to the ACFTU have been reported in other industrial centers like Shanghai, Beijing, and Shenzhen (Feng 1996, p. 27). Apprehensive about these reported workplace abuses while being aware that both the state and the Chinese workers attach a high premium to the lucrative employment opportunities that these enterprises afford, the ACFTU has responded by enhancing its organization work in this type of workplace. The ACFTU places its faith upon the presence of grass-roots unions as the most efficacious safeguard in protecting the legitimate rights and interests of the Chinese employees. Part of the trade union center's national agenda laid down at its 12th National Congress in October 1993 propagated, accordingly, the importance of strengthening the work of the Chinese trade unions in the foreign-funded enterprises (ACTFU 1994, p. 35).

The ACFTU Agenda and Foreign-Invested Enterprises

The 12th National Congress detailed an elaborate set of guidelines for the Chinese labor movement and its union organs in dealing with FIEs. The instructions for governing labor-management activities in this sector were, in summary:

1. Trade unions should be established at the earliest opportunity in enterprises already in operation, while preparatory work of organizing unions should be started simultaneously with the preparation of any new enterprise.
2. The political status and legitimate rights of the workforce in FIEs are "naturally" protected by the State Constitution, as masters of the country.
3. Trade unions are to safeguard the legitimate rights and interests of workers and staff members in these enterprises; and to cooperate and work together with investors in order to strive jointly for the development of the enterprise "to serve the masses of workers and staff members" and to contribute to promoting reforms and opening to the outside and the economic construction"; moreover, "trade unions should support the legitimate operations of enterprises."
4. Trade unions should sign collective contracts with enterprises on workers' behalf with enterprises and help workers and staff members to sign individual labor contracts with enterprises and supervise the implementation of these contracts.
5. Trade unions should check and supervise the implementation of state laws and regulations on wages, working hours, social insurance, labor protection, safety in production, the special protection of female workers, and training.
6. Trade unions should attend the full or nonvoting members' board meetings and working meetings of management in these enterprises to voice the opinions and demands of their workers and staff members.
7. A system of consultation or bargaining should be established "in exclusive foreign-funded enterprises and private enterprises" and the participation of the unions in the management of these enterprises should be constantly explored.
8. The workers' congress system should be conserved and improved in those Sino-foreign equity and contractual joint ventures where such a system has been established and in existence already.
9. The work of organizing grass-roots unions should be enhanced in those foreign participating enterprises because problems such as serious law-breaking, preventing workers from organizing unions, violating the human rights of workers and staff members, and arbitrarily extending

working hours, deducting wages and firing workers and staff members and the lack of labor protection measures, and so on, were more serious and abhorrent in enterprises where trade unions are not yet organized.

10. The Chinese trade unions in foreign-funded enterprises should seek to cultivate stable labor relations and promote the healthy development of these enterprises, while the overall role of the ACFTU in participating in labor policy and law formulation should be strengthened for safeguarding the interests and rights of the workers and staff members in these enterprises.

THE DILEMMA OF THE CHINESE TRADE UNIONS

Behind the clear official concern of the ACFTU in holding the personnel and industrial relations situation "under rein" among foreign-funded businesses is an apparent yet subtle paradox of a dualistic agency role which the Chinese trade unions are expected to perform. The context is historical, rooted in China's century-long "chiliastic" encounter with the West. The union's role is now two-sided, due to the imperatives both to modernize the nation industrially and to conserve the state under the sacrosanct ideology of socialism with Chinese characteristics. First, the union's role is to serve the state in dealing with and receiving foreign capital and business, a role now enhanced because of the nation's instrumental and steady move away from past tradition, inspired by the soviet model of self-austerity, of restricting and containing strenuously foreigners' interests and investment. The state's design for the union now is to act with hospitality toward guest investors and foreigns partners from overseas, and act for the Chinese trade unions with a quasi ambassadorial role in the workplace. The union also undertakes a "chaperone" role, to educate Chinese workers to accommodate an alien employer and at the same time to protect them from Western "spiritual contamination." This diplomatic-cum-guardian task is especially conspicuous where the FIEs are exempt from representation by such organs as the Party and the workers' congress.

> Where the Party abstains from the workplace of the FIE, it is likely that the grass-roots union organization will fill the gap by acting as its proxy. One of these tasks, consistent with the state's policy of working with foreign capital, is for trade unions to educate workers and staff in supporting the enterprise administration. Even though "some of them do not understand the policy of opening to the outside world and feel that they are selling their labour in those enterprises," the trade unions endeavour to "help workers and staff members realize that they are equally masters of the country and that running well those enterprises is beneficial to China's modernization drive and therefore conforms with the fundamental interests of the working class" (Ng 1994, p. 20).

The second role, liable to be in conflict with the first one where the alien capital is a "secondary sector" employer at the lower end of the labor market, but now high on the ACFTU's newly revitalized and popularized agenda, is its mission to act and haggle on behalf of the labor force in order to shield them from the excesses of unscrupulous overseas employers.

In this connection, a greater challenge of increasing urgency for the ACFTU has been the growing problems of workplace tensions and vulnerabilities uncovered in this hybrid and heterogeneous FIE sector. The increasingly visible syndrome of depressed working conditions, workers' grievances or even open agitations, together with widely publicized industrial accidents (fires and explosions in ill-equipped factories), has created such embarrassing examples of capitalist sweatshop exploitation inside socialist China that the ACFTU could no longer stay lukewarm and ignore such phenomena as just trivial "teething troubles" of third world industrialization. Pressure on the foreign employers by the ACFTU was unequivocal and uncompromising, when the state was about to rebuild, after the upheavals of June 4, 1989, a more rationalized, sensitive, and humanized industrial system of institutional safety valves to address workplace grievances, in part to stabilize the administration and in part to preempt any undesirable drift toward an alternative underground labor movement. In a public statement published in 1994 the ACFTU leadership articulated its "greatest concern" over the recent frequent violations of the legitimate rights and interests of the workers in some overseas-funded enterprises in an interview with the *Workers' Daily*. Zhang Dinghua, the vice-chairman and first secretary of the ACFTU, lamented that in these enterprises there existed:

- Serious violation of China's labor legislation and neglect of safety in production, putting in jeopardy workers' personal safety and health;
- Abuse of workers. Some have violated the workers' human dignity, imposed corporal punishment on them, and even encroached their civil rights;
- Forced overtime work. Some overseas-funded enterprises have forced workers to work 10 to 12 hours a day, in defiance of the 44-hour work week system as defined in China's law;
- Failure to implement the minimum wage standard as set by the local governments. Some overseas-funded enterprises have arbitrarily cut down or pocketed workers' wages; and
- Refusal to sign labor contracts with the workers in an attempt to show legal responsibilities (Zhang 1994, p. 2).

What has compounded the human and industrial relations pattern in joint ventures, however, is the relatively privileged conditions and employment opportunities that modern corporate employers in this sector are liable to offer in China's vast employment market, especially the comparatively advanced and scientific managerial practices in human resources and associated activities at the upper levels of the Chinese labor market, in what are considered model overseas enterprises. Apart from the reputation enjoyed by visiting multinational corporations for their abilities to pay high wages, these foreign businesses have been typically rated superior as the preferred employers in the areas of employment and personnel practices, notwithstanding those dire conditions of industrial deprivation identified at the other end of the spectrum, as mentioned earlier. The stereotyping is by now well defined but it is still useful to make a brief reference to the Sino-foreign differentials in human relations and management approach which are observable in the context of investigating workplace industrial relations among the FIEs and state-run enterprises inside China today. As Child comments:

> ...the Chinese conception of the personnel management role is quite at variance with that normally held by foreign managers today. The personnel management role in Chinese organisations is geared towards the maintenance of control and conformity, supplemented by an ideological appeal to the virtues of work. This clearly contrasts with the foreign concept that the personnel function exists to provide a service to management through assisting the selection, training, assessment, motivation and organisation of employees, doing this systematically with reference to their contribution to organisational effectiveness.
>
> Differences between foreign and Chinese personnel practices appear in a number of areas within joint ventures. A combination of the control over staff just mentioned with traditional attitudes means that Chinese managers tend to emphasise negative discipline: punishment, restrictions and personnal loss of face. By contrast, many foreign managers today favour positive (or self-) discipline: motivation through praise and reward, and encouragement of initiative.
>
> Foreign personnel management tends to rely on standard practices for selection, appraisal, time-keeping, assessment of attitudes and discipline (Child 1994, p. 259).

In short, the human and industrial relations configuration that can be construed from these reports is so complex and heterogeneous that any generalizations are necessarily simplified. One has to consider, for instance, the role of such corporate features as the ethnic character of the foreign investment and the style and cultural traits associated with it; the collaborative strength and linkage between the Chinese and foreign partners dependent not only on the formal business contract but also on such hidden influences as norms of reciprocity, *guanxi* (networking), and face relationship; and the cultural mix of the workforce in joint ventures due to its nature as an ethnic coalition. Again, such diversities raise interesting questions as to the prospect of and propensities toward convergence, not only between state-owned and foreign-funded sectors but also internally among various clusters and subgroups within the industry of overseas investment, including those derived from Hong Kong, Taiwan, and Macau, in terms of their industrial relations development. Moreover, to the extent that the nation's labor market is segmentalized with increasing evidence of a "primary-secondary" divide between the privileged bureaucratic employers at one end and the marginal labor shops at the other, it is also problematic to ascertain the relative location of the FIE employers on this spectrum, vis-à-vis such home establishments as state-owned enterprises, township and village enterprises, as well as labor contract shops.

The myth once enshrining the joint venture and the wholly foreign-owned enterprise as trendsetting model employers is now increasingly emasculated, and the nexus of workplace relations between the managed and the manager is now the marketplace one between mercenary capital and waged labor. There is, thus, an emerging arena of industrial conflict and wage haggling, workplace grievance and discipline, organizational commitment, and labor force stabilization. And in the context of China's dualistic structure of state-owned and foreign-funded sectors, a basic issue is how vulnerable are joint venture enterprises toward moving into this syndrome which is characteristic of industrial relations in capitalist systems of production and social relations?

It may still be assumed that in spite of the compounding features that the FIE sector is far more varied and internally differentiated than it appears as a source of employment; and empirical evidence suggesting the beginnings of convergence in human resource management, in part due to recent statutory labor standards (especially the 1994 Labor Law), between joint venture and state-owned enterprises (Warner 1996, p. 31), the imagery of the foreign business as "primary sector" employers in China's labor market generally prevails today. In spite of the growing fluidity and interorganizational mobility of key managerial and professional personnel which guest transnational corporations are likely to experience, it is suspected that the work bureaucracies of visiting capital, mostly carriers of relatively advanced hardware technologies and managerial practices, are mostly able to conserve themselves as the elitist "enclaves," demarcating themselves with relatively distinct boundaries of their consolidated (if not privileged) internal labor markets.

> Since these foreign-funded businesses...are able to offer their workers and staff members better wages and conditions of employment than other employers, they may be described (in the language of Western theories on labour market segmentation) as "primary sector" employers. Further, insofar as they are able to attract and retain the more highly trained personnel from China's manpower reservoir, these enterprises may be seen as potentially creating a quasi layer of "labour aristocracy" more advantaged than the average mass of the working proletariat inside China (Ng 1994, p. 24).

However, it must be reiterated that the FIE sector is not made up entirely of the standard-bearing sector of efficient and problem-free employers to be emulated by the Chinese home enterprises in human and industrial relations. Warner was able to identify, in his 1995 study in Beijing of a comparative sample of joint ventures and SOEs, "numerous problems" which "beset the foreign managers in Sino-foreign JVs."

> Employee appraisal was confounded by job demarcation; tightening up on time-keeping was spoilt by lax practices in the organisational culture; promotions were not easily accepted due to the egalitarian norms founded locally and so on. Dismissing workers was still resisted in most JVs' experiences according to such studies. It was thus easier to transfer "hard" technology than its "soft" counterparts: this clearly delayed improvements in productivity and overall enterprise performance (Warner 1996, p. 28).

Earlier, Tsang had documented extensively on aspects of problematic wages, and human and industrial relations in his review of Sino-foreign joint ventures. Apart from the much reported legacies of official and other institutional constraints on the nominal abilities of these firms to hire, transfer, and discharge freely according to the rules of the contract and the influence of the market, it was the once highly structured and now liberalized wage domain that was probably most vulnerable to glaring discrepancies and problems of equity and equality, as well as of cost effectiveness and incentives.

> Although many investors are attracted to China by the low labour costs, the whole remuneration package is more expensive than expected when compared with other developing countries. The Chinese regulations stipulate that the wage level of a joint venture is to be set at 120 per cent to 150 per cent of that of state enterprises in the same line of business and same locality....The complete wage package consists of the basic wage, bonuses, and subsidies; take-home pay, which includes the basic wages plus bonuses, amounts to about three-quarters of the package. The subsidies—insurance, welfare, pension and housing funds—are paid to the Chinese partner or local authorities....The introduction of the bonus system...is meant to provide monetary incentives....Owing to the ideological legacy of egalitarianism, bonuses have been distributed rather evenly to all workers within a work group or production floor. This practice of "collective assessment" has made bonuses less effective as a motivational tool....Remuneration of expatriates presents another problem. In Beijing Jeep, it is said that the great difference in remuneration received by local versus foreign staff has been the cause of resentment. Each Chinese worker is highly aware that the compensation package for one foreign expatriate is several hundred times the annual salary and benefits that he or she receives (Tsang 1994, pp. 8-10).

WORKPLACE RELATIONS AND THE UNION RESPONSE

Understandably, many of the problems documented previously are endemic to the dualistic characteristics of the managerial structure of joint ventures and the problems of their internal governance hence implied. Compounding the dialectics of labor-capital interests in these enterprises is now also the "us-and-them" divide separating foreign and local (but which may unify the managed and the manager) identities—which is still reputed to cause a sizable amount of managerial strain and intra-organizational strife (Pearson 1991, p. 174). In this context, the FIEs have been a fertile breeding ground, in spite of their good reputation as a better paying employer, for workplace grievances, industrial strife, and worker agitation, and this has worried the national labor movement. As an example of such a conflict, the ACFTU related the situation of a work stoppage affecting a overseas-funded company:

> On June 21 this year, more than 300 workers of its paint spraying workshop went on strike, demanding better working conditions. Soon after receiving the workers' complaints, the Shenzhen Federation of Trade Unions sent an investigation team to the company, heeded workers' opinions and investigated their workshops and accommodation. They discovered that more than 30 workers lived in a simple living quarters of 30 square meters, with bad ventilation and lighting and without any fireproof installations. In the company with a workforce of more than 1,000, there was no dining hall so the workers had to eat in the open. The paint spraying workshop was full of poisonous gas and there were not any protection measures for workers' safety and health. The company never provided medical examinations to them.
>
> Workers were paid 80 yuan (US$10) less than the minimum wage of 280 yuan (US$33) as defined by the local government, and worked 100 extra hours every month without any extra pay (Wei 1994b).

These workers' grievances were investigated and the ACFTU subsequently instigated union organization of the workplace. The Shenzhen Trade Union Council convened a preparatory team for a grass-roots trade union to be created, at the request of the workers, in order to institutionalize its agency role of representing their job interests and safeguards on a proper footing. In this narrative, the leverage role of the Chinese trade union both as a protector of labor as well as in policing the workplace conduct of the overseas and foreign funded business is emphasized:

> ...the Shenzhen Federation of Trade Unions...would, in co-operation with other relevant departments, continue to urge the Shenzhen Guangyue Industrial Co. Ltd. to enforce laws and regulations till it has corrected its wrong-doing and the first Trade Union Committee comes in being...the company was urged to meet [the demands] within one month. Otherwise, it would demand the municipal government to punish it according to law (Wei 1994b).

Indeed, the shifting terrain of workplace industrial relations in these joint venture enterprises attests to a creeping yet noticeable redefinition inside China of the official view in interpreting and approaching strikes, as its reformed economy evolves toward the practice of market socialism. Previously, trouble with "managerial bureaucratism" was the only officially sanctioned reason for a strike; "in socialist China, the workers and staff members are the masters of the country and the enterprises [so that] under ordinary conditions there is no need for them to achieve their end through strikes" (Ng 1995, p. 68). However, the admission into the nation of foreign capital has epitomized and instituted a new and distinctive configuration of workplace relations by virtue of the dualistic character of foreign business for being (1) alien and (2) capitalistic in employing Chinese labor on the wage nexus. At the beginning of the 1990s the ACFTU began to acknowledge formally that in FIEs the workers' identity and interests could be so intrinsically distinctive from the employers' that these workplaces featured labor-capital relations analogous to what are typical of Western capitalist societies (Lao 1990, p. 7). Even in relatively well-managed model joint venture businesses such as the Fujian Hitachi TV Set Corporation Ltd., labor-management relations cannot be freed from its intrinsic paradoxical antagonistic-cooperative relationship—which gives Chinese workers a new legitimacy to strike in order to extract a better deal from the "mercenary" capitalists. This was because of and consistent with the adjusted strategy which the ACFTU adopted, in part proactive but largely responsive, that the "Chinese trade unions would establish a new type of labour relations. That is to say, they could safeguard the vital interests of workers while upholding the legitimate interests of enterprises as a whole" (ACFTU 1991, p. 9).

However, even such an enhanced industrial role has remained constrained by the concern of the state to continue to attract and retain foreign and overseas investment, and in this connection the strategic function of a "workplace ambassador" role to be played by the Chinese trade unions, conciliatory rather than adversarial, cooperative rather than conflictual or antagonistic. Trapped in such a dualistic role and the dilemma it hence poses, it is still probably true that the ACFTU, in spite of its increasing and vocal zeal in articulating employees' interests and grievances encountered in the workplace, has and will continue to treat industrial militancy stemming from labor-capital conflict as damaging to transnational industrial collaboration and, hence, to be abhorred in general. Inasmuch as the Chinese trade unions continue to opt for the consultative approach of dialogue building and conflict resolution as the preferred style of structuring the joint venture system of workplace industrial relations, it may be suspected that in the event of industrial conflict, they are more inclined toward a stance of reasoned and restrained intervention to remove misunderstandings, accommodate differences, and resolve shop-floor disputes. Indeed, such an image was propagated in the early 1990s when the ACFTU reported amicable dispute settlements due to its mediation, of which the following is typical:

> On Spring Festival, the Japan Sanyo Corporation in Shenzhen decided that workers and staff members would have five days off. But some workers and staff members demanded to have 15 days off so that they could stay longer together with their families. Learning of the matter, the trade union of the corporation explained to those workers and staff members that the Sanyo Corporation had not violated the stipulations of three days of holiday during the Chinese Spring Festival, so that they should respect the decision of the corporation. The workers and staff members accepted the advice of the trade union and gave up their demand (Gong 1990, p. 4).

However, what appears to be a hiatus in more recent developments of workplace industrial relations in this non-state sector has been the more sceptical and less accommodating attitude of the national labor movement toward capital and its hiring malaise and defaults allegedly uncovered on a glaring scale by the ACFTU. The reason could be quasi political: in giving the trade union organ the raison d'etre to enhance its agenda of organizing, with greater interventionist rigor, the industrial plants and business enterprises of foreign and overseas capital. However, the growing visibility of workplace issues detailed by the ACFTU in its recent disclosures could also be a disturbing sign suggesting the drift of inhospitality or even exploitative intentions harbored by visiting capital against the Chinese working masses. Indeed, the indictments brought up by the ACFTU in its recent reports against the vicissitudes of alien capital did not look frivolous and were well corroborated by coverage in the press (both domestic as well as outside the nation, notably in Hong Kong). The poor level of industrial safety has been lamented by the nation's trade union center:

> The findings report reveals that some overseas-funded enterprises, small ones in particular, have neglected safety in production with noise, toxic gases and pollution well above the standards set by the State. In a toy factory solely funded by a Hong Kong businessman, a big fire broke out, burning 84 women workers to death. Investigation into the tragedy shows that it was because the workers were forced to work in precarious conditions. With almost all exits sealed off, the workers could not manage to escape with their lives quickly (Wu 1994, p. 3).

A series of surveys conducted by the ACFTU, at both national and local levels of the provinces and muncipalities, has indicated the vulnerability of Chinese women workers in particular in these workshops in the non-state sector. Examples of industrial deprivation were reported in several areas. Discrimination included risk of dismissal for maternity reasons and failure to protect women during pregnancy and postnatal childcare. The denial of the protection of a regular work contract was common: in Guangdong, the survey revealed that 33-87 percent of women questioned had no work contracts, and that 23-46 percent of signed contracts had not been testified. Many overseas investors recruit only single women aged between 18 and 25 on short-term contracts of three years or less (Wu 1994, p. 3). Other examples include low and inferior pay compared with their male counterparts; no overtime pay for work outside the scheduled hours; working in overcrowded, congested, and fire-prone conditions on the shop floor; and subject to abuse, insults, beatings, and sexual harrassment (Wu 1994, p. 3).

Following such reports of alleged maltreatment and impoverishment of working women, it apparently became an urgent case for the ACFTU to extend its organizational realm to cover those foreign-funded enterprises still not unionized or still resistant to unionization. The presence of the trade unions was imperative in this context in order to protect otherwise inarticulate and unrepresented women workers when they were being disadvantaged or exploited. As pledged by the national trade union center:

> The ACFTU report stresses that "women workers in overseas-funded enterprises, like their counterparts in other enterprises, are the masters of the country, and their political status, economic interests, personal dignity, civil liberty and other lawful rights and interests allow for no infringement." It urges trade unions at various levels to carry out careful inspection of the implementation of legislations on labour protection for women workers together with the labour and public health departments,...In accordance with China's Trade Union Law and other relevant legislations, the Chinese employees in overseas-funded enterprises are entitled to establish trade union organizations, and women workers' organizations should be set up in enterprises with 25 female workers or above. The report urges the setting up of trade unions and committees for women workers in overseas-funded enterprises at a faster pace in order to safeguard the workers' legitimate rights and interests organizationally and forge a link between the workers and the management so that labour relations can be stabilized (Wu 1994, p. 3).

Given this sensitivity and alertness of the national labor movement toward the problematic nature of labor conditions and industrial relations in FIEs, are these workplaces prone to industrial conflict and disputes? The ACFTU suggests a potentiality of such a drift:

> What merits attention is that collective labour disputes are on the rise. Statistics compiled by the ACFTU show that mediation committees across the country handled 14,313 collective labour disputes in 1993. The collective disputes in some provinces have multiplied several times, bringing about a considerable increase in stoppages, strikes and their participants.
>
> Xiao Zhenbang, a member of the ACFTU Secretariat, attributes the direct causes for labour disputes to the problems in labour remuneration, insurance, welfare, and the punishment of workers. In 1993, 35,208 labour disputes were related to wages and insurance benefits, representing 41.5 per cent of the total....Xiao said that most labour disputes had been caused by the workunits' infringement of the legitimate rights and interests of labourers. This is more striking in overseas-funded enterprises (Wei 1994a, p. 8).

The ACFTU did not hesitate to name the non-state sector, essentially funded by overseas capital, as the primary source of the troubled current industrial relations situation as it observed that these employers' defaults in their duties and responsibilities have "resulted in tense labour relations, including many disputes and occasional strikes in some overseas-funded enterprises" (Wu 1994, p. 3). Concluding that this sector is vulnerable to labor abuses and exploitation that can, in turn, breed widespread shop floor discontent and agitation, the ACFTU has apparently viewed it as a proper corrective and an urgent lever to intervene by organizing the inarticulate Chinese workers. Such accentuated intervention would be consistent with the state's directive issued in 1983 ratifying the right of the ACFTU to unionize the workforce hired in every FIE.

And it has been deemed imperative now in the light of accumulated experiences indicating workplace deprivation and injustice which need addressing promptly in order to help stabilize industrial relations in these enterprises. This recognition gives explanation to the urgency with which a deadline for unionization in overseas-funded enterprises was added to the ACFTU's agenda in 1994:

> trade unions should be set up in all overseas-funded enterprises in the coastal provinces that had started business before June 1994. As to other cities, regions and provinces, trade unions should be organized in over 60 per cent of the overseas-funded enterprises by that time (Wei 1995, p. 6).

The vice-chairman of the ACFTU also made explicit his instructions that:

> the setting up of trade unions in newly founded overseas-funded enterprises shall be written in agreements or contracts according to the Chinese relevant laws, the prescription for the setting up of enterprises and trade unions shall be done at the same time, and when the enterprises start business, trade unions shall be organized simultaneously or no later than one year (Wei 1995, p. 7).

PROPENSITY TO UNIONIZE FOREIGN-INVESTED ENTERPRISES: RESISTANCE AND CHALLENGE?

The appeal by the ACFTU's vice-chairman to the Chinese trade unions to work harder to make a breakthrough in organizing trade unions in FIEs betrayed signs that such unionizing efforts by the national center may have encountered a certain amount of resistance in previous years. This would probably explain the sluggish pace with which the ACFTU has been advancing in organizing the non-state sector. That grass-roots union organizations are not universally found in all FIEs but are relatively erratically distributed among local districts was noticeable at the beginning of the 1990s as the ACFTU reported:

> In Guangdong province, which has three economic zones, 41.9 per cent of foreign-funded enterprises that have opened for business had set up trade unions and 43 per cent of workers and staff members in those enterprises have joined the trade unions. In Shenzhen Special Economic Zone, 96 per cent of foreign-funded enterprises employing over 25 people have trade union organizations (Gong 1990, p. 2).

However, the scope of unionization in FIEs had, by the mid-1990s, remained stable at a more or less comparable level in spite of the rigors with which the ACFTU has pursued the task on its agenda. This is symptomatic of the relatively equivocal profile of the Chinese trade unions' penetration of these workplaces which has been elucidated by the ACFTU:

> Recently the ACFTU has conducted investigations on the unionization in such provinces and municipalities as Jiangsu, Shangdong, Guangdong and Shanghai, where overseas-funded enterprises are comparatively concentrated. The investigation showed that 52,340 overseas-funded enterprises had started business in these provinces and municipalities by the end of June 1994. Among them, 17,477 trade unions had been set up, accounting for 33 per cent of the number of the enterprises. Compared with December 1993, 4,017 new trade unions were set up and unionization rate increased 4 percentage points. In Jiangsu Province, the number of trade unions in overseas-funded enterprises increased from 2,800 at the end of 1993 to 4,260 at the end of last June, and in Shangdong Province, the number increased from 1,690 to 2,632 (Wei 1995, pp. 6-7).

Two factors can perhaps help explain such a dubious situation of unionization in FIEs. First is the scepticism, if not resistance, of such employers as the multinationals, especially those from the United States, which are known for their apathy or hostility toward unionism posing as a challenge and alternative to the nexus of managerial prerogative. Foreign investors participating in joint ventures "are likely to feel apprehensive about a labour organization belonging to the central quasi-official bureaucracy of the ACFTU, especially since the JV law enables the union to participate in the enterprise's decision-making process by direct access to the board of directors" (Ng 1994, p. 18).

A common strategy adopted by foreign management in coping with the Chinese workplace unions has hence been one of containment. Pearson observed that "foreign managers...were able to confine LO [labor organization] activity to after regular work hours," reducing it in some cases to just a nominal "friendly society" which concentrates on organizing sports activities (Pearson 1991, p. 186). The suspicion of foreign partners in joint ventures toward the influence of Chinese trade unions is acknowledged by the ACFTU, which laments that "most foreign investors looked on trade unions with distrust. They believed that trade unions would organise strikes, and interfere with their work, thus giving a negative effect on production and performance" (Huang and Bao 1991, p. 10).

The official perception of foreign capital's unease and anxiety with Chinese trade unions (which are conceivably not difficult to appreciate in the context of historical legacies from, for instance, the militant challenge of the Chinese labor movement in the turbulent decade of the 1920s) has bred and nurtured its policy dilemma, which has chronically beset the state leadership ever since it launched on the Four Modernizations and opened up the nation again to investment abroad. That is the basic contradiction between a wealth-oriented strategy: on the one hand, to attract, welcome, and accommodate with Western (and Japanese) advanced industrial capital and, on the other, maintain the moral, ideological, and nationalistic imperative of controlling and keeping the Western visitors cautiously at a distance.

In this ambivalent context it is conspicuous that the Chinese labor movement at the local level have adopted a nominally active yet intrinsically lukewarm stance toward the agenda of organizing the FIEs, in order to avoid confronting and antagonizing these foreign partners. Such a prudent inactivity has worked, presumably, in the past because of a quiescent Chinese labor force. However, industrial affluence made possible now by the nation's advances toward the market economic system has apparently increased shop-floor workers' expectations and heightened their awareness of the vicissitudes of industrial hazards, inhospitable working conditions, and other abuses of workers' rights and benefit entitlements. This is the second factor affecting industrial relations in the overseas-funded sector.

> Such a "pluralistic" industrial syndrome features a rising level of workplace antagonism together with the augmented shopfloor power of factory management as a result of the State's decision to devolve managerial prerogative down to the operational unit of the factory. The implications of these developments for workplace industrial relations are reflected in the inflated propensity of Chinese enterprises (in both the state and non-state sectors) towards shopfloor grievances and labour disputes....Grievances are rooted in a psychology of insecurity associated with the development of "contractual" hiring and sharp income disparities resulting from the "competitive" wage system. Contrary to the socialist ideology still officially upheld, individuals, enterprises, industries, occupations and localities are swiftly stratified into those "well-off" and "privileged" at one end and those "impoverished" and "disadvantaged" at the other end of the spectrum (Ng 1995, pp. 70-71).

That there is now a drift toward an increase in the amount of workplace unrest in the non-state sector, which has caused alarm in the state leadership, is attested by reports in the Chinese press in mid-1994 that China registered officially as many as 260 strikes in FIEs in 1993 (Associated Press 1994). The CCP General Secretary, Jiang Zemin, stated in May 1994 that workers' strikes were deplored by the state as the most harassing item among the "eight hidden perils" now besetting the nation and its stability (BBC 1994).

The state responded to this escalating industrial relations syndrome in the PRC by promulgating in August 1994 the *Regulations on Labour Management in Foreign-funded Enterprises* under the joint jurisdiction of the Labour Ministry and the Ministry of Foreign Trade and Economic Co-operation. This code lays down the following guidelines:

1. The Labour Ministry is responsible for supervising the enterprise's staffing, training, pay, insurance, worker safety and hygiene, as well as fringe benefits in this sector.
2. The enterprise is allowed to recruit its workforce through the local employment agencies and labor service companies approved by the Labour Ministry.
3. The hiring of child labor is prohibited.

4. The enterprise is required to recruit only Chinese workers but is allowed to hire recruits from Taiwan, Hong Kong, and Macau, and from abroad provided approval is given by the local labor bureau and in conformity with the relevant state regulations.
5. A minimum wage must be prescribed for the workforce on the basis of wage guidelines stipulated by the Labour Ministry or the local labor bureau.
6. Employment benefits such as holidays, old-age insurance, maternity, sickness, and workmen's compensation, and the rules governing overtime work and pay and those regulating the dissolution of labor contracts, must be rationalized and standardized in the enterprise.
7. The publication and cirulation to the workforce of a "labor handbook" (or "employee handbook") will be mandatory.
8. An array of official sanctions must be instituted to censure the enterprise for breaches of these regulations (Guoji 1995).

THE DIALECTICS OF FOREIGN CAPITAL AND THE CHINESE LABOR MOVEMENT: PROSPECTS FOR INDUSTRIAL RELATIONS IN FOREIGN-INVESTED ENTERPRISES

The growing unease articulated by the ACFTU about the vulnerabilities of Chinese workers hired in the FIE sector are probably neither new nor or surprising. Ideologically, at least, the distinct and defensive apprehension expressed by Chinese trade unions about the exploitative potentials inherent in the cash nexus epitomized by the evolving system of waged employment relations in these enterprises were consistent with mainstream Marxist socialism, still officially upheld as sacrosanct. Indeed, the embattled experiences of the Chinese labor movement in the early days, especially during the decade of upheavals of the 1920s, has always been a patent reminder to the ACFTU leadership, even today, of the vicissitudes of Western mercantile activities that were and are both alien and capitalistic. Historical examples of unequal treaties and labor strife, such as the seamen's strike of 1922 and the Hong Kong-Canton Strike-Boycott of 1925-1926, have always been reminders in the background alerting the state and its union organs to both the industrial benefits and the plight of impoverishment implied by the "opening-up" policy of inviting foreign capital operations into the country.

The situation is, however, paradoxical—and compounded by the specifically Chinese character of unionism in the Mainland. Chinese trade unions have not evolved through analogous experience, as mature Western unionism has developed to its present status as an adversarial industrial institution, basically enshrining and buttressing the capitalist system of waged production and economic relations. The history of the Chinese labor movement (during the pre-World War II era of gestation and antiforeign struggles, and then in their subsequent configuration as soviet-prescribed socialist unions after the 1949 liberation) attests sparsely, if at all, to Anderson's definition of the notion of trade unionism by the standards of Western "conventional wisdom":

> Trade unions are an essential part of a capitalist society because they incarnate the difference between capital and labour which defines the society...trade unions are dialectically both an opposition to capitalism and a component of it....As institutions, trade unions do not challenge the existence of society based on a division of classes, they merely express it (Anderson 1967, p. 264).

Chinese society basically lacks such a structural history and hence the Chinese unions, albeit emulative in organizational forms, have never seen that type of spontaneous workers' joining together to espouse a defensive working class solidarity to respond to and challenge the ills of industrial capital. China's trade unions in their pre-World War II heyday achieved their unusual strength of workers' solidarity and militancy not because of their commitment to a class struggle against capital (they were virtually political allies to the patriotic Chinese capitalists and merchants, who provided even worse working conditions that their Western counterparts trading in China), but because they were the vanguard in a nationalistic crusade against Western and foreign aggrandisement and imperialistic assaults on China, the nation, and its sacrosanct interests. After liberation in 1949 socialism replaced nationalism as the nexus of cementing the organization of the Chinese labor movement. The imperative of reacting to and containing the alien power of capitalism has never been the raison d'etre of the nation's trade unionism.

The implications of this for the present situation of workplace industrial relations in the foreign-funded sector are not necessarily negative. Ironically, this intrinsic and historical character of the Chinese unions can be viewed as a blessing in disguise. Paradoxically, the Chinese trade unions have always been allies to or agencies for the established order and political (often governing) elite, rather than as alien institutions or alternative power centers that need to be incorporated, as hypothesized in such celebrated theories as those of "union integration" and "union incorporation." Inasmuch as the Chinese trade unions are always located within the mainstream of the establishment (in spite of their "chiliastic" agitations against foreign capital in the 1920s), the authenticity and applicability of recently popularized arguments in Western literature that the postmodernization Chinese union's are increasingly becoming "corporatist" can be severely doubted (Chan 1993), simply because, unlike the situation in the capitalist Western world, the institutional integration of the union system has never been problematic in the Chinese milieu.

This probably means that a collaborative relationship of "mutual partnership," basically instrumental and tactical, is more readily attainable in workplaces where the tradition has not been conducive to the workers' and their unions' antagonistic opposition of and challenge to managerial authority, insofar as its exercise has been mandated and sanctioned by the state. Up to the present such an official strategy of accommodating and offering foreign capital and business a hospitable investment environment has seemingly been upheld and continued. In spite of the unequivocal signaling now by the ACFTU that the labor movement cannot be expected to stay acquiescent about devious attempts by foreign businesses to exploit cheap labor unscrupulously inside China, the official policy has appeared intact, by and large, that the union organ shall continue to sustain "an ambassadorial role towards the visiting capital, exemplifying the State's policy on mutual nonconflictual co-operation" (Ng 1994, p. 25), in order to "help foreign investors acquaint themselves with the national conditions and relevant policies of China so that they can run entrprises without any worries within the scope provided by China's law and encouraged by China's policies" (Gong 1990, p. 5).

CONCLUSION

All these observations, albeit tentative and cursory, are tantamount to suggesting that the increasing tendencies for foreign multinationals to import into China the classic MNC attitude of avoiding trade unions or aversion from any contacts or dialogues with them could be an excessive antiunion phobia unwittingly transferred from their home societies. Yet the Chinese trade unions have not been nurtured, historically, as adversarial industrial institutions or antagonistic bargaining agencies of the workforce against the enterprise's management or employing capital. Where the structural conditions are not intrinsically associated with the adversarial model of Western industrial relations there exists a potential for China to evolve, through its experience gained from union-management relations, to crystallize from the trendsetting workplaces in the foreign-funded sector, an imaginative and inspiring Asian approach to a nonconflictual model of labor-management collaboration, instead of confrontation, as in other exemplary cases of Japanese or Singaporean practices. That such an option may be attractive is made apparent by both the current doldrums in which the adversarial tradition in Europe and the United States of Western-style trade unionism is trapped, and the recognition by Thurley and other industrial relations specialists of the distinct prospect of an alternative Asian model of industrial relations and unionism:

> Asians often reject the conflictual, adversarial basis of Western industrial relations argument. Asians...are frequently horrified by strikes and attached to values of co-

> operation, mutual commitment and harmony. Collective bargaining, itself, is seen as overlapping with consultative discussions. If this is true, then, of course, the basis of trade unions in Asian countries is indeed very different from that current in the West, certainly in the United Kingdom (Thurley 1988, p. 26).

Evidently, there are substantial constraints handicapping such a prospect of a new model industrial relations style emanating from FIEs in China. Of these, two factors are perhaps most strategic. The first is the level of suspicion that the state may espouse, at varying times, toward the aggrandisement of "obscure interests and ambitions" of foreign business and capital in China. Such distrust is historical and has never disappeared totally. Fed on nationalistic sentiments, its explosion into antiforeign hostility can be erratic and cyclical. And the industrial relations arena is potentially vulnerable, if the state were to increase its intervention into this type of workplace.

The second condition is probably more endemic to the shop floor itself, suggested by the ACFTU's conspicuous anxiety now to enhance its activities in the workplace and its organization, otherwise it might invite disillusion at the grass-roots level of the laboring masses with its authentic image as the entrusted spokesman of their occupational interests and grievances. The pressure from the shop floor for the ACFTU to "deliver the goods" has become increasingly evident, given "its newly discovered role of assisting the State to absorb and cushion any emerging agitation which now appears imminent in the urban areas under the impact of accelerated industrial growth" (Ng 1995, p. 72). Indeed, the credibility crisis for this giant union bureaucracy is liable to explode, if the ACFTU consistently demonstrates its incapacity to cope effectively with the alienative syndrome of workers' disaffection and deprivation precipitated by the apparent success of the nation's economic reforms, namely, in generating socioeconomic issues such as "the inflated expectations and the creation of diverse interests stimulated by economic affluence and its uneven distribution in the populace" (Ng 1995, p. 72).

Where a wide spectrum of varying work and employment conditions exist among FIEs it is arguably a prudent strategy for the national trade union to attach its priority of the present work agenda to the harmonized improvement of working conditions in this sector. Failure in this respect might lead to the formation of an alternative and "undesirable" worker movement, were the competence of the ACFTU as the bona fide representative agency of the Chinese worker to be seriously questioned. This prospect has, up to now, hardly been tenable, but it would be alarmingly costly and traumatic for the nation in its present rigor of accelerated reforms. The ills of deprivation and other economic vicissitudes arising from the accelerated advances of industrial affluence need to be held in check by the ACFTU in its celebrated role as an important state organ for the sake of conserving the stability of the nation, its people, and its newly developed wealth.

NOTE

1. In its orthodoxy, the "one country, two systems" design of accommodating the disparities of dichotomous institutional arrangements within the sovereign domain of China is now attributed to Deng Xiaoping. Such an idea has been extended to reckon the possibility of pursuing marketplace pluralism under the new vision of market socialism which signifies the economic-cum-social reforms of China. The implications appear to be the tolerance of capitalist institutions in the economic sphere but the conservation of socialism in the politico-ideological arena.

REFERENCES

All-China Federation of Trade Unions (ACFTU). 1994. *The Twelfth National Congress of Chinese Trade Unions*. October 1993. Beijing: All-China Federation of Trade Unions.

Anderson, P. 1967. "The Limits and Possibilities of Trade Union Action." Pp. 263-280 in *The Incompatibles*, edited by R. Blackburn and A. Cockburn. Harmondsworth, UK: Penguin.

Associated Press. 1994. News bulletin, June 22.

British Broadcasting Corporation (BBC). 1994. *Summary of World Broadcasts*. BBC Monitoring Service, May 24.

Chan, A. 1993. "Revolution or Corporation? Workers and Trade Unions in Post-Mao China." *Australian Journal of Chinese Affairs* 29: 31-61.

Child, J. 1994. *Management in China during the Age of Reform*. Cambridge, UK: Cambridge University Press.

Deng, X. 1985. *Building Socialism with Chinese Characteristics*. Beijing: Foreign Languages Press.

Feng, T. 1996. "The Reconstructed Labour Force and Unions' Reconstructed Strategy in the New Context." *Workers and Trade Unions under the Market Economy: Perspectives from Grassroots Union Cadres. Chinese Sociology and Anthropology* 28 (3): 25-53.

Gong, Y. 1990. "Trade Union Organizations in Foreign Funded Enterprises Play an Important Role." *Chinese Trade Unions* 1 (February): 2 5.

Guoj, S. 1995. Cited in *Summary of World Broadcasts*. BBC Monitoring Service, March 30.

Huang, M.Y., and W.W. Bao. 1991. "The First Federation of Trade Unions in Foreign Owned Enterprises in China." *Chinese Trade Unions* 2 (February).

Kerr, C., J.T. Dunlop, F. Harbison, and C.A. Myers. 1973. *Industrialism and Industrial Man* (2nd ed.). Harmondsworth: Penguin.

Lao, S. 1990. "Trade Unions Help Joint Ventures Develop Production." *Chinese Trade Unions* 1 (February): 7.

Ng, S-H. 1994. "Industrial Relations in Joint Ventures in China." Pp. 13-28 in *Joint Ventures in the People's Republic of China: Advances in Chinese Industrial Studies, Volume 4*, edited by S. Stewart. Greenwich, CT: JAI Press.

Ng, S-H. 1995. "A Current Note on the Chinese Labour Movement." *International Journal of Employment Studies* 3 (2): 61-75.

Pearson, M.M. 1991. *Joint Ventures in the People's Republic of China: The Control of Foreign Direct Investment Under Socialism*. Princeton, NJ: Princeton University Press.

Sit, Victor S.F., and S-L. Wong. 1990. *Changes in the Industrial Structure and the Role of Small and Medium Industries in Developing Countries: The Case of China*. Tokyo: Institute of Developing Economics.

Thurley, K. 1988. "Trade Unionism in Asian Countries." Pp. 24-31 in *Labour Movement in a Changing Society: The Experience of Hong Kong*, edited by Y.C. Jao, D.A. Levin, S-H. Ng, and E. Sinn. Hong Kong: Centre of Asian Studies, University of Hong Kong.

Tsang, E.W.K. 1994. "Human Resource Management Problems in Sino-foreign Joint Ventures." *International Journal of Manpower* 15 (9/10): 4-21.

Warner, M. 1996. "Joint Ventures Vs. State-owned Enterprises: Management and Human Resources in China." Working paper of the Judge Institute of Management Studies, University of Cambridge, Cambridge (March).

Wei, M. 1994a. "Labour Dispute Settlement on the Make." *Chinese Trade Unions* 5: 7-9.

Wei, M. 1994b. "Trade Unions Flex Muscles in Overseas-funded company." *Chinese Trade Unions* 5: 11.

Wei, M. 1995. "ACFTU's Deadline for Unionization in Overseas-Funded Enterprises." *Chinese Trade Unions* 1: 6-7.

Wu, J. 1994. "Protection of Women Workers Rights in Overseas-Funded Firms Urged." *Chinese Trade Unions* 5: 3-4.

Zhang, D. 1994. "Overseas-Funded Enterprises to be Unionized." *Chinese Trade Unions* 5: 2.

PART IV

STRATEGY AND PERFORMANCE

THE EFFECT OF OWNERSHIP ON PERFORMANCE IN SINO-FOREIGN JOINT VENTURES

Yanni Yan

INTRODUCTION

The joint venture is considered to be one of the best means to gain rapid access to resources, technology, and markets within a competitive and rapidly changing global economy. The People's Republic of China (PRC) is the major example of this today. During the last 20 years in China 120,000 foreign-funded enterprises have begun operation and 260,000 projects have been approved. The successes reported by the *Sino-Foreign Investment Journal* suggest that most Sino-foreign joint venture (SFJV) partners are satisfied and are meeting their strategic objectives. Only 33 percent of joint ventures in China have failed.

The environment in China presents special conditions to foreign investors. Although Chinese joint venture law requires the foreign investor to take a minimum 25 percent equity stake, it does not stipulate what constitutes equity. A foreign partner usually contributes a combination of cash and new and/or used equipment, as well as advice in the procurement of resource components

Advances in Chinese Industrial Studies, Volume 5, pages 219-247.

ISBN: 1-55938-961-3

from the international market. Chinese national law does not cover technology injected as capital. In some parts of the country approval authorities have not allowed the value of technology to be capitalized as equity when it exceeds 20 percent of the foreign partner's total equity contribution.

The Chinese partners tend to bring land, buildings, existing equipment, and plants to the joint ventures. Performance would be expected to vary according to the nature of the joint venture's regional environment within China and its resource capability (Child and Stewart 1996). This depends on the differences in levels of local government support, economic development, and business culture. An investor's decision about the configuration of ownership inputs into a joint venture, including noncapital contributions valued as equity, ownership inputs, both with and without contract, is usually determined by the strategic objective: to produce a certain product or service, and to obtain market share in China.

Evaluating the performance of a joint venture is an important challenge. No consensus on the appropriate measure of the concept of performance has yet emerged. Relatively little of the research relating to joint venture performance has directly examined joint ventures between firms from market economies and those from China (Daniels, Krug, and Nigh 1985; Yan and Gray 1994a, 1996). Jaeger (1980), Lecraw (1984), and Schaan (1983) indicate that it is more difficult to achieve satisfactory joint venture performance in developing than in developed countries. Lee and Beamish (1995) point out that performance problems are costly not only to the parent companies, but also for the recipient country itself, due to the social costs and economic disturbances associated with such problems. A major controversy over the measurement of joint venture performance appears to be in finding an appropriate yardstick (Doyle 1994). The debate revolves around whether to use financial criteria, such as return on capital investment and growth on sales, or whether other economic development criteria, such as technology transfer and the learning of managerial expertise, are more appropriate. Obviously, the inadequate performance evaluation of joint ventures may affect the efficiency of their resource acquisition and utilization, and this could eventually lead to stress or de-motivation among managers, simply because the owning companies are applying inadequate performance criteria (Scott 1973; Shapiro 1982; Emmanuel and Otley 1985; Demirag 1988; Anderson 1990).

Geringer and Hebert (1991) developed and tested several hypotheses regarding the reliability and comparability of a range of objective and subjective measures of joint venture performance. Glaster and Buckley (1994) extended this work by considering the effect of national cultural differences on the relationship between objective and subjective measures of joint venture performance. They developed their work by examining the ways in which measures of performance are affected by differences in perception on the part of the parent companies. In this paper both subjective and objective measures are used to examine the ownership effects on performance. Six indicators of performance are presented and the pattern of relationships among them is examined in order to infer the underlying dimensions of performance.

The remainder of this chapter is structured as follows: first, a broader definition of ownership in the new context of joint venture is described. Second, the relationship between ownership inputs and performance is examined in terms of (1) partner contributions in ownership investment at the joint venture's formation and (2) the dependency on transactional resources supplied by foreign and local partners to the ongoing management. Finally, performance outcomes are discussed in relation to the ownership inputs of the partners.

OWNERSHIP PATTERNS IN SINO-FOREIGN JOINT VENTURES

In formal terms ownership is the legal possession of assets. It is normally defined in terms of three fundamental rights: (1) the right to possess an asset and/or its financial value; (2) the right to exercise influence over the use of the asset; and (3) the right to information about the status of what is owned (Pierce, Rubenfeld, and Morgan 1991). Other rights are those to transfer assets and to receive an income or return from them.

In joint venture business equity constitutes the conventional concept of ownership. However, ownership in the context of joint ventures can be categorized in a way that goes beyond the conventional. First, there are ownership rights associated with the range of inputs valued as equity investments committed by the owning companies; second, the structure of contracts governing the range of ownership inputs committed by the partners usually depends on the local legal system, social customs, and the technical attributes of the assets involved in the exchange; third, the range of ownership inputs provided on a noncontractual basis represents the level of continuing commitment by the owning companies to the joint venture. Foreign and local partners providing resources, skills, and knowledge additional to their equity and contractual contribution enjoy de facto property rights through the expertise and moral influence these inputs generate.

The essential feature of the ownership rights structure in joint ventures in the PRC is that owning companies have a restricted right to use their assets to generate income, but they are required to maintain the value of the assets under the framework of local laws and regulations on joint ventures. Usually the allocation of the joint venture's dividend and net income are regulated by the two parties: foreign partner and local partner. The enforcement of ownership equity rights involves the level of use of the range of scarce technological and managerial resources committed by the partners. The value of ownership equity rights also depends on the cost of enforcing those rights.

Yan and Gray (1994a, 1996) regard equity as the provision of a "capital resource" to a joint venture by its partner companies, typically through finance and sometimes through land and buildings. They distinguish between these types of resource and what they categorize as "noncapital resources." Noncapital resources include technology, management expertise, local knowledge, raw material procurement channels, product distribution and marketing channels, and global service support. The author has made a further distinction within the category of noncapital resources, namely between resources that are provided to a joint venture on a contractual basis, and those that are provided on a noncontractual basis (Yan 1994).

This last distinction has important theoretical and policy implications for the basis on which resource providers may exercise control and influence within joint ventures (Yan, Child, and Lu 1995). Some noncapital resources may be provided under terms that are set out in formal contracts. Such contracts typically convey formalized rights to exclusive control over the use of, and/or benefit from, assets including technology and brands. Contracts expressing technological property rights include patents and licence agreements and they are particularly important in the case of China (Guo and Ackroyd 1996). These rights derive from the provision of inputs to a joint venture by its owners, and hence they may be termed "contractual" inputs. These inputs can be interpreted as a network of contracts specifying the benefits and costs that arise out of the cooperation of the partners in management and technology. Dunning and McQueen (1981) explain that contractual equity control can avoid these costs by giving authority to local investors, who probably have an absolute advantage in the knowledge of local conditions. This leaves the foreign investing companies free to meet their own objectives through contract-based expansion and control. Hall and Eppink (1992) indicate that partners of joint ventures can get combined power via the contractual equity inputs to optimize the utilization of available capacity.

Ownership structures are evaluated with respect to the contribution by the owning companies toward the enhancement of the joint venture's capability. Pfeffer and Salancick (1978) identify that power is derived from commanding critical resources, and is the basis of control for within and between organizations. The owning companies' strategy on equity resource inputs into joint ventures provides the potential for earning rents. Schulze and Meyer (1991) suggest that the actual and sustained earning of rents depends on factors internal to the firm. The range of ownership inputs at the joint venture's formation is important, as the structure of the joint venture contract depends on the legal system, social customs, and the technical attributes of the assets involved in the exchange by the foreign and Chinese partners. The more detailed the legal framework and the stronger the ties of custom and social control, the less specific are the written contracts.

Noncapital resources can be provided to joint ventures by their owners outside of any formal contracts. These include technological know-how, management systems, professional services, and training. They may be termed "noncontractual inputs." With the development of joint ventures in particular, and of globalization in general, noncontractual ownership inputs have assumed increasing importance as an important key to success. Success now lies in the knowledge and skill of managing complex interdependencies within and across joint venture boundaries and in the ability to manage multicultural units (Ohmae 1993; Nonaka and Takeuchi 1995). The provision of noncontractual inputs normally reflects a high level of commitment to joint ventures on the part of the parent company (Beamish 1988; Cullen, Johnson, and Sakano 1995). These inputs are likely to give rise to de facto ownership rights through claims to expertise, and the goodwill and cultural capital which they generate. The partner that is able to accrue goodwill, trust, and the loyalty of the personnel, adds significant value to its original equity.

With regard to the logic of ownership, in establishing joint ventures to exploit complementarities between themselves, the partners provide resources, skills, and knowledge in addition to their equity contribution. These assets, which are within the possession of partner firms, have an intrinsic value, and amount to ownership inputs with property rights. This distinction is an important one because assets such as technology, market channels, and management expertise have become increasingly recognized as ownership factors, especially in the formation of joint ventures, where they may constitute more important complementary assets than can be measured purely by financial contributions. In joint ventures the organizational capability is enhanced by transfer of knowledge experientially with the partner in a learning-by-doing fashion. Knowledge and skill transfer occurs not at top management level but as the result of daily interaction among employees at the operations level (Hamel, Doz, and Prahalad 1989).

Joint ventures are especially suited to knowledge transfers. They may provide scope for learning and capability accumulation (Hamel 1991). The partners can extend those limits outward by building up trust and learning through operating noncontractual equity inputs to a joint venture at its formation. A joint venture generates exposure to different routines, through exchange of personnel and other forms of interaction, and this can facilitate a higher level of learning between partners. The noncontractual equity inputs can be based on the use of informal mechanisms to build partners' motivation and commitment.

A comprehensive concept of ownership, applicable to joint ventures, would therefore incorporate equity, contractual, and noncontractual inputs (Yan 1994). The distinction between these three categories of ownership inputs is likely to be a significant one for the understanding of joint venture performance because of the different nature and scope of the power which stems from each of them. Equity share, and especially a majority share, confers certain legal rights to determine the overall direction of a joint venture. When noncapital resources are provided through contracts, these can specify rights as to the use and possibly the management of such resources. When noncapital resources are provided on a noncontractual basis they may still confer powers to the providing company either because intrinsically they create a dependency on its expertise and/or because they generate the moral authority which derives from the way they evidence commitment.

OWNERSHIP-PERFORMANCE RELATIONSHIP

The relationship between ownership and performance has taken on a new aspect in recent years with the rapid growth in numbers of joint ventures. Ownership in joint ventures is typically concentrated as ownership is shared between two, or very few partners, who will in most cases be legally formed companies rather than individuals. Performance is usually measured in relation to the various objectives established for a joint venture. As a result, it is necessary for joint venture research to examine performance-related issues from the perspective of the individual partners (Hill and Hellriegel 1994).

Beamish (1984), Geringer and Hebert (1989), and Harrigan (1987) have examined joint venture performance by using perceptual measures. This approach allows managers to rate how effective a given joint venture has been in meeting the goals established for it. Performance targets tend to be based on the perspective of an individual parent company, and are relevant to their own resource base and capabilities (Harrigan 1987; Doyle 1994). The empirical work of Schaan (1983) and Beamish and Banks (1987) measures performance on the basis of managerial assessment. They suggest that only when both partners are satisfied is the joint venture considered successful. In contrast, Anderson (1990) argues that joint ventures should be evaluated primarily as stand-alone entities seeking to maximize their own performance, without reference to the parents.

The problem stems from the fact that each of these performance measures conflicts with others. Maximizing one measure implies minimizing others. Basically, it has been argued that the process of realizing ownership commitments by partners tends to generate a conflict of interest. Finding an appropriate measure of the relationship between ownership inputs to a joint venture at its formation and its subsequent performance in the market is extremely difficult. This deficiency may be due to a number of reasons, such as the complexity of the structure of joint ventures involving two or more owning companies, or the lack of data available at industry and firm-specific levels. In addition, many problems may be associated with the "gap" between the identification of mutual long-term resources, capabilities, and actual commitment of the partners.

The outcome of the ownership inputs between joint venture partners will only be satisfactory to the partners if contributions and expected benefits of the two companies are kept in balance. Robinson (1969) observed two things: first, the joint venture relationship can not be a zero-sum game, or else the two partners would not commit ownership inputs at all, and second, each of the partners must expect to gain from the partnership. Robinson concluded that the stability of the joint venture was dependent, to a certain degree, on the balance of benefits the partners achieve from the performance of the joint venture. If the joint venture is in a "win-lose" situation the likelihood of instability is high.

Harrigan (1988) examined the control and influence of partner asymmetries on joint ventures on the basis of duration, survival, and managers' assessments. The results indicate that joint ventures with symmetric partnerships tend to gain a better performance than those with asymmetric partnerships. Lee and Beamish (1995) found that control was the most important factor in determining the performance of Korean joint ventures. Their results suggest that, in the case of Korea, the partners' needs regarding a joint venture were significantly related to joint venture performance. Killing (1983, 1985) suggests that joint ventures dominated by one partner are more successful than shared-control partnerships. Beamish (1985) uses Killing's scale analysis in developing countries and finds that shared-control joint ventures are more successful. Similarly, Beamish also finds that partner needs and commitment are good predictors of performance.

The legal format of ownership provides the framework within which the range of inputs by the partners can be made. Strategic and operational control is mediated through local legal institutions and social relations. The effective possession of critical resources and competence by the joint venture's parent companies may be constructed in a way that does not correspond to the prevailing legal format. As an owning company faces the problem of protecting the use and integrity of its investments when collaborating with a joint venture partner, it has a strategic objective of seeking a certain level of control through legal institutions and social relations. When the two aspects of property rights and social relations are not dissociated it is possible to distinguish the "range of ownership inputs" to a joint venture at its formation, which provides rights at strategic and operational levels. This allows owning companies to achieve strategic objectives and provide economic development incentives as a return. The range of ownership inputs conveys control and influence over a joint venture both through the formal terms of any contracts by which they are provided and through the less formal influence that derives from the partner's possession of resources and capabilities.

Overall, identification of key variables associated with performance has been perceived very differently between partners. Developing countries tend to favor joint ventures with local partners as the main channel for foreign direct investment. The government indicates its preferences with a combination of restrictive regulations and economic incentives for equity joint ventures. Local government presents special conditions on legal provisions, taxation structuring, and approval of expansion plans, which highlight the significance of joint venture performance criteria from the local perspective. Performance requirements imposed by developing countries often include local content and employment policies. Foreign investing companies are asked to commit themselves to a schedule of increasing the locally produced content of the final product over a stated period of time. But countries like China may have to pay a high price for having local content when local markets cannot supply good quality parts, components, and materials.

HYPOTHESES RELATED TO OWNERSHIP INPUTS

Universalistic Approach

The universalistic approach holds that high joint venture performance will be the result of a combination of (a) ownership inputs; (b) transactional resources; (c) control; and (d) duration. A range of ownership inputs may constitute the major resource for a firm's strategy in establishing its strategic presence in the foreign market. Joint venture transactional resources can affect owning companies' access to resources, cost of production factors, and receipt of favorable local policy treatment. Control can influence several dimensions of joint venture performance; and the length of time the joint venture has been in operation is associated with the collaboration and integration of the owning companies.

With regard to examining ownership inputs in relation to performance, Lee and Beamish (1995) found that multinational company (MNC) executives from low-performing joint ventures regarded their local partners' contribution as unimportant, while those from high-performing ventures considered their partners' contributions important. Buckley and Casson (1988) indicate that committed partners have more efficient joint ventures. This implies that greater commitment of resources leads to higher performance. The work of Killing (1983, 1985), Schaan (1983), and Beamish (1985) suggests an ownership inputs hypothesis where the relative technological and managerial capability between the foreign and local partners affects the pattern of performance. Barney (1991) suggests that resources and core competencies generate competitive advantage and superior performance. Pfeffer and Salancick (1978) and Murray, Kotabe and Wildt (1995) suggest that the availability of alternative sources of supply is one factor that allows joint ventures to switch from one supplier to another or to use substitute products without incurring high switching costs. Yan and Gray (1994b) use five components of bargaining power in their analysis technology, market access and marketing skills, local knowledge, managerial expertise, and equity share. Their findings suggest that the five components have a positive impact on the strength of the partners possessing them.

Hypothesis 1. The more comprehensive the range of ownership inputs relative to the scale of the joint venture operations, the better will be the performance of the JV.

From a parent companies' transactional resource perspective, how well the joint venture performs will depend on the proportion of resources supplied from the parent companies and how much parent companies themselves rely on such supplies. Hennart (1982) notes that the exchange is costly because the buyer cannot know the characteristics of what he is buying without appropriating it. With regard to transactional resource dependence, the proportion of inputs and outputs provided by parent companies is used to predict the extent to which the level of protection and guarantees are committed by the partners. Ghoshal and Bartlett (1990) suggest that the vertical distribution of power within the parent-joint venture managerial network will depend on the density of the transaction and information network within its own organization set. The greater this density, the more restricted will be the hierarchical power of the parent company. Conversely, the greater the density of the network between the joint venture and parent company, both informational and transactional density, the more restricted will be the autonomy of the joint venture. Therefore, performance may be influenced by the density of the distribution of transactional resource between owning companies and its subsidiaries.

Hypothesis 2. The higher the proportion of joint venture transactional resources supplied by the parent companies, the better will be the performance of the JV.

Blodgett (1991) and Lecraw (1984) suggest that a crucial factor determining the return parent companies can expect is the amount of control the parent is able to exert on the joint venture. With a sample of 71 joint ventures in India and Pakistan, Tomlinson (1970) found that joint ventures evidenced higher levels of profitability when their UK parents assumed a more relaxed attitude toward control. Using a sample of 169 U.S. MNCs involved in more than 1,100 joint ventures, Franko (1989) examined how parents exercise control over joint ventures. Franko's main argument is that different strategies have different control requirements, and these influence the stability of joint ventures. Buckley and Casson (1988) note that dominant control is a mechanism for reducing the risks associated with coordination, potential conflicts, and disclosures and, consequently, for minimizing transaction costs and stabilizing the joint venture. Killing (1983) notes that the return to a parent company is not based solely on the joint venture's profits, but also on transfer prices, royalties, and management fees not included in traditional financial performance measures. With regard to the ownership-performance relationship a distinction is made on how a parent can use its resources and its core competence to gain a higher level of overall control, which in turn may lead to a better performance. These arguments appear to support Killing's (1983) view that shared control constitutes the major source of management difficulties, while dominant partner joint ventures are easier to manage and consequently more successful.

Hypothesis 3. The higher the level of control exercised by one partner, the better will be the performance of the joint venture.

The performance achieved by joint ventures seems to vary over time, though this has rarely been studied. Harrigan (1988) finds that joint ventures of longer standing tend to achieve more successful performance. The reason is that the gap between the mutual knowledge of foreign and local partners concerning the economy, technology, politics, and culture is reduced by the actual operating of the joint venture. Learning foreign business practices and experience can reduce the totality of cost of doing business in the foreign countries.

Hypothesis 4. The longer the joint venture has been in operation, the better will be the performance of the joint venture.

Contingency Approaches

The next two hypotheses are generally associated with the nature of "fit" or "match" between characteristics of joint ventures as an influence on their performance. Indeed, a parent firm may adopt very different ownership input commitments to each of its subsidiaries in order to establish an optimum strategic presence vis-à-vis competitors. It is important to consider the role of the parent firm ownership input in the influence and exercise of power in joint ventures, and how these can be attributed to the ownership positioning.

The empirical work conducted by Hill and Hellriegel (1994) suggests that complementarity actually has a negative impact on several dimensions of joint venture performance. Qualitative data suggest that joint venture partners with distinctive competencies in different operational areas may experience difficulties in implementing potential complimentarities due to problems of integration and the danger of segmentation. Yan and Gray (1994a) suggest that equity structure is not equivalent to management control. Once equity structure is agreed, it delineates the relative positions of the partners and sets the tone for successive negotiations over management structure and control.

Previous studies that use ownership as a proxy for management control must be questioned. Schaan (1983) concluded that joint venture success, or the extent to which parent expectations for the joint venture were met, is a function of the fit with three variables: the parent's criteria for success, the activities or decisions it controls, and the control mechanisms that are utilized. He concluded that joint ventures in which a parent achieved this fit will evidence better performance. Jaeger (1980) and Child, Yan, and Lu (1997) also suggest that joint venture success should be enhanced when the joint venture's structure fits the owning company's strategy.

Hypothesis 5. The more the configurations of ownership inputs and control match, that is, the more that control matches the level of ownership resource commitment, the better will be the joint venture's performance.

Very few studies have focused on the relationship between transactional sourcing and various dimensions of market performance (Murray, Kotabe, and Wildt 1995). Based on an examination of existing literature, the following contingency factors are identified for use in this study: bargaining power of suppliers (Porter 1980) and elements of transaction costs (Williamson 1979). For each of these factors the ownership inputs can be explained by evaluating the overall transactional control aspects and the nature of the joint venture structure. Transactional resource input and output supplied by the partners have been regarded as the indicators of performance. The unit of analysis for the study should be decided by examining the relationship between the partners' sourcing strategy and the joint venture's performance, and the influence of control factors on this relationship.

Hypothesis 6. The higher the level of the joint venture's transactional dependence on its parent companies and the more control matches the level of resource dependence, the better will be its performance.

METHODOLOGY

Data Collection

The researcher, working with colleagues from the International Technology and Economic Research Institute of the PRC State Council, and the University of Cambridge, gathered information from a total of 212 foreign and Chinese senior managers of 67 participating Sino-foreign joint ventures. Mandarin Chinese was the language used in interviews with local and overseas Chinese respondents, while English was generally used with foreign respondents. An interpreter was required in the case of some Japanese managers. The senior managers from each side (usually the general manager and deputy general manager) were interviewed, together with the heads of two or three functions: typically operations, HRM, and technology or marketing depending on the sector and availability. The interviews were conducted between May 1994 and April 1995. Interviews with general managers and deputy general managers normally lasted two hours or more, while those with other managers usually lasted between one hour and 90 minutes.

Sample Characteristics

The sample consists of 67 joint ventures formed between Chinese and foreign parent companies. The foreign share of their equity ranges between 25 and 95 percent. Thirty-three of the joint ventures are located in the advanced nondomestic electronics sector (mostly microcircuitry and telecommunications), while 34 are located in the fast-moving consumer goods (FMCG) sector.

The choice of these two sectors took into account several considerations. First, the pattern of joint venture investment in China is influenced by the Chinese economic and political climate. Chinese policy has shifted from emphasizing heavy industry to the development of light industry, such as the FMCG and electronics sectors. Choosing these two sectors reflects the importance of Chinese government policy influence. Second, these two sectors contain quite large populations of foreign companies operating in China, and this ensured a reasonable population from which to select the sample. The results of the study are thus likely to apply quite widely. Third, the particular primary business needs of these sectors are expected to generate different ownership configuration patterns and control priorities. In advanced electronics technology transfer and its management are a key factor, with product design being a focus of competence. In FMCG brand management and marketing are particularly important, and technological competence is more likely to rest in the process rather than the product.

The sample is also stratified to provide equal numbers of foreign parent companies from regions that some of the literature claims have different approaches to management—the United States and United Kingdom (Anglo-Saxon), continental Europe, Japan, and ethnic (overseas) Chinese. The joint ventures chosen were located in three areas of China: Beijing-Tianjin, Shanghai-Hangzhou, and Guangzhou-Shenzhen. With the Chinese open-door policy on foreign direct investment, regional effects on joint ventures indicate significant important impacts on joint venture management.

Variables

Equity: The shares of equity held by foreign and Chinese parent companies; the composition of equity distinguishing between contributions in the form of cash, product and production technology, land, buildings and equipment, brand names, and marketing/distribution support.

Contractual ownership inputs: Inputs or resources that parent companies have a contract to provide to the joint venture in addition to their equity contributions—with particular reference to product design, production technology, management systems, professions services, and training. Provision and non-provision are scored in a binary manner.

Noncontractual ownership inputs: Inputs or resources that parent companies have provided to the joint venture on a noncontractual basis—covering the same items as contractual inputs and any other noncontractual inputs. Provision and non-provision are scored in a binary manner.

Transactional dependence: Percentage of inputs and outputs by value supplied and received by the foreign and Chinese partners.

Perceived achievement of parent company objectives: Twelve items of foreign strategic objectives and 17 items of Chinese strategic objectives are presented in this study. A maximum of five items from the two sets of strategic objectives respectively are chosen. The achievement ratings are assessed by the interviewee managers (1 = not achieved at all, to 5 = fully achieved).

Subjective performance measures: How the joint venture managers perceived its profitability and growth (1 = not satisfied at all, to 5 = fully satisfied).

Operational profile of the joint venture: The operational trend of the joint venture in the last three years, if applicable, that is, growth in sales, growth in profit, and profitability.

In order to simplify an examination of the possible connections between ownership and performance, tests of internal reliability were conducted on the multi-item categories of ownership inputs, such as items valued as equity, contractual inputs, and noncontractual inputs. The results in Table 1 indicate that aggregation into composite measures is acceptable for indicators of contractual and noncontractual ownership inputs, but not for indicators of noncash contributions made to equity by Chinese and foreign parent

Table 1. Alpha Coefficients for the Aggregation of Ownership Indicators into Composite Scale

Aggregation	*Alpha Coefficient*
Noncash equity inputs from Chinese parent companies	.53
Noncash equity inputs from foreign parent companies	.57
Contractual inputs from Chinese parent companies (excluding managerial services)	.72
Contractual inputs from foreign parent companies	.71
Noncontractual inputs from Chinese parent companies	.67
Noncontractual inputs from foreign parent companies	.74

companies. Composite measures were constructed for contractual and noncontractual inputs, based on binary (0/1) scores which indicate the provision or not by either the Chinese or foreign parent companies of each of the five items.

RESULTS

Table 2 shows that of all the performance measures subjective profitability appears to have the most significant correlation with perceived achievement of foreign and Chinese parent companies' strategic objectives. With regard to current performance criteria the subjective measures of performance tend to cluster together, but not with the objective measures of organizational performance such as profitability and growth in profit and sales.

The results appear to support Geringer and Hebert's (1991) argument that objective measures have failed adequately to reflect the extent to which a joint venture has achieved its objectives. One reason may be that if joint ventures have exceeded the parents' expectations they are considered successful by one or all of the parents. The subjective assessments of foreign strategic objectives are correlated with its performance measures on profitability and growth. It suggests that no single strategic objective is adequate for judging the performance of joint ventures. The reason is that each performance measure suffers from strategic and operational conceptual problems; specifically, because each concentrates on a limited perspective. For example, some foreign investing companies may focus on long-term business profit or growth; in contrast, Chinese strategic objectives are more oriented toward profitability. The other reason may be that subjective measures tend to be connected to the present time, whereas, objectives are calculated over several years. The criteria of performance for strategic objectives in this study may be more appropriately used to evaluate a very long-term performance horizon.

Hypothesis 1

Hypothesis 1 identifies the comprehensive range of ownership resources committed by the partners, equity, contractual, and noncontractual, as determinants of performance. Table 3 reports correlations between the owning companies' ownership commitment and indicators of performance. The subjective and objective measures of performance yield different results for the Chinese and foreign groups. Most of the correlation coefficients between Chinese ownership commitment and measures of joint venture performance are virtually zero. Among the correlations between each indicator of performance and the three subcategories of ownership commitments there is only one positive correlation for subjective measures between Chinese strategic

Table 2. Correlations between International Joint Venture Performance Measures ($N = 67$)

Performance Measures:	*1*	2	3	4	5	6	*7*
1. Achievement of Foreign Strategic Objectives		.39**	.40***	.61***	-.004	-.02	-.10
2. Achievement of Chinese Strategic Objectives			.44***	.28*	.002	.10	.11
3. Subjective Measurements: Profitability				.49***	.19	.39*	.02
4. Subjective Measures: Growth					-.04	-.09	-.11
5. Objective Measures: Profitability $N = 39$						.12	-.60***
6. Objective Measures: Growth in profit $N = 39$							-.07
7. Objective measures: Growth in sales $N = 47$							

Notes: * $p < 0.05$, ** $p < 0.001$, *** $p < 0.000$.

Table 3. Correlations between Performance Indicators and Resource Commitment by Partners ($N = 67$)

	Performance Measures					
		Subjective Measures		*Objective Measures*		
Equity Commitments	*Strategic Objective Achievement*	*Profitability*	*Growth*	*Profitability*	*Growth in Profitability*	*Growth in Sales*
Equity						
Chinese	.34**	-.12	-.18	.07	-.04	.13
Foreign	-.02	-.11	.18	-.06	.04	-.14
Contractual Input						
Chinese	.12	.03	-.08	-.07	-.04	-.04
Foreign	-.03	-.02	-.04	-.09	.09	-.04
Noncontractual Input						
Chinese	.10	.04	-.02	.07	-.07	-.04
Foreign	-.04	-.12	-.05	-.21	-.008	.15

Notes: * $p < 0.05$, ** $p < 0.01$, *** $p < 0.00$.

objectives and Chinese equity input. Most of the Chinese firms in this study have achieved their equity position by investing land, existing buildings, plant, and equipment, which have been arbitrarily valued for equity share purposes. Chinese partners tend to contribute "resource input" and, as this does not constitute a critical impact on the technology and management of joint ventures, it could eventually lead to the Chinese partners having a low level of bargaining power to establish priorities for technology and management. On the whole, the Chinese strategic objective achievement has its positive significant correlation in relation to equity in this study. Very few foreign firms contribute to equity share through a valuation of their technology. Foreign firms usually emphasize their need in a number of key areas, such as technology transfer, marketing, and finance. Expertise is likely to be located primarily within the foreign company. Therefore, foreign investing companies tend to invest in product and production technology, management systems, and services to joint ventures on both a contractual and noncontractual basis.

Seventy-five percent of the firms sampled have more than two-and-a-half years' operational experience. According to Chinese joint venture law, joint ventures enjoy a three-year tax holiday once they start producing profits. This may encourage managers to report no profits in the early years. The main contractual ownership inputs in this study are from the foreign partners. However, if we examine the detailed items of noncontractual ownership inputs, one by one, the results indicate that joint ventures exhibit a very marginally better profit performance when the partners' production and product technology are taken into account.

This is consistent with the opinions of most of respondents in this study; that noncontractual managerial and technical resources committed by the foreign partners are most effective in the areas of quality control and professional service. The most important Chinese noncontractual inputs committed to joint ventures are concerned with liaison with local Chinese authorities. On the whole, however, Hypothesis 1 receives no support in terms of examining a range of ownership configurations by the partners on the performance.

Hypothesis 2

The transactional dependence of joint ventures on their parent companies indicates the importance of the input and output resources which the latter supply. Table 5 suggests that the impact on performance of resource inputs supplied by the foreign partners appears to vary between objective and subjective measures. The percentage resource input provided by the foreign partners correlates with the subjective measures of joint venture performance, but not with the objective measures. Evidence gained from the respondents indicates that most foreign partners tend to have direct control over the

Table 4. Correlations between Performance Indicators and the Technological Noncontractual Inputs by Partners

	Performance Measures					
		Subjective Measures		*Objective Measures*		
Noncontractual Commitments	*Strategic Objective Achievement*	*Profitability*	*Growth*	*Profitability* N = 39	*Growth in Profit* N = 39	*Growth in Sales* N = 47
Production Technology						
Chinese	.14	.06	.14	.08	-.09	-.04
Foreign	-.17	-.08	-.03	-.14	-.13	.11
Product Technology						
Chinese	.17*	.17	.09	.16	.07	-.03
Foreign	-.13	-.04	-.03	-.10	-.19	.05

Notes: * $p < 0.05$, ** $p < 0.01$, *** $p < 0.001$.

Table 5. Correlations between (1) Indicators of Trasnsactional Resources Provided by the Foreign and Chinese Partners (2) Joint Venture Performance ($N = 67$)

	Range of Ownership Resources	
Performance Meaures	*Percentage Input Supplied by Foreign Parent Companies*	*Percentage Output Going Directly to Foreign Parent Companies*
Foreign Strategic Priorities Achievement	.21*	.17*
Subjective Measures: Profitability	.30**	-.16*
Subjective Mesures: Growth	.22*	.16
Objective Measures: Profitability $N = 39$	.18	-.36*
Objective Measures: Growth in profit $N = 39$	-.08	.18
Objective Measures: Growth in sales $N = 47$	-.13	-.08
	Percentage Input Supplied by Chinese Parent Companies	*Percentage Output Going Directly to Chinese Parent Companies*
Chinese Strategic Priorities Achievement	.21*	.10
Subjective Measures: Profitability	.19*	.30**
Subjective Measures: Growth	.24*	.10
Objective Measures: Profitability $N = 39$	.13	.18
Objective Measures: Growth in profit $N = 39$	.05	.04
Objective Measures: Growth in sales $N = 47$	-.23*	-.08

Notes: * $p < 0.05$, ** $p < 0.01$, *** $p < 0.00$.

resource import from the international market. Foreign partners also appear to control international distribution networks. The results from Table 5 indicate that when resource input is supplied by the foreign partners, there is a greater likelihood of satisfactory performance. This is consistent with the possibility that resource inputs supplied by foreign partners provide them with benefits from transfer pricing. Some Chinese managers admit that when using existing foreign channels for resource inputs, joint ventures will benefit from improved quality control of resource inputs, lower transactional costs, and gaining a preference in claiming technological support from the foreign parent companies.

When a higher proportion of resource input is supplied by the Chinese partner, there is a positive correlation with subjective indicators of performance, but not with the objective measures. Most of the respondents in this study shared the same belief that the Chinese partners are forced into a "passive" position regarding local sourcing issues due to poor Chinese supplier capabilities. Several respondents acknowledged that Chinese local sourcing and domestic distribution in the past tended to be based on personal relationships. As localization increases and the joint venture itself progresses the joint venture has to face the transition from dependence on the existing Chinese partners for distribution to using the Chinese market network infrastructure. A significant imbalance in sourcing control appears to occur at an early stage between the partners. As the Chinese domestic supply of materials and components improves the foreign partners are able to gain greater access to and control of the sourcing of material and components, even in the Chinese market. The extent of the proportion of resources supplied by the partners can, however, affect performance. The decision whether to obtain resources through the foreign or Chinese parent companies largely depends on price, and this determines the costs of raw materials and also the quality aspects of the components supplied. This control facilitates the management of the costs of production, reduces production disruption, and leads to increased market performance.

As shown in Table 5 the correlation between the percentage of outputs taken from parent companies and its respective six indicators of performance receive weak but inconsistent support. One exception is that a moderately positive correlation is evident between the proportion of output taken by the Chinese partners and objective measures of performance on profitability. A positive influence can be attributed to performance when the outputs account for a large proportion of turnover. Hypothesis 2 receives support in terms of a higher proportion of joint venture transactional resources supplied by the parent companies.

Hypothesis 3

The sample of joint ventures were divided into those in which one partner had dominant control and those where the partners shared control. This distinction was drawn as follows. Thirteen items of control and influence of owning companies on managing joint ventures are identified in the study: use of profit; allocating senior managerial positions; setting strategic priorities; product pricing; training and development policies; reward and incentive policies; financial control; reinvestment policy; purchasing policies; production planning; sales and distribution; technology innovation; and quality control. The level of influence exercised by the foreign and local parties in each of the above control areas was assessed, on the scale of 1-5 (1 = very little, 2 = minor, 3 = some, 4 = considerable, 5 = very considerable). The result is worked out from the total of 13 foreign influence areas and the total of the Chinese influence areas. Thirty-one joint ventures out of the 67 are identified as shared control and 36 as dominant control. Using *T*-test analysis Table 6 examines the extent to which the distribution between dominant and shared control predicts joint venture performance. Of seven indicators of performance used only the objective measure of profitability is weakly related to dominant versus share control. Table 6 shows that the higher performance mean scores tend to appear

Table 6. Dominant versus Shared Control of Joint Venture and Performance Exercised by Foreign and Chinese Parent Companies ($N = 67$)

	Mean Scores		*T-test for Independent Samples*	
Performance Measures	*Dominant* $N = 36$	*Shared Control* $N = 31$	*F-value*	*P-level*
Chinese Strategic Priorities Achievement	3.73	3.34	.99	.32
Foreign Strategic Priorities Achievement	3.40	3.42	.61	.44
Subjective Measures: Profitability	3.59	3.04	.13	.72
Subjective Measures: Growth	3.45	3.50	.43	.51
Objective Measures: Profitability $N = 39$	.16	-.09	3.7	.06
Objective Measures: Growth in profit $N = 39$	1.84	1.79	.12	.72
Objective Measures: Growth in sales $N = 47$	2.11	2.08	.01	.94

within the dominant groups (in five out of seven instances). Hypothesis 3 receives no real support, but the differences are not significant.

Hypothesis 4

The joint ventures are categorized into two groups according to their duration (length of operational history), that is, three years or less, and greater than three years; the reason for this split being that under PRC law joint ventures enjoy three years of tax exemption. It divided this sample into two roughly equal groups. The results shown in Table 7 indicate that joint venture duration has a significant relationship only with the "objective" measures of performance, the timescale for which is limited to the two years previous to the date of the study. The group with at least three years' operation has moderately higher means in comparison with the other group. The result of analyzing the objective measures of profitability indicates that joint ventures that have been operating for more than three years have better performance results than the joint ventures which are three years old or less.

Explaining the relationship between the accumulated business experience of joint ventures and their performance, the author maintains that with increasing knowledge and experience in China, foreign firms acquire greater confidence in collaborating with their Chinese partners, understanding the Chinese market, gauging customer needs, and estimating costs and returns. The uncertainty in the Chinese market is reduced only through actual experience of operating in the market, because foreign firms have more chance

Table 7. Performance and the Duration of Joint Venture Operation ($N = 67$)

Subjective and Objective Performance Measures	*Duration Mean Scores*		*T-test for Independent Samples*	
	Less and Equal Three Years (N = 30)	*Over Three Years (N = 37)*	*F-value*	*P-value*
Chinese Strategic Priorities Achievement	3.38	3.69	.051	.82
Foreign Strategic Priorities Achievement	3.29	3.50	2.09	.15
Subjective Measures: Profitability	3.05	3.58	.058	.81
Subjective Measures: Growth	3.20	3.70	.071	.79
Objective Measures: Profitability N = 39	-.12	.15	6.66	.014
Objective Measures: Percentage growth in profit N = 39	2.56	1.49	8.59	.006
Objective Measures: Percentage growth in sales N = 47	2.57	1.80	1.91	.173

to secure the appropriate information to enable them to operate the business effectively.

Hypothesis 5

Hypothesis 5 integrates the concepts of ownership inputs and control and treats them as interdependent factors. It claims that a better fit between them positively influences joint venture performance. In other words, it suggests that when a greater range of ownership inputs committed by the partners is matched by a higher level of control, a better level of performance will result. Higher and lower performing joint ventures are distinguished in Table 8. Four performance measures, that is, growth and profit on subjective and growth in sales and profitability on objective, are used to compare the performance in joint ventures achieving higher and lower performances. Higher performing joint ventures are identified as above level 3 in subjective performance measures on growth and profit and above 1.12 percent in objective performance measures on growth in sales and profitability. Thirteen items of control are aggregated by the foreign and Chinese partners. Correlations are respectively for foreign ownership inputs with foreign control, and Chinese ownership inputs with Chinese control. These are based on four performance indicators categorized by higher and lower performing joint ventures.

As shown in Table 8, there are high correlations between the four indicators of performance and the strength with which the ownership and control variables are correlated. The results show that higher performing joint ventures have a stronger correlation between ownership and control. This is consistent

Table 8. Comparison of Performance the Fit Between Ownership Inputs and Control in Joint Ventures Achieving Above and Below Average Levels of Growth and Profit

	Ownership Inputs Correlation with Overall Control[1]			
	Subjective		*Objective*	
Performance Measures	*Growth* $N = 67$	*Profit* $N = 67$	*Growth in Sales* $N = 47$	*Profitability* $N = 39$
Higher Performing Joint Venture				
Foreign equity	.68***	.74***	.67**	.58**
Foreign Contractual Inputs	.37*	.60**	.09	.31
Foreign Noncontractual Inputs	.46**	.49**	.43*	.12
Chinese equity	.72**	.81***	.71***	.76***
Chinese Contractual Inputs	.17	.37*	.14	.33
Chinese Noncontractual Inputs	.51**	.47**	.65**	.65*
Lower Performing Joint Venture				
Foreign equity	.49**	.48**	.68**	.48*
Foreign Contractual Inputs	.19	.06	.62**	.54*
Foreign Noncontractual Inputs	.35*	.36*	.11	.31
Chinese equity	.62**	.57***	.63*	.23
Chinese Contractual Inputs	.25	.09	.39*	.42*
Chinese Noncontractual Inputs	.54**	.58***	.37*	.21

Notes: * $p < 0.05$, ** $p < 0.001$, *** $p < 0.000$.
[1] Correlation are respecitively for foreign ownership inputs with foreign influence and control, and Chinese ownership inputs with Chinese influence and control, categorized by higher and lower performing joint ventures.

for both the subjective profitability measures and objective measures such as growth in sales and profitability as the performance criteria. When the equity committed by foreign and Chinese partners is presented in terms of lower and higher performing joint ventures, there is a reasonably consistent pattern among the variables. Correlations between foreign equity and control variables are positive and significant among the higher performing joint ventures. The main exception is the objective measure of growth in sales which tends to show lower levels of fit when contrasted with the lower performing joint ventures. For the Chinese equity in higher and lower performing joint ventures, there are clear indications that when the Chinese ownership inputs valued as equity are more closely matched to the local Chinese control policies, then the Chinese partners will perceive a better performance of joint ventures. Overall, it can be suggested that when the range of contributions valued as equity committed by the partners is matched to the level of control perceived by the partners, a better joint venture performance will result.

Correlations between (1) the fit of contractual inputs with levels of control, and (2) the four indicators of performance measures, are generally positive and statistically significant. The correlations between foreign contractual inputs and control measures show a clearer distribution between higher and lower performing joint ventures in comparison with the pattern of the Chinese contractual ownership inputs. The results may imply that there is a significantly lower reliance on contractual inputs from Chinese companies in joint ventures in terms of technology and management. The performance results indicate that when foreign contractual inputs fit or match the overall foreign control and influence, then the joint venture will have a better performance.

When Hypothesis 5 is tested for the level of fit between foreign noncontractual inputs and the foreign control and influence there is a clear differential pattern in higher and lower performing joint ventures. Most of the correlations are stronger and significant at the 0.01 level or less in higher performing joint ventures. The findings associated with Chinese noncontractual inputs are slightly surprising in that the correlations between the subjective measures and Chinese noncontractual inputs in lower performing joint ventures show slightly higher correlations. It is worth noting that, on the whole, the contractual and noncontractual inputs committed by foreign partners show a clearer pattern in higher and lower performing joint ventures in comparison with the Chinese group. Hypothesis 5 receives partial support in terms of fit between ownership and control.

Hypothesis 6

Higher and lower performing joint ventures are distinguished in Table 9 to compare the transactional resource dependency supplied by the owning companies. Four performance measures, growth and profit on subjective and growth in sales and profitability on objective, are used. Higher performing joint ventures are identified respectively as above the mid-point on the scale of the subjective performance measures for growth and profit, and objective performance measures on growth in sales and profitability. Thirteen items of control are aggregated by the foreign and Chinese partners. Correlations are respectively for foreign ownership inputs with foreign control, and Chinese ownership inputs with Chinese control. These are based on four performance indicators categorized by higher and lower performing joint ventures.

Table 9 indicates that there is a stronger correlation between the inputs supplied by foreign partners and their overall control among joint ventures with higher (objective) profitability. Foreign resource output correlations are positive and statistically significant subjective performance measures on growth and profitability among higher performing joint ventures. The fit between foreign transactional resource supply and foreign joint venture control is greater in higher performing joint ventures than it is among lower performing

Table 9. Comparison of the (1) Fit between Transactional Dependency and Overall Control and (2) Performance

	Resources Transaction[1] Correlation with Overall Control[2]			
	Subjective		*Objective*	
Performance Measures	*Growth*	*Profitability*	*Growth in Sales*	*Profitability*
Higher Performing Joint Ventures				
Input from foreign partner	.27	.04	.28	.73***
Input from Chinese partner	.18	.15	.56*	.29
Output go the foreign partner	.35*	.39*	.44	.41
Output go to Chinese partner	.60*	.36*	.60*	.39
Lower Performing Joint Ventures				
Input from foreign partner	.17	.27*	.21	-.04
Input from Chinese partner	-.24	-.13	-.35	-.31
Output go the foreign partner	.36*	-.18	.17	.32
Output go to Chinese partner	.33*	.40*	.37*	.12

Notes: * $p < 0.05$, ** $p < 0.001$.

[1] Correlation between resource transaction supplied by the foreign and Chinese partners and overall control, categorized by higher and lower performing joint ventures.

[2] Correlation are respectively for foreign inputs and output percentages with foreign influence and control, and Chinese ownership inputs and output percentage with Chinese influence and control.

ones. With regard to Chinese transactional resource dependency, the results suggest a higher association between the output taken by the Chinese partner and their overall control among the higher performing joint ventures. For Chinese resource inputs correlations with objective performance indicators on growth in sales is statistically significant. On the whole, the fit of Chinese overall control with the level of resource inputs supplied by the Chinese partners is stronger in higher performing joint ventures than in lower performing joint ventures.

CONCLUSION

This paper indicates that the differences in ownership inputs provided by foreign and Chinese partners do have implications for the performance of the joint venture. There are universalistic and contingency approaches that explain these findings based on resource dependency theory. A universalistic approach on performance measure is when the range of ownership input, transactional resource, control, and business experience contributed to joint ventures by its owning companies helps the resource to be put to better use. This is because the owning companies contribute their expertise to the operation of the joint venture. A contingency approach on performance measure is when joint venture performance is good, and the level of overall control provision is matched respectively by the foreign and Chinese partners' ownership input. These include ownership inputs valued as equity share, contractual and noncontractual ownership inputs. The insights of achieving better performance are due to lower transactional costs for the resource by the owning companies and quicker access to the domestic and international market.

The findings related to the universalistic hypotheses identify a number of issues. The results indicate that the definition of ownership in the context of joint ventures does matter. The classification of ownership with its three categories into contributions valued as equity, contractual and noncontractual input, appears to be a useful way to examine their effects on performance. As the range of ownership configurations is very different between foreign and Chinese partners, failure to appreciate this point would result in misleading findings.

Attention to the details of resource transaction supplied by partners is important in this area of investigation. The findings suggest that when transactional resource inputs are supplied directly by the foreign partners, joint ventures will enjoy better performance. Other evidence from this study suggests that when a higher percentage of resource inputs are supplied by foreign owning companies, those companies' global sourcing strategies focus on the areas of quality control, product pricing, and international sales. When output goes directly to the Chinese partners joint ventures tend to achieve a better performance, as Chinese partners can reduce transactional costs, speed access to the Chinese domestic market, and assist in the handling of local regulations.

There is no clear performance difference between joint ventures having dominant and shared control in the 67 sample firms. The results may imply that the development of joint ventures in the PRC is still at too early a stage to judge their performance with regard to the two categories of dominant and shared control. The contrast in duration (three years or less and greater than three years) in terms of associations between objective and subjective performance measures is of some apparent consequence for joint venture performance.

With regard to the argument that better fit will enhance performance, it was found that the joint ventures tended to achieve higher performance not so much when they received a more comprehensive range of ownership inputs, as when these inputs were matched by a corresponding level of parent control. In addition, those joint ventures in which the foreign partners actively engage the support of their Chinese partners, in terms of resource inputs, tend to be more successful. The findings are consistent with research done by Geringer and Hebert (1989); that partners are likely to focus control efforts in the areas critical to their company. The findings show that coefficients for control and influence over joint ventures in relation to the range of ownership inputs supplied by the partners are in general statistically significant among higher performing joint ventures, rather than among lower performing joint ventures. Moreover, when transactional resources are supplied by the parent companies rather than by the market, joint ventures tend to achieve better performance. On the whole, a relatively high degree of correlation is found in higher performing joint ventures between the resource inputs supplied by the foreign partners, resource outputs taken by the Chinese partners, and their respective overall fit with control and influence.

ACKNOWLEDGMENTS

Grateful acknowledgment is made of the funding toward the cost of research by the Economic and Social Research Institute of the State Council, PRC, the Hong Kong Research Grants Council, and the Guinness plc. The author also wishes to thank the following for their valuable comments: John Child, John R. Fawn, Yuan Lu, Sally Stewart, and Ingmar Björkman.

REFERENCES

Anderson, E. 1990. "Two Firms, One Frontier: On Assessing Joint Venture Performance." *Sloan Management Review* (Winter): 19-30.

Barney, J. 1991. "Firm Resource and Sustained Competitive Advantage." *Journal of Management* 17 (1): 99-120.

Beamish, P.W. 1984. *Joint Venture Performance in Developing Countries.* Unpublished Doctoral Dissertation, University of Western Ontario, London, Ontario.

Beamish, P.W. 1985. "The Characteristics of Joint Ventures in Developed and Developing Countries." *Columbia Journal of World Business* (Fall): 13-19. Beamish, P.W. 1988. *Multinational Joint Ventures in Developing Countries.* London: Routledge.

Beamish, P.W., and J. C. Banks. 1987. "Equity Joint Ventures and the Theory of the Multinational Enterprise." *Journal of International Business Studies* 18 (2): 1-16.

Blodgett, L.L. 1991. "Partner Contributions as Predictors of Equity Share in International Joint Ventures." *Journal of International Business Studies* 22: 63-78.

Buckley, P.J., and M. Casson. 1988. "A Theory of Co-operation in International Business. Pp. 31-53 in *Co-operative Strategies in International Business*, edited by F. Contractor and P. Lorange. Lexington, MA: Lexington Books.

Child, J., and S. Stewart. 1996. "Regional Differences in China and their Implications for Sino-foreign Joint Ventures." Paper presented at the Conference on Managing Joint Ventures in the People's Republic of China, University of Hong Kong, April 9-12.

Child, J., Y. Yan, and Y. Lu. 1997. *Ownership and Control in Sino-Foreign Joint Ventures.* In *Co-operative Strategies: Asia-Pacific Perspectives*, edited by P. Beamish and J.P. Killing. New York: Lexington Press.

Cullen, J.B., J.L. Johnson, and T. Sakano. 1995. "Japanese and Local Partner Commitment to IJVs: Psychological Consequences of Outcomes and Investments in the IJV Relationship." *Journal of International Business Studies* 26: 91-115.

Daniels, J.D., J. Krug, and D. Nigh. 1985. "US Joint Ventures in China: Motivations and Management of Political Risk." *California Management Review* (Summer): 46-58.

Demirag, I.S. 1988. "Assessing Foreign Subsidiary Performance: The Currency Choice of UK MNCs." *Journal of International Business Studies* 19 (Summer): 257-275.

Doyle, P. 1994. "Setting Business Objectives and Measuring Performance." *European Management Journal* 12 (2): pp. 123-132.

Dunning, J.H., and M. McQueen. 1981. "The Eclectic Theory of International Production: A Case Study of the International Hotel Industry." *Managerial and Decision Economics* 2: 197-210.

Emmanuel, C., and D. Otley. 1985. *Accounting for Management Control.* UK: Van Nostrand Reinhold (UK) Co. Ltd.

Franko, L.G. 1989. "Use of Minority and 50-50 Joint Ventures by United States Multinationals during the 1970s: The Interaction of Host Country Policies and Corporate Strategies." *Journal of International Business Studies* 20 (1): 19-40.

Geringer, J.M., and L. Hebert. 1989. "Control and Performance of International Joint Ventures." *Journal of International Business Studies* 20 (Summer): 235-254.

Geringer, J.M., and L. Hebert. 1991. "Measuring Performance of International Joint Ventures." *Journal of International Business Studies* 22 (Second Quarter): 249-263.

Ghoshal, S., and C.A. Bartlett. 1990. "The Multinational Corporation as an Inter Organizational Network." *Academy of Management Review* 15 (4): 603-625.

Glaister, K.W., and P.J. Buckley. 1994. *Measures of Performance and Success Factors in UK International Joint Ventures.* Unpublished working paper.

Guo A., and R. Ackroyd. 1996. "Overcoming Barriers to Technological Transfers into China." In *Management Issues in China International Enterprise*, edited by J. Child and Y. Lu. London: Routledge.

Hall, W., and J.D. Eppink. 1992. "Strategic Alliance in the Airline Industry." *Journal of Strategic Change* 1: 341-348.

Hamel, G. 1991. "Competition for Competence and Inter-partner Learning within International Strategic Alliances." *Strategic Management Journal* 12: 83-103.

Hamel, G., Y.L. Doz, and C.K. Prahalad. 1989. "Collaborate with your Competitors - and Win." *Harvard Business Review* 5: 567-575.

Harrigan, K.R. 1987. "Joint Ventures and Competitive Strategy." *Strategic Management Journal* 9: 141-158.

Harrigan, K.R. 1988. "Strategic Alliances and Partner Asymmetries." Pp. 141-158 in *Co-operative Strategies in International Business*, edited by F.J. Contractor and P. Lorange. Lexington, MA: Lexington Books.

Hennart, J.F. 1982. *A Theory of Multinational Enterprise.* Ann Arbor, MI: University of Michigan Press.

Hill, R.C., and D. Hellriegel. 1994. "Critical Contingencies in Joint Venture Management: Some Lessons from Managers." *Organisation Science* 5 (4): 594-607.

Jaeger, A.R. 1980. *Organisation of International Joint Ventures.* New York: The Conference Board.

Killing, J.P. 1983. *Strategies for Joint Venture Success.* New York: Praeger.

Killing, J.P. 1985. "How to make a Global Joint Venture Work." *Harvard Business Review*: 120-127.

Lecraw, D.J. 1984. "Bargaining Power, Ownership, and Profitability of Transaction Corporations in Developing Countries." *Journal of International Business Studies* 15: 27-43.

Lee, C., and P.W. Beamish. 1995. "The Characteristics and Performance of Korean Joint Ventures in LDCs." *Journal of International Business Studies* 26 (Third Quarter): 637-654.

Murray, J.Y., M.K. Kotabe, and A.R. Wildt. 1995. "Strategic and Financial Performance Implication of Global Sourcing Strategy: A Contingency Analysis." *Journal of International Business Studies* 26 (First Quarter): 181-202.

Nonaka, I., and H. Takeuchi. 1995. *The Knowledge-creating Company.* New York: Oxford University Press.

Ohmae, K. 1993. "The Global Logic of Strategic Alliances." In *Collaborate to Compete: Using Strategic Alliances and Acquisitions in the Global Marketplace*, edited by J. Bleeke and D. Ernst. New York: John Wiley.

Pfeffer, J., and G.R. Salancick. 1978. *The External Control of Organizations: A Resource Dependence Perspective*. New York: Harper and Row.

Pierce, J.L., S.A. Rubenfeld, and S. Morgan. 1991. "Employee Ownership: A Conceptual Model of Process and Effects." *Academy of Management Review* 16: 121-144.

Porter, M.E. 1980. *Competitive Strategy: Techniques for Analysing Industries and Competitors*. New York: Free Press.

Robinson, R. 1969. "Ownership Across National Frontiers." *Industrial Management Review* 1 (Fall): 41-65.

Schaan, J-L. 1983. *Parent Control and Joint Venture Success: The Case of Mexico*. Unpublished doctoral dissertation, University of Western Ontario.

Schulze, W.S., and G.D. Meyer. 1991. "The Relationship between Resource, Capabilities, and Sources of Competitive Advantage as a Unifying Construct in the Field of Business Strategy." Working paper, University of Colorado.

Scott, G.M. 1973. "An Introduction to Financial Controls and Reporting in Multinational Enterprises." *Studies in International Business*. Bureau of Business Research, Graduate School of Business, The University of Texas at Austin, August 1.

Shapiro, A.C. 1982. *Multinational Financial Management*. Newton, MA: Allyn and Bacon.

Tomlinson, J.W.C. 1970. *The Joint Venture Process in International Business*. Cambridge, MA: The MIT Press.

Williamson, O.E. 1979. "Transaction Cost Economics: The Governance of Contractual Relations." *Journal of Law and Economics* 22: 233-262.

Yan, A., and B. Gray. 1994a. "Bargaining Power, Management Control, and Performance in United States-China Joint Ventures: A Comparative Case Study." *Academy of Management Journal* 37: 1478-1517.

Yan, A., and B. Gray. 1994b. "An Empirical Investigation of a Negotiation Model in American-Chinese Joint Ventures." Paper given at the Conference on Management Issues for China in the 1990s. St John's College, Cambridge, March.

Yan, A., and B. Gray. 1996. "Linking Management Control and Inter Partner Relationships with Performance in US-Chinese Joint Ventures." In *Management Issues for China: International Enterprises*, edited by J. Child and Y. Lu. London: Routledge.

Yan, Y. 1994. *Ownership and Control in International Joint Ventures*. First-year Report Doctoral Programme, Judge Institute of Management Studies, University of Cambridge.

Yan, Y., J. Child, and Y. Lu. 1995. "Ownership and Control in International Business: An Examination of Sino-foreign International Joint Ventures." Discussion paper at Conference of Academy of International Management, Canada (August 8-14).

PROFITABILITY AND TECHNICAL EFFICIENCY:

A PERFORMANCE EVALUATION OF INTERNATIONAL JOINT VENTURES IN SHANGHAI'S MANUFACTURING INDUSTRIES

Clement Chow Kong Wing and Michael Fung Ka Yiu

INTRODUCTION

For the past 15 years competition has been the centerpiece of economic reform in the People's Republic of China (PRC). The entire decade of industrial reform can be understood as an effort to "marketize" the industrial sector (Byrd 1992; Byrd and Lin 1990; Perkins 1988). One major feature of the Chinese reform process is the massive entry of non-state enterprises (McMillan and Naughton 1992). In 1978 just before the implementation of economic reform, state-owned firms accounted for 78 percent of China's industrial output. The state share of industrial production had been declining steadily and at the end of 1990 it accounted for roughly 50 percent of industrial output. If agriculture and services were included, the state share of China's output was less than 25 percent

Advances in Chinese Industrial Studies, Volume 5, pages 249-267.

ISBN: 1-55938-961-3

(*The Economist* 1992). The substantial expansion of the non-state sector is probably one of the prominent features of Chinese economic reform, besides her spectacular economic growth: her average GDP was growing at 9 percent per year during the period of 1978-1992 (Solimano 1993). The non-state sector is dominated by collective-owned enterprises, especially in the industrial sector. These collective enterprises are usually small in size and developed originally from the cooperatives before the economic reform. Another major type of non-state enterprise is the foreign invested enterprise, mainly joint ventures. Given the success of the open-door policy, foreign direct investment increased from a total of US$15.50 billion in the decade 1979-1989 to US$11.16 billion in the single year of 1992. This rapid change in the Chinese economy has resulted in a wide variety of ownership structures. What are the determinants of profitability of these different Chinese enterprises? Do enterprises of varyimg ownership structure perform differently? Does ownership structure affect the determinants of profitability? These are the questions we want to study.

The determinants of profitability are extensively investigated in the literature of finance and industrial organization.[1] The objective of this paper is to investigate the determinants of profitability and their relations with ownership structure of different enterprises in the Chinese economy in transition, which is neglected in the literature. The study will be carried out using enterprise-level data in Shanghai's industrial sector during the period 1989 to 1992. Our data set covers four types of enterprises: collective-owned enterprises, state-owned enterprises, international joint ventures, which include equity joint ventures and contractual joint ventures, and other enterprises,[2] which include state and collective jointly owned enterprises and private enterprises. Since the central government gave Shanghai more freedom in planning its economic development in 1990, Shanghai has been one of the hottest choices of foreign direct investment in China. The results of this study can provide overseas investors with a better understanding of the profitability of Shanghai's manufacturing enterprises. Moreover, given the rapid development of enterprises in the non-state sector, the results of this study are relevant in the evaluation of reform policy in China.

This chapter is organized as follows: first, related research on different types of enterprises in the Chinese economy are surveyed; second, details of the data set are described; third, the research methodology of this study is provided; and fourth, the empirical results are discussed followed by some concluding remarks.

STATE-OWNED, COLLECTIVE-OWNED, AND FOREIGN-INVESTED SECTORS

The rapidly booming non-state sector in China is dominated by a special type of organization called collective enterprises, or township and village enterprises

(TVE) in rural areas, which evolved from the cooperatives during the central planning era. These collective enterprises are "vaguely defined cooperatives," basically communal organizations and far removed from a well-defined ownership structure. The presence of these collective enterprises makes the Chinese economy different from the rest of post-socialist economies. By Western standards a collective enterprise or TVE is collectively owned by all the people, usually the workforce in that enterprise, in the community where it is located. Collective enterprises are controlled by local government while state enterprises are controlled by central government. However, these collective enterprises developed spontaneously under few government regulations and most of them are small or medium-sized enterprises.

In contrast with state enterprises that can easily obtain input materials, energy, and loans from central government (these inputs are under the control of central government), these collective enterprises have to rely on the market to obtain these input factors. In addition, products are sold in some form of market rather than being allocated by the state planning bureau. In terms of governance inside enterprises, rules governing operations, major decisions, and appointments of top managers are determined democratically by a workers' general meeting or equivalent. Finally, these collective enterprises are ultimately theoretically responsible for their own profits and losses. Therefore, their budget constraints are far from being soft (Lockett 1988; *The Economist* 1992). As a result, collective enterprises are very much "marketized," but their ownership structure is far from the Western concept of a private firm. These collective enterprises contribute substantially in improving the competitiveness of the economy; at the same time they also increase the flexibility and adaptability of the whole economy because of their small size.

The rapid expansion and growth of collective enterprises has forced reluctant state enterprises to move in the direction of market-oriented behavior. Jefferson and Rawski (1994) and Singh, Ratha, and Xiao (1993) show that profitability within the state industry is lowest in provinces where the output of non-state industry has grown more rapidly. In addition, Singh, Ratha, and Xiao also find that large provincial shares of non-state industrial output are associated with higher levels of total factor productivity[3] in state industry. This result suggests that strong growth of the non-state sector both squeezes profits and motivates greater efficiency in the state sector.

Faced with so much competition from non-state enterprises, the Chinese government introduced some new measures to improve the productivity of state enterprises. The reform measures included the following changes: first, a higher degree of autonomy is given to an enterprise's manager in input, output, and pricing decisions; second, a manager's rewards are linked to the enterprise's performance; third, a bonus from profits is given to workers; and fourth, more contract workers are employed to replace permanent workers so as to add more flexibility to the labor force (Groves, Hong, McMillan, and Naughton 1994).

After the introduction of these new measures the total factor productivity (TFP) growth rate in state-owned enterprises was 3.4 percent during the period 1980-1984 (Chen, Jefferson, Rawski, Wang, and Zheng 1988). In addition, the TFP of the state-owned sector continued to grow at about 3 percent during the period 1984-1988 (Jefferson, Rawski, and Zheng 1992) and 2.5 percent during the period of 1988-1992 (Jefferson and Rawski 1994).

However, in comparison with collective enterprises the improvement of state enterprises is still not good enough. The annual average TFP growth rate of the collective sector was about 5 percent in the period 1980-1988 and 4.7 percent during 1988-1992 (Jefferson and Rawski 1994). These TFP growth rates were higher than the TFP growth rate of state enterprises (Jefferson, Rawski, and Zheng 1992). In a similar study on the collective sector in Jiangsu Province for the period 1981-1988, the TFP growth rate of collective enterprises was 6.2 percent, which was also higher than the national level (Prime 1992). In addition, by using industrial census data, McGuckin and Nguyen (1993) show that the TFP growth rate of collective enterprises was six times higher than that of state enterprises for the period 1981-1984. According to Weitzman (1993) these collective enterprises are actually the driving force behind the rapid economic growth. They are now the second largest sector of the national economy (after the state sector), constituting over 40 percent of total industrial output, while they accounted for only 20 percent of industrial output before the economic reform.

Since the opening up of the Chinese economy in 1978 the PRC has been one of the hottest choices for foreign direct investment. Joint ventures, which were the only allowed form of foreign investment until the early 1990s, include two different kinds, namely equity joint ventures and contractual joint ventures. Undoubtedly, China's objectives in forming JVs are technology transfer, learning new techniques in production, management, marketing so as to improve productivity, and creating jobs to absorb surplus labor in the loss-making state-owned sector and rural areas. For example, in order to develop its aerospace technology the Chinese government uses the coproduction ventures as a condition for continuing to purchase from its giant overseas corporate partners like Boeing and McDonnell-Douglas (Engholm 1989). According to Beamish (1993), no country had more equity joint venture formation than China during the 1980s. Although joint ventures in China have been developing rapidly, their proportion is relatively small compared with domestic enterprises because of numerous problems encountered, such as government restrictions, long and complicated negotiation processes (Eiteman 1990; de Bruijn and Jia 1993), cultural differences, and communication problems (Beamish 1993). Despite the rapid development of JVs, research in this area has been developing at a much slower pace. Most research concentrates on the business and management issues of these foreign-invested firms in China (Schroath, Hu, and Chen 1993; Shan 1991). Chow and Fung

(1996a, 1996b, 1996c) focus on measuring the technical efficiency of joint ventures in comparison with other types of ownership like state and collective enterprises. On the aspect of firm growth, Chow and Fung (1996d, 1996e) prove that there is a negative relationship between firm growth and firm size, that is, smaller firms or joint ventures tend to grow faster than their larger counterparts. However, little research has been done to measure their productivity and profitability in comparison with domestic enterprises. This paper intends to fill this gap of knowledge by considering the issue.

DATA

The data set, supplied by the Shanghai Economic Commission, covers 2,131 enterprises in Shanghai and includes the input-output information of these enterprises. This data set contains the enterprises' net industrial output values (value added, measured at current prices in Chinese yuan), gross industrial output values, original values of fixed assets (in Chinese yuan), net values of fixed assets, types of ownership, and total profits (in Chinese yuan). There are four types of enterprises in this data set: state-owned enterprises (SOEs), collective-owned enterprises (COEs), joint ventures (JVs), and other enterprises (OEs).

Shanghai, a metropolitan city of 14 million people, was chosen because it has a large number of experienced engineers, a well-educated labor force, and is the technological leader in many fields of manufacturing in China. The city was of commercial and industrial importance before and after 1949. According to different issues of Shanghai's *Statistical Yearbooks*, the city's share in the national industrial output was very high: an average of 15 percent from 1949 to 1979 and about 7 percent in the post-reform period, although Shanghai accounts for only 1 percent of the national population.

Despite the superior conditions that Shanghai enjoyed, the central government gave little autonomy to Shanghai's government in managing its political and economic affairs. One reason for the central government's reluctance to give Shanghai more economic freedom in the earlier part of reform is that Shanghai has a sophisticated and relatively efficient taxation bureau, and the highest industrial formation and per capita national income, all of which implies a stable and substantial tax revenue for the central government. Again, although Shanghai accounts for only 1 percent of the national population, the central government relies on the city for 15 percent of its revenues (*The Economist* 1995). The central government feared that if things went wrong, its revenue would be lost; if things went right, Shanghai would keep the money. As a result, the central government was unwilling to give more economic freedom to Shanghai.

This situation changed dramatically when Jiang Zemin (ex-party chief and mayor of Shanghai) was elected as the chairman of the Chinese Communist

Party in 1989 after the Tiananmen Square incident. Since 1990 Shanghai has been given a lot more autonomy in making economic and administrative decisions. The Shanghai government can now plan and invest at its own pace. A massive Pudong project was launched to speed up the economic development and to attract foreign direct investment. Of all other locations in China, Stelzer, Ma, and Banthin (1992) reported that Shanghai offered the highest returns on investment, measured by five-year average returns on investment, to joint ventures. Now Shanghai is one of the most favorable locations chosen by U.S. investors. This study can help provide timely information to understand which factors determine the profitability of its manufacturing enterprises.

Among all Shanghai's manufacturing industries, two labor or less skill intensive industries (textile, clothing) and two capital or skill intensive industries (machinery and equipment, electronics and telecommunication equipment) are considered in our study. This panel data set covers 651 firms (268 SOEs, 216 COEs, 25 JVs, 142 OEs) in the textile industry, 335 firms (33 SOEs, 189 COEs, 12 JVs, 101 OEs) in the clothing industry, 971 firms (420 SOEs, 431 COEs, 13 JVs, 107 OEs) in the machinery and equipment industry, and 174 firms (50 SOEs, 97 COEs, 12 JVs, 15 OEs) in the electronics and telecommunication equipment industry. This panel data set tracks these groups of firms from 1989 to 1992.

METHODOLOGY

Given the significant increase in total factor productivity of Chinese enterprises during economic reform, we want to know whether this successful improvement of technical efficiency can contribute to the enterprise's profitability. The procedures to estimate total factor productivity are described as follows. For any firm in an industry, a simple Cobb-Douglas production technology is assumed. The estimation of total factor productivity follows Schmidt and Sickles's (1984) model of estimating stochastic production frontier with panel data,

$$y_{it} = a + X_{it}\alpha + e_{it} - \epsilon_i \tag{1}$$

where y = output, X = input, e = statistical noise with zero mean and finite variance, and $\epsilon_i > 0$ is a firm effect representing technical inefficiency. This model can obviously be put in the form:

$$y_{it} = a_i + X_{it}\alpha + e_{it} \tag{2}$$

where $a_i = a\text{-}\epsilon_i$ is the measure of technical efficiency of firm i and it is also the target of our analysis. The larger the a_i, the more technical efficient the firm i is.

This study adopts Cornwall, Schmidt, and Sickles's (1990) framework to estimate the total factor productivity of each firm, a log linear Cobb-Douglas production function is considered as the regression model:

$$y_{ijt} = a_{ij} + \alpha_{Kj}k'_{ijt} + \alpha_{Lj}l_{ijt} + \alpha_{Mj}m_{ijt} + u_{ijt},\ i = 1,\ldots,n_j,\ t = 1,\ldots,T \qquad (3)$$

where y_{ijt}, k'_{ijt}, l_{ijt}, m_{ijt}, and a_{ij}, are logarithms of output (Y_{ijt}), capital (K'_{ijt}), labor (L_{ijt}), materials (M_{ijt}), and index of technical efficiency (a_{ij}). u_{ijt} is a random error with mean zero and finite variance σ^2. Y_{ijt} is the gross industrial product of firm i in industry j at constant prices at the end of year t which is calculated by deflating the values measured at current prices by its product price index using 1980 as the base year. L_{ijt} is the number of workers employed by firm i in industry j at the end of year t. K'_{ijt} is the capital stock of firm i in industry j at the end of year t measured by net fixed assets deflated by a capital price index. Following McGuckin and Nguyen (1993), the capital price index is computed from the weighted average of product price indexes of five capital goods manufacturing industries: machinery and equipment, automobile and transport equipment, electric appliances, electronics and communication equipment, and apparatus and instrument-making (using 1980 as the base year). Materials or intermediate inputs are computed from the definition of gross industrial product (GIP), GIP = NIP+CC+MRF+MAT, where NIP, CC, MRF, and MAT are net industrial product (value added), annual fund for capital consumption (depreciation), and major repair fund, respectively. Based on a 1988 enterprise survey, enterprises accumulate major funds amounting to almost exactly one-half of annual depreciation figures. Therefore, we adopt the method used by Jefferson, Rawski, and Zheng (1992): MRF is assumed to be one-half of CC and material inputs, MAT, are equal to GIP-NIP-1.5CC, all terms are measured at 1980 constant prices.

McGuckin and Nguyen (1993) suggest that the TFP computed from value added will have substantial upward biases even where constant returns to scale technology and constant materials to output ratios are assumed. The presence of this bias is also confirmed by the study of Chow and Fung (1996a). As a result, technical efficiency is estimated from gross industrial values.

The values of net fixed assets are calculated from the sum of investment in the previous year minus the accumulated depreciation without any adjustment for inflation. Given the higher inflation rates in the 1980s, our deflation of net fixed assets by using the capital price deflator may not be good enough. We follow the approach suggested by Jefferson, Rawski, and Zheng (1992) to adjust for the measurement errors of reported values of capital stock. Besides the adjustment for inflation, their approach can also capture the vintage effect of investment. Since the more recent capital equipment may embody updated and more efficient technology, such newer equipment should have higher productivity than the older one. Suppose k' represents the logarithms of efficiency-price adjusted measure of the values of net fixed assets, following Jefferson, Rawski, and Zheng (1992), k'_{ijt} is expressed as:

$$k'_{ijt} = k_{ijt} + \theta_j v_{ijt} \tag{4}$$

where k_{ijt} and v_{ijt} are logarithms of firm i's values of original fixed assets deflated by capital price index and the ratio of the net fixed assets to original fixed assets at the end of year t. If the inflationary effect dominates (is dominated by) the vintage effect, we may expect a negative (positive) θ_j. For estimation purposes, the equation of k'_{ijt} is substituted into equation (3),

$$y_{ijt} = a_{ij} + \alpha_{Kj} k_{ijt} + \alpha_{Lj} l_{ijt} + \alpha_{Mj} m_{ijt} + \alpha_{vj} v_{ijt} + u_{ijt} \tag{5}$$

where $\alpha_{vj} = \alpha_{Kj}\theta_j$. The estimate of a_{ij} in (5) is the average technical efficiency of firm i in the industry j during the period 1989-1992.

The productivity of both SOEs and COEs has been increasing since the implementation of industrial reforms. In such a dynamic environment it is important to know how these firms are performing over time and what are the intertemporal shifts of their technical efficiency. In order to find out whether they are experiencing steady increases or decreases in technical efficiency, it is necessary to compute estimates of time-varying technical efficiency of each firm. Unfortunately, owing to insufficient annual observations for each firm, the desired firm-specific time-varying technical efficiency cannot be obtained. Instead, the ownership specific time-varying technical efficiency is estimated. There are four types of ownership: SOEs, COEs, JVs, and OEs. The regression model is as follows:

$$\begin{aligned} y_{ijt} = {} & a_{ij} + b_{s1j} t_{sj} + b_{s2j}(t_{sj})^2 + b_{c1j} t_{ct} + b_{c2j}(t_{cj})^2 + b_{f1j} t_{fj} + b_{f2j}(t_{fj})^2 + b_{o1j} t_{oj} \\ & + b_{o2j}(t_{oj})^2 + \alpha_{Kj} k_{ijt} + \alpha_{Lj} l_{ijt} + \alpha_{Mj} m_{ijt} + \alpha_{vj} v_{ijt} + u_{ijt} \end{aligned} \tag{6}$$

where $i = 1,\ldots,n_j$; t_z and $(t_z)^2$, $z = s,c,f,o$ are simply the linear and quadratic time trends of the corresponding enterprises (SOE (s), COE (c), JV (f), and OE (o)), that is, t_z and $(t_z)^2$ take zero values except for their own type of ownership. These time trend variables pick up the over time variations of the total factor productivity.

The time-varying technical efficiency estimates of firm i in industry j is obtained as follows:

$$a^*_{ijt} = a_{ij} + b_{z1} t_z + b_{z2}(t_{zj})^2,\ z = s,c,f,o \tag{7}$$

according to their types of ownership.

Given the impressive improvement of total factor productivity of Chinese enterprises in the 1980s, it is interesting to know whether this significant increase in technical efficiency is one of the determinants of profitability. After we get the estimates of technical efficiency, we can investigate the relationship between technical efficiency and profitability. A significantly positive relationship implies that a technically more efficient firm enjoys higher profit. However, do firms with different ownership structures manage the technological advantage to generate profit differently? We are going to test the existence of interaction effect between technical efficiency and ownership structure.

Based on the competitive process of Joseph Schumpeter (1934, 1950), competition from imitating firms should successfully and rapidly erode excess profit positions, that is, in the long run the economic rents should be zero. However, according to Mueller (1990) and Geroski and Jacquemin (1988), there exists persistence of profits over time in the United States, France, West Germany, and the United Kingdom, that is, a firm earning high profits in this period is more likely to also earn a high level of profits in the next period. As the Shanghai government conducted a massive economic reform program in 1990, such a program is similar to a market liberalization scheme which allows state firms to have more freedom in resource allocation and to compete in the marketplace. At the same time, more new firms were also allowed to enter the market. All these changes should make competition keener than before and erode profits more rapidly according to Schumpeterian competitive process. However, do enterprises in Shanghai have higher or lower persistence in their profits? Do different types of ownership exhibit different degrees of persistence? The answers to these questions will be provided by testing the interaction effect between lagged profits and ownership structure.

It has been shown in various studies that market share plays a significant role in the determination of profitability. The classical view (labeled according to Schmalensee 1985), following Bain (1951, 1956), suggests that high profitability is derived from high concentration (occupying high market share) which results from the presence of barriers to entry. Thus, there is a positive measured correlation between market share and profitability. On the other hand, the revisionist view suggests that all markets are competitive and scale economies are absent. Within some industries there are persistent efficiency differences among firms. Those efficient firms, together with their market shares, grow faster at the expense of the others. As a result there is a positive correlation between market share and profitability which is actually caused by the persistent efficiency difference and not by barriers to entry (Demsetz 1973; Jovanovic 1982; Lippman and Rumelt 1982; Peltzman 1977). In this chapter we are trying to separate the effect of efficiency from the factor of market share and to examine whether the pure market share effect (which measures the concentration caused by barriers to entry) can still account for the profitability of manufacturing enterprises in Shanghai. Moreover, we also investigate how the ownership structure affects the magnitude of the market share effect.

Our unrestricted model is as follows:

$$PROF_{ijt} = \alpha_0 + \sum_{k=1}^{3}\alpha_{Ik}DIk + \sum_{k=1}^{3}\alpha_{Tk}DTk + \sum_{k=1}^{4}\theta_k DTPROF_{kij,t-1} + \sum_{k=1}^{4}\beta_k DTEFF_{kijt} + \sum_{k=1}^{4}\gamma_k DTMS_{kijt} + e_{ijt} \tag{8}$$

where $PROF_{ijt}$ is the accounting profits of firm *i* in industry *j* at the time *t* divided by its net fixed assets. The firm *i*'s accounting profit is deflated by its product price index using 1980 as the base year. Following McGuckin and Nguyen (1993), we compute the capital price index from the weighted average of product price indexes of five capital goods manufacturing industries: machinery and equipment, automobiles and transport equipment, electrical appliances, electronics and telecommunication equipment, and apparatus and instrument-making industries (using 1980 as the base year). There has been a lot of controversy in measuring profitability of a firm and accounting profit to book values of stockholders' equity is commonly adopted (Scherer and Ross 1990). Unfortunately, it is impossible to measure stockholders' equity values in China because the Chinese ownership structure in general does not conform to the Western one. For example, the ownership of the state and collective enterprises, which are the majority in the industrial sector, is defined vaguely and obscurely. In this paper, our profitability indicator, PROF_{ijt}, is defined as net profits to capital ratios according to Scherer and Ross (1990) and Schmalensee (1985).

Lagged profits, $DTPROF_{kij,t-1} = DTi \cdot \mathrm{TPROF}_{ij,t-1}$, $k = 1,\ldots,4$ (1 is for state-owned enterprises, 2 is for collective-owned enterprises, 3 is for joint ventures, and 4 is for other enterprises), which is assumed to vary according to types of ownership, is added to capture the persistence of profits over time. The estimate of $DTPROF_{kij,t-1}$ is the speed of adjustment of *k*th type of company's profits in industry *j*. The larger (smaller) this estimate, the slower (faster) the short-run economic rents erode over time.[4] DTk, DIk, $k = 1,2,3$ are the dummy variables for the four types of ownership and four industries respectively (one dummy from each set is deleted to prevent perfect multicollinearity). $DTEFF_{kijt} = DTk \cdot \mathrm{EFF}_{ijt}$ and $DTMS_{kijt} = DTk \cdot \mathrm{MS}_{ijt}$, $k = 1,\ldots,4$, are the interaction factor among the dummies of types of ownership, technical efficiency, EFF_{ijt} (time varying technical efficiency obtained from equation (7)) and market share, MS_{ijt} (defined by its gross output share of the total gross output in its industry). The estimate of $DTEF_{kijt}$ ($DTMS_{kijt}$) is the magnitude of technical efficiency (market share) effect on the profits of *k*th type of firm in industry *j*. In addition, the proposition that the effects of lagged profits, technical efficiency, and market share vary according to types of ownership can be tested by examining whether the coefficients of $DTEFF_{kijt}$ or coefficients of $DTMS_{kijt}$ are all identical (H_0: $\beta_1 = \ldots = \beta_4$ or H_0: $\gamma_1 = \ldots = \gamma_4$) by an F test.

Since economic reform in Shanghai was speeded up substantially in 1990, the implementation of this policy is likely to create a structural break in the market structure. As a result, a Chow (1983) test is used to test the presence of any structural break created after 1990. If the reform program really changed the market structure, the structural parameters estimated during the period 1989-1990 should be different from those estimated during the period of 1991-1992. By dividing the samples into two groups, 1989-1990 and 1991-1991, and by running two separate regressions on these two subsamples, this should lead to two separate sets of parameters. Therefore, the hypothesized model is as follows:

$$Y = XB + U,\ Y = \begin{bmatrix} Y_1 \\ Y_2 \end{bmatrix},\ X = \begin{bmatrix} X_1 & 0 \\ 0 & X_2 \end{bmatrix},\ B = \begin{bmatrix} B_1 \\ B_2 \end{bmatrix},\ U = \begin{bmatrix} U_1 \\ U_2 \end{bmatrix} \tag{9}$$

Dependent var., Predictor var., Parameters Error
Y-Nx1 vector, X-Nx2k matrix, B-2kx1 vector, U-Nx1 vector,
Y_1-N_1x1 vector, X_1-N_1xk matrix, B_1-kx1 vector, U_1-N_1x1 vector,
Y_2-N_2x1 vector, X_2-N_2xk matrix; B_2-kx1 vector; U_2-N_2x1 vector,

where $N = N_1 + N_2$. If the program has no effect on market structure, the two sets of parameters should be identical, that is, $B_1 = B_2$. Running regression using the whole sample should be equivalent to running two separate regressions as there is no structural break. As a result, the null hypothesis is that market structure is not affected by the reform program,

$$H_0\colon B_1 = B_2.$$

The test statistics is as follows:

$$F = \frac{(RSSR - USSR_1 - USSR_2)/k}{(USSR_1 + USSR_2)/(N-2k)} \tag{10}$$

$RSSR$, $USSR_1$, and $USSR_2$ are the restricted sum of squared residuals, unrestricted sum of squared residuals of 1989-1990 subsample, and 1991-1992 subsample, respectively. F is distributed as a $F(k,N\text{-}2k)$ distribution.

Equation (6) is estimated by using the panel data estimation procedure of LIMDEP version 5.1. The rest are done by using SAS version 6.0. After lagging accounting profits for one year our data set has 2,131 enterprises from 1990 to 1992, and altogether 6,393 observations.

Table 1. Estimating the Technical Efficiency from Gross Industrial Product for Each Industry (1989-1992)

Variables[a]	*Textile*	*Clothing*	*Machinery and Equipment*	*Electronics and Telecommunication*
t_s	-0.0100	-0.0456	-0.0832**	-0.2049*
	(0.0167)[b]	(0.0546)	(0.0166)	(0.1046)
t_s^2	-0.0001	0.0108	0.0204**	0.0443*
	(0.0033)	(0.0107)	(0.0033)	(0.0205)
t_c	-0.0963**	-0.0491*	-0.1512**	-0.2198**
	(0.0187)	(0.0232)	(0.0166)	(0.0764)
t_c^2	0.0175**	0.0121**	0.0360**	0.0473**
	(0.0037)	(0.0045)	(0.0033)	(0.0149)
t_f	-0.0530	0.1388	0.1419*	0.0579
	(0.0547)	(0.0904)	(0.0935)	(0.2165)
t_f^2	0.0170	-0.0232	-0.0083	0.0136
	(0.0107)	(0.0178)	(0.0184)	(0.0420)
t_o	-0.0382	-0.0247	-0.1100**	-0.0584
	(0.0231)	(0.0313)	(0.0328)	(0.1901)
t_o^2	0.0073	0.0050	0.0259**	0.0222
	(0.0045)	(0.0061)	(0.0064)	(0.0373)
l_{it}	0.1297**	0.1002**	0.2165**	0.3471**
	(0.0191)	(0.0259)	(0.0211)	(0.0828)
k_{it}	0.0448**	0.0432**	0.0547**	0.1370*
	(0.0089)	(0.0109)	(0.0124)	(0.0531)
v_{it}	-0.0046	0.0180	0.0145	0.2475*
	(0.0181)	(0.0219)	(0.0192)	(0.1177)
m_{it}	0.7864**	0.7491**	0.6317**	0.3192**
	(0.0069)	(0.0092)	(0.0069)	(0.0159)
adj. R^2	0.9920	0.9816	0.9872	0.9508
Firm no.	651	335	971	174
Total obs	2604	1340	3884	696

Notes: [a] The estimates of fixed effects are not presented here because there are too many estimates for each industry.

[b] The values in parentheses are the standard errors of the corresponding estimates.

* and ** imply that the estimates are statistically significant at 5 and 1 percent level of significance respectively.

EMPIRICAL RESULTS

The estimation of equation (6) with gross industrial output as dependent variables are presented in Table 1.

By using equation (7), technical efficiency estimates are obtained. Three observations can be obtained from Table 1. First, the specification for production function is acceptable in both cases because the coefficients for inputs are significant in general and both tables show that adjusted R^2's are relatively high. Second, the technical efficiency is changing in the sample period

Table 2. Testing for the Presence of Ownership and Industry Effects on Intercepts and Slope Estimates

F-test Values	*(1)*[a] *1990*	*(2)* *1991-1992*
Structural break		27.84**
Ownership Effect[b] on Intercept	3.137*	1.271
Industry Effect on Intercept	8.628**	29.23**
Ownership Effect on $PROF_{kij,t-1}$	25.80**	465.1**
Ownership Effect on *EFF*	1.569	1.017
Ownership Effect on *MS*	0.471	0.762

Notes: [a] Model (1) and (2) are obtained from equation (8).

[b] Ownership effect on intercept: H_0: estimatses of *DTi*, $i = 1,2,3$ are zero. Ownership effect on $PROF_{kjt,t-1}$: H_0: estimates of $DTPROF_{ijt,t-1}$, $i = 1,\ldots,4$ are all identical. Ownership effect on *EFF*: H_0: estimates of $DTEFF_{kijt}$, $i = 1,\ldots,4$ are identical. Ownership effect on *MS*: H_0: estimates of $DTMS_{jij,t-1}$, $i = 1,\ldots,4$ are all identical. Similar interpretation holds for industry effect on intercept.

* significant at 5 percent level.

** significant at 1 percent level.

because some coefficients for time trend are significant. This time-trend effect is very strong in machinery and equipment and electronics and telecommunication equipment industries. Third, only the most high-tech sector (electronics and telecommunication equipment) shows the existence of vintage effect. The superior performance of the electronics and telecommunication equipment industry is reported in Table 1 that the coefficient of v_{ijt} (vintage effect variable) is positive and statistically significant. This result suggests that the quality of investment goods rose more rapidly than their costs. It is probably a result of an aggressive upgrading of technology in this industry.[5]

Table 2 reports the results of a number of tests that examine the statistical relationship between profits and ownership effects. Models (1) and (2) are estimated from equation (8). First, the F-test statistics for structural break is 27.84 for equation (8). This result strongly rejects the null hypothesis (H_0: $B_1 = B_2$) that the market structure is unaffected by the reform policy. As a result, splitting the sample into two groups (1989-1990 and 1991-1992) is necessary to yield unbiased estimates.

In addition to the stability test, the ownership effects on the intercept and slope coefficients are also tested. According to Table 2 there are significant ownership effects on the intercept term and the adjustment coefficient. However, the ownership effects on the slope coefficients of market share and technical efficiency effects are insignificant.[6] We shall discuss these ownership effects later.

Based on the results of these tests that accept some of the null hypotheses imposed on the unrestricted versions of model (1) and (2), restricted versions of model (1) and (2) (incorporating those accepted null hypotheses) are estimated and the results are reported in Table 3.

Table 3. Estimation of Restricted Profitability Model

Variables	*(1)*[1] *1990*	*(2)* *1991-1992*
Constant	-6.125**	-3.332**
	(1.364)[b]	(0.420)
DI1	4.443**	2.316**
	(0.952)	(0.293)
DI2	3.999**	2.048**
	(0.801)	(0.248)
DI3	2.796**	1.549**
	(0.613)	(0.189)
DT1	-0.257	
	(0.142)	
DT2	0.100	
	(0.136)	
DT3	-0.731*	
	(0.281)	
$DTPROF_{-1,1}$	0.267**	0.586**
	(0.045)	(0.031)
$DTPROF_{-1,2}$	0.052**	0.515**
	(0.008)	(0.014)
$DTPROF_{-1,3}$	1.235**	1.169**
	(0.158)	(0.036)
$DTPROF_{-1,4}$	0.316*	0.027*
	(0.158)	(0.012)
EFF	0.925**	0.478**
	(0.196)	(0.059)
MS	-16.67	-2.480
	(8.791)	(1.956)
Adj. R^2	0.095	0.432
F	19.66	360.9
Total obs	2131	4242

Notes: [a] Models (1) and (2) are obtained from equation (8).
[b] Values in parentheses are the correspondening standard errors.
* Significant at 5 percent level.
** Significant at 1 percent level.

We can find the determinants of profitability of Shanghai's industrial enterprises and their relations with ownership structure from the results reported in Table 2 and 3. The estimated adjustment coefficients of profits for different types of enterprises are all positive and significant. It implies a persistence of profits of enterprises in our sample. However, there are significant variations in the magnitude of the coefficients of different types of enterprises. The adjustment coefficients of joint ventures are the largest for both models (1) and (2) and are above 1. These may indicate that the accounting profits of joint ventures are highly persistent relative to state- and collective-owned enterprises.

Table 4. Average Profitability[a] of Shanghai Enterprises Across Four Industries During 1989-1992 Period (by Ownership)

Years	*State*	*Collective*	*Joint*	*Other*
1989	0.557	1.206	0.733	0.533
1990	0.281	0.491	0.842	0.549
1991	0.237	0.395	0.883	0.281
1992	0.126	0.278	1.363	0.249

Note: [a] Profitability is measured by profit to net fixed asset ratio.

High persistence of profits of joint ventures is not a surprising result, for the following reasons. First, they have been receiving preferential treatment from the government, such as tax reductions and exemptions, and priority access to raw materials and credit. This is a direct result of the government policy of attracting overseas investors. Second, joint ventures usually possess more advanced technology and management skill. These factors support that JVs can earn persistently higher profits. Chow and Fung (1996c) show that international joint ventures are in general more technically efficient than domestic manufacturing enterprises. Moreover, the technical efficiency gaps between joint ventures and domestic enterprises are widening in our sample period although the industrial reforms and active technology policies have improved the productivity of domestic enterprises (Simon 1990). Given the superiority of joint ventures in the areas of technical efficiency and preferential treatment from government, they are likely to make more profits in comparison with domestic enterprises.

Interestingly, after the massive economic reform in Shanghai during 1991-1992 the persistence of profits does not decline uniformly across all types of firms. The persistence of profits in joint ventures and other enterprises is decreased while the persistence of profits in state and collective enterprises is increased. This does not imply that these enterprises are doing better than joint ventures. The reality may lie in the fact that state and collective enterprises are steadily suffering from declines in profits for the whole period of 1989-1992, as shown in Table 4. These two groups of enterprises are actually persistently making low profits during the period of 1991-1992. On the other hand, joint ventures are doing so well that their profitability is steadily increasing during the whole period of 1989-1992.

The effects of technical efficiency on accounting profits do not vary according to the types of ownership but have statistically significant impact on profitability. For models (1) and (2) improvement in technical efficiency does raise company profits. Accordingly, we find enterprises of different ownership structure that are technically efficient are equally capable in keeping good profitability. There is no statistically significant market share effect on profitability of different types of enterprises in our sample. This may provide some support for the revisionist view that persistent efficiency differences are the ultimate source of higher profitability.

CONCLUSION

According to Beamish (1993), no country had more equity joint venture formation than China during the 1980s. Of all Chinese cities, Shanghai has been the most favorable location for foreign direct investment since the central government gave Shanghai more freedom to plan for its economic development in 1990. Although Shanghai has been attracting numerous foreign investors, little is known about the profitability of its manufacturing enterprises. This paper attempts to make a contribution in this area by studying the relationship between profits and a group of factors like ownership, industry effects, technical efficiency, and market shares of manufacturing firms in Shanghai from 1989 to 1992. In addition, the presence of these effects and structural break caused by the speeding up of the reform program in Shanghai after 1990 are also tested.

Our empirical study provides the following results. First, when the Shanghai government speeded up their economic reform by further relaxation of its controls on the economy, our empirical test confirms that such an act creates a structural break in the market structure of the industries included in this study. In addition, the goodness of fit of our model is much higher during the period 1991-1992 than the previous period, 1989-1990. Second, the estimates of lagged profit, $PROF_{ij,t-1}$, suggest that the coefficient of adjustment in profits varies significantly across different types of ownership and industries. Profits of joint ventures are more persistent over time compared with the rest. This may result from the preferential treatment received from the government and their superiority in areas of technical efficiency. In addition, contrary to the prediction that profits would be eroded more rapidly after the Shanghai government implemented a massive economic reform program in 1990, the profit persistence of state and collective enterprises is increased. Third, ownership effects are tested to be present and the effect of technical efficiency on measured profits does not vary according to types of ownership. Technical efficiency is a statistically significant factor in explaining profitability while pure market share has a statistically insignificant effect on profitability. This may support the revisionist view that persistent efficiency difference and not market concentration is the important factor that accounts for the profitability of firms. Therefore, higher profits of joint ventures compared with domestic enterprises are due to their higher technical efficiency as they have more advanced technology, better management, and marketing skills.

NOTES

1. An excellent review of this huge literature can be found in Scherer and Ross (1990, chap. 11).

2. Other enterprises include a variety of non-state and non-collective enterprises, mainly privately owned enterprises and some state and collective jointly owned enterprises.

3. Total factor productivity is a standard and widely used measure of technical efficiency of manufacturing firms (for example, Caves and Barton 1990). This indicator of technical efficiency is therefore adopted in this analysis.

4. Since only four years are covered in this data set, given such a short time horizon, readers are cautioned to interpret the adjustment coefficients of profits.

5. This partly confirms that the technology policy of the Chinese government is paying off. In the early 1980s Shanghai and central government leaders decided to create small "Silicon Valleys" in China: the Minhang and Caohejing Economic and Technological Development Zone in Shanghai is one. Since the government offered preferential treatment such as tax reductions and exemptions to priority access to raw materials and credit, and this area is equipped with better infrastructure, high skilled labor, and experienced engineers, the lion's share of U.S. direct foreign investment in Shanghai has been centered in this zone (Simon 1990).

6. These results are based on the testing of the following null hypotheses: Ownership effect on intercept: H_0: estimates of DTi, $i = 1,2,3$ are zero. Ownership effect on $PROF_{kij,t-1}$: H_0: estimates of $DTPROF_{kij,t-1}$ are all identical. Ownership effect on EFF: H_0: estimates of $DTEFF_{kijt}$, $i = 1, \ldots, 4$, are all identical. Ownership effect on MS: H_0: estimates of $DTMS_{kijt}$, $i = 1, \ldots, 4$, are all identical.

REFERENCES

Bain, J.S. 1951. "Relationship of Profit Rate to Industry Concentration: American Manufacturing, 1936-1940." *Quarterly Journal of Economics* 65: 293-324.

Bain, J.S. 1956. *Barriers to New Competition*. Cambridge, MA: Harvard University Press.

Beamish, P.W. 1993. "The Characteristics of Joint Ventures in the People's Republic of China." *Journal of International Marketing* 1: 22-48.

de Bruijn, E.J., and X. Jia. 1993. "Transferring Technology to China by Means of Joint Ventures." *Research-Technolgy Management* 36: 17-22.

Byrd, W.A. 1992. "Chinese Industrial Reform, 1978-1989." Pp. 1-32 in *Chinese Industrial Firms Under Reform*, edited by W.A. Byrd. New York: Oxford University Press.

Byrd, W.A., and Q. Lin. 1990. "China's Rural Industry: An Introduction." Pp. 3-18 in *China's Rural Industry: Structure, Development, and Reform*, edited by W.A. Byrd and Q. Lin. New York: Oxford University Press.

Caves, R.E., and D.R. Barton. 1990. *Efficiency in U.S. Manufacturing Industries*. Cambridge, MA: MIT Press.

Chen, K., G.H. Jefferson, T.G. Rawski, H. Wang, and Y. Zheng. 1988. "Productivity Change in Chinese Industry: 1953-1985." *Journal of Comparative Economics* 12: 570-91.

Chow, G.C. 1983. *Econometrics*. New York: McGraw-Hill.

Chow, K.W., and K.Y. Fung. 1996a. "Firm Size and Performance of Manufacturing Enterprises in the People's Republic of China: The Case of Shanghai's Manufacturing Industries." *Small Business Economics*.

Chow, K.W., and K.Y. Fung. 1996b. "Technical Efficiency and Firm Size of International Joint Ventures in Shanghai's Manufacturing Sector." *Journal of Global Business*.

Chow, K.W., and K.Y. Fung. 1996c. "Measuring the Technological Leadership of International Joint Ventures in a Transforming Economy." *Journal of Business Research*.

Chow, K.W., and K.Y. Fung. 1996d. "Firm Dynamics of International Joint Ventures in Shanghai's Manufacturing Sector: Testing the Validity of Gibrat's Law." *Journal of Applied Business Research.*

Chow, K.W., and K.Y. Fung. 1996e. "Firm Dynamics and Industrialization in the Chinese Economy in Transition: Implications for Small Business Policy." *Journal of Business Venturing.*

Cornwall, C.P., P. Schmidt, and R.C. Sickles. 1990. "Production Frontier with Cross-sectional and Time Series Variation in Efficiency Levels." *Journal of Econometrics* 46: 185-200.

Demsetz, H. 1973. "Industry Structure, Market Rivalry, and Public Policy." *Journal of Law and Economics* 16: 1-10.

The Economist. 1992. "A Survey on China." November 28: 1-18.

The Economist. 1995. "A Survey on China." March 18th: 1-24.

Eiteman, D.K. 1990. "American Executives' Perceptions of Negotiating Joint Ventures with the People's Republic of China: Lesson Learned." *Columbia Journal of World Business* 25: 59-67.

Engholm, C. 1989. *The China Venture.* Glenview, IL: Scott Freeman & Co.

Geroski, P., and A. Jacquemin. 1988. "Dominant Firms and their Alleged Decline." *International Journal of Industrial Organization* 5: 1-28.

Groves, T., Y. Hong, J. McMillan, and B. Naughton. 1994. "Autonomy and Incentives in Chinese State Enterprises." *Quarterly Journal of Economics* 109: 183-209.

Jefferson, G., T.G. Rawski, and Y. Zheng. 1992. "Growth, Efficiency, and Convergence in Chinese State Enterprises." *Economic Development and Cultural Change* 40: 239-266.

Jefferson, G., and T.G. Rawski. 1994. "Enterprise Reform in Chinese Industry." *Journal of Economic Perspectives* 8: 47-70.

Jovanovic, B. 1982. "Selection and the Evolution of Industry." *Econometrica* 50: 649-670.

Lippman, S.A., and R.P. Rumelt. 1982. "Uncertain Imitability: An Analysis of Interfirm Differences in Efficiency under Competition." *Bell Journal of Economics* 13: 418-438.

Lockett, M. 1988. "The Urban Collective Economy." Pp. 118-137 in *Transforming China's Economy in the Eighties*, edited by S. Feuchtwang, A. Hussain, and T. Paircult. Boulder, CO: Westview Press.

McGuckin, R.H., and S.V. Nguyen. 1993. "Post-reform Industrial Productivity Performance of China: New Evidence from the 1985 Industrial Census Data. *Economic Inquiry* 31: 323-341.

McMillan, J., and B. Naughton. 1992. "How to Reform a Planned Economy: Lessons from China." *Oxford Review of Economic Policy* 8: 130-143.

Mueller, D.C. 1990. "The Persistence of Profits in the United States." Pp. 35-57 in *The Dynamics of Company Profits*, edited by D. C. Mueller. Cambridge, UK: Cambridge University Press.

Peltzman, S. 1977. "The Gains and Losses from Industrial Concentration." *Journal of Law and Economics* 20: 229-263.

Perkins, D.H. 1988. "Reforming China's Economic System." *Journal of Economic Literature* 26: 601-645.

Prime, P.B. 1992. "Industry Response to Market Liberalization in China: Evidence from Jiangsu Province." *Economic Development and Cultural Change* 41: 27-50.

Scherer, F.M., and D. Ross. 1990. *Industrial Market Structure and Economic Performance.* Boston, MA: Houghton Mifflin & Co.

Schmalensee, R. 1985. "Do Markets Differ Much?" *American Economic Review* 75: 341-351.

Schmidt, P., and R. C. Sickles. 1984. "Production Frontier and Panel Data." *Journal of Business and Economics Statistics* 2: 36-74.

Schroath, F.W., M.Y. Hu, and H. Chen. 1993. "Country-of-origin Effects of Foreign Investment in the People's Republic of China." *Journal of International Business Studies* 24: 277-290.

Schumpeter, J.A. 1934. *The Theory of Economic Development*. Cambridge, MA: Harvard University Press.

Schumpeter, J.A. 1950. *Capitalism, Socialism and Democracy* (3rd ed.). New York: Harper & Row.

Shan, W. 1991. "Environmental Risks and Joint Venture Sharing Agreements." *Journal of International Business Studies* 22: 555-578.

Simon, D.F. 1990. "Shanghai's Lure for High-tech Investor." *China Business Review* (March-April): 44-49.

Singh, I., D. Ratha, and G. Xiao. 1993. "Non-state Enterprises as an Engine of Growth: An Analysis of Provincial Industrial Growth in Post-reform China." Working paper, Transition and Macro Adjustment Division, The World Bank.

Solimano, A. 1993. "The Post-socialist Transitions in Comparative Perspective: Policy Issues and Recent Experience." *World Development* 21: 1823-1835.

Stelzer, L.C., C. Ma, and J. Banthin. 1992. Gauging Investor Satisfaction." *China Business Review* (November-December): 54-56.

Weitzman, M.L. 1993. "Economic Transition: Can Theory Help?" *European Economic Review* 37: 549-555.

FOREIGN INVESTMENT IN THE RETAIL SECTOR IN THE PEOPLE'S REPUBLIC OF CHINA

C.S. Tseng

INTRODUCTION

More and more business attention has been concentrated on the People's Republic of China (PRC) in recent years. China is one of the world's fastest-growing economies, with an average double-digit GDP growth (Hang Seng 1994). *Time* (1993) and *Business Week* (1993) predict that China will be "the next superpower" and the "emerging economic powerhouse of the twenty-first century." The PRC was the second largest recipient of foreign direct investment (US$26 billion) after the United States in 1993 (United Nations Conference on Trade and Development figures).

The decision was made at the third plenary session of the 14th Central Committee of the Communist Party, held in November 1993, to establish a socialist market economic structure and open wider to the outside world. With a population of 1.19 billion, one-fifth of the world's population, China has the biggest market in the world. Chinese consumers have a higher disposable

Advances in Chinese Industrial Studies, Volume 5, pages 269-287.

ISBN: 1-55938-961-3

income than statistics may suggest, as most of their living essentials are heavily subsidized, and many of them also have other secondary incomes.

REFORMS IN DISTRIBUTION AND RETAILING

Before the period of economic reform the retail distribution of consumer goods in the PRC was under a state monopoly: the "three-tier" structure, consisting of specialized corporations under the Ministry of Commerce or local commercial bureau, divided along product lines to handle specific categories or groups of goods. The distribution of household electrical appliances, for instance, was under the control of the metals, transport, electrical, and chemical companies, a corporation under the first commercial bureau. The three-tier structure comprised the First Level Purchasing and Supply Enterprises (FLPSEs), the Second Level Purchasing and Supply Enterprises (SLPSEs), and the Third Level Wholesalers (TLWs). The FLPSEs were located in three cities only, namely Tianjin, Shanghai, and Guangzhou, and reported to the Ministry of Commerce in Beijing and the local commercial bureau. They purchased goods from all over China, and accepted imported goods, and then distributed them to the SLPSEs who operated at the provincial level; each reported to the commercial bureau of the province and also to the local government department taking charge of commercial matters. The SLPSEs were normally located in the capital cities of the provinces, and were responsible for the purchase of goods from the FLPSEs and their distribution to the TLWs in the various cities and counties. In turn, the TLWs redistributed goods to local retailers, normally state-owned enterprises. The supply and distribution of goods in rural areas was under the control of supply and marketing cooperatives. Regional protectionism characterized this system. The retailers were allowed to buy only from wholesalers within the dictated region; supplies from elsewhere were brought in only as a very last resort. Figure 1 shows the distribution structure before the reforms; Figure 2 shows the distribution structure in Shanghai before the reforms.

The central government has introduced, since 1979, a series of reforms of distribution systems. Enterprises from noncommercial systems, such as production enterprises, as well as private and collective enterprises, were gradually allowed to participate in the distribution and retailing of consumer goods. Until the late 1980s distribution and retailing of household electrical appliances could be handled by different types of companies; for example, the distribution of Philips' Domestic Appliances in Shanghai was handled by a company under the agricultural bureau.

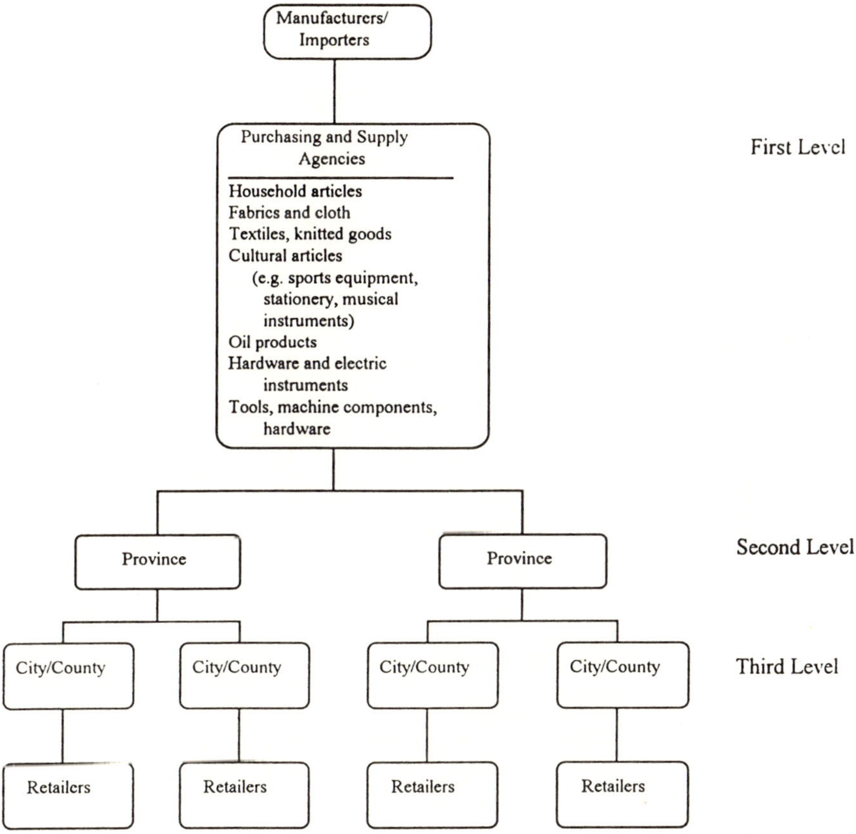

Figure 1. Traditional Distribution Channels

FOREIGN PARTICIPATION IN DISTRIBUTION AND RETAILING

Access to China's consumer market was restricted to domestic enterprises before 1991. Foreign companies were not allowed to set up direct retail outlets. All foreign manufactured consumer goods had to be imported by the foreign trade corporations, subject to a high tariff and licensing requirements where applicable. An alternative was to set up a manufacturing plant either in the form of contract manufacturing, joint venture, or wholly owned venture, where part of the product may be permitted to be distributed in China if domestic sales rights are granted. Since consumer goods were not considered as priority

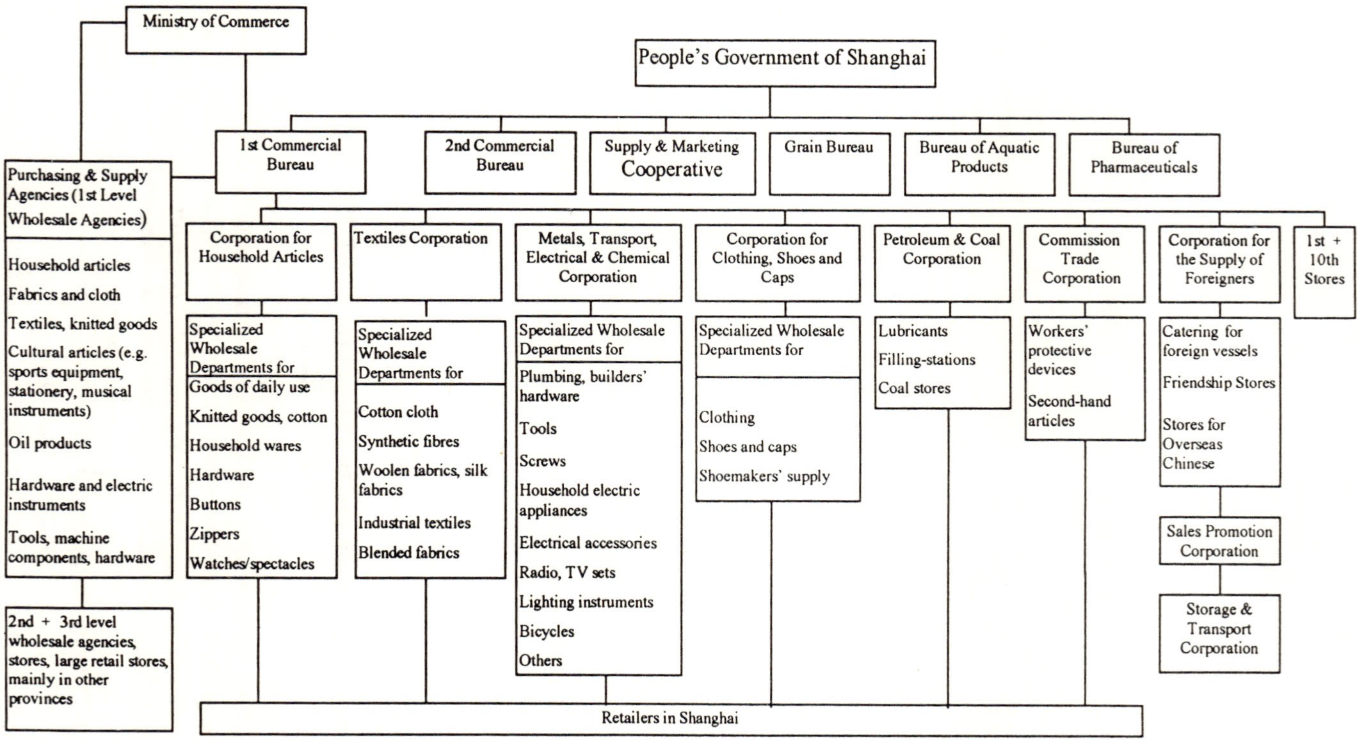

Figure 2. Distribution of Consumer Goods under the Commercial System before Reform in Shanghai

projects, however, export to the PRC or setting up a manufacturing plant there usually met with many obstacles.

The PRC decided to open up the retail sector to foreigners in 1992. The policy statement of June 16, 1992 (Document No. 5) issued by the Communist Party and State Council urged provincial and local authorities to take bolder measures to utilize foreign capital, know-how, and technology and develop distribution channels (State Council 1992).

Following this, in October 1992 the State Council announced that a maximum of two large-scale joint venture department stores would be allowed to operate in six cities and the five Special Economic Zones (SEZs) on a trial basis. The six cities are Beijing, Shanghai, Tianjin, Dalin, Qingdao, and Guangzhou, and the SEZs are Shenzhen, Xiamen, Zhuhai, Shantou, and Hainan. These joint venture department stores were to be approved by the central government (*Hong Kong Economic Journal* 1993) and they would be allowed to sell a full range of merchandise and enjoy certain import and export rights. They would be able to import goods for sale limited to general merchandise, with a value not exceeding 30 percent of their total annual turnover, and would have to balance their own foreign exchange needs (HKTDC 1994).

By December 1995 14 large-scale joint venture department stores had been approved by the State Council. Examples include the Beijing Yansha Shopping City (a joint venture between the Friendship commercial enterprise group, a state-owned corporation, and Sin Cheng (Holdings) Pte Ltd from Singapore; and Yaohan in Pudong, Shanghai, a joint venture between Yaohan International of Japan and Shanghai Number One Department Store. Details of these 14 joint venture projects are shown in Table 1. The table shows that four joint venture projects have been approved for Shanghai; this is partly because Pudong is considered a new development zone where special preferential treatment is given to promote foreign investment. Moreover, the so-called foreign partners of two of the projects are Chinese enterprises from Hong Kong: the China Resources Group was set up by the Ministry of Foreign Trade and Economic Co-operation (MOFTEC) in Hong Kong, and Shanghai Industrial is the window company of the Shanghai municipal government in Hong Kong. The joint venture partners are mainly from Asia, that is, Singapore, Japan, Malaysia, Thailand, and Hong Kong; however, new policy directives specify that in order to gain more advanced know-how and management skills in retailing, future joint venture partners should be big North American, European, and Japanese stores or groups.

In addition to those mentioned, local governments can approve joint venture retailing projects on a smaller scale, but projects approved under this category do not possess import rights. Existing examples include Sincere, Shui Hing, Carrefour, Printemps, and Isetan (Shanghai), Seibu (Shenzhen), and Park'N Shop (East China and Shanghai).

Table 1. 14 Sino-Foreign Retail Joint Venture Projects Approved by the State Council (up to December 1995)

City	*Project*	*Chinese Party*	*Foreign Party*	*Investment*
Beijing	Yansha Friendship Xinchang Co. Ltd.	Friendship Commercial Center Group	Sin Chang (Holdings) Co. Ltd., Singapore	RMB 150 million
	Xin Dongan Co. Ltd.	Dongan Group	Sun Hung Kai Co. Ltd., Hong Kong	US$300 million
Shanghai	Shanghai No. 1 Yaohan	Shanghai No. 1 Department Store Co. Ltd.	Yaohan Group, Hong Kong; Yaohan, Japan	US$230 million
	Shanghai run Hau	Shanghai Hua Lian Group	China Resources Group, Hong Kong	US$100 million
	Shanghai Orient Shopping Center	Shanghai Commercial Development Co.	Shanghai Industrial Co. Ltd., Hong Kong	RMB 71.9 million
	Shanghai Jusco	Shanghai Shen Hua Industrial Co. Ltd.	Jusco, Japan; CITIC (Hong Kong)	RMB 94.6 million
Tianjin	Hua Xin Shopping Bazaar	Tianjin Hualian Shopping Bazaar Co. Ltd.	Xinde Gruop Co., Hong Kong	RMB 700 million
	Chia Tai International Chopping Center	Tianjin Leader (Group) Co.	Chia Tai Group, Thailand	RMB 700 million
Guangzhou	Hualian Broaday	Guangdong Sugar, Ciagreet and Liquor Group	Broadway Int'l Development, Hong Kong	RMB 150 million
	Zhengjia Enterprises (Commercial) Co. Ltd.	Jiajing Commercial Trading Development Co.	Chia Tai Tian He Investment, Hong Kong	US$35 million
Qingdao	Qingdao No. 1 Department Store	Qingdao No. 1 Department Store	Lion Group, Malaysia	RMB 780 million
	Qingdao Jusco	Qingdao Supply and Marketing Cooperative	Jusco Co. Ltd., Japan	US$38 million
Dalian	Dalian International Commerical Center	Dayun Shopping Center Co. Ltd.	Nichii Co. Ltd., Japan	RMB 900 million
Shantou	Shantou Jinyindao Trading Co. Ltd.	Tianjin Hualian, Shantou China Travel Service	Chen Shi Xian, Thai-Chinese	HK$100 million

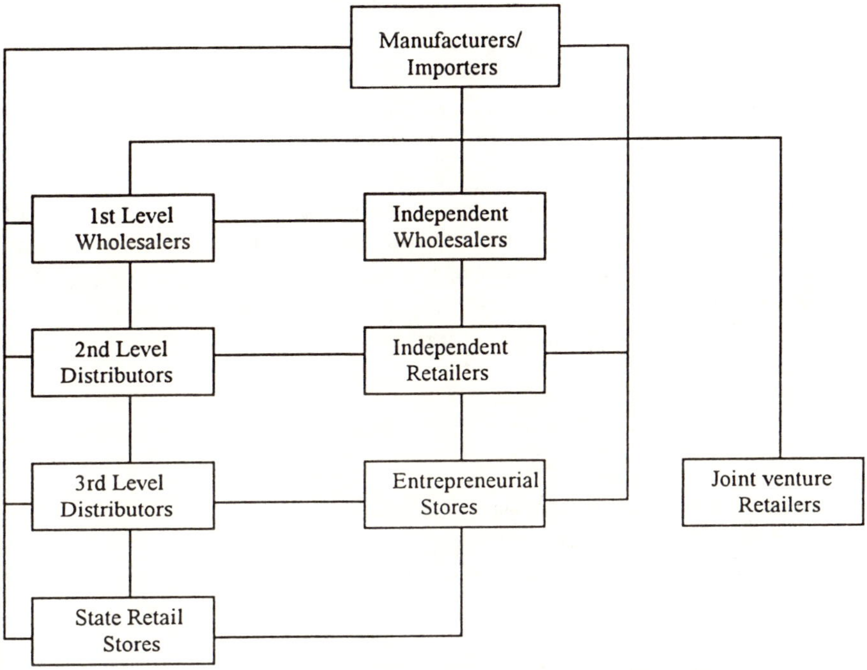

Figure 3. The Distribution System as at 1994

Another objective of Document No. 5 is to encourage state enterprises to set up service subsidiaries so that excess staff and workers can be redeployed. As a result, many newly set up tertiary industry organizations (TIOs) have entered the wholesale and distribution sector, and together with an increasing number of collective and private players entering the industry, the distribution system in the PRC is undergoing great change. In a move to streamline government structure the Ministry of Materials and Equipment (in charge of supplying raw materials and equipment to industrial organizations) and the Ministry of Commerce (in charge of the distribution of commodities to consumers) were combined to form the Ministry of Internal Domestic Trade in March 1993 (*SCMP* 1993). In November 1993 the Central Committee of the Communist Party decided to establish a socialist market economic structure (*China Economic News* 1993), and the monopolistic state-owned distribution system was further broken down. In order to support the application to rejoin GATT, a Ministry of Internal Domestic Trade official revealed that foreign investors would be given the green light to do wholesale business (*China Daily Business Weekly* 1993). The 1994 distribution system in China is shown in Figure 3. More details about the distribution and retailing reforms in China can be found in Tseng, Kwan, and Cheung (1994).

CHANNELS USED BY FOREIGN COMPANIES TO ACCESS CHINA'S CONSUMER MARKET

As mentioned earlier, foreign companies wishing to access China's consumer market before 1991 could do so only through export or local manufacturing. With the 1992 reforms permitting limited foreign participation, more channels were made available: the following is a summary of channels foreign companies use to access the Chinese consumer market.

Duty-Free Organizations

Consumer goods may be imported through the China National Duty-free Merchandise Corporation, which is responsible for the import, distribution, and retailing of consumer goods to retail outlets in key international airports, ferry terminals (Guangzhou, Shenzhen, and Zhuhai), railway stations (Guangzhou and Shenzhen), and duty-free stores for diplomats and returning overseas Chinese spending hard currency in China or through China Travel in Hong Kong (a company under the overseas Chinese office of the State Council) for consumer durables such as color televisions or motorcycles. Up to 1994 overseas Chinese (including Taiwanese) were entitled to import one item every year for their relatives in the PRC. They could purchase a voucher for a particular item in Hong Kong, the voucher would be stamped at any port of entry by Chinese customs for duty-free purposes, and delivery could be taken at any major city. In 1994, however, this privilege for overseas Chinese (except Taiwanese) was abolished.

Export Through Trading Organizations in Hong Kong or China

Many foreign consumer goods manufacturers who do not have manufacturing facilities in China have been using trading organizations with import licences to bring their products into the PRC market. For high-value products such as expensive brands of spirits or electrical appliances, which carry high import duties, the trading organizations in Hong Kong are able to negotiate a lower tariff, or use other means such as unofficial channels to import products into one of the SEZs and then distribute them to other parts of China. Many state-owned department stores and wholesalers and distributors will approach the trading organizations in the SEZs rather than the foreign trade corporations, to avoid paying high tariffs.

The Hong Kong Trade Development Council Promotion in Department Stores

The Hong Kong Trade Development Council (HKTDC) has been active in organizing in-store exhibitions, called "Hong Kong Showcase," in department stores in China. During promotion periods participating manufacturers can, under the management of the department store, operate wholesale and retail activities of their products and the HKTDC will provide marketing and promotional services including advertising, product display, and counter design. The first event of this kind was held in May 1989, and was jointly organized with the Nanfang Building Department Store in Guangzhou. The promotion period was two years. Since then the HKTDC has organized similar events in coastal cities such as Shanghai, Beijing, Dalian, Shenyang, and Tianjin, and inland cities such as Wuxi, Wuhan, Zhengzhou, Nanjing, Chongqing, Harbin, and Hangzhou. The HKTDC is now focusing on other inland cities, such as Chengdu, Changsha, and Qingdao since Hong Kong businessmen are now quite familar with the coastal cities. Promotional periods are now adjusted to last for about three months, and participating manufacturers are able to use this opportunity to decide whether their products are "acceptable" in the China market and whether to rent a counter in the store.

Exclusive Counters in Department Stores

Consumer goods manufacturers or suppliers may directly rent a counter in a department store by signing a contract permitting the store to manage the sales activities. Alternatively, instead of paying rent for the counter, the supplier may sell the merchandise to the store at an agreed discount. Goldlion, for example, a Hong Kong-based manufacturer and retailer of upmarket men's accessories, operates 460 Goldlion counters in major cities and urban areas such as Guangzhou, Tianjin, Shanghai, Beijing, Xian, and Shenzhen. It sells its merchandise to the stores at a discount of 20 percent (Davies 1994).

Joint Venture Retailing Outlets

A wholly owned or joint venture manufacturer may set up another joint venture retailing outlet with a domestic company that has a shop in a prime location and possesses a retailing licence. Foreign companies without manufacturing facilities in China may also set up joint venture retailing outlets with companies under former commercial systems. For example, Park'N Shop's parent company, the Watson Group, formed a joint venture with Zhuhai Development Store Group to set up a supermarket in Zhuhai.

Granting Franchise to Local Mainland Retailers

Franchising is still a relatively new concept in China, and it can be very difficult to convince the Chinese to pay royalties for "soft technology," such as ideas in store decoration, management, and marketing know-how. Many international fast-food groups generally use franchising as a form of market entry in the internationalization of their operations, but have had to modify their strategy in China. For example, McDonald's first restaurant in Beijing is in the form of a joint venture.

Franchising is difficult to translate into Chinese. The usual translation, *liansuodian*, or "chain store," is a term that does not have a legal definition in China. Franchising operations can be established under three legal options: the equity joint venture law, the cooperative (or contractual) joint venture law, and licensing legislation (U.S. Foreign and Commercial Service 1994). Western companies, because of the lack of familiarity with the business environment structure in China, usually find it very difficult to franchise directly to a domestic company in the PRC. Moreover, since these companies are not familiar with the Chinese environment their corporate cultures do not allow executives to enter into any contract that is not legally binding.

Western companies, therefore, usually franchise an operation to Hong Kong or Taiwanese companies, and these companies then franchise or set up joint ventures in China. One example is Walt Disney, which has franchised children's clothing to a Taiwanese company which then grants franchises to local mainland retailers. The Taiwanese company provides Walt Disney products and, also, store decoration and marketing and management know-how. The retailers sell the franchised products exclusively. Other examples are Giordano, Benetton, Crocodile, and Bossini stores, and Printemps of Paris, which has franchised the name and departmental operations to Topform, a listed company in Hong Kong. Topform then set up a joint venture department store in Huaihai Zhong Lu, a prime shopping area in Shanghai, with Yimin Departmental Group, a company listed on the Shanghai stock exchange.

Chain Stores

The chain store, or *liansuodian*, is the latest form of officially promoted retail operation in China. Restaurants, fast-food outlets, supermarkets, convenience stores, jewellery shops, photo-finishing shops, speciality boutiques, and optical shops are all seen as businesses that could be developed feasibly into chain stores, or *liansuo jingying*, in China. With the rapid urbanization and changing lifestyle in major cities, and in order to improve operational efficiency, small staple and non-staple food stores, including wet markets under the commercial system, have embarked on major reforms, and many supermarket/retail outlets in the form of chain stores are being set up. For example, up to 1995 there were 21 supermarket groups (with centralized purchasing, packaging, and distribution centers) in Shanghai with 700 retail outlets. The Shanghai municipal government has set a target to have more than 1,000 chain store outlets in Shanghai by the year 2000, and there should be four or five big supermarket groups, each with more than 100 big retail outlets (*Jiefang Daily China Economic News* 1996). As chain stores have extensive coverage in the distribution of products, foreign consumer goods manufacturers should explore the feasibility of distributing products through this channel, and should start to establish business contacts and *guanxi* with potential big chain store operators.

Foreign companies can also set up chain stores themselves. Several Hong Kong companies have plans to establish joint venture chain stores in China, including Fotomax photo-finishing shops, Hong Kong Optical, City Chain, and Fortei. It is important to note that up to now there is still no central body to issue retail licences to enable a company to operate a chain store operation throughout the whole of the PRC. The operator needs to make separate applications with different joint venture partners in each city.

Supermarkets/Hypermarkets

Foreign investors can also engage in supermarket operations which involve retail sales of foodstuffs and small household items. In the past, entry was usually in the form of a joint venture located in hotels for foreign visitors, but nowadays foreign investors can form joint ventures with corporations under the commercial system which own shops in strategic locations convenient for domestic customers. For example, the A.S. Watson Group (Hutchison Whampoa), parent of Park'N Shop, established a joint venture called Park'N Shop Shanghai Ltd (PNSS) with Lu Wan Non-Staple food company. The first store opened in Qu Xi Lu, Lu Wan District on October 15, 1994, and up to December 1995 Park'N Shop had 10 stores in Shanghai.

Hypermarkets and big discount shops have also set up joint ventures. For example, Carrefour from France has concluded a joint venture agreement with Shanghai Lian Hua Supermarket Ltd and is planning to set up its first store in Qu Yang Road, Shanghai. Wal-Mark Store Inc., the biggest U.S.-based discount retailer, was also planning to set up stores in Shengzhen, Shenyong, and Shanghai, all scheduled to open in the latter part of 1996.[1]

Department Stores

As mentioned before, foreign investors may engage in large-scale projects in the six cities and five SEZs, subject to State Council approval. They may also engage in smaller scale department store projects (less than US$30 million investment) without import and export rights.

Property Development Projects

Foreign companies engaged in the development of commercial/office/shopping complexes, in particular in prime urban locations, can, upon completion of the projects, either lease space to local retailers in conjunction with local partners, or indirectly engage in retailing business, utilizing the licence of their joint venture partners. Examples include Henderson, Hang Lung, and Hysan in Shanghai's Xujiahui district and Ryoden's Shanghai Square project.

Direct Marketing

Foreign companies may be involved in direct marketing: examples include Avon and Amway. However, credit cards are not popular in the PRC, and government policy does not encourage this type of activity.

Wholesaling

Officially, foreign companies are not allowed to engage in wholesaling activities in China. However, in provisions on foreign investment in retailing (issued by the State Council in November 1992) the differences between retailing and wholesaling are not specified exactly. Wholesaling may be described as "retailing in bulk quantities"; this is a grey area of the law. In the PRC, however, as long as the law does not specifically prohibit something, the chances are that you can get away with it. At present, foreign companies may engage in "retailing in bulk quantities" through the following channels.

The International Fashion Center

This center, located in Panyu and organized by the HKTDC, assists Hong Kong garment manufacturers to distribute their products in China. The HKTDC plans to develop the center into a national distribution center for garments in China. The center accommodates shops, showrooms, meeting rooms, and warehousing facilities under one roof. Hong Kong garment manufacturers can also make use of the promotional expertise of the HKTDC to build up their product image.

The Industrial Park with Distribution Facilities

Manufacturers of light industrial products can make use of the industrial park, also located in Panyu, developed by Li and Fung Development (China) Ltd. Foreign companies can make use of this channel to carry out manufacturing and distribution in bulk orders at the same time.

The International Merchandise Mart (IMM)

This is a large distribution center in Mei Long, on the outskirts of Shanghai, invested by Yaohan and opened in 1994. It is similar to one already operating in Singapore (a joint venture between the Trade Development Board of Singapore and Yaohan, for the distribution of goods for the South East Asian region). In addition to wholesaling the IMM carries out retail business. Foreign companies may make use of this channel for the distribution of their goods in China, especially for the Yangtze Delta region.

PROBLEMS AND PRACTICES

Payment Terms

Long payment terms are very popular in China. The retailer will owe the distributor, and the distributor will owe the manufacturers or the importers, which means that foreign companies must have effective means for dealing with cash-flow problems. The majority of wholesalers do not have the resources to provide credit facilities, and prefer consignment arrangements. Long payment periods (e.g., 150 days instead of the usual 60 days) are widely practiced. Foreign companies have little option but to agree to this arrangement, and should be very careful to select wholesalers that are economically viable.

Geographic Differences

The PRC is comprised of provinces that are at different stages of economic development, and it would be difficult (and very costly) for a company to set up a retail network throughout the country. The purchasing power of people in the coastal provinces is much higher than in the interior, and it has been the usual practice for companies to go to the cities with higher incomes first, perhaps planning to explore others areas later.

Companies should also take into account the fact that customers differ in buying behavior from city to city. The author was involved in a study on consumer behavior in the three most developed cities (Guangzhou, Shanghai, and Beijing) in 1993. It was found that consumers preferred, in order, imported foreign brands, then joint venture-made foreign brands, and then local brands. It was also found, however, that the attitudes of consumers in these areas varied in some aspects. Consumers in Guangzhou are more Westernized due to their proximity to Hong Kong, and more ready to accept new things; they are also the wealthiest group of customers in China and so are more selective in purchasing goods. Shanghai consumers appear to be more "calculating";

although they perceive that foreign brands are of better quality, they sometimes cannot accept the immense difference in price, and also like to examine the product carefully before making any purchase. Beijing consumers are very emotional and quite receptive to advertising messages. Companies should adopt and adapt their marketing strategies accordingly.

Different cities also have different styles in dealing with foreign companies. Shanghai has been reported as the city with the best cooperative attitude to overseas investors. Perhaps this is because Shanghai was one of the first cities opened to foreign businessmen, and the municipal government leaders are young, open-minded, and energetic. In Beijing everything must go by the book; foreign investors have no alternative but to follow the regulations. One good point about this is that at least companies receive a clear direction as to what course to follow. In the south the central government is remote and control is lax, thus companies may sometimes have difficulty sometimes in figuring out what is feasible and what is not.

Availability of Market Information

Market information is vital for business success. A company cannot formulate its strategies without knowing consumers' needs and competitors' strategies. Unfortunately, there is not much published material on China available. Neither is there an organization such as a trade promotion board to provide assistance to foreign businessmen. Companies wanting to explore the Chinese market usually have to gather information first-hand, rather than rely on secondary data. When Philips, for example, first planned to enter the Chinese market they used a very primitive method of sourcing the appropriate retailers to handle their electrical appliances. Having purchased a map of the targeted city they traced all the department stores and visited them one by one, observing the environment, the traffic, the atmosphere, and the buying behavior of customers and talking to the employees. They evaluated all these factors and then made their decisions. It turned out to be an effective approach: it was not difficult to obtain information from the staff, such as sales figures. As China is still a developing country, staff often do not realize the importance of sales figures and do not treat them as confidential. If one shows a sincere attitude, and the stores are not busy, staff are likely to be willing to engage in conversation and give information about sales. The author has carried out consultancy research in China and was able to write down the prices of various products and take photographs of displays without being interrupted.

Logistic Problems

The transportation infrastructure in China is not yet well-developed and thus the physical movement of goods is rather inefficient. The highway system is not comprehensive, linking only the coastal cities, and most distributors have to use the rail system for long-distance transport. However, the rail system is closely controlled and priority is often given to goods that are still under central government control, such as coal and agricultural products. Distributors are left to compete for the remaining space and those who enjoy a good relationship with the rail office are likely to get better service. Therefore, in some provinces it is better for companies to use the centralized distribution system rather than setting up their own. Philips uses a dual system for its product distribution. In the big cities, which are linked by highways, it has set up its own network; in other provinces it uses the centralized system.

Warehousing is another problem. Although space is usually available, it may not be in good condition and the protection for goods is minimal. Thus many companies choose to build their own warehouses and handle their own products. There are also domestic independent distributors who have experience in handling particular kinds of goods.

Relationships

Guanxi (relationships) is the key for business success in China. Companies with good *guanxi* with government officials can enjoy advantages such as the speedy processing of documents and ready approval of permits. However, one should be very cautious. It may be simplistic to think that there is only one clique with whom to establish *guanxi* in China. Having good relations with one clique which may be the rival of another may cause problems. There are no rules of thumb in building *guanxi*, and employing someone who knows the Chinese market may well be the best solution. The *guanxi* phenomenon can also be applied to managing retailers. A company can enjoy many privileges if it has a good relationship with its retailers. For instance, because of its good relationship with retailers in Tianjin General Foods was able to get better shelf positions than, say, Nestle: staff in department stores were in the habit of pushing Nestle's products to the back. Similarly, through personal influence Philips was able to have its promotion posters placed in prominent positions in Jing Pin Shang She (a big department store situated on Nanjing Road in Shanghai). Ways of establishing good *guanxi* with retailers and ensuring favorable treatment include incentives to staff, frequent visits, and showing trust and a sincere attitude.

Staffing

The focus group study carried out by the author also revealed that Chinese consumers rely heavily on suggestions by salespeople in making their purchase decisions; it appears that in choosing products consumers often do not know exactly what they are looking for. The reliability and the credibility of the sales message very much depends on the salesperson's knowledge of the product, and therefore it is very important to train salespeople to know about the products they are selling, as well as teaching them about the concept of service and attitude toward consumers. However, it is advisable to bear in mind that transforming attitudes is not possible overnight. It should be considered as a long-term investment.

The appointment of a well-qualified marketing team is a major problem. As China is a relatively newly opened economy the concept of marketing is a new phenomenon, and therefore it is difficult to recruit people with a marketing background. According to the General Manager of Houghton (China) Co. Ltd, marketing staff recruited in China do not really possess the "marketing concept," but adopt the "product concept": they believe that a good product will speak for itself. Moreover, they rely on past sales contacts rather than adopting more innovative ways of attracting customers.

Differences in attitudes are observed not only in consumers but also in employees in different parts of China. In interviews with the author managers reported that junior-level staff in the north are easier to manage than those in the south, perhaps because those in the south are more influenced by the Hong Kong culture; there are more job opportunities and the turnover rate is much higher.

CONCLUSIONS

For foreign manufacturers or retailers entering the China market is a process of internationalization, with different stages through which a company may pass as it develops into foreign markets. The process normally begins with direct or ad hoc exporting, moves on to active exporting and/or licensing to active exporting, licensing, and joint equity investment in foreign manufacturing, and finally to full-scale multinational marketing and production (Root 1987). Figure 4 illustrates the typical sequence a company is believed to follow as it internationalizes.

A number of studies support this model. Johanson and Wiedersheim (1975) and Johnanson and Vahlne (1977) found that Swedish firms expanded abroad in small steps, the typical pattern extending from exporting via an agent to the establishment of a sales subsidiary and, finally, to production abroad. Buckley and others (Buckley, Berkova, and Newbould 1983; Buckley, Newbould, and Thurwell 1988), in studies of small UK firm first-time investors and small continental European investors in the UK, found that only 15 percent of the combined sample of companies omitted the exporting phase en route to foreign manufacturing; of these, one-half were prevented from exporting by-product-transport costs, or a high service element effectively excluded exporting.

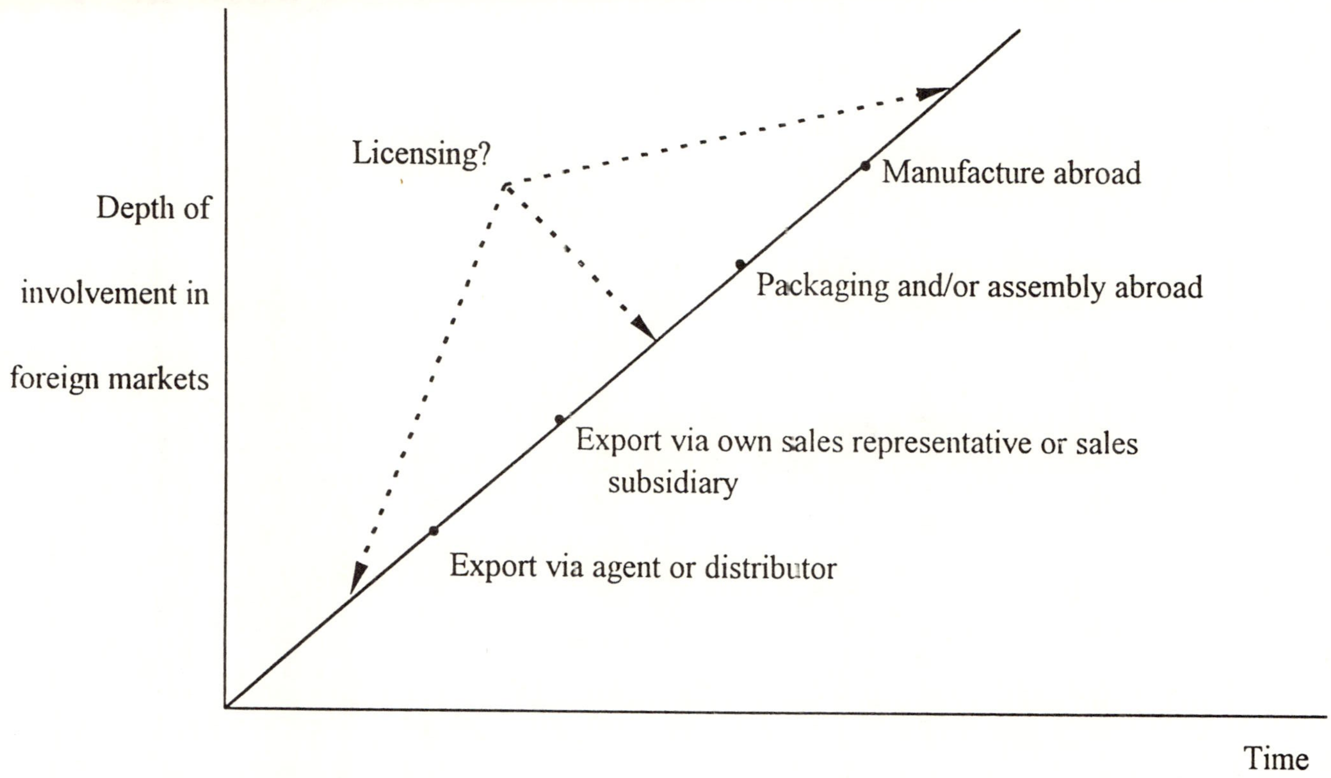

Figure 4. The Process of Internaticnalization

Foreign manufacturers, in theory, may make use of the stepwise process to acquire the knowledge of the foreign market gradually, or enter directly into joint ventures, because of export or licensing restrictions for certain products and government incentives for foreign direct investment. But as retailing is a service that requires direct interaction with customers, retailers have to enter directly into joint ventures, and thus the risk involved is very much higher. It would be valuable to look into the strategies manufacturers and retailers adopt when entering the Chinese market, and how successful they are in adapting strategies to suit the environment. Discovering what exactly the right strategy might be is a challenge to both retailers and researchers in this field.

NOTE

1. Wal-Mark Stores Inc. initially teamed up with C.P. Pokphand Co., a Hong Kong-listed affiliate of the Charoen Pokphand Group (CP Group), a pioneer among foreign investors in China with major interests in agriculture and motorcycle production, to venture into the China market. CP was expected to help Wal-Mark with the regulatory complications of business in China, and Wal-Mark would provide expertise in the operation of a huge warehouse-style discount store. However, the joint venture is not without its problems; according to the *Asian Wall Street Journal* (January 11, 1996, pp. 1, 5), the two companies have ended their venture and are going their separate ways in China's retail market. Under the terms of dissolution, Wal-Mark is keeping the Shenzhen venture while CP will take over the rest of the venture's holdings in Shanghai and Shenyang.

REFERENCES

Buckley, P.J., Z. Berkova, and G.D. Newbould. 1993. *Direct Investment in the United Kingdom by Small European Firms.* Basingstoke, UK: Macmillan.

Buckley, P.J., G.D. Newbould, and J.C. Thurwell. 1988. *Foreign Direct Investment by Small U.K. Firms: The Success and Failure of First Time Investors Abroad.* Basingstoke, UK: Macmillan.

Business Week. 1993. May 17, p. 20.

China Daily Business Weekly. 1993. December 11-17, p. 1.

China Economic News. 1993. November 29.

Davies, K. 1994. "Foreign Investment in the Retail Sector of the People's Republic of China." *Columbia Journal of World Business* (Fall).

Hang Seng. 1994. *Hang Seng Economic Monthly* (August).

Hong Kong Economic Journal. 1993. March 21.

Hong Kong Trade Development Council (HKTDC). 1994. *China's Consumer Market.* (August).

Jiefang Daily China Economic News. 1996. January 8.

Johanson, J., and J. E. Vahlne. 1977. "The Internationalization Process of the Firm: A Model of Knowledge Development and Increasing Foreign Market Commitments." *Journal of International Business Studies* 8: 23-32.

Johanson, J., and P. Wiedersheim. 1975. "The Internationalization of the Firm: Four Swedish Cases." *Journal of Management Studies* 12: 305-322.

Root, F.R. 1987. *Entry Strategies for International Markets.* Lexington, MA: Lexington Books.

South China Morning Post (SCMP). 1993. March 16.

State Council. 1992. "Decision to Accelerate Development of Tertiary Industries." In *Important Strategic Decision-Accelerate Development of Tertiary Industries* (Beijing Zhong Guo Zheng Fa Da Xue Chu Ban She). Beijing: PRC State Council.

Time. 1993. "Special Report: China." May 10, p. 17.

Tseng, C.S., P. Kwan, and F. Cheung. 1995. "Distribution in China: A Guide Through the Maze." *Long Range Planning* 28 (1): 81-95.

U.S. Foreign and Commercial Service in Beijing. 1994. "Franchising in China." *East Asian Executive Reports* (April): 6-13.

STRATEGIC ISSUES FOR SINO-HONG KONG JOINT VENTURES

Danming Lin

INTRODUCTION

The international joint venture (IJV) has become an important form of foreign direct investment (FDI) over the last few decades. From an academic point of view, what is equally important is the emergence and development of a vast and growing body of studies on IJVs. The IJV literature represents a profound extension to the traditional FDI theories, which tend to provide only one satisfactory reason for establishing a wholly owned subsidiary (Contractor 1990). It is expected that many practical implications can be drawn from IJV studies, since the IJV has been adopted by more and more multinational enterprises (MNEs) and even become the dominant form of FDI in developing countries (Beamish and Banks 1987).

At a country-specific level some authors note that the People's Republic of China (PRC) has received more FDI in the form of equity joint ventures than any other country in the context of the reform and Open Door era (Campbell and Zhang 1994). It is therefore not surprising to record the increasing amount of research published on topics related to Sino-foreign joint ventures (SFJVs).

Advances in Chinese Industrial Studies, Volume 5, pages 289-302.

ISBN: 1-55938-961-3

A brief literature survey suggests, however, that most current studies place an emphasis on SFJVs in a strict sense, that is, SFJVs funded by investors from foreign countries, especially those from Western countries and Japan. Few, if any, systematic studies have been conducted in SFJVs funded by investors from Hong Kong, Taiwan, and Macao, which have so far appeared as the vast majority of SFJVs in official PRC statistics. In short, there remains an imbalance between SFJV studies and SFJV realities.

This paper examines a number of critical issues revolving around Sino-Hong Kong joint ventures (SHJVs), that is, SFJVs funded by the arguably "foreign" investors from Hong Kong who constitute the single largest source of SFJV investment (Campbell and Zhang 1994). The paper partially adopts a strategic management angle to examine key strategic issues accompanying SHJVs, notably motives and competitive advantages of SHJV partners, as well as their interactions. A comparative approach is also incorporated so as to highlight possible variations between SHJVs and SFJVs funded by investors from other places. It is hoped and believed that such a study can add insights to the current knowledge base on the SFJVs.

LITERATURE REVIEW AND RESEARCH HYPOTHESES

Parkhe (1993), in a review of the literature on IJVs, classifies the core theoretical dimensions of existing research streams as (1) the motives for IJV formation; (2) the issues of partner selection/characteristics and control/conflict; and (3) IJV instability/performance. Beamish (1993), taking a strategic management point of view, proposes a similar yet more comprehensive analytical framework for IJVs as follows: (1) strategic issues; (2) structural and organizational issues; and (3) performance issues. While such analogies can be applied to SFJVs, this section emphasizes reviewing current SFJV literature at the level of strategy in light of the purpose and scope of this study.

As previous studies (Anderson 1990; Harrigan 1985) suggest IJV strategic issues and their interactions are incorporated and implied in the IJV formation process. Such issues can mainly be examined through aspects of the motives of the IJV partners, the competitive advantages of each party behind those motives, and the interactions involved.

The purpose of foreign operations may be either (1) to serve foreign markets or (2) to attain some resource not found at home under the same favorable conditions (Daniels and Radebaugh 1992). In PRC business dealings the specific configuration of SFJV foreign partners' business strategic focuses tends to vary somewhat in degree according to the source of the foreign investment and the sector in question (Child 1994). For investors from the Western world, notably those from the United States, entry into the PRC market is mainly for market expansion rather than for seeking resource based on the "dollar-per-person" hypothesis (Daniels, Krug, and Nigh 1986; Tai 1988).

While Japan, the United States, and other Western investors pursue their market expansion strategy in China by investing in capital-intensive, high-technology, import substitution projects, investors from Hong Kong and Taiwan tend to favor the resource-seeking strategy and concentrate mainly on export-oriented, processing/assembling operations. In fact, the synergy of the PRC's cheap labor and land with Hong Kong and Taiwan's know-how and capital has been the main factor behind China's spectacular export drive (Huan 1992; Schroath, Hu, and Chen 1993; Sung 1992). Thus current literature suggests that Hong Kong partners in SHJVs are mainly motivated to launch export platforms by China's cheaper factors of production (Sung 1992). In light of the dynamic change in the PRC's political economy, however, this needs to be supported by up-to-date evidence. Therefore, a research hypothesis is formulated:

Hypothesis 1. The Hong Kong partners of SHJVs are mainly motivated by the advantage of cheaper production factors.

From the standpoint of the PRC government the motives for trying to attract foreign investment are no different from those of governments elsewhere. The influx of investment under specific conditions may bring in advanced technology and management know-how, fill a local capital gap, promote the export of local products, conserve foreign exchange, and create jobs (Brunner, Koh, and Lou 1992; Li 1992; Thoburn, Leung, Chau, and Tang 1990). Although PRC companies may have similar motives to those of the government, there are other considerations for these local companies, such as gaining advantageous competitive position in the local market (Aiello 1991) and to escape from numerous governmental interventions (Daniels, Krug, and Nigh 1986). Since foreign investment has usually been attracted into China by Chinese companies and local authorities wishing to work in partnership with foreign firms, not by the national government, possible conflicts between the interests of local partners and those of the host nation need to be considered (Thoburn, Leung, Chau, and Tang 1990). Furthermore, interactions between governmental agents and enterprises, in the context of the PRC's transitional economy, remain rather intra-organized (Boisot and Child 1994), leading to intensive and complex policy-related corporate behavior. The motives of the local partners of SHJVs can be examined in detail by testing the following hypothesis:

Hypothesis 2. The motives of local firms for establishing SHJVs significantly interact with the policies and behaviors of governmental agents.

The competitive advantages of partners in SFJVs can generally be placed in the context of IJVs. As elaborated by many IJV studies, the competitive advantages of traditional MNEs from the Western world compared to local firms and host governments in developing countries lie in their control of the skills and resources critically needed by those countries. Among the important advantages are sufficient investment capital or the capability of raising it on the international financial market, access to a flow of advanced technology, highly developed management, marketing skills, strong brand names and trademarks, scale of economy, risk reduction ability, and a global perspective (Farge and Wells 1982; Lecraw 1984).

Studies on third world multinational enterprises (TWMNEs), which are of growing importance in the world economy, show a different picture. The competitive advantages of these MNEs from the developing world are characterized by their special abilities to undertake flexible, low-cost, and labor-intensive manufacturing of standard products, with technology appropriate to the developing countries in the context of high unemployment and limited host developing markets, good opportunities for local procurement, better access to foreign markets, first-hand familiarity with working conditions in developing countries due to similar regulatory contexts and family/ethnic connections, and less host government interference due to the lower profile of these TWMNEs (Chen 1983; Wells 1983). It is argued that, applying these notions in the context of SHJVs, investors from Hong Kong are likely to have substantial competitive advantages because they enjoy geographic and cultural proximity with Mainland China. This proximity can be of great help in overcoming various barriers and obtaining favorable concessions. Furthermore, the medium-level technology possessed by the Hong Kong firms may be more suited to the PRC's level of development and could enhance China's bargaining power in acquiring technology from the developed countries (Sung 1992).

Studies on the competitive advantages of local firms in developing countries are relatively few. According to the limited literature, a local firm's competitive advantages mainly come from their access to local human resources, especially a cheap labor force, and raw materials (Zurawicki 1975), knowledge of the local business environment (Beamish 1987), and connections with host governmental authorities and institutions (Reynolds 1984). These last two categories may prove of special relevance to local partners of SHJVs, given the fast-changing nature of the PRC's transitional economy, as well as the significant governmental interventions and the proliferation of *guanxi* in doing business in the PRC.

Thus, current studies can be taken as guidelines for surveying the competitive advantages of SHJV partners, but other problems remain to be researched. Specifically, while most studies on the motives and competitive advantages of IJV partners indicate, explicitly or implicitly, possible matches between the two, little, if any, empirical work has been done on this aspect. By its very nature and from an interactive perspective such a "matching" question can be formulated as to whether the motives of one partner are compatible with the competitive advantages of the other partner. An exploratory research hypothesis, therefore, is proposed:

Hypothesis 3. There are compatible matches between SHJV partners.

METHOD

Sample

Sixty manufacturing SHJVs were included in the field survey, which was undertaken during mid-1994. The SHJVS were selected by what may be viewed as a step-step process. First, we selected two Special Economic Zones (SEZs), namely Shenzhen and Shantou, and four cities, Guangzhou, Foshan, Chanzou, and Chaoyang, in Guangdong province, as potential sites for survey. Formal contacts with the associations of foreign-invested companies (AFIC) in the sites were then established. After an introductory letter was issued by the local AFIC, we visited 10 SHJVs in each SEZ and city. The local and Hong Kong partners were asked to answer specific questions related to their respective strategic motives and advantages by filling in survey questionnaires, to be returned within two months. To ensure prompt and serious responses, regular telephone contacts were maintained by the author until the questionnaires were received.

Completed questionnaires were received from 42 SHJVs in Guangdong province, operating in the SEZs of Shenzhen (6) and Shantou (8), and the cities of Guangzhou (8), Foshan (7), Chaozhou (7) and Chaoyang (6).

After the completed questionnaires were received, face-to-face interviews were conducted in addition with 10 SHJVs willing to cooperate in this way. For the other 32 SHJVs double-checks on the returned questionnaires were carried out by telephone conversations. While such a sampling method could be regarded as acceptable for the purpose of this exploratory study, the lack of randomness does limit the extent to which the findings are applicable.

Measures

A four-item measure, rather than the customary five- or seven-point "Likert scales," was used for the survey questions. This decision was made after a pilot test in which a five-point Likert scale was used and the interviewees responded to most questions by giving a rating of three, falling exactly in the middle of the scale. As the interviewees explained, "ticking the middle" is typical behavior for (Mainland) Chinese respondents whenever they encounter uncertainties, such behavior stemming from the deeply entrenched Confucian tradition of the "neutral rationale" (*Zhong Yong Zhi Dao*). Furthermore, the Likert scale itself seems unpopular with Mainland China respondents, who are less exposed to standard social science survey practice. Accordingly, the four-item measure was introduced as an alternative, so as to obtain more reliable responses.

Two simple but effective statistical methods, namely mean ranking and Spearman correlation, were employed as major data analysis methods to extract relevant information from the questionnaire data. The mean ranking method was employed to measure the degree of importance of different factors relating to the motives and competitive advantages of the SHJVs. Respondents were asked to rank factors on a scale of 1 (unimportant) to 4 (most important), therefore, the higher the mean ranking, the greater the degree of importance of the factor. Tabulation or cross-tabulation including the mean rankings were also made to assess the difference among various factors. The inclusion of correlation analyses was inevitable due to the need to test the matches between motives and competitive advantages between SHJV partners. In light of the ordinal nature of the questionnaire data we had to rely on Spearman correlation analysis, which limited the flexibility of statistical analysis to a certain extent. It should be noted that there were also considerable qualitative ingredients in the data analysis process because records of the face-to-face and telephone interviews were also elaborated and presented.

RESULTS

Table 1 illustrates the motives of the Hong Kong partners in initiating their PRC investment, and provides a number of interesting observations. Specifically, the motive of using cheaper production factors (labor, land, etc.) to maximize profits appears as the most important motive for the foreign partners' investment decisions. In other words, research hypothesis 1 is confirmed: *the Hong Kong partners of SHJVs are mainly motivated by the advantage of cheaper factors of production.*

To a large extent such resource-oriented behavior of the Hong Kong partners reflects not only the labor-intensive pattern of these SHJVs but also that pattern among the Hong Kong parent firms, which is discussed in detail elsewhere (Chen 1983).

To better understand the configuration of the Hong Kong partners' motives, other findings presented in Table 1 should also be taken into account. First, Hong Kong investors rely heavily on favorable FDI policies. Adopting the notion that cultural similarities and ethnic linkages are helpful for adaptation to the local environment (Cai 1994; Sung 1991), the above finding seems to suggest that the implication of adaptation can be extended from more easily overcoming entry barriers to understanding and even exploiting fully favorable environmental conditions. Second, exploiting the PRC market and preempting

Table 1. Importance of Hong Kong Partners' Motives

Factor	*Mean*
Using cheaper production factors	3.333
Seeking favorable policies	3.214
Exploiting China market	2.833
Preempting rivals	2.690
Exploiting suitable technology	2.405
Diversifying investment risks	2.286

Note: 1 = unimportant; 2 = less important; 3 = rather important; 4 = most important.

rivals—two significant strategic issues influencing the China business decisions of Western companies (Wang 1992; Dong 1991)—were ranked by Hong Kong business people as being important, albeit less so than the advantage of cheaper production factors and of seeking favorable policies. As many respondents suggested, however, the mainland market and competition considerations are likely to continue to increase in importance, in the light of the fact that the bulk of Hong Kong business people are continuing to move their manufacturing activities into the fast-growing mainland China market and that competition in the international marketplace is becoming ever more intense.

It was also found that the motives of diversifying investment risks and exploiting suitable technology, presumably significant objectives for traditional MNEs and TWMNEs respectively, received relatively less emphasis. This finding is, to a certain degree, an indicator of the Hong Kong partners' smaller scale operations, narrower operational scope, and less technological orientation.

In short, there are both static and dynamic interpretations of the findings presented in Table 1. The static interpretation is that Hong Kong partners are currently mainly motivated to use the cheaper production factors in Mainland China. More significantly, the dynamic interpretation is that these Hong Kong investors will, in the long run, be motivated by other market and competition related factors. Hypothesis 1 should in this dynamic sense be considered as confirmed provisionally but subject to validation, even modification, by future studies.

Table 2 outlines the motives of the local partners in launching SHJVs, and shows that all the factors listed except that of absorbing labor were regarded as of some importance. The objectives of seeking favorable policies, promoting exports, and injecting capital were interestingly ranked higher than those of introducing technology and managerial skills. This result reflects a certain departure from the state government's intentions in absorbing FDI, where the introduction of advanced technologies and managerial skills were considered

Table 2. Importance of Local Partners' Motives

Factor	*Mean*
Utilizing favorable policies	3.143
Promoting exports	3.071
Injecting capital	3.024
Introducing technology	2.905
Introducing managerial skills	2.881
Absorbing labor	2.214

Note: 1 = unimportant; 2 = less important; 3 = rather important; 4 = most important.

as of highest priority. The emphasis on taking advantage of favorable SFJV policies has in fact been a widespread phenomenon among local partners of SFJVs established with investors from Hong Kong, Macao, and Taiwan. Sometimes this policy-seeking motive even becomes the ultimate reason for the JV establishment (Cai 1994; Wang 1992). An explanation related to the findings presented in Table 2 was provided by the general manager of an SHJV operating in the Shenzhen SEZ as follows:

> Foreign advanced technologies and managerial skills are more attractive and important to the large [local] firms with formal organizational structures than to the medium and small ones, which tend to carry out simple production with simple management. As you [the author] know, most of the enterprises in Guangdong are medium and small ones....Being able to export something is a prime target of most Guangdong enterprises because we are living in an externally-oriented economy (in Guangdong).

The manager of a state-owned enterprise, the local parent company of an SHJV operating in a small town in east Guangdong, put forward another frank comment:

> Things like the introduction of technologies and managerial skills and the possible advantages for easing the employment pressure (through the introduction of FDI) are mentioned and only of concern to the government. For me, the foremost reason to join this JV is to take advantage of being a partner of an SFJV. New business activities have been created by setting up the SHJV. Tax burden has been reduced. The supply of water and electricity has been normalized.

Similar feelings were in fact shared by a large number of the local partners. In a sense, this finding highlights the inconsistencies between the strategic intentions of the government and those of the local firms in the process of introducing FDI. Further interviews with local administrative staff even suggested that there are some differences between the strategic intentions of central government and that of the local authorities. While central government clearly states its intense interest in introducing advanced technologies and managerial skills via FDI, the local authorities tend to be more concerned with the potential benefits FDI can bring for promoting local exports and easing local employment pressures. In short, there is a hierarchy of strategic intentions on FDI along the line of central government/local authorities/local partners, and the interactions of strategic intentions at various levels of that hierarchy may be traced to the decentralization process that has occurred since economic reform. In other words, the survey findings on the motives of SHJV local partners relate the strategic behavior of the local parties to the transitional context of China's political economy.

Overall, the above analysis provides supportive evidence to hypothesis 2: *the motives of local firms for establishing SHJVs significantly interact with the policies and behavior of governmental agents.*

Combining the findings from Tables 1 and 2, the motives of local and Hong Kong partners provide a basic picture of the mutual interaction of the partners' strategic intentions concerning the formation of SHJVs. Such interactions have certainly occurred in the context of Sino-Hong Kong economic links, especially the Guangdong-Hong Kong economic relationship. The common interests of SHJV partners in seeking favorable FDI policies specifically remind us of a "platform" explanation (Aiello 1991), which views the SFJV as a temporary platform built by partners from two sides. As Aiello explained:

> Each party has its own particular agenda for entering into the relationship (similar to Western joint ventures). However, the maximization of dividend income from the venture is not a top priority for either party (unlike Western joint ventures). The...platform thus acts as an interface or medium through which both shareholders extract what they can get from the other party (Aiello 1991, p. 50).

It is also true that each party in an SHJV has its own particular agenda for entering into the relationship. We are not sure at this stage whether the maximization of dividend income from the venture is a top priority for either party. The key and interesting point, however, is that both partners share an agenda—seeking favorable FDI policies—and give it high priority. The SHJV platform is, moreover, likely to serve as an interface from which both partners can extract policy-related benefits from the government, which is arguably a third party. In other words, findings on the SHJVs seem to extend the implications of the platform explanation.

Partners must have some sort of competitive advantage, or potential contributions, to the ongoing SHJVs in order to start cooperation. According to Table 3, access to export markets and greater flexibility and adaptability were ranked as the Hong Kong partners' most significant competitive advantages, while technology and scale economy were considered as moderately important advantages. This finding is, by and large, in accordance

Table 3. Importance of Hong Kong Partners' Advantages

Factor	*Mean*
Access to export markets	3.262
Adaptability and flexibility	3.024
Managerial skills	2.857
Capital	2.786
Technology	2.548
Scale economy	2.500

Note: 1 = unimportant; 2 = less important; 3 = rather important; 4 = most important.

with previous studies on the multinational activities of Hong Kong firms (Chen 1983) and on other TWMNEs (Wells 1983).

Linkages to administrative bodies, or *guanxi*, were considered to be of highest importance to local partners as a competitive advantage (see Table 4), while local market access, a factor identified as one of the most important contributions to be made by the local partner in the context of a developing country IJV (Beamish 1988) and that of Sino-Western JVs (Dong 1991), was relatively less emphasized in this survey. The advantage of the existing facilities of the local partners was ranked the lowest. In other words, the competitive advantages of the local partners rely more on the invisible, or soft, factors than on the visible, or hard, ones. From a strategic management point of view (Porter 1990), those invisible advantages possessed by the local partners are location (China) based, rather than system based.

Linking findings from Tables 2 and 3, it is worth pointing out that the better export access of the Hong Kong partners matches the strong desire of the local partners for promoting exports through SHJVs. The relatively lower rankings given by the Hong Kong partners to technology and scale economy also coincide with the less strong intentions of the local partners with regard to

Table 4. Importance of Local Partners' Advantages

Factor	*Mean*
Linkages to administration	2.952
China business experience	2.714
Local information	2.595
Local market access	2.548
Existing facilities	2.524

Note: 1 = unimportant; 2 = less important; 3 = rather important; 4 = most important.

Table 5. Analysis of the Relationship between Local Partners' Motives and Hong Kong Partners' Advantages (One-tailed Spearman Correlation)

Correlated Variables	*Spearman Correlation*
DMEXP-HAEXP	.4393**
DMTEC-HATEC	.5550**
DMMAN-HAMAN	.5196**

Notes: **: $p <= .01$
DMEXP: promoting export as local partner's motive.
HAEXP: export market access as Hong Kong partner's advantage.
DMTEC: introducing advanced technology as local partner's motive.
HATEC: Advanced technology as Hong Kong partner's advantage.
DMMAN: Introducing managerial skills as local partner's motive.
HAMAN: Managerial skills as Hong Kong partner's advantage.

these two factors. Further correlation analyses also provide moderate support to these observations concerning the relationship between local partners' motives and the Hong Kong partners' corresponding advantages, as Table 5 shows.

Accordingly, research findings are found, from the perspective of the local partner, to be supportive for hypothesis 3: *there are compatible matches between SHJV partners.*

More precisely, the behavior of rational partner selection is observed from the local perspective: based on their business motives and firm-specific advantages, potential local SHJV partners identified and selected their Hong Kong counterparts intentionally, resulting in relatively compatible "matched pairings." To a certain extent, this partial-hypothesis testing sheds insights on studies on IJV partner selection in the sense of exploring the actual behavior of partner selection, rather than relying on the normative descriptions of partner selection criteria.

The above finding can also be contrasted with some previous studies (Lin and Zao 1991; Wu 1991), where the local partners were criticized for their blindness and lack of understanding in seeking foreign joint venture partners. A further implication is that, given the rational partner selection behavior and, subsequently, compatible matchings between SHJV partners, there should be less organizational complexity among the SHJVs. The following mini-case is an example of this matching process:

> Mr. Li, the manager of the No. 2 Food Processing Factory in city Y, was attracted by a news report in 1986 that there was a huge demand for eels in Japan. Li felt that he could make use of this opportunity. "We had several fish farms. The environment here is wonderful for eel reproduction. The problem was how to get the eels exported," Li recalled.

So Li asked some friends working in Hong Kong's China-invested companies to seek suitable joint venture partners for his factory. A month later, Li was introduced to the manager of a Hong Kong company which had some business experience in and export channels to Japan. A joint venture deal was finally launched.

DISCUSSIONS

This paper has examined strategic issues revolving around SHJVs by testing a number of relevant hypotheses and elaborating further research findings. In so doing it represents an initial step toward systematically studying SHJVs, which constitute a group of major SFJV players, yet which have received comparatively little research attention.

The research findings and corresponding analyses presented raise a number of questions which need further study. Some discussions are proposed below.

As a strategic issue for the local side, it is noted that there is a hierarchy of motives for introducing FDI among the three levels of central government, local government, and local SHJV parent firms. At the various levels there are different yet sometimes overlapping motives. Based on the survey findings and other previous studies, potential conflicts among motives at different levels can be suggested. For example, the local government's concern with easing local employment pressure may lead its strategic focus on introducing FDI toward the labor end, hence labor-intensive FDI, which is in contrast to the central government's preference for introducing advanced technologies via FDI.

Taking a broader view, different motives or strategic intentions may stem from different strategic coverage at different levels: the central government intends to introduce FDI to spur national economic growth, while local governments and local SHJV parent firms are mainly concerned with the possible gains in wealth for the regions and the firms, respectively. In short, the formulas used in joint venture cost/benefit analysis are different. In a transitional economy like the PRC this seems to be a matter of hybrid arrangements with immense hierarchical and personal interactions occurring amid the process of economic decentralization. The specific configuration of the parties at the three levels in that hybrid system will accordingly decide to a large extent the strategic focus of the local side in the SHJVs and, broadly, the SFJVs. The motives of the local side for joint ventures must, therefore, be explored in future studies of SFJVs by taking a multi-perspective and interactive approach with special attention paid to the dynamics of the PRC's economic transition, since a single-perspective and rather static approach, as largely reflected in the current IJV literature, may prove inappropriate.

This study suggests that influence from central and local governments is decreasing, and the motives of the local parent firms are more significant. Given the rather liberal context for strategic decision making, the local partners demonstrate a rational pattern in the selection of their Hong Kong counterparts. Such findings should, however, be interpreted cautiously because of the following considerations.

First, the sample for this survey was selected only from Guangdong, the province that has the most developed market economy in the PRC and where the intervention of the state or local governments thus tends to be less; the situation in other regions may be different. Second, since the SHJVs are operating on a small scale and labor-intensive basis, they are less likely to be of concern to the central government because of the limited role these firms play in the overall industrial structure, and governmental intervention would therefore be less. In short, the dynamic interactions among the governmental bodies and the local firms in the formation of local SHJV strategies will be contingent on the two variables of location and industry. This would seem to apply to all SFJVs and, for this reason, future SFJV studies conducted on interregional and/or intersectorial bases should be useful for clarifying relevant strategic issues.

REFERENCES

Aiello, P. 1991. "Building a Joint Venture in China: The Case of Chrysler and the Beijing Jeep Corporation." *Journal of General Management* 17 (2): 47-64.

Anderson, E. 1990. "Two Firms, One Frontier: On Assessing Joint Venture Performance." *Sloan Management Review* (Winter): 19-30.

Beamish, P.W. 1987. "Joint Venture in LDCs: Partner Selection and Performance." *Management International Review* 27 (1): 23-37.

Beamish, P.W. 1988. *Multinational Joint Ventures in Developing Countries*. London: Routledge.

Beamish, P.W. 1993. "The Characteristics of Joint Ventures in the People's Republic of China." *Journal of International Marketing* 1 (2): 29-48.

Beamish, P.W., and J.C. Banks. 1987. "Equity Joint Ventures and the Theory of Multinational Enterprise." *Journal of International Business Studies* 18 (2): 1-16.

Boisot, M., and J. Child. 1994. "China's Emerging Economic Order: Modernization Through 'Weak' Markets and Quasi-Capitalism?" Paper presented to the Conference on Management Issues for China in the 1990s, Cambridge, UK, University of Cambridge, April 9-12.

Brunner, J.A., A. Koh, and X. Lou. 1992. "Chinese Perceptions of Issues and Obstacles Confronting Joint Ventures." *Journal of Global Marketing* 6 (1/2): 97-127.

Cai, S. 1994. "Comparative Study on Investment Strategies of Firms from Hong Kong, Taiwan, Japan, US, and Europe" (in Chinese). *Guo Ji Mao Yi Wen Ti* (*International Trade Issues*) 5: 31-36.

Campbell, N., and J. Zhang. 1994. "The Pattern of EJVs in China 1979-89." Pp. 3-12 in *Joint Ventures in the People's Republic of China: Advances in Chinese Industrial Studies, Volume 4*, edited by S. Stewart. Greenwich, Conn.: JAI Press.

Chen, E. 1983. "Multinationals from Hong Kong." Pp. 88-136 in *The New Multinationals*, edited by S. Lall. Chichester, NY: John Wiley.

Child, J. 1994. *Management in China during the Age of Reform*. Cambridge, UK: Cambridge University Press.

Contractor, F.J. 1990. "Contractual and Cooperative Forms of International Business: Towards a Unified Theory of Modal Choice." *Management International Review* 30 (1): 31-54.

Daniels, J.D., J. Krug, and D. Nigh. 1986. "U.S. Joint Ventures in China: Motivation and Management of Political Risk." *California Management Review* 27 (4): 46-58.

Daniels, J.D., and L.H. Radebaugh. 1992. *International Business.* Reading, MA: Addison-Wesley.

Dong, D. 1991. "Joint Venture Strategies of the US Companies in China" (in Chinese). *Guan Li Shi Jie* (*Management World*) 5: 168-171.

Farge, N., and L.T. Wells, Jr. 1982. "Bargaining Power of Multinationals and Host Governments." *Journal of International Business Studies* (Fall): 9-23.

Harrigan, K.R. 1985. *Strategies for Joint Ventures.* Lexington, MA: Lexington Books.

Huan, Y. 1992. *China's Industrialization and Foreign Direct Investment* (in Chinese). Shanghai: Shanghai Academy of Social Sciences Press.

Lecraw, D.J. 1984. "Bargaining Power, Ownership, and Profitability of Transnational Corporations in Less Developed Countries." *Journal of International Business Studies* (Spring/Summer) 1: 27-43.

Li, Z. 1992. "Managerial Mechanism of Sino-foreign Joint Ventures" (in Chinese). *Guan Li Shi Jie* (*Management World*) 1: 152-155.

Lin, D., and Y. Zao. 1991. *Practice of Enterprise with Foreign Investment* (in Chinese). Guangzhou: Guangdong Tourism Publishing House.

Parkhe, A. 1993. "'Messy' Research, Methodological Predispositions, and Theory Development in International Joint Ventures." *Academy of Management Review* 18 (2): 227-268.

Porter, M.E. 1990. *The Competitive Advantage of Nations.* New York: The Free Press.

Reynolds, J.I. 1984. "The 'Pinched Shoe' Effect of International Joint Ventures." *Columbia Journal of World Business* (Summer): 23-29.

Schroath, F.W., M.Y. Hu, and H. Chen. 1993. "Country-of-Origin Effects of Foreign Investments in the People's Republic of China." *Journal of International Business Studies* (Second Quarter): 277-290.

Sung, Y-W. 1991. *The China-Hong Kong Connection.* Cambridge, UK: Cambridge University Press.

Sung, Y-W. 1992. "The Economic Integration of Hong Kong with China in the 1990s: The Impact on Hong Kong." Research Paper No. 1, University of Toronto and York University, Joint Centre for Asia Pacific Studies.

Tai, Lawrence S.T. 1988. "Doing Business in the People's Republic of China: Some Keys to Success." *Management International Review* 28 (1): 5-9.

Thoburn, J.T., H.M. Leung, E. Chau, and S.H. Tang. 1990. *Foreign Investment in China Under the Open Policy: The Experience of Hong Kong Companies.* Aldershot: Avebury.

Wang, Z-M. 1992. "Managerial Psychological Strategies for Sino-foreign Joint Ventures." *Journal of Managerial Psychology* 7 (3): 10-16.

Wells, L.T., Jr. 1983. *Third World Multinationals.* Cambridge, MA: MIT Press.

Wu, C. (Ed.). 1991. *Survey Report on Foreign Direct Investment in China* (in Chinese). Beijing: China Finance and Economics Press.

Zurawicki, L. 1975. "The Cooperation of the Socialist State with the MNCs." *Columbia Journal of World Business* (Spring): 109-115.

STRATEGIC INTENTIONS OF PARENT COMPANIES AND PROPERTY RIGHTS IN JOINT VENTURES

Zhang Shiquan

INTRODUCTION

The joint venture (JV) is a most important part of world economic integration. It is also a way of bringing into play foreign direct investment (FDI) or "equity investment." For parent companies, in terms of their strategic intentions for operating and development, controlling and influencing joint ventures' strategic decisions and management becomes the objective in the formation of JVs. We want to analyze several related questions. First, what are the differences between the strategic intentions of the Chinese and foreign parent companies? Second, can parent companies' strategic intentions be fully understood by all sides and carried out? What are the contradictions within the enterprise? Third, what kind of arrangements would be adopted in order to strengthen influence and control from parent companies?

Through analysis of these questions I intend to discover some clues showing the relations between parent strategic intention and the structure of property rights in JVs.

Advances in Chinese Industrial Studies, Volume 5, pages 303-310.

ISBN: 1-55938-961-3

ANALYSIS OF CHINESE AND FOREIGN PARENT COMPANIES' STRATEGIC INTENTIONS

Joint ventures in China have developed very quickly. Not only have they become the most important of foreign invested enterprises (FIEs), but they have also had huge effects on the Chinese macro economy. As a new economic form, the JV has more power than other economic forms. So the question we should consider is, how do managers representing different economic systems and different cultural backgrounds cooperate in JVs?

Generally speaking, as parent companies adopt a kind of international business strategy entering into the target nation's market, they may be constrained by their scale, sector, strength, product advantage, and factors in host countries such as economics, society, and politics. If these are acceptable the strategic intentions of FDI can be separated into three basic parts: resource orientation, market orientation, and lower labor cost orientation. The abundant resources, vast market, lower labor costs, along with measures made by government at all levels for improving FIEs' external environment, are the reasons for attracting FDI and allowing investors to obtain benefits in China. Through investigation and analysis we found that market orientation is the most important factor. The reasons are as follows. In recent years serious inflation has already offset the advantage of resources; under the traditional system workers in many state-owned units have no efficiency in production, and these weaknesses do not complement lower labor costs and vast resources. So, comparing the two orientations (labor cost and market), market orientation is the main strategic intention.

In a survey of 67 JVs distributed in the sectors of electronics and fast-moving consumer goods, we found within the strategic intentions of foreign parent companies that they are attracted by the Chinese market, the opportunity for good long-term profits, and gaining strategic position in China vis-à-vis competitors, and establishing strong business credibility in China. These were the priority of goals of foreign managers in the JVs. These aims have been achieved more and more in the practice of business in recent years. So we can conclude that keeping and enlarging the market share is the primary target for foreign parent companies.

In negotiating the formation of JVs, Chinese partners aimed to absorb technology and management experience transferred from the foreign side, then to have the output produced by the JVs exported to the world market or returned to foreign parent companies. Foreign partners usually did not dissent, but most JVs in China could not achieve this original export objective: even high-tech products were still sold in the internal market. Of course, there were some valid reasons for this, but it suggested that foreign parent companies had insufficient incentives for promotion to the external market; they intended to occupy the Chinese market with their JV's products, where they might extend their influence enthusiastically.

Nowadays, JV products, particularly high-tech products, still have considerable attraction for Chinese consumers. They have more functional advantages, although their prices are higher than internal products. As the Chinese market upgraded, foreign JV managers intended to occupy or monopolize it. Some observers have already pointed out that market promotion, followed by production and research and development is the order of priority in which foreign parent companies conduct their JV business in China.

Chinese parent companies have different strategic intentions. They emphasize changing the enterprise system and rebuilding the enterprise's property rights. The results of our investigation demonstrated that as far as their purpose for JVs is concerned, obtaining the factors of production and managerial software that the Chinese partner lacks, enhancing the resources of the enterprise to operate efficiently, raising the power of competition for more profits—these were definitely normal characteristics of the strategic intentions of most Chinese parent companies. Questionnaire items such as technology transfer, obtaining foreign currency, opening up the internal market, and learning managerial experiences, all were commonly confirmed by managers on the Chinese side, and had a higher degree of achievement. In addition, system reform was also a requirement for Chinese parent companies.

With regard to state-owned enterprises being transformed into modern companies in terms of the enterprise system, there are two paths. One is to use foreign capital, meaning that the enterprises let foreign partners have some sort of equity share or hold a certain proportion of equity with foreign partners, introducing scarce factors of production from abroad. The other is so-called "local reform," meaning that the original ownership is retained, transforming state-owned enterprises into legal entities. For most Chinese parent companies the first path is the more attractive, because they get the necessary factors and preferential policy for development and system reform, and workers can get more income. Therefore, having accepted the idea of FDI, the Chinese side usually keeps an active attitude toward JV formation. At present, Chinese parents can use either a complete enterprise or just part of an enterprise for a joint venture with a foreign partner. Whichever method is used, after formation JVs must operate in terms of the requirements of market economics, giving up the constraints of the old system. Chinese parent companies just require lip service to decision making on JVs, and do not intervene in JVs' business administration, giving managers full autonomous rights. At present, 100 percent of the JVs surveyed have been prepared for full collaboration with the foreign partner. This proves that Chinese parents do change their system to fit in with JV partners.

Hence, we can say that Chinese parent companies setting up JVs have two objectives. The first is to achieve the enterprise's normal objective, such as getting the necessary factors of production, occupying the market, and maximizing profits; the second is to reform the enterprise system. This dual objective for Chinese parent companies is different from other JVs, and it means that not only each parent company has different strategic intentions, but also Chinese parent companies and Chinese managers have different strategic thinking on the development of JVs. This leads to difficulties in coordination. Foreigners can usually carry out the intentions of their superiors without any problem. But the distance between Chinese managers in JVs and their parent companies is great. Managers wish for more and more autonomous rights. So, how do JVs carry out the parent companies' intentions? Which is more important, the agreement between Chinese managers in JVs and their superiors, or that between the parent companies of different nationalities.

Undoubtedly, JVs are useful for both Chinese and foreign companies. As partners for development in the Chinese market, both obtain some advantages, seeking common points and avoiding differences as far as possible. This is strategic intention compatibility.

STRATEGIC INTENTIONS AND PROPERTY RIGHTS

The right to obtain revenues could be called "property rights." Compared with ownership, this sort of property rights is a broader concept. It can include creditor's rights, equity rights, and invisible rights. Property rights can be put into some specific functions such as dealing with factors of production, allocation, and use. The strategic intentions of parent companies are outside the property rights structure.

Strategic Intentions and the Pattern of Control

The formation and operation of Sino-foreign JVs rely on a kind of artificial arrangement. Each parent company participates in negotiations to allocate personnel, factors of input, and so on. Each side wishes to obtain long and stable revenues by their investment, but each side has its own restrictions for property rights allocation. One contradiction that might occur would be that between one and many strategic intentions. The main characteristic of foreign companies' strategic intentions is market orientation, the occupation of the market in order to achieve maximum profits. But JVs should also bear some social functions, such as increasing employment, retirement benefits, and housing arrangements, which are considered by foreigners as burdens. Chinese parent companies, however, require JVs to bear their share of the relevant social functions, not leave them to the state-owned enterprises. Once they have made the decision to form a JV, they have already started to change the original system. They must meet the contradictions in maximizing profits while handling society.

The contradictions between the single strategic intention of foreign parent companies and the multiple ones of Chinese parent companies affect all sides of the JV and cause a pattern of crosswise relationships at the managerial level. Vertical relations between parent companies and JVs have to be maintained, so managers from each side must know how to carry out their parent companies' strategic intentions while consulting with the other side; mutual understanding becomes the key to collaboration. Cultural differences and opposing viewpoints are real barriers, however, not easily overcome. From our investigation it seems that foreign managers in JVs succeed in carrying out the decisions of both parent companies, particularly the Japanese managers in Sino-Japanese JVs. But the Chinese side has more difficulty, because of the differences in systems between the JV and the parent companies. JVs are given autonomous rights, so they have their own intentions, different from those of the parent companies: they look for independent development, free from restrictions and emphasizing the value to themselves of competition and market economics. Chinese managers try to extend their influence beyond the contract frame when bargaining with parent companies, achieving much more than was intended. So, the relationship between foreign JV managers and their parent companies can be described as strategic intention centralized vertically, and the relationship between Chinese JV managers and their parent companies can be called strategic intention duality vertically. In order for managers to improve their crosswise relationships, the foreign side should understand the changeable structure of benefits caused by reform. The Chinese side must adjust the relationship between the parent company and the JV. The more JVs have autonomous rights, the better managers are able to solve the contradictions caused from different ideas and systems.

Exclusiveness of Property Rights Ownership

There are two more questions worth discussion. First, with their ownership of factors of production, parent companies take part in the negotiation of JV formation and seek control through equity share. In high-tech enterprises the Chinese side owns the low-cost labor and workplace, but since the foreign side owns know-how and special skills, they have more advantage. At the end of the contracted fixed term of operation the foreign sides of several high-tech JVs have extended their equity share and are on the way to complete ownership.

Second, parent companies put factors owned by themselves into JVs and negotiate with the other side, confirming that these factors belong exclusively to themselves, according to law, but this conflicts with the unanimity of strategic intentions and the demands on partners by parent companies. For example, foreign parent companies may own know-how that is their intellectual property right exclusively. In a JV, however, to achieve the strategic intentions of both parent companies and obtain common benefits for both sides, the exclusiveness of intellectual property rights should not be defended to the last. We found in our survey that managerial experience and market channels do not retain their exclusiveness; parent companies and their agents in JVs could not meet the huge transaction costs for their transferral. Thus, Chinese parent companies and managers are faced with the problem of how to keep the opposite side's exclusiveness to a minimum.

In the survey we found that foreign parent companies strictly controlled their contributions in know-how and some skills. In addition, few JVs have R&D departments themselves, apart from some product exploration in relation to the Chinese market. This means that JVs were doing little to change parent companies' products in order to enter or occupy the Chinese markets, the core technology or skill always being viewed as central by the foreign side. Consequently, foreign experts continue to head technical departments. We understand exclusiveness as the process of control factors of production. The stronger the exclusiveness, the greater the transactional fee, the larger the collaborational cost, the less certain the future of the collaboration.

"Dual Agent" Relations and Strategic Intentions

The agent relationship existing between parent companies and subsidiaries is defined as duality. This refers to the way in which the board of directors acts for the benefit of shareholders (parent companies) and managers act for the benefit of the board. With regard to the different extents of separation between rights of ownership and of doing business, the relationships are divided into two types: close and scattered. For instance, Limited Holding Company belongs to the scatter pattern: there are many shareholders owning a small number of stocks who do not directly control or manage the enterprise, but who elect the board of directors. The directors recruit managers according to requirements. Here the rights of ownership represented by shareholders and the rights of business represented by managers are separate, with both parties seeking different (or opposite) benefits and targets. In contrast, the Limited Duty Company belongs to the close pattern, with only a few shareholders. The board of directors consists of partners in terms of their proportion of equity inputs, and managers, particularly at the general or executive level, are usually members of the board.

In JVs in China the strategic intentions and interests of parent companies can be better achieved using the close pattern rather that the scatter pattern. Representations of shareholders, directors, and managers are concentrated in one person or group so that there should be fewer contradictions. Two problems stand out, however. First, the distances between different nationalities, cultural backgrounds, and particularly strategic intentions of parent companies are easily seen in the way that managers have to adjust to the contradictions of the two partners and deal with internal conflicts, and become what are called dual agents, carrying out each parent's intentions and maintaining the JV's operation. Second, of the strategic intentions of Chinese parent companies, the reforming of the old system of JVs is very important. Even though a manager in the parent company and a Chinese manager in the JV may be one and the same person, his or her behavior will be different in the different systems. We think that is a very interesting phenomenon.

The position of managers in JVs is located at the junction point horizontally and vertically: Chinese managers not only represent the Chinese parent company's interests, they also have to take account of the foreign side's interests, and not only looking after the development of their own enterprise, but also following the objective requirements of enterprise reform. With their dual status they are able to carry out the parent companies' intentions and maintain their own autonomous rights under this convenient condition. So we can say that good agent relationships between parent companies and JVs are the results of managers who use their personal skills.

The main function of the board of directors composed from both parent companies is strategic decision making and exercising control and monitoring managers. The managers organize and are in charge of the enterprise's operation, and put suggestions for development to the board. Because of the dual status of managers who are also directors, the requirement and monitoring from the board of directors depends on the managers themselves. Whether or not managers and parent companies have trust in each other vertically is important for the JV's development and operation. For example, according to the common rule the board of directors should meet at least four times a year, perhaps as often as once a month at the beginning of operation. But our investigation has shown that meetings are held on average only once or twice, maybe three times a year. Further, many JVs hold meetings at irregular intervals: if they have nothing to discuss no meeting is held. So, the kind of monitoring judgment system mainly depends on the loyalty of managers to parent companies' intentions. The agent relationship between parent companies and JVs may diminish to a minimum. The foreign side's managers have changed more frequently than those of the Chinese side so their rate of recruiting is higher. So the foreign side exercises tight control in a dynamic way. The foreign side has relatively more methods to solve the vertical contradictions, therefore, the horizonal relations (with the Chinese side) are viewed by them as more important.

In contrast, Chinese managers seek autonomy and value in cooperation with the foreign side. The serious contradictions caused by Chinese-foreign cooperation can lead to JV disintegration, although this happens less and less. If JVs collapse the reasons are usually attributed to the change in the macroeconomic environment. Many managers who have dual status thought that they could cooperate well with foreigners, but meanwhile had more differences of opinion with their parent companies in such areas as profit distribution, human resources allocation, and targets. The problems on the Chinese side occur in respect of vertical trust. Because of their dual status, the managers become the "lubricant" in relieving system friction. Many contradictions on the Chinese side are connected with change, and the foreign side should understand this. Moreover, although at the macroeconomic level there are many different opinions on JVs, at the microeconomic level most entrepreneurs desire to work with foreigners. The main reason for this is that entrepreneurs have the spirit for reform and imagination, rejecting former vertical systems. Even after JV formation Chinese managers are often dissatisfied with their supervisors, and this condition should be understood by foreigners. Generally, the more autonomy Chinese managers have, the easier they can solve the problems involved in partnership.

CONCLUSION

To sum up, the strategic intentions of Chinese parent companies in JVs is enterprise reform. This depends on the dual status of managers. This can be compared with the obvious market orientation and internal integration of the foreign sides, and the Chinese side is usually therefore the weaker side. The strategic intentions of parent companies is a definite factor in property rights in JVs. If we want to make the relationship of property rights structure more reasonable, we should look to the strategic intentions. The latter are, however, restricted by the macro environment, politics, laws, and the power of the companies themselves. To improve the environment for JVs and promote stronger collaboration, the government should improve the macro environment, and enterprises should strive to enhance their performance.

PART V

ALTERNATIVE MODELS

FOREIGN INVESTMENT IN CHINA:
B-SHARE MARKET VERSUS JOINT VENTURES

Liping Deng

INTRODUCTION

Joint ventures (JVs) and their variants, such as contractual and wholly foreign-owned enterprises, have for more than a decade been a major channel attracting foreign investment to the People's Republic of China (PRC). In December 1991 the Chinese government announced the opening of domestic stock markets (Shanghai and Shenzhen Securities Exchanges) to foreign investors. So-called "B-shares," defined as foreign currency denominated shares for foreign investors only, thus created another channel for foreign capital inflows.[1] In addition there were so-called "A-shares," local currency denominated shares which could be held only by PRC nationals. Thus, the pattern of attracting foreign private investment to the PRC has consisted of two major channels: direct investment (primarily in the form of JVs) and indirect or portfolio investment (including B-share transactions).

While there have been an increasing number of studies on Sino-foreign JVs, the analysis of the B-share market is at an early stage. Some authors have provided an institutional description of the B-share market (Sen 1994; Xu 1995;

Advances in Chinese Industrial Studies, Volume 5, pages 313-329.

ISBN: 1-55938-961-3

Spencer 1995). Others have focused on the comparative performance of A- and B-shares (Lin 1994). This paper will analyze the B-share market from a different perspective by examining its relationship with JVs. Two main questions will be asked. First, can the B-share market be (or has it already been) a complementary channel to JVs as a means of attracting foreign investment? Second, to what extent can JVs play a role in helping the development of the B-share market? These questions have theoretical and practical significance for both the Chinese authorities and foreign investors.

During the author's field trips to China in the summer of 1994 and the winter of 1995, aggregate data of the B-share markets were collected and case studies in the Shanghai Securities Exchange were made. The following sections will begin with a theoretical analysis of the relationship between the B-share market and JVs, followed by a brief discussion of the performance of the B-share market in the light of its ability to absorb foreign capital. A profile analysis of the B-share listing companies in the Shanghai Securities Exchange will then be reported, primarily with respect to the possible contributions of JVs to the development of the B-share market. The paper ends with a discussion of conclusions and policy implications.

B-SHARE MARKET VERSUS JOINT VENTURES: A MACRO ANALYSIS

Necessity of B-Share Market

The functions of a stock market (or a capital market in general) in a reformed socialist and developing economy like the PRC have been widely debated (Nuti 1989; Bowles and White 1992). Predictably, this debate has generally focused on two fronts. One is whether a stock market might be consistent with socialist principles, and the other is whether a stock market could help the economic growth of a developing country. Up to the early 1990s while certain controversies remained, the mainstream view in China tended to recognize a consistency between a stock market and reformed socialism, and the contribution of a stock market toward economic development. It was believed that a stock market should perform some basic functions in a socialist economy, such as a pool for the society's dispersed savings, a channel to direct these savings to companies with the best investment opportunities, and a mechanism to promote the efficient use of capital (Singh 1990; Levine 1996).

The aforementioned functions aside, there have been two particular objectives in China in the establishment of a stock market. The first was to create another channel to attract foreign investment. It was recognized that in the early 1990s the growth of indirect investment had surpassed that of direct investment as a major form of capital flow on a global basis. For developing

Table 1. Percentage Share of Foreign Investment in China, 1985-1992

	1985	*1986*	*1987*	*1988*	*1989*	*1990*	*1991*	*1992*
Direct investment	84.8	83.6	87.4	85.4	89.9	92.9	93.6	97.5
Other investment	15.2	16.4	12.6	14.6	10.1	7.1	6.3	2.5

Note: Other investment includes portfolio inflow, compensation trade, processing, and leasing.
Source: *China Statistical Yearbook.* Various issues. China's State Statistical Bureau.

countries, private capital flows have tripled since 1990 to over US$113 billion in 1993, the highest level since the debt crisis of the early 1980s. About half of these flows were accounted for by private portfolio investment (stocks and bonds), reaching US$55.8 billion in 1993 (Claessens and Gooptu 1994). It has been noted that foreign direct investment is driven by multinational companies' intensified pursuit of worldwide production and resources. Foreign direct investment flows have also increased in response to the market potential offered by rising incomes and trade liberalization processes in developing countries. History has shown that China has done quite well in attracting foreign direct investment. Table 1 reflects this success; it tabulates the percentage share of overall foreign private inflows to China.

In the case of private portfolio flow, foreign investors have been highly selective, particularly in developing countries. They invest in a portfolio only if the marginal returns from it are higher than those of the home country after allowing for factors such as the risk and stability of the host country. Since 1989 more than half of such flows have gone to Latin America, and five countries (Argentina, Brazil, Korea, Mexico, and Turkey) accounted for two-thirds of the flows (Claessens and Gooptu 1994). As shown in Table 1, the relative size of "other investment" in the PRC has been small and decreasing. It should be noted that in Chinese statistics "other investment" is a category defined more widely than portfolio investment, so the actual figures of portfolio investment in China are much smaller than the table suggests. Clearly, as a latecomer in this competition there has been an urgent need for the PRC to speed up this process. Moreover, as it would have taken an even longer period for China to extend its bond market to foreign investors, the opening of a domestic stock market to foreign investors turned out to be the more feasible choice.

The second objective of having a stock market was to find an alternative way to reform the existing enterprise structure in China. Enterprise reform has been a key, but thus far the most difficult, component of Chinese reform. Attempts at reform were speeded up in the early 1990s with numerous efforts to find a suitable and efficient enterprise structure. Currently, there are four major categories of enterprise in China: (1) state-owned enterprises in various forms; (2) non-state-owned enterprises; (3) enterprises with foreign direct investment (JVs and their variants); and (4) joint stock companies. The major purpose of establishing joint stock companies was to diversify enterprises' sources of financing, to create a system of corporate governance without relying on bureaucrats, and to make domestic enterprises behave more consistently in line with international standards. It was hoped that joint stock companies could provide an additional element for the new enterprise structure in a market-oriented economy. In addition to the use of domestic financial resources, foreign participation in joint stock companies was welcome. The opening of the B-share market was the first step in this direction. In July 1993 China also issued H-shares in Hong Kong, and in August 1994 N-shares in New York on a trial basis.

B-Share Market Versus Joint Ventures

As we have seen, the objective of JVs was similar to that of the B-share market. On the one hand, the establishment of JVs and other forms of foreign direct investment brought in foreign capital, and on the other hand, it provided a new option for the existing enterprise structure in China. Given that both the JVs and B-share market were expected to fulfill the same dual objective (absorbing foreign investment and helping enterprise reform), the similarities and connection between JVs and the B-share market are obvious. It was therefore natural for the Chinese government to expect the B-share market to become a channel complementary to JVs.

Such a similarity, or connection, has actually been reflected in the evolution of the B-share market. In the late 1980s and before the B-share market was officially established there had already been experiments to allow foreign participation in domestic joint stock companies. In 1988 the Jinbei Automobile Co. Ltd. in Shenyang became the first enterprise in China to issue shares to foreigners with the purchase price and dividends payable in foreign currencies. Following this example, numerous JVs were transformed into joint stock companies with shares issued to foreign investors. To some degree joint stock companies with foreign portfolio investment participation could be considered as a special type of JV. The opening of the B-share market in the early 1990s can be seen as an extension of these experiments and a reflection of the inherent connection between the two forms.

The Chinese authorities have attempted since the early 1990s to promulgate a set of laws and regulations to manage joint stock companies in general and the B-share market in particular. A brief evaluation of these laws and regulations reveals a close connection between the B-share market and JVs. In May 1992 a legal document known as the *Standard Opinion on Companies Limited by Shares* was issued to regulate all joint stock companies incorporated in the PRC. This document was later replaced by the "Company Law," which became effective on July 1, 1994. Based on the Company Law the State

Commission for the Restructuring of the Economic System (Reform Commission) and other governmental agencies further adopted a series of supporting regulations in connection with taxation, management of land and properties, accounting systems, financial management, state-owned assets, labor and remuneration management, management of human resources, material supply, and auditing. Local governments also established certain regulations applicable to joint stock companies under their jurisdiction.

At the time of the field studies connected with this paper, there had been no comprehensive national securities law in China. The "Interim Regulation on Securities" adopted on April 22, 1993 served as a basic law to control the issuing and trading of B-shares nationwide. Four governmental agencies of the State Council—the Securities Commission, the Planning Commission, the Economic and Trade Commission, and the Reform Commission—were designated as the final approving authorities for B-shares. The issue, trading, and settlement of B-shares in both Shanghai and Shenzhen were also subject to local rules and regulations issued by the local governments, local branches of the four Central Commissions, and local Securities Exchanges.

One key aspect of these laws and regulations is associated with the permission given to a joint stock company to issue B-shares. A joint stock company applying for B-share listing must meet a number of requirements. For example, such a company should have at least RMB100 million net capital, should hold a record of continuous profitability for the previous three years with expected profit margin greater than the bank deposit rate, and should prepare financial statements consistent with international accounting standards.

According to the existing regulations joint stock companies can be either newly established enterprises, with governmental agencies and other state-owned entities being the major shareholders, or transformed existing state-owned enterprises. In order for these joint stock companies to issue B-shares they are required to have special permission from the relevant governmental agencies to utilize foreign investment. Once certain conditions have been met such a joint stock company can be treated as a special type of JV.

There are also regulations that directly provide a linkage between a JV and a B-share company. As specified earlier, a joint stock company can be created from an existing JV through a structure reorganization. Alternatively, it can be done by a two-step transformation procedure in which a state-owned enterprise can first become part of a JV, then later be reconstructed as a joint stock company. While there are no special requirements with respect to the approval of the B-share listing application from these JV-related or JV-transformed joint stock companies, there are certain advantages for JVs that actually make it easier to obtain permission; for example, JVs are already in an industry where foreign participation has been permitted. A JV finds it easier to meet other requirements as well; for instance, regulations require that an applicant joint stock company should have a stable and adequate source of foreign exchange revenue in order to secure dividend payment. Comparatively speaking, a JV-transformed joint stock company has advantages in this regard since it has more foreign exchange in hand and its use of foreign exchange is generally subject to a low degree of government control.

Another aspect of the laws and regulations is related to foreign participation in a joint stock company after permission to issue B-shares has been given. General requirements include, for example, restrictions on who may hold B-shares for a joint stock company. The subscription and trading of B-shares are limited to (1) foreign investors, (2) investors from Hong Kong and Taiwan, and (3) other investors outside the PRC if approved by the relevant governmental agencies. Other special regulations pave the way to link the B-share market and JVs more closely.

One such regulation is the so-called "25 percent rule." It is stated that if foreign portfolio investment (in the form of B-share holding) has accounted for more than 25 percent of the registered capital of a joint stock company, this company can apply to be treated as a JV. If such an application is approved the company can enjoy the preferential policies normally applied to JVs. In practice, such a B-share listed company may be better off than either an ordinary JV or a standard joint stock company, because it can simultaneously enjoy the preferential treatments given both to JVs and to joint stock companies. For example, the 25 percent rule qualifies a B-share listing company to export its products directly and to retain all foreign exchange earnings from such exports. Dividends on the company's B-shares can be paid out by these earnings. Furthermore, if the earnings are not sufficient to pay dividends, the company can purchase foreign exchange from authorized banks with the approval of the State Administration for Exchange Control.

Another case in point is the regulation that permits B-share listed companies to enter into new JVs. As an equal partner, a B-share company can set up a new joint venture with foreign direct investment. A B-share company can also acquire the existing JVs as its subsidiaries through the means of shareholding. The regulations provide certain policy incentives and special treatments to encourage B-share companies to enter new JVs, particularly those B-share companies with state-owned enterprises as their precursors.

Other regulations make a clear distinction between foreign participation (both B-shares and JVs) and domestic activities (A-shares) in the stock market. As previously noted, there are strict requirements on the separate holders of A- and B-shares. As the B-share market and JVs are treated as two related parts of foreign capital inflows, funds in existing JVs can be used to purchase B-shares, but these funds are not to be used to trade A-shares. By the same token, funds from domestic sources are not permitted to be used for trading in B-shares.

Consideration must be given to the differences between the B-share markets and JVs. The respective features of the B-share markets and JVs point to the fact that they are complementary, rather than substitute, channels. JVs bring into the PRC foreign capital, accompanied by additional resources such as technology, management know-how, and access to export markets. B-share companies, on the other hand, can absorb foreign capital without being accompanied by real flow. From this unique perspective, the B-share market and JVs should be treated as equally important.

However, as far as the function of helping enterprise reform is concerned, there are still ideological or systemic constraints on the development of the B-share market. For example, how far would the PRC government like joint stock companies to be a major form of the new enterprise structure? How far would the government allow the shares of joint stock companies to be controlled by foreigners? Which industries will be allowed to have foreign involvement? These questions do not have obvious answers and therefore the Chinese authorities have taken a more cautious approach toward foreign portfolio investment, compared with its policy toward direct investment.

Experience suggests that the authorities have maintained a much tighter control over the B-share market than over JVs. The so-called "5 percent versus 35 percent" rule is a good case in point. This rule states that (1) the purchase by any investor of B-shares in excess of 5 percent of a company's total shares should be subject to approval from governmental agencies; and (2) the prescribed ratio of B-shares to total shares cannot exceed 35 percent of the company's capital source unless otherwise approved. As indicated by interviews with governmental agency officials, it is still the government's position that JVs should continue to play a more important role in attracting foreign capital than the B-share market for the present time. As a result, JVs continue to receive preferential treatment over B-share companies.

In summary, the development of the B-share market has been subject to concurrent supports and constraints from the Chinese government, an approach that is guided by caution. The lack of experience in the early stages further complicates the issue. As a result, the B-share market has not yet become a major channel of absorbing foreign investment in comparison to JVs.

The Comparative Performance of the B-Share Market and JVs

The evolution of the B-share market in the past few years as a channel to attract foreign investment has not yet been successful. The size of the B-share market in terms of the composition of stock market capitalization in China is comparatively small. By the end of 1994 A-shares were by far the largest segment of the stock market, with a capitalization value of about US$43 billion, while the capitalized value of listed B-shares was about US$2 billion. Considering the fact that the Chinese stock market has accounted for only 4 percent of overall stock market capitalization in East Asia emerging markets in 1994 (Dalla and Khatkhate 1996), the contribution of the B-share market in attracting foreign investment to China is quite limited.

Moreover, the performance of the B-share market has fluctuated widely. In February 1992, when B-shares were first issued, foreign investors showed considerable interest, and turnover, while initially low, appeared to be improving. However, the enthusiasm of foreign investors vanished in 1993 when B-share liquidity all but disappeared and prices fell sharply. Stock values slid 60 percent in the first seven months of 1993.[2] Since that time, while there were some short periods of recovery, B-share markets have consistently been poor performers and this trend is expected to continue for some time. Table 2 gives the major price index of B-shares in Shanghai and Shenzhen Securities Exchanges.

In sharp contrast, JVs have continually maintained strong growth and have remained a major channel to attract foreign investment to the PRC. In 1990 foreign direct investment was US$3.49 billion, and in 1995 this amount significantly increased to US$36.5 billion. At that point, China's absorption of all foreign direct investment in developing countries accounted for 42 percent. During the period 1991 to 1995 accumulated direct investment flows to China reached US$114.2 billion. In comparison, the inflows of foreign capital through the B-share market were quite small. By the end of December 1994 the cumulative face value of B-shares accounted for only 2 percent of overall foreign capital inflows, an insignificant number compared to direct investment (nearly 68%) and bank loans (around 29%). With regard to the composition of B-share purchasing, Hong Kong and Taiwan investors comprised the vast majority of purchasers, followed at some distance by Japanese and American investors.

There have been several studies into the reasons why the B-share market has not yet become an important channel for attracting foreign investment (Shal 1994; Sen 1994; Xu 1995; Spencer 1995; Wang and Liu 1996). The field studies indicate several issues worth noting. One is potential foreign investors' lack of confidence in the reliability of the B-share market in particular and the stability of the PRC economy in general. Second, the procedure for trading B-shares is highly complex and there is a great deal of uncertainty surrounding the legality of governing rules. Third, a paucity of information leads to the failure to observe regulations. For example, the requirements for disclosing relevant information to potential investors has not yet been precisely observed by quite a number of B-share companies. In practice, some companies have even misused the proceeds of B-shares issued by speculating in real estate, or simply by on-lending the foreign exchange they received. A combination of these factors has contributed to the "wait and see" approach of foreign investors toward the B-share market while they rely more on JVs and other forms of direct investment.

Table 2. B-Share Market Performance, Major Price Index, 1992-1995

	End of 4Q 92	*End of 1Q 93*	*End of 2Q 93*	*End of 3Q 93*	*End of 4Q 93*	*End of 1Q 94*	*End of 2Q 94*	*End of 3Q 94*	*End of 4Q 94*	*End of 1Q 95*	*End of 2Q 95*
SH B	66	82	58	73	103	65	68	82	63	57	53
q-o-q	n.a.	23.8%	-28.9%	25.9%	39.8%	-36.8%	4.2%	20.6%	-22.9%	-9.0%	-6.5%
SZ B	112	137	98	109	141	112	104	119	87	74	66
q-o-q	n.a.	22.4%	-28.2%	10.4%	29.8%	-20.4%	-6.9%	13.6%	-27.0%	-14.5%	-10.5%

Note: SH B = Shanghai B-share; SZ B = Shenzhen B-share; 1Q = first quarter, and so forth; q-o-q = growth over last quarter.
Sources: *Securities Reports.* Various issues. Shanghai International Securities Ltd.

B-SHARE MARKET VERSUS JOINT VENTURES: A PROFILE ANALYSIS IN SHANGHAI

The previous sections have addressed the relationship between the B-share market and JVs at the national level. This section attempts a micro analysis in Shanghai to explore how the B-share market and JVs are institutionally related in practice, and how JVs may make contributions to the development of the B-share market. There are several ways to approach such an analysis. One could examine the comparative contributions of the B-share listing companies and JVs toward the growth of the Shanghai local economy. One could also analyze the financial performance of the B-share companies and JVs as two separate groups. Due to the nature of the field study data, this section intends to take a narrower perspective by analyzing the profile of the B-share companies listed on the Shanghai Securities Exchange up to the middle of 1995.

B-Share Listing Companies and JVs: An Institutional Profile

As previously noted, the existing laws and regulations specify several paths through which a joint stock company can be granted the right to issue B-shares, and each of these paths has a particular relationship with JVs. An institutional profile analysis of 32 B-share companies listed on the Shanghai Securities Exchange helps to illuminate how such regulations have been implemented in practice. Four types of B-share listed companies attract attention in this regard.

Type I

There were three government-controlled B-share listed companies (Type I = 9% overall): Shanghai Jinqiao Export Processing Zone Development Co. Ltd., Shanghai Lujiazui Finance and Trade Zone Development Co. Ltd., and Shanghai Wai Gaoqiao Free Trade Zone Development Co. Ltd. These companies were also related to the development of the Pudong Development Zone, a special area being given "most preferential policy treatment." The relationship between these B-share companies and JVs was somewhat indirect. Interviews with managers of these companies conveyed the impression that the major purpose of setting up such companies was to obtain foreign capital in the form of B-share purchasing to finance infrastructural and other facilities in the Development Zone, which would encourage more JVs and other forms of direct foreign investment to come into Pudong.

Shanghai Wai Gaoqiao Free Trade Zone Development Co. Ltd. (Wai Gaoqiao) was the first joint stock company of this type. It was established in 1990 as a joint stock company to develop the Outer Gaoqiao Free Trade Zone in Pudong. Wai Gaoqiao was principally engaged in land requisition, site formation, and, in some cases, construction of industrial, office, and residential premises. By mid-1995 the company was selling or leasing premises in the First Phase of the Free Trade Zone and engaging in investment activities both within and outside the Free Trade Zone. Up to mid-1995 the Shanghai Municipal Government had been the largest shareholder (with 65.8% of the overall share), while other domestic sources owned around 28 percent and foreign shares (B-shares) accounted for only 5.7 percent.

Type II

There were 14 B-share listed companies that had been directly transformed from existing state-owned enterprises (Type II = around 44% overall). The predecessors of these companies were generally large or medium-sized, core state-owned enterprises with a solid performance, a good financial record, promising markets, and long-standing government support. Among this group were some household names in China: Shanghai Chlor-Alkali Chemical Co. Ltd., China Textile Machinery Co. Ltd., Shanghai Industrial Sewing Machine Co. Ltd., Shanghai Hero Co. Ltd., Shanghai Phoenix Bicycle Co. Ltd., and Shanghai Forever Bicycle Co. Ltd. From interviews with managers of these companies and local government officials, it seems that the major purpose of allowing these companies to be listed was to convince foreign investors to participate in Chinese enterprise reform, and to improve foreign investors' confidence in the B-share market. By allowing foreign participation in these formerly state-owned enterprises, the Chinese authorities actually created a special type of JV.

China Textile Machinery Co. Ltd. is a good example of this group. The company was the largest manufacturer of textile machinery in China, with an estimated market share of more than 60 percent. It had been a state-owned enterprise since 1949 and was reorganized as a joint stock company in 1992 with both B- and A-shares listed that year. This company, as well as the entire textile industry, had constantly been backed by the Chinese government in the form of special policy treatment and various other supports. As indicated from the field study, the major reason for allowing this enterprise to be reorganized as a joint stock company was to diversify its financial sources so that the company would be in a better position to beat increasing competition from foreign companies. In mid-1995 the government owned 52.9 percent of total shares, other domestic sources owned around 33 percent, while foreign holding was 12.6 percent. Two years after being listed this company had not only continued to dominate the Chinese textile machinery market, but had also significantly increased its exports.

Type III

There were 11 B-share listed companies that established new relationships with JVs after being listed (Type III = 34% overall). The typical path was first to transform the state-owned enterprise into a joint stock company, and then to become part of a new JV. In general, companies who took this path and particularly those companies with a certain degree of foreign participation, gained in the capacity to become engaged in new joint ventures.

Shanghai Sanmao Textile Co. Ltd. (Sanmao) is a good case in point. The forerunner of this company was the state-owned Sanmao Textile Factory. It was reorganized into a joint stock company in mid-1993 (Shanghai State Assets Administration Bureau was a major shareholder with 49.3% of the overall shares); A-shares were offered and listed shortly thereafter. B-shares were offered and listed in December 1993 and January 1994, respectively. Immediately after the B-shares were listed Sanmao entered into three new JVs with French and Italian partners and became a supplier to each JV. Data from the field studies showed that the combined sales to these JVs accounted for about 20 percent of Sanmao's turnover in 1995.

Shanghai Erfangji Co. Ltd. (Erfangji) provides another example. Erfangji was one of the largest producers and distributors of various machinery equipment in China. It was transformed from a state-owned enterprise to a joint stock company in 1992 (with a state share of 46.3%) and during that year both A- and B-shares were issued and listed on the Shanghai Securities Exchange. Such a transformation enabled Erfangji to diversify its operations by entering into two new JVs with Swiss investors in 1994, and to increase its export by a significant amount in the same time period.

The case of Shanghai Refrigerator Compressor (SRC) Co. Ltd. is also interesting. After SRC became a joint stock company (with a state share of 47%), it entered into a new JV with the Hitachi Corporation of Japan for the production of air conditioner compressors. As the product was originally imported from Japan, a new joint venture relationship enabled SRC to produce it according to international standards but at lower prices than existing Japanese competitors. As a result, SRC came to have a large share of the domestic market for this product.

Type IV

Four B-share listed companies belonged to the JV-transformed category (Type IV = around 13% overall): Shanghai Haixin Co. Ltd., Shanghai Lian Hua Fibre Corporation, Dajiang Co. Ltd., Yaohua Pilkington Glass Co. Ltd., and Shanghai New Asia (Group) Co. Ltd. Three of these companies were directly transformed from existing JVs.

The case of Haixin can be used as an illustration. Haixin was a JV formed in 1986 between three Chinese state-owned enterprises and two Hong Kong companies. It was directly converted into a joint stock company in November 1993 before it was listed. By mid-1995 three Chinese enterprises accounted for approximately 42.4 percent of total shares, and the two Hong Kong companies had a share of 29.5 percent. This company was not entering into any new JVs.

New Asia (Group) provides a somewhat different case. New Asia was a JV principally engaged in the hotel, fast-food, and restaurant business in Shanghai. It was converted into a joint stock company with its core company Shanghai New Asia (Group) Ltd. holding 48.8 percent of the shares. After being listed, the company continued to enter into new JVs. For example, in April 1993 the company signed a new JV contract with Tomson (China) Co. Ltd. of Hong Kong to construct the Shanghai New Asia Tomson Hotel.

Observations

Clearly, each of these four types of B-share companies had a direct or indirect relationship with JVs to differing degrees. There are some interesting observations here. First, the majority of the existing B-share listed companies were either directly organized by the government (Type I) or transformed from former state-owned enterprises retaining the government as the major shareholder (Type II). To some extent, this is a strategy of "picking the strongest," which clearly demonstrates the Chinese government's intention to control the development of the B-share market rather than let the market fully determine the issuers. Second, a great number of joint stock companies have gained an improved financial ability to enter new JVs after having been listed (Type III). This practice provides a close linkage between B-share listed companies and JVs, suggesting that the formation of the B-share market could help to promote the further development of JVs. Third, it is interesting to note that JV-transformed B-share listed companies (Type IV) have not yet become an important element of the B-share market. As indicated by the field studies, one reason may be that foreign investors do not benefit more from a B-share company than from a JV. The other reason may be that while the regulations in place have attempted to make such a transformation easier, in practice the procedures for approval were still rather complicated.

Comparative Performance of Four Types of B-Share Companies

There have been several comprehensive studies of the financial performance of B-share companies as a group in Shanghai (Lin 1994; Deng 1996). The following analysis will simply use three indicators to examine the comparative performance of these four types of B-share companies. The results of this analysis may further clarify the issue of whether JVs can make contributions to the further development of the B-share market.

Table 3. Selective Indicators of Four types of B-Share Companies

	Companies			
Indicators	*Type I*	*Type II*	*Type III*	*Type IV*
1. B:A-share price discount	78.0%	69.5%	66.1%	53.0%
2. B/Total market capitalization	7.8%	13.2%	16.5%	21.3%
3. B-share yield ratio	3.8%	3.6%	3.9%	4.0%

Source: Calculated from *China Fund Managers' Digest*. Various issues. Shanghai H.K. International Securities Ltd.

The first indicator is price-related, namely the *B:A-share price discount ratio*. This ratio is defined as (1 - B-Price/A-Price). A positive ratio suggests a higher A-share price than B-share price for a given transaction date. The second indicator is associated with the relative size of foreign involvement, namely the *ratio of B-share capitalization over total market capitalization*. This is an accumulative value; the larger the number the higher the level of foreign participation in a given joint stock company. The third indicator is a three-year average *B-share yield ratio*. Table 3 presents a group average of these three indicators for the four types of companies based on the data as at July 10, 1995.

With regard to Indicator 1, Type I has the largest price differential between its A- and B-share prices on average, followed by Types II and III, with Type IV averaging the lowest of all the groups. In theory, if the operation of joint stock companies is primarily based on the market mechanism, the prices of the A- and B-shares should be almost the same after the rate of foreign exchange is taken into consideration. A lower discount ratio, other things being equal, may suggest that price performance of JV-transformed or JV-related companies is more related to the market environment, while the price movement of Type I (government-supported companies) is further removed from market determination. Moreover, the largest price discount rate for Type I companies may suggest that this group suffered most when the stock market was hit by the sudden collapse of foreign investors' confidence. By the same token, this factor may also have influenced foreign investors to be more confident in the performance of the JV-transformed B-share companies.

Indicator 2 represents a comparison of foreign participation in all four types of joint stock companies. As seen in Table 3, Type I has the lowest foreign participation ratio, which may suggest the difficulty of attracting foreign investors to this type of joint stock company. In contrast, Type IV has the highest foreign participation ratio. This phenomenon could be partially attributed to foreign investors having more confidence in investing in those JV-transformed joint stock companies. Types II and III again occupy a middle position, with Type III having a higher ratio. It is interesting to note that none of these four types of companies passed the 25 percent rule on average, but Type IV had approached this mark.

With respect to Indicator 3, there are no significant differences among the four types of companies. Type IV has the highest B-share yield ratio, which may imply that JV-transformed B-share companies have a better financial performance, other things being equal. Type III is again ranked second in this category, followed closely by Types I and II.

One should interpret the above results with caution. Certain nonperformance-related factors may also account for the differences between types. More indicators are needed in order to understand fully the bases of differences. However, the above comparison does indicate that JV-transformed or JV-related B-share companies may have a relatively better performance in attracting foreign investment than their counterparts and that their operation appears to rely more on the market mechanism. This finding suggests that if more JV-transformed or JV-related joint stock companies were listed on the B-share market, the performance of the B-share market could be improved to some degree.

CONCLUSIONS

Several conclusions can be reached from the above analysis. First, while there has been progress in utilizing the B-share market to attract foreign investment, there is still a long way to go before such a market can function as an effective channel. In the foreseeable future, JVs and other forms of direct investment will continue to play a key role in absorbing foreign private capital to China. Second, there is a close connection between the B-share market and JVs, both theoretically and institutionally. In practice, there are several patterns which indicate that B-share companies and JVs are interchangeable and can enhance each other's performance. Third, as observed primarily by the performance of JV-transformed or JV-related B-share companies in Shanghai, one can reasonably argue that there is still a considerable role for JVs to play in helping the future development of B-share markets.

The policy implication for the Chinese government is straightforward. While continuing to rely on JVs and their variants as a major channel to attract foreign investment, more effort should be made to strengthen and improve the existing B-share market. It is advisable to allow the market mechanism to play a more important role in the operation of the B-share market. Moreover, certain regulations should be modified to encourage further the involvement of JVs in the development of the B-share market.

The suggestions for foreign investors are twofold. On one side, investment opportunities created by the B-share market should not be ignored or passed by, at least in the long-term perspective, but on the other, given the performance and problems in the existing B-share market, caution is advisable when one attempts to make portfolio investments in China. JVs and other forms of direct investment may still be a more feasible and reliable choice to enter the Chinese market.

ACKNOWLEDGMENTS

The author is grateful to the Shanghai Securities Exchange, Shanghai International Securities Ltd., and Securities College, Financial University of Shanghai for their assistance during the field study. The author accepts the final responsibility for the interpretation of the data.

NOTES

1. More precisely, they are "special local-currency denominated shares" but should be traded in foreign exchanges.
2. Parallels are drawn with the 1970s, when the developing countries first caught the imagination of investors, a romance which finally led to the international debt crisis of the early 1980s.

REFERENCES

Bowles, P., and G. White. 1992. "The Dilemma of Market Socialism: Capital Market Reform in China—Part II: Shares." *Journal of Development Study* 28 (4).

Claessens, S., and S. Gooptu. 1994. "Can Developing Countries Keep Foreign Capital Flowing In?" In *Finance & Development* (September). Washington: IMF & World Bank.

Dalla, I., and D. Khatkhate. 1996. "The Emerging East Asian Bond Market." In *Finance & Development* (March). Washington: IMF & World Bank.

Deng, L. 1996. "Financial Performance of B-Share Companies in Shanghai: An Empirical Study Based on Merton-Smibud-Mendelson Model." Working paper, Department of Economics, Mount Allison University, Sackville, NB, Canada.

Levine, R. 1996. "Stock Markets: A Spur to Economic Growth." In *Finance & Development* (March). Washington: IMF & World Bank.

Lin, M. 1994. "Determination of Contributing Factors to the Prices of A- and B-Shares" (in Chinese). *Shanghai Securities Weekly* (July 29).

Nuti, D. 1989. "Remonetisation and Capital Markets in the Reform of Centrally Planned Economies." *European Economic Review* 33 (2/3).

Sen, R. 1994. "Current Status and Prospects of Shanghai B-Share Market." A paper presented at an international conference on China's stock market in Shanghai, October 27.

Shal, T. 1994. "A China Puzzle." *Euromoney* (June).

Singh, A. 1990. "The Stock Market in Socialist Economy." In *The Future of Financial System and Services*, edited by E. Gardener. Basingstoke, UK: Macmillan.

Spencer, M. 1995. "Securities markets in China." In *Finance & Development* (June). Washington: IMF & World Bank.

Xu, L. 1995. "An Overview of China's B-Share Market: Challenges and Opportunities." In *Global Business in Transition, Prospects for the Twenty-First Century, Volume 2.* Hong Kong: Lingnan College and City University of Hong Kong.

Wang, L., and L. Liu. 1996. "Joint Stock Companies in China and International Capital Market" (in Chinese). *World Economy* (1).

SOME PRC PERSPECTIVES ON CONGLOMERATION OF ENTERPRISES

Yu-min Chou

INTRODUCTION

Conglomeration of enterprises may assume many forms. It can be in the shape of a vertically integrated group, as has been exemplified by the mergers to achieve backward and forward integration in the steel and oil industries. Some, which take the form of horizontal integration in the same industry, reduce the number of remaining firms and create a monopoly or an oligopoly. A cartel, which is a monopoly, is another form of horizontal conglomeration in the same industry formed by a voluntary association of independent firms.

The Japanese-style conglomerate, known as a *keiretsu* group, is formed by cross-equity share holding among the member enterprises and includes both vertical and horizontal conglomerates. The Toyota Group is a vertically integrated group in which Toyota Motors serves as the core enterprise for other related businesses in the automotive industry but is also at the same time a member of the Mitsui Group—a horizontal *keiretsu* group comprising major firms (each of which heads a vertically integrated group of its own) in diverse fields. Then there is the U.S.-style conglomerate which is a grouping of

Advances in Chinese Industrial Studies, Volume 5, pages 331-341.

ISBN: 1-55938-961-3

enterprises in a variety of industries brought under the control of a single firm through mergers and acquisitions.

Why does conglomeration take place? The literature on merger activities in the United States up to 1980 offers several hypotheses. These include (1) the attempt to wrest control from inefficient, entrenched management; (2) the attempt to limit competition and gain market power; (3) the attempt to benefit from market inefficiency that leaves corporate equity undervalued; and (4) tax considerations (Warshawsky 1987). With regard to hypothesis 2, conglomeration, while gaining market power for the conglomerate, may or may not limit competition in the context of a globalized market. In the case of Japan's *keiretsu*, the primary motives behind conglomeration would appear to be the desire to preserve (or increase) the *keiretsu* members' competitiveness in the market and to reduce business risk for each member (Okumura 1990).

Conglomerates are coming into existence in the People's Republic of China (PRC) today. It may be worth examining whether there are significant differences or similarities between these groupings in the PRC and those in the United States and in Japan. This leads to further questions as to why conglomeration is taking place in the PRC and why it is assuming particular forms. Little research seems to have been conducted to see whether the Chinese approach to conglomeration is unique; what new problems may arise as a result of it; what part the privatization of the state-owned enterprises plays in this development; and what role overseas Chinese enterprises assume in the conglomeration, and so on. This paper attempts in the following sections to address these issues.

IMPETUSES TO CONGLOMERATION IN THE PRC

Conglomeration of enterprises in China would not have been possible without the economic reform that started in the PRC in the mid-1970s. The economic reform was intended to transform a static economy into a dynamic one and this required an overhaul of the PRC's industries which could only be achieved by a comprehensive restructuring and rationalization of enterprises. Among the measures used to expedite this overhaul was the opening of the economy to foreign investment so that firms in China could acquire capital, technology, and business know-how from foreign investors. The opening started from the four Special Economic Zones (SEZs) in the southern coastal region and then spread to the entire coastal regions and, recently, further inland. Much of the foreign investment initially came from overseas Chinese investors, who through their direct subsidiaries and joint ventures with local PRC enterprises contributed to the rise of a market mentality in China's businesses and provided some global linkages. In particular, these foreign investments, most of which are small to medium in scale, transferred technology, management know-how, and global linkages to collectively owned township and village enterprises of a similar size. Domestically, the growth of these semiprivate enterprises and the new privately owned enterprises (which emerged as a result of the economic reform) exerted new competitive pressures on the state-owned enterprises and forced the latter to restructure and regroup for survival.

The state-owned enterprises employed at least two approaches in their responses to the new market pressure. One was a search for foreign linkages, through inward foreign investments and later by actively seeking foreign linkages through their presence in Hong Kong. The other was to privatize state-owned enterprises and, in the process, foster entrepreneurship in the management of the state-owned enterprises. The latter, the privatization, can also be used as a vehicle to promote conglomeration of enterprises.

Since conglomeration of enterprises, by creating a group, also expands the power base of the management, it was thought that the management of a conglomerated group, with its larger power base and newly acquired entrepreneurial skills, would be able to counteract government interference in the business affairs of the enterprise more effectively than could the management of a single enterprise. Thus, conglomeration of enterprises became a strategy in the economic reform package (Chung Guo 1992, pp. 92, 578).

There were also other objectives in the conglomeration of enterprise groups in the PRC. It was pointed out earlier that economic reform requires an overhaul of the PRC's industries and that enterprise conglomeration was thought to be a route to achieving this objective. Conglomeration permits strong enterprises to take over the control of the weaker ones and thus to energize the latter. By integrating different levels of economic activities backward and forward, the conglomeration internalizes all activities, such as research and development, engineering, manufacturing, distribution, and financing; and this internalization aims to improve the coordination of these activities and eliminate duplication of activities at the same time. Also, conglomeration via backward and forward linkages under one single conglomerate management integrates not only enterprises that formerly were placed under the jurisdiction of different ministries (as, for example, an aircraft manufacturer, under the jurisdiction of the Ministry of Aerospace Industry, and its subcontractor, a machine and tool maker under the jurisdiction of the Ministry of Machinery and Electronics) but also enterprises that were administered by various local (such as provincial) authorities. While this kind of conglomeration is a form of vertical integration, enterprises have also been encouraged to diversify into other industries in their group on the lines of Japan's horizontal *keiretsu* groups. In the words of a senior official whose responsibility is to oversee the restructuring of the state-owned enterprises, these measures will ultimately create large, China-based conglomerate groups that are efficient, dynamic, and internationally competitive (*World Tribune* 1995; Chung Guo 1992, pp. 89-95, 577-579).

TYPES OF CONGLOMERATION

A multinational company in the United States can be a form of conglomerate when its value chain is vertically integrated. For example, General Motors internalizes many of its activities forward and backward and its vertical integration is demonstrated by the fact that the company procures 70 percent of its supplies internally. General Electric is another well-known multinational company that is also a conglomerate because its business is spread over diversified products. The Japanese forms of conglomeration are usually referred to as vertical and horizontal *keiretsu* conglomerates but they are, however, somewhat different in form from General Motors or General Electric. In the Japanese types of conglomerates the control of the value chain in the vertical *keiretsu* group is not internalized; and in the case of the horizontal *keiretsu* group enterprises form a group by swapping equity shares among themselves (i.e., cross-equity share holdings), with each enterprise in the group retaining its independent identity as well as its managerial independence. An examination of the configuration of the PRC's conglomerates compared with U.S. and Japanese models may shed light on the competitive potential of China-based conglomerates in the global economy.

There are several forms (or methods), both horizontal and vertical, of conglomeration in the PRC (Liu 1992, pp. 154-158; Chung Guo 1992, pp. 398-402) and they can be categorized as follows: finance-based conglomerates, trading company-based conglomerates, and manufacturing-based conglomerates.

Finance-based Conglomeration

In this type of conglomerate the core member is a major financial institution. By providing capital, in the form of loans, seed money, and via equity participation, this core member extends its financial linkages to other firms that are dependent on the supply of capital from the core enterprise, much as companies in a bank-centered Japanese *keiretsu* group do. The most notable examples of such groups are the China International Trust and Investment Company (CITIC) Group and the Bank of China Group.

Take the CITIC Group, for example. It is a vast financial institution established under the jurisdiction of the State Council (central government) in 1979 to promote the growth and the globalization of the PRC's enterprises. CITIC performs these roles by providing capital to selected enterprises, by loans and by equity capital participation directly or through a holding company (such as CITIC Pacific of Hong Kong) it controls. With these means at its disposal, CITIC has acted as an intermediary or as a direct participant to put together domestic as well as foreign enterprises in various forms of coalition networks. CITIC has, through these linkages, brought under its umbrella diverse groups of enterprises over a wide range of industries, both inside and outside China. It is in this sense that the CITIC Group can be regarded as a finance-based horizontal enterprises conglomerate, similar to a Japanese bank-centered *keiretsu* group.

Unlike the bank *keiretsu* group of Japan in which the core member is a commercial bank, however, CITIC is not a commercial bank. Nor is it a U.S.-style investment bank whose principal intermediary role usually remains in the realm of underwriting securities. A better analogy for CITIC is the Industrial Bank of Japan (IBJ) before the latter was allowed to expand into commercial banking activities in the late 1980s. IBJ started as a central government-sponsored specialized bank, designed to act as a development bank (not as a commercial bank) to promote the development and growth of Japan's industries. Through various forms of loans and equity participation that permitted the bank some control over the management of the beneficiary enterprises, IBJ has formed since the Second World War a network of affiliated enterprises that spans a wide range of industries. It is this type of finance-based conglomeration that CITIC and the Bank of China groups have attempted to emulate. In the case of the Bank of China Group, however, conglomeration has targeted financial institutions, creating what amounts to a banking *keiretsu* group.

Trading Company-based Conglomeration

This form of conglomeration centers around a foreign trading company that has worked in a foreign trade monopoly. In the centrally planned economy of the past, foreign trade was centrally controlled and enterprises in an industry that were involved in foreign trade had to work through a specialized foreign trading company specifically established for that industry. Thus, foreign trading companies, such as the Sinochem Group for petrochemical products, Minmetal Group for nonferrous metals, CMNC for nonmetallic materials, CNCOF for cereals, oils, and foodstuffs, and China Hua Ruenn Group for energy-related products, came into existence. Economic reform, however, has now broken down the barriers that used to protect the trade corporations from competitors.

Given the need to diversify the trading company's activities to meet the competition from the entry of new competitors and the need to accommodate the outward push (permitted by the opening of China's economy) of the enterprises in the group, the former foreign trade monopolies are forming trading company-centered conglomerates a la the Sogoshosha-led (multinational, multi-products trading company) Japanese conglomerates, such as the Mitsui Group and the Mitsubishi Group. The Sogoshosha played an active role in the formation of the post-Second World War horizontal *keiretsu* groups in Japan by acting not only as a marketing intermediary but also as a financier and as a deal maker; and by taking equity interest: it thus assembled under its umbrella companies spanning a wide range of industries. This would seem to be the model for the PRC's trading company-centered conglomerates, as is shown, for example, by Sinochem, which via direct equity participation has now diversified into banking, building of industrial projects, maritime shipping, retail outlets, and even owns a movie studio in Shanghai. With a total revenue of US$15 billion, it ranked 26th in *Fortune* magazine's 1994 ranking of international companies (*Wall Street Journal* 1995).

Manufacturing-based Conglomeration

There are numerous enterprise groups in the PRC whose primary activities are manufacturing, and in this type of conglomeration the group is formed by linking firms in a related manufacturing industry to the dominant manufacturer in that industry which then serves as the core enterprise of the conglomerate. In some of these, especially those that are involved in the development of high-technology products, members of the group also include research institutes and universities. Thus, the linkages in a manufacturing-based conglomerate comprise all stages of manufacturing, ranging from research and development, supply of raw materials, supply of parts and components, and terminal manufacturing to distribution. These linkages are cemented voluntarily, or by fiat of the state bureaucracy, and assume forms such as technical assistance, equity participation, financial assistance by the core enterprise to the peripheral members, or by joint ventures and other cooperative arrangements. What has thus emerged under this category is a pyramid of a vertically integrated group akin to a vertical *keiretsu* group.

The PRC's State Council approved in 1991 the formation of 55 enterprises groups (Chung Guo 1992, pp. 398-402). While a few are found in service industries, such as those in foreign trade and transportation, the large majority of these conglomerates are manufacturing-based and encompass numerous sectors, ranging from automotive, machines, and equipments firms, to those in mining and metallurgy, textiles, energy, chemicals, pharmaceuticals, construction and forest products, and the emerging aerospace manufacturing industry.

Some of the manufacturing conglomerates have now become well known outside the PRC, including groups such as First Automotive, Second Automotive, Shanghai Automotive, Great Wall Computers, Shanghai Aero-Space, and Xi An Aerospace, because of their business alignments with foreign enterprises. The Shanghai Automotive Group, the country's largest auto manufacturer (1994 total revenue of over US$4 billion) is, for example, well known outside China for its partnership with Volkswagen of Germany and General Motors of the United States. It is a vertically integrated group of enterprises engaged in activities that cover all aspects of the automotive industry (*Wall Street Journal* 1995). There is also the Shougan Group (the Capital Iron and Steel Corporation) which, with the authorization of the State Council, formed a vertically integrated conglomerate in the steel industry long before 1991.

Another development in the conglomeration in the manufacturing industries is that, through the conglomeration of enterprises, the state has attempted to insulate a conglomerate against meddling by the state bureaucracy by forming a state corporation or a holding company to oversee the business affairs of a conglomerate. Since the executives in the state corporation and directors in holding companies are appointed by the state, the conglomerate's ties to the latter have not, however, been truly severed. The Xi An Aerospace Group (which has a McDonnell-Douglas joint venture connection) is, for example, overseen by a state corporation, China Aerospace Corporation, which has its headquarters in Beijing. Under instructions from China Aerospace in Beijing (and that instruction presumably reflects the wish of the Ministry of Aerospace), Xi An Aerospace has assembled formerly independent aircraft parts manufacturers and automotive parts manufacturers as well (*World Tribune* 1995a).

THE MECHANISM OF CONGLOMERATION

In a system in which enterprises are state-owned, conglomeration of enterprises can be effected by administrative fiat that emanates from government authorities at national, provincial, or municipal level. A directive by an appropriate government authority (e.g., a cabinet ministry through a state corporation in the Xi An Aerospace example) to consolidate the several independent plants it controls under the management of a core plant will lead to the formation of a conglomerated group of enterprises. This type of consolidation may eliminate duplication of facilities and reduce the cost of the group's manufacturing activities, but it still leaves the government with control over the consolidated group of enterprises. Such an outcome defeats one of the objectives of the economic reform, which is to free enterprises from management by government bureaucracy. Another method is to integrate the activities of related enterprises under a core enterprise via various forms of collaboration, such as supply-distribution and exclusive subcontractor-terminal manufacturer linkages. But if these forms of collaboration are voluntary and if the managements of each enterprise remain independent of each other, the collaboration is at best unstable.

For a conglomeration to be effective and solid, there must be shared ownership among the enterprises that constitute a conglomerated group. Furthermore, for it to operate efficiently and become globally competitive, its management must be freed from the administrative control of government bureaucracy. These considerations call for the development of a mechanism by which ownership can be transferred and exchanged, and in doing so the free spirit of entrepreneurship will grow in the management ranks. That mechanism is to be found in the privatization of state-owned enterprises, which, by attracting foreign capital inflow and inward technology transfer, also extends the global linkages of China-based conglomerate groups. How effectively these objectives can be met depends partly on the methods of privatization that are adopted; there are basically two of these methods: privatization via sale of equity shares, and direct transfer of an enterprise's assets.

Privatization Via Sale of Equity Shares

In order to facilitate the sale of equity shares, two stock exchanges were established in Shanghai and in Shenzhen (a new city located in the SEZ north of Hong Kong) in 1991. Two classifications of equity shares were issued in these markets: A-shares and B-shares. A-shares are listed in the PRC, sold only to Chinese citizens, and can be paid for only in local currency (RMB). B-shares are also listed in the PRC but can be sold to foreign citizens and paid for in foreign currencies, notably in U.S. dollars. In addition, equity shares of some selected enterprises are also listed on the securities markets in Hong Kong (known as H-shares) and New York (known as N-shares). While one of the motives behind this complex method of selling equity shares is the desire to attract capital from many sources, security trading also expedites conglomeration of enterprises and, through foreign ownership of securities, it also extends the global linkages of China-based conglomerate groups.

Direct Transfer of An Enterprise's Assets

An enterprise may acquire another enterprise, wholly or partially, in one of the Assets Transfer Centers (or Property Exchange Centers) located in almost every major city in China. This form of acquisition is akin to a takeover of a firm in the form of "merger and acquisition" practiced in the United States. When a state-owned enterprise acquires another state-owned enterprise using this form of acquisition, theoretically there is no privatization taking place but, on the other hand, when a state-owned enterprise is a partner to a joint venture with a foreign firm an element of the private sector enters into the merged enterprise under this form of acquisition. Furthermore, China's private enterprises, which are expanding both in number and in size, may also acquire state-owned enterprises and foreign enterprises; they may also take over state-owned enterprises by the direct acquisition route. These examples in reality transform a state-owned enterprise into a private enterprise.

Normally, in a country with a well-developed capital market, mergers and acquisitions are consummated by transfer of equity shares in a securities market. One might view the presence (or the rise) of the Assets Transfer Center as a reflection of the underdevelopment of the capital markets in China. To fill this void, direct transfer of assets through the Assets Transfer Centers has facilitated the consolidation of enterprises at the local level and many village and township enterprises, which are collectively owned by the local community and are too small to list equity shares in the securities markets, have used this channel to consummate mergers and acquisitions (*China Times Weekly* 1994).

It must be pointed out, however, that the PRC's privatization of state-owned enterprises is characterized by being deliberately gradual, selective, and partial. It is gradual and selective in that the state selects the enterprises for privatization and puts them on the block gradually. It is partial in that only a portion of the equity of an enterprise selected for privatization is sold to private investors (Rawski 1995).

To understand the PRC's approach toward privatization, one must examine the functions and responsibilities assumed by state-owned enterprises. In the context of the PRC's formerly centrally planned economy, a state-owned enterprise is more than a business firm in the Western sense. It is also a mini-government and is expected to provide, in addition to guaranteed employment for employees, social services such as housing, health care, and education for employees' families. These tasks cannot be simply passed on to a private enterprise (when a state enterprise is privatized) unless the state subsidizes the private enterprise to perform these tasks. But, if the state has to subsidize the private enterprise in this regard, then the privatization of state-owned enterprises loses its relevance. In addition, enterprises in industries that are considered the backbone of the economy—energy, transportation, communication, and so on—will probably not be fully privatized (Dong and Hu 1995). All these considerations mean that the state, through its full or partial ownership of state-owned enterprises, will for the foreseeable future remain a partner (sometimes a major partner) in the conglomeration of enterprises.

CONCLUSION

Conglomeration of enterprises in China is a relatively new development and their forms and configuration are still in a state of flux. With respect to the types or kinds of conglomerate that are in the making, China's approach has much in common with that of the post-Second World War *keiretsu* Japanese groups. It is, in fact, the Japanese model which the PRC is attempting to emulate. In China's case, however, the state is directly involved in the conglomeration of enterprises, in part because many of those taking part in the process are state-owned enterprises, whereas in Japan the state used an industrial policy (an indirect approach) to guide the restructuring of the *keiretsu* groups in the years following the Second World War (after the break-up of the pre-Second World War *zaibatsu* groups).

In the earlier period of *keiretsu* group formation (from 1950 through most of the 1970s), the internationalization of the *keiretsu* groups was achieved via the direct presence of the *keiretsu* enterprises' presence overseas, that is, through their direct foreign investment, while at the same time inward direct foreign investment into Japan was restricted. In other words, transactions with foreign enterprises were kept at arm's length, in the forms of export and import. This model of conglomeration is still in vogue in the *keiretsu*'s entry into Southeast Asia, where a *keiretsu* group, through the direct investment of its member enterprises, divides the manufacturing tasks of the host countries and creates a vertically integrated value chain tied to the *keiretsu*'s home base in Japan. The PRC's approach to conglomeration is, in contrast, aided by the privatization of state-owned enterprises and provides room for foreign partnership, in inward and outward direct foreign investment, from the beginning. It is an approach that emphasizes networking with overseas Chinese enterprises as well as non-Chinese enterprises and the creation of a global network of linkages.

The U.S. conglomerate model is not exactly transferable to China because the U.S. legal system does not allow equity ownership of the peripheral enterprises by the core enterprise in the same industry and this is one way in which the conglomeration of enterprises is achieved in the PRC. Furthermore, the U.S.-style conglomeration that is accomplished through mergers and acquisitions is motivated by objectives that include tax considerations and capturing the value of undervalued securities (due to temporary market inefficiency). Transactions to achieve such objectives are pure financial transactions that leave no lasting effects on the efficiency and competitiveness of a conglomerate.

Conglomeration of enterprises in the PRC is still in a state of flux, as stated earlier. State ownership of conglomerated enterprises, even if that ownership is partial, will remain a fact for the conglomerates for a long time to come. How this state presence will be harnessed in ways that will permit the conglomerates' management independence is a vital key to how the configuration of the conglomerated enterprises will evolve. It remains to be seen whether the state, in spite of its ownership stake, will be merely a passive investor in the conglomerate. It needs to be pointed out that many state-owned enterprises in China are huge enterprises with privileged access to the supply of resources (human resources, transportation, and communication services). There are also enterprises directly controlled by the military that are in the process of conversion into civilian production, and are, therefore, candidates for conglomeration. These power bases are bound to affect on the competitiveness of PRC-based conglomerate groups in a global context.

REFERENCES

China Times Weekly (a Chinese language newspaper published in New York). 1994. March 27, p. 29.

Chung Guo Chi Yeh Guan Li Nen Chien Editorial Committee (Chung Guo). 1992. *Chung Guo Chi Yeh Guan Li Nian Chien* (*The Yearbook of China's Enterprises*). Beijing: Chi Yeh Guan Li Publishing Company.

Dong, J.L., and J. Hu. 1995. "Mergers and Acquisitions in China." *Economic Review* (November-December): 15-29.

Liu, Y. 1992. *Kua Guo Kong Su Yu Chung Guo Chi Yeh Guo Chi Hua* (*Multinational Enterprises and the Internationalization of China's Enterprises*). Beijing: Chung Shin Publishing Company.

Okumura, H. 1990. "Seitoka Dekinai Keiretsu No Gohlisei" ("The Rationale of the Keiretsu Cannot Be Legitimized"). *Ekonomisto* (July 10): 78-89.

Rawski, T.G. 1995. "Implications of China's Reform Experience." *The China Quarterly* 144: 1150-1173.

The Wall Street Journal. 1995. July 5, p. A6.

Warshawsky, M.J. 1987. "Determinants of Corporate Merger Activity: A Review of the Literature." *Federal Reserve System Staff Study* 152.

The World Tribune (a Chinese language newspaper published in New York). 1995a. March 1, p. A17.

The World Tribune. 1995b. July 4, p. A12.

PART VI

CONCLUSION

CONSEQUENCES OF CHANGE FOR JOINT VENTURES IN CHINA

Erik J. de Bruijn, Xianfeng Jia, and Ina Konterman

INTRODUCTION

Developments in global competition and rising production costs in traditional industrialized and newly industrialized countries have led companies to widen their areas of operations, particularly to developing countries. The emerging consumer and industrial markets, and the need to be close to these markets for competitive reasons, contributed to this trend. For these reasons, many U.S. and European companies are now concentrating on the Asian markets, and the People's Republic of China (PRC) is one of the main countries of interest.

With the rapid development of (parts of) the Chinese economy—and the further development of China's open-door policy—foreign enterprises have seized the opportunity to obtain a share of the market. The most effective way to obtain a foothold has proved to be to create a joint venture (JV) with a Chinese business partner. The foreign partner provides, in general, the technical expertise, machinery, and part of the financing. The Chinese partner of the JV contributes facilities (which may, however, be technologically obsolete), the

Advances in Chinese Industrial Studies, Volume 5, pages 345-363.

ISBN: 1-55938-961-3

labor force, contacts with central and local government officials, and access to the market. The Chinese economy has benefited to a large extent from the creation of joint ventures.

A negative aspect, however, has been the loss of a very large amount of foreign exchange because of JVs. The Chinese government is trying to minimize this negative effect and to keep developments in the foreign investment field under control. This has led to a drastic change in the rules for the formation and operation of joint ventures. Both new JVs and existing ones have to cope with the changing situation. They are confronted with unforeseen measures which greatly affect their operations and profitability.

FOREIGN INVESTMENT IN THE PRC

Foreign Investment 1990-1995

After the shock of 1989,[1] the growth in investments of past years stagnated, but recovery was swift. Since 1990 the inflow of foreign investment has been taking place at an increasing pace. Foreign investment was further stimulated by Deng Xiaoping's announcement in 1992 of the intention to speed up the reform of the economy and to grant easier access for foreign enterprises. The stimulation of foreign investment is illustrated by the approval of 47,000 foreign-funded projects by the Chinese government in that year, which was 3.8 times the number approved in 1991. A total of US$11.16 billion was actually invested in 1992. Three years later, by the end of 1995, the total number of approved foreign-funded enterprises had increased to 258,903. More than 120,000 foreign projects are in operation at the time of writing. The growth in the numbers of foreign investment projects over recent years, and in actual foreign investment, is illustrated in Table 1 (*People's Daily* 1994; Ji 1996).

Total actual foreign investment from 1991 to 1995 was more than US$111.37 billion. During the last five years China has received the largest actual foreign investment of non-Western countries. Worldwide, China is second with its amount of actual foreign investment, after the United States.

Table 1. Foreign Investment Projects and Actual Foreign Investment in China 1991-1995

	1991	*1992*	*1993*	*1994*	*1995*
Total number of approved projects	36,800	84,600	167,000	206,000	258,903
Actual foreign investment in US$ billion	4.3	11.1	27.5	33.8	35

The increasing importance of foreign investment can be illustrated by the situation in Shanghai, where foreign investments contribute 30 percent of the local GDP. Between January and May 1996 the output of foreign-invested enterprises in Shanghai was about US$7.36 billion, which is 32.3 percent of its local industrial output in total (Xia 1996).

Direction and Impact of Foreign Investments

A study of the direction and impact of foreign investment developments, we discern the following important factors:

- The scope of investments is widening. In the past it concentrated on the sectors of electronics, food, construction materials, machinery for the chemical industry, textiles, pharmacy, and agricultural processing. Recent additions to these sectors are power generation, transportation, communication, banking, insurance, and the educational.
- The tendency to enter into small and medium-sized investments only is changing in favor of larger ones. Many multinational enterprises are aiming to gain access to the Chinese market by investing there. By the end of 1995 more than 200 large international companies were investing in China. This increases the average amount invested by foreign-funded projects. In 1990 the average investment of each project was less than US$1 million, while in 1994 it was US$1.71 million and up to US$2.45 million in 1995 (Ji 1996).
- There is an increase in economic participation. Foreign investments and the output related to these investments are becoming significant in terms of the total Chinese economy. By the end of 1995 more than 120,000 foreign-funded enterprises were operating in China, with 12.6 million employees. The total enterprise tax was over 7.56 billion RMB in 1995, an increase of 57.1 percent since 1994 (US$1 = 8.3 RMB). Foreign-funded enterprises contributed over 15 percent of the total GNP of China in 1995 (Ji 1996). The export of these enterprises is also increasing. In 1995 foreign-funded enterprises generated a total export revenue of US$109.8 billion, 25.3 percent more than in 1994 (*People's Daily* 1996).
- Actual foreign investment increases. At the beginning of the 1980s actual foreign investment was only a few hundreds of millions US$. Since 1992 foreign investment has developed rapidly, and the figure was up to near US$72.3 billion from 1992 to 1994. In the first half of 1995 actual foreign investment was US$16.3 billion, 10.3 percent more than during the first half of 1994.
- Foreign investment is concentrated on the southeastern coastal area. Until the beginning of 1994 only 4,913 of the 167,000 foreign-invested projects (about 3%) were in the middle and western parts of China (Li 1994).

- An increasing number of investors are from Western Europe (Germany, France, Italy, and the U.K.) and the United States, as well as from some developed countries in the Asia-Pacific region (Japan, Singapore, and Australia).

CHALLENGES TO FOREIGN INVESTMENT

Joint ventures in China are confronted with new challenges. It is not only the shift in the government's attitude toward JVs but also the changing economic, industrial, and cultural circumstances in China which provide a new situation for these enterprises.

Developments in the Economy

There are three major relevant economic issues for JVs in the PRC: the chronic losses made by state-owned enterprises, high inflation, and developments in the relative strength of the currency.

Because of their inflexibility and resistance to change, and the very tough competition in China, state-owned companies are experiencing chronic losses. The severe competition is caused by booming private and collective enterprises, contributing from 10 percent of GDP in 1992 to more than 50 percent of GDP in 1995. The government is considering privatizing—at least partially—state-owned enterprises, hoping to revitalize these industries and to reduce government losses.

Inflation is another important economic issue. Prices of consumer goods increased by 24.1 percent in 1994 (*People's Daily* 1994). The effects of inflation are especially severe in western areas. In the southern coastal area negative effects are diminished by the high local production growth rate of around 20 percent. In 1995 the Chinese government made great efforts to lower inflation by controlling the investment mechanism, especially in "bubble sectors" such as the stock market and real estate. As a result, inflation was lower in 1995, at about 15 percent (Li 1995; Ji 1996).

The third economic issue is related to the hardness of the currency and the SWAP market. Before 1994 China had a SWAP market for the exchange of foreign currency. JVs committed themselves to achieving a balance between inflow and outflow of foreign exchange within two or three years (de Bruijn and Jia 1993a, 1993b). If this foreign exchange could not be earned with exports, which was often the case, JVs had to purchase foreign exchange at the SWAP market, paying a relatively high price. At the beginning of 1994 the Chinese government closed the SWAP market and lowered RMB from 5.8 to 8.7 against the U.S. dollar. Very soon, however, it became clear that the value of RMB was underestimated by the government. RMB turned out not only to be stable but even to increase to an exchange rate of 8.3 against the U.S. dollar in March 1995. RMB is a relatively hard currency and could have easily been raised in value to 7 RMB = US$1 in 1995 (Yang 1995). China's exports increased from 1994 onwards, and the government had to buy foreign exchange in order to keep the exchange rate stable. As a result, more RMB was placed in the Chinese economy, which gave a high demand in the consumer industry and kept inflation relatively high.

Developments in the Industry

A major development in Chinese industry has been the narrowing gap in technology levels between Chinese and foreign firms. This is especially noticeable in the passenger car industry and in the production of color televisions, telecommunication systems, and elevators. The latest technology is increasingly employed in the production of these items. For new JV entrants being able to offer state-of-the-art technology is a major competitive advantage in getting approval for the setting up of the venture.

Another issue is the increasing significance of the concept of quality. A survey by Arthur Andersen & Co. which investigated more than 70 foreign-funded enterprises in China (Gao 1995), found that the quality concept is becoming more important, even more important than *guanxi* (personal relationships). It was found that companies which had good relations with their local partner and the government and good quality products (27% of the sample) made a profit. In contrast, companies that had good relations with the local partner and the government, but were not concerned about quality (40% of the sample), made a loss.

A final point of consideration is related to the labor costs in production in China. The advantages of cheap labor are gradually disappearing; between 1993 and 1995 the labor costs in foreign-funded enterprises increased by 35 percent (Gao 1995).

In summary, technological development and quality considerations are essential tools for surviving in China in the long term; special favorable circumstances, such as cheap labor costs, can be counted upon less and less.

Cultural Changes

Foreign companies benefit not only from the change of the planned economic system toward a more market-oriented system, but also from a general change of business practices. There is more relief from day-to-day frustrations, caused by poor infrastructure, high levels of bureaucracy, and lack of effective management, which were still hampering operations considerably as recently as the early 1990s (de Bruijn and Jia 1993a, 1993b). Business people in China are in general becoming more realistic and consider profit as the key issue as far as business is concerned. More people take the view that to make money is more attractive and more interesting than being involved in political affairs. This can be illustrated by the observation that a number of the participants involved in the "6.4 event" in 1989 are now in business in China, and some of them are very successful.

NEW REGULATIONS

The PRC government recognizes the trends concerning the functioning of the JVs and their effects on the economy and has developed accordingly a new attitude toward existing and new JVs. The government still has the aim to attract foreign investment, but it wants the structure of the investments to be more effective and more advantageous for the economic development of China itself. To achieve this objective, the following measurements have been taken.

Limit Numbers of JVs in Certain Industries

This first important change means that in some types of industries further foreign investment projects are not permitted. This concerns especially TV manufacturing and the car industry. The reason for this measure is that, according to the government, there are already too many JVs in these sectors. Furthermore, the government wants to reformulate the investment structure to sectors that are more beneficial for the economic development of the country. At the beginning of 1996 the government was wanting to encourage foreign investment projects in sectors such as infrastructure building, energy, transportation, telecommunications, and specific high-tech industries (such as the computer, biochemical, and space industries). As a result of this governmental support, an increasing number of foreign investments are being made in these sectors. In 1994, 56 percent of approved foreign-funded projects were in electronics, telecommunications equipment, machinery, chemicals, and textiles.

Tax Reforms

Tax reforms are a major part of the changed regulations of the PRC government. Since 1979 China has used two corporate tax systems, one for state-owned firms and the other for foreign investment projects. As a part of the policy to attract foreign investors, the tax rate for foreign investment projects was lower than the tax rate for indigenous companies. Foreign JVs paid 15 percent corporate tax—which included value-added tax, income tax, and government tax—in China's Special Economic Zones, 24 percent in some 400 areas "open" for investment, and 30 percent elsewhere, while state-owned companies paid tax at a rate of 55 percent.

In 1994 the tax system for foreign projects was changed. The objectives of this tax reform were to create a more equal tax basis for local firms and JVs, to simplify the tax system, to increase the share of taxes for central government, and to have a better instrument to steer economic development. The new system consists of a total of 12 taxes, of which the most important are value-added tax (VAT), consumer tax, commercial tax, resource-added tax, real estate tax, company and individual income tax, and car/ship tax. Most significant for companies is VAT, currently at a rate of 17 percent. For basic consumer goods, agricultural, and stationary products the VAT rate is 13 percent.

As a result of these tax reforms a number of favorable regulations for JVs have been ended. One consequence is that JVs will have to start paying duty and VAT on imports of capital machinery. Duties could run as high as 20-35 percent, while VAT would take an additional 17 percent. This would result in an increase of 40 percent or more to be paid for import duties (Forney 1995). Furthermore, the Chinese government is planning to decrease the VAT rebate allowed for manufactured inputs that are later exported. Up to July 1, 1994 companies could reclaim the full 17 percent VAT. After that date the restitution was lowered to 14 percent, and from January 1, 1996 only 9 percent can be claimed. Finally, since April 1, 1996 companies in the Special Economic Zones, the high-tech parks, and other beneficiary zones have to pay the full amount of import duties and other charges for imported goods. Before this date they were exempted from these charges. All these regulations have been established in order to reduce the inequalities in conditions for foreign and domestic firms, what governmental regulating bodies might call "leveling the playing field" (Walker 1995; Forney 1995).

Banking Reform

The changed attitude of the government toward foreign investment projects has resulted in new policies for banks. Under the State Council there are five major banks: the People's Bank of China, the Bank of China, the Industrial & Commercial Bank of China, the People's Construction Bank of China, and the Agricultural Bank of China Rural Credit Co-operatives. Until 1994 the activities of these banks were "guided" by government policy. They all invested in state-owned enterprises in accordance with plans issued by the government. In addition, the Bank of China and the Industrial & Commercial Bank of China were instructed to support foreign-funded projects by providing loans to those projects.

In 1994 the PRC government instructed the Central Bank to give each of these banks greater independence (Bank for International Settlements 1994). Gradually the five major banks converted into commercial banks, and one of the results of this is that these banks are now not obliged to give loans to foreign-funded projects, and can choose to give loans only to those projects they judge to be profitable ones. Sometimes banks may decide to participate in JVs in order to obtain an insight in the development of its operations, but in general it will be more difficult for JVs to obtain loans from banks. Another result of the commercialization of the banks is the increasing interest rate, from 11 percent in 1994 to between 14 percent and 15 percent in 1995.

Contracts Procedure

The procedure for the approval of the joint venture contract has been changed. In the past all documents concerning the feasibility study, contracts, and articles of associations, were submitted to the Ministry of Foreign Trade and Economic Co-operation (MOFTEC) or to its local representative. If there were no items in the documents that were in violation of the JV law and regulations, the JV was approved. Nowadays the foreign partner must submit a financial certificate to the local authority to show that it has the financial means to invest in China. The foreign partner's contribution in cash, machinery, or the evidence of know-how must be physically transferred to China. All quotations to the JV must be examined by local authorities and a check is made to ensure no overcharging takes place. In some provinces the foreign-funded enterprise gets a copy only of the business licence instead of the original document until the foreign party's capital is transferred. If that doesn't occur within a certain period, usually six months, the business licence can be canceled.

Fake Joint Ventures

The government has decided to tackle the problems concerning "fake JVs," and has had some success. Fake JVs are enterprises established to gain the benefits of favorable tax regulations, and are discussed below. In 1992 and 1993 one-third of all JVs could be counted as fake JVs, but in 1994 and 1995 the figure was less than 10 percent. The government has reached this success by critically checking the financial ability and the actual contribution of the foreign partner. Between April and November 1995 MOFTEC canceled the business licence of any JV in which the foreign partners had not placed registered capital within the specified time and in which there was no real foreign investor. A large number of fake JVs business licences were revoked during this period (MOFTEC 1995).

REASONS FOR THESE CHANGES

There are no formal documents available with regard to this subject, but two underlying reasons are regarded as the driving forces behind the new government regulations.

Increasing Numbers of Fake JVs

In 1984 local firms were required to pay VAT, while foreign projects were exempted. This resulted in increased competitiveness of JVs, while indigenous firms suffered: particularly hard hit were the export-oriented businesses. In this situation it was attractive to set up fake foreign-investment projects in order to obtain tax advantages. The most prominent ones were those that aimed at a (hopefully) profitable enterprise for the foreign partner without any capital outlay. The benefits for the Chinese partner were the favorable tax treatment, cars free of import duty, and an increase in political clout, having acquired a foreign-funded project. The growth in numbers of foreign-funded projects was therefore to a large extent the result of this measure. Two types of fake JV construction can be identified.

The Foreign Partner does not Transfer Money to the JV

Many fake JVs are established without real money transfer by the foreign partner. The basic idea is that the equipment brought in by the foreign partner is sold to the JV at a price above its real cost, and which covers the contractual capital outlay of the foreign partner. The following example illustrates the process.

A Western and Chinese firm have decided to cooperate in a JV with a total registered capital of US$200,000. The Western partner buys machinery for the JV in a Western country for US$100,000 and reports to the Chinese partner that the price of the machinery was US$200,000. In return for this investment the Western partner wants a share in the JV of 30 percent. The Chinese partner knows that the cost price of the machinery is not US$200,000, but accepts it and pays 70 percent, which is US$140,000. For both partners in the JV this agreement is advantageous. The Western partner earns US$40,000 and has a "free" share in a JV of 30 percent, since they "paid" US$60,000 as registered capital to buy the machinery. The Chinese partner benefits even more. They will have a considerable tax advantage as being part of a JV, which includes three years exemption from income tax, followed by two years of 50 percent income tax. In addition, the Chinese partner will have an exemption on import duty for the machinery.

The Chinese Company Opens a Subsidiary Abroad

Another type of fake JV emerges when a Chinese company opens a subsidiary abroad and uses this "foreign" subsidiary to invest in a JV. In this way there is no real foreign partner, but the Chinese company gains the previously mentioned tax advantages.

Attempts by JVs to Maximize Tax Advantages

The tax advantages to JVs are related to their profits and losses. Organizations have only a limited exemption from taxes after a profitable year, and therefore many JVs try to keep a loss in their books, even though they may in fact be profitable. In 1994 it was estimated that about 50 percent of foreign-invested enterprises reported a loss in Fujian Province (southern China), while half of this number actually made a profit. Some companies continuously reinvest and add people to the payroll in order to avoid becoming profitable. For example, one JV in Xiamen, established in 1991 with a total investment of US$900,000, never reported a profit, but registered an increase of capital to US$1.5 million in 1994 without adding external funds to its capital base.

CONSEQUENCES FOR MANAGING JOINT VENTURES

The recent developments in China have a major impact on the way in which JVs are managed. The following case studies will show some typical internal problems that have been caused by the changed circumstances. General internal difficulties that have no direct relation toward the changes, for instance, quality control, are not explored here.

Less Working Capital Available

Since the reform of the Chinese banking system, banks are no longer obliged to hold specific regulations for JVs, such as the provision of loans with favorable conditions. The central bank, the People's Bank of China, is still greatly influenced by central government, but provincial banks have become quite independent from local governments. These provincial banks have acquired more autonomy in their investment decisions and are consequently more critical toward the provision of loans. Because of this attitude, JVs experience serious problems in obtaining sufficient funds. It became even more difficult for JVs to acquire enough financing when the provincial banks were forced—by the central bank—to restrict their investments in industry. The central bank had been instructed by central government who, in response to the high inflation of 24.1 percent in 1994 and 15.4 percent in 1995, wanted to keep a tight rein on investment policy. The imposed investment restrictions, together with the more critical attitude of the banks, created serious problems for JVs with respect to their financial situation. The available working capital for JVs was found to be in practice far less than the amount expected and initially agreed upon with the banks.

The Dong Ping Heavenly Hemp Co. Ltd. experienced a serious lack of working capital. Dong Ping is a Chinese-U.S. JV (the partners being Dongping Hemp mill [75%] and Naturetex [25%]). It produces mainly hemp cloth. The JV had a total investment of US$10 million, had established a production capacity of 3.62 million meters (including hemp blends) and employs about 2,500 people. When the JV contract was signed (in September 1993) the Bank of China made a commitment to lend 30 million yuan (US$3,600,000) in order to support the JV with enough working capital. After the bank reforms at the beginning of 1994 the bank became more critical toward the provision of loans, and reduced the loan to 15 million yuan. This created a serious lack of working capital for the enterprise, which couldn't buy the necessary raw materials for producing the amount of fabric that was initially planned. As a consequence, the production capacity was not fully utilized and the sales income was insufficient for the JV to operate. The situation deteriorated and in June 1996 the JV was two to three months late with the salary payments. The general manager is shocked that the change in banking policy should reduce a sound and profitable project to an almost bankrupted JV. In order to have any chance for the future, the JV is now looking for investors to buy shares in the enterprise. Only in that way will the JV be able raise enough working capital to survive.

Change in Ownership of Chinese JV Partners

Because of the chronic losses experienced by state-owned enterprises, the PRC government was stimulated into privatizing these enterprises, at least partially. A number of these newly privatized enterprises are partners in Chinese-Western joint ventures. The transformation of the Chinese partners has a number of implications for the JVs. The arrival of new shareholders and new directors in the JV board is the most obvious one. The agreements made with former directors of the JV partner may not necessarily be accepted by the new ones. The directors of the new partner may want to introduce new rules and may have a different attitude and style of working. Furthermore, when a director leaves an enterprise in China, their assistants and colleagues often leave at the same time, so that a large group of employees needs to be replaced.

The PRC government also encourages the merging of profitable state-owned enterprises with less successful state-owned enterprises. It may happen that the parent company of a Chinese JV partner is taken over by a more profitable state-owned enterprise. In this case, the new parent company will become the owner of the Chinese JV partner, which has the same kind of implications for the JV as in the case of privatization.

When a state-owned enterprise (being a JV partner) is unable to repay a bank loan, the bank practically becomes the owner of the enterprise. The loan is usually guaranteed by fixed capital, such as machinery and buildings. If the loan is repaid on time, the bank will obtain the fixed capital and is likely to behave as a kind of shareholder of the enterprise, influencing the decision-making processes within the enterprise and also within the JV, particularly where the Chinese partner is the majority shareholder. The bank is likely to control finances rigidly and be critical toward new investments. Even minor financial decisions in the JV may have to be examined and approved by the bank, since the bank controls all money transactions.

The Baotou Saitic Leather Products Co. Ltd. is a Chinese-Dutch JV (the partners being Baotou No. 2 leather product factory [75%] and Saitic [25%]). The JV produces leather jackets and made a total initial investment of US$500,000. It has a production capacity of 100,000 and employs 240 people. When the JV was established in 1994 its major difficulty was the lack of financial means to modernize the production line of the Chinese partner. Fortunately, the local government encouraged local enterprises to establish foreign cooperation (partly in order to obtain political credit from the central government) and, therefore, the Chinese partner was able to obtain a loan of US$350,000 at an interest rate of 9 percent. The JV decided to import Italian machinery, which cost US$450,000. This major purchase required an extra loan from the bank of US$250,000, but because of the commercialization of the Chinese banks, the interest rate for this loan was 13 percent. In 1995 the JV had some serious operational problems, primarily due to the lack of financial means, and the Chinese partner could not repay its loan on time to the bank. The bank therefore became the owner of the fixed capital and started to control rigidly the financial affairs of the Chinese partner. Whenever the JV needed to spend money, even for everyday activities, it had to get approval from the bank. The JV is now searching for other financial resources. One of the opportunities is the newly established commercial units of the local government, which provide loans against critical conditions, with interest rates as high as 15 percent. If these loans with the high interest rates are accepted, the JV will again have difficulties with repayment and thus easily get into a negative vicious circle.

Production Volume

Low production volumes mean that JVs are not able to become competitive. High production volumes are necessary to reach economies of scales, but in the Chinese situation the following issues are even more important. First, with a low production volume it might become difficult to find suitable local suppliers. Some Western technology or products are not yet available in China and local suppliers are not willing to purchase the technology or products, unless it is clearly beneficial. A small production volume, and a resulting small demand of (local) input, will not motivate local suppliers to produce the desired components or parts. The alternative—to import the needed input—

is too costly in the Chinese situation. Second, the level of production volume is indirectly related to the support of the government. One of the most important criteria for the government to approve and support JVs is its planned localization rate. Localization is the process of increasing the local parts content of finished products, and is very difficult to accomplish with a low production volume, since low quantities are not attractive for local suppliers.

The importance of the production volume can be shown by the differences in approach and results of Shanghai Volkswagen Autmotive Co. Ltd. and the Beijing Jeep Corporation. The JV contract of Shanghai Volkswagen (SVW) was signed in October 1984 between China National Automotive Industry Corporation, the People's Bank of China, Shanghai Trust and Consultancy Co., and Volkswagen AG. The Chinese partners and Volkswagen AG each own 50 percent of the stock. The major products are the Volkswagen Santana cars and engines (4-cylinder 1800 CC). The JV has invested US$185 million and installed new equipment with an annual capacity of 60,000 cars and 100,000 engines. The Beijing Jeep Corporation was set up in 1984 by the partners American Motor Corporation (AMC), Beijing Automobile Industry Corporation (BAIC), and Beijing Municipality. When the American Motor Corporation merged with Chrysler in 1987, Chrysler automatically became the foreign partner of this JV (Chrysler 31% and the Chinese partners 69%). In 1990 the share of Chrysler increased to 45 percent by buying shares from the Chinese partner. The main products are Cherokee Jeeps and the BJ212. A total of US$51.03 million is invested in the JV and the company has an annual capacity of 20,000 Cherokee jeeps.

SVW started with a production capacity of 60,000 cars per year, while Beijing Jeep started with a production capacity of only 20,000 Cherokee jeeps. Both JVs reached their production capacity in 1992. SVW made a good profit and planned to double its production volume by merging with Shanghai Auto-Works. The company got considerable support from local government, and without this government contribution, the merger could not have been realized. Because of the large production volume of SVW, the company attracted many local suppliers, making production cheaper in the long run. In 1995 the output of SVW was already 120,000, with 80 percent local content. In contrast, the production volume of Beijing Jeep remained at the initial low level. It was very difficult for the JV to gain support from local suppliers, because of the low production volume. In 1995, the output of Beijing Jeep was only 21,000, with a local content of less than 50 percent. For SVW, Beijing Jeep, and the local suppliers, economies of scale are expected to be reached at a production volume of about 100,000 units per year. Table 2 compares the production volume of the two enterprises.

Table 2. Actual Production Volumes at SVW and Beijing Jeep

Production Volume (Units)	*1987*	*1990*	*1992*	*1995*
SVW (Santana)	11,000	18,537	60,500	120,000
Beijing Jeep (Cherokee)	3,002	7,500	20,001	21,000

Flexible Strategy

JVs in China need to have a clear strategy, explicitly adapted to the Chinese circumstances. Many JVs lack such a strategy, which complicates critical management activities such as marketing, transfer of technology, and decisions on the desired localization rate. Even more important than a clear strategy is flexibility in the long term. The strategy needs to be adaptable to the continually changing business environment in China.

Hua Fei Colour Display Systems is a Chinese-Dutch JV, set up by Philips Electronics South-Asia Holding, Novel Technical Development Co., and the Huadon Electron Tube Factory. The JV manufactures color TV tubes. The JV invested US$180 million and employs 1,500 people. Its production target was 1.6 million color TV tubes per year by 1992. Hua Fei holds a technology-oriented strategy, while the Chinese market requires a more customer-oriented approach. Because of the focus on technology, the JV adjusts its marketing strategy only slowly to the (fast changing) needs of the Chinese customers. This has had severe consequences in the production of the color TV tubes. The JV planned to manufacture 17″ and 21″ tubes, and carried out product selection research beforehand (see Table 3).

The JV concluded that the product was appropriate to the Chinese market, government policy, and the goals of the partners. Unfortunately the market circumstances changed and the JV could not adapt its strategy quickly enough. The market demand changed from the small-size tube TV (14″-18″) to the large-size tube TV (21″-29″), which made the future potential of the 17” tube very poor. The fact that Hua Fei Colour Display couldn't adapt its strategy to the customers' need resulted in a delay of two years before the desired production level (in comparison with competing companies) was reached.

CONCLUSION

Dealing with the New Circumstances

The issues discussed show clearly that the circumstances for JVs have changed considerably since 1994. Until that time the government offered attractive regulations concerning taxes, import duties, and financing, but these

Table 3. Criteria of Production Selection for Color Television Picture Tubes

Criteria	Color TV Tubes (17" and 21")
Phase 1: identification of possibilities	
* environmental factors	
— market situation	+
—local supply	—
— government policy	+
* goals/preferences of the partners	
— profit concern	+
— more competitive position	+
— preference for type of product	+
* key internal factors of Chinese partners	
— existing production technology level	—
— market position	+

favorable regulations are quickly disappearing. The general economic, cultural, and technological climate in China is also changing fast and will have a substantial impact on the profitability and functioning of JVs. This leads to the following main conclusions.

Chinese JV Business becomes "Normalized"

The basis of the new government regulations is that JVs are to be treated according to "normal" international business practices. The relative financial advantages have almost completely disappeared as a result of the rigorous tax reforms. Special loans with low interest rates are becoming rare and even regular loans are more difficult to obtain, since the five major banks have converted into commercial banks and can make their own choices as to whether to make loans to foreign-funded projects. The attitude of the government toward JVs in general has become less flexible. The procedures for the approval of joint venture contracts have become very strict and in certain types of industries foreign investment projects are no longer permitted. In addition government control on fake JVs has been tightened.

Chinese JV-Partners are Changing

A number of Chinese JV partners are private enterprises converted from state-owned enterprises. With the change in ownership comes (slowly) change in management characteristics. The privatized Chinese partners focus more on profit and pay less attention to political and social aspects. This greater focus on profit is part of a general cultural trend in China; people are getting more "realistic" in business and old attitudes with respect to values of time and money and the organization of labor are (again slowly) changing. The banks can become practically the owners of JV partners, if the enterprise is unable to repay its loans. In this case, the bank will obtain the fixed capital and will behave as a shareholder, exercising considerable influence on the management of the JV.

The Chinese Task Environment is Becoming more Demanding

JVs are confronted with a number of changing circumstances. In 1994 inflation in China was 24.1 percent and a devaluation occurred of the dollar against RMB. The advantage of low labor costs in China is gradually diminishing. The economic developments have resulted in relatively higher production costs. Even though inflation has declined and RMB is getting harder, production costs are increasing; this is also due to other factors, such as a deficient infrastructure. Bank reforms have had a significant impact on the functioning of JVs. The more critical attitude of the banks toward investments creates serious financial problems, with the available working capital being far less than the amount originally expected and agreed upon with the banks. As Chinese industries become more competitive, foreign JVs are confronted with a decline in their competitive edge on the Chinese market. This is due partly to the narrowing gap in technology level between Chinese and foreign industries, and partly to the considerable effort China is putting into the improvement of quality.

Recommendations

The following recommendations can be made in order to help JVs to adjust to the changing circumstances in China.

Start as Soon as is Feasible

Once a company has decided to enter into a JV in China, it is advisable to do so as soon as possible. JVs still get important tax advantages, but there are strong indications that this may end soon. "Grandfather clauses," which mean that on a limited scale the benefits of the past can still be enjoyed, can provide considerable benefits (Forney 1995). Even in cases where there are no such clauses, special circumstances can be negotiated.

Obtain a Reliable Foothold and Compete with Basic Business Processes

In order to survive and even prosper in the changing circumstances a number of conditions are necessary. JVs need to have a reliable foothold, and Chinese partners who who understand exactly the ways of doing business in China and the developments in these activities. JVs also need to be competitive in basic business processes, not relying on uncertain relative beneficial treatment. This means that the basic elements as price, quality, service, and suitable products for the market are more than ever becoming critical issues for the profitability of enterprises.

Search for Alternative Financial Sources and Keep a Good Relationship with Government Officials

Following the banking reforms, JVs should focus on alternative financial sources. Possibilities are the large Chinese state-owned companies, with whom JVs are cooperating, or private relationships with organizations or individuals. Again it is necessary to have a local key player with knowledge about the actual situation and how negotiation with financial sources can be executed successfully. Although the financial relations with banks and government regulation bodies tend to be normalized from a Western point of view, help from government officials remains important. Special relations with officials do not necessarily mean more bureaucracy, and often benefit the organization and can contribute to the smooth operation of the JV.

Be Prepared for the Privatization of the JV Partner

As a partner of a state-owned company it should be decided in advance what might happen should the Chinese partner be privatized. It is essential to ensure in the contract that the Western partner has the preferential right to buy shares, otherwise other parties can buy shares and exert influence, diluting the share of the foreign partners. After the privatization process, both partners should review the initial motives for setting up the JV; if these have changed drastically due to the privatization, the question is whether and how the two parties can adapt to the new circumstances or whether the partnership should be discontinued.

Be Prepared to Adapt Organization Methods

As a result of the Chinese partner's changing attitudes, it may be necessary to adjust organization methods, in order to maintain the highest efficiency. A pragmatic approach is advisable; neither making do with the old situation nor introducing the latest/leanest methods is recommended, since cooperation with the local partner is likely to break down in either case.

Improve Competitiveness

The general economic and technological developments in China have caused, on the one hand, the necessity of being aware of cost aspects and on the other the need to invest sufficiently in technology and quality in order to compete successfully in the Chinese market. Marketing strategies have to be adapted continually to the fast-changing business environment. Existing JVs have to consider how production volume can be augmented, in order to obtain lower production unit costs, but also how to obtain government support and attract local suppliers to produce components and parts for the JV (localization). They might also consider whether it would be cheaper to import components instead of purchasing them in the Chinese market: JVs still have easy access to hard currency which makes it relatively easy to import products. New entrants offering state-of-the-art technology have a main competitive advantage in obtaining approval for the setting up of a JV, especially when the technology can be applied in sectors in which the government particularly wants to attract foreign investment projects.

Be Cautious with Value Matters

Although the value of RMB has increased during the last few years, JVs have to be cautious about exchanging dollars into RMB. At the moment, RMB is stable or increasing in value, but the China market is not yet mature and a sudden devaluation of RMB might happen. In addition, political risks with Hong Kong or Taiwan might seriously disrupt the situation.

NOTE

1. This refers to the "6.4 event" (June 4, 1989), when students were protesting against the government. An initial result of this was that a large number of Western countries banned trade with China and loans from all Western banks were discontinued.

REFERENCES

Bank for International Settlements. 1994. *64th Annual Report*. Basle.

de Bruijn, E.J., and X. Jia. 1993a. "Managing Technology Transfer to China by means of Joint Ventures: A Survey of Critical Issues." *Research Technology Management* 36 (1): 17-22.

de Bruijn, E.J., and X. Jia. 1993b. "Managing Sino-Western Joint Ventures: Product Selection Strategy." *Management International Review* 33: 335-360.

Forney, M. 1995. "You Never Know: Foreigners Fret Over Possible Chinese Tax Changes." *Far Eastern Economic Review* (December 21): 56-57.

Gao, K. 1995. "Foreign Investment in China needs to Improve Quality." *People's Daily* (Overseas Edition) November 24: 2.

Ji, X. 1996. "Foreign Investment is Promising." *People's Daily* (Overseas Edition: January 10): 2.

Li, A. 1995. "The Goal of Price Adjustment is Expected to be Achieved." *People's Daily* (Overseas Edition) December 11: 2.

Li, G. 1994. "More Need Foreign Investment in the West of China." *People's Daily* (Overseas Edition) April 21: 2.

MOFTEC. 1995. *Internal Report* (Document No. 1995-391). Beijing: July 11: 3.

People's Daily. 1994. "News on Foreign Investment." Overseas Edition, July 28: 1.

People's Daily. 1996. "Increase of Foreign Investment 1991-1995." Overseas Edition, January 10: 2.

Walker, T. 1995. "China Tax Policy Changes Could Hit Foreign Investors." *Financial Times*: November 28: 18.

Xia, R. G. 1996. "Foreign Investment Enterprises Take 30 percent of Local GDP in Shanghai." *People's Daily* (Overseas edition) July 9: 2.

Xu, Z. 1994. "Foreign Trade." *People's Daily* (Overseas Edition) July 28: 1.

Yang, J. 1995. *Trend of Exchange Rate in China*. Beijing: China Futures Association.

FUTURE DIRECTIONS FOR RESEARCH ON SINO-FOREIGN JOINT VENTURES

Sally Stewart and Anne Carver

The increase in the number of joint ventures in the People's Republic of China (PRC) in recent years has been paralleled by a surge in academic interest in the whole topic of joint ventures. Recent issues of the *Journal of International Business Studies* clearly demonstrate the international academic interest generated by Chinese joint ventures. There has also been a steady stream of commercially organized seminars on practical aspects of Sino-foreign joint ventures, including, for example, the implications of changes in the tax system and rates, human resource management, and legal problems such as how to dissolve a joint venture. There are still, however, many gaps in the knowledge that is being built up and important areas for research still remain.

One particular gap still to be filled is detailed PRC research on the contribution of Sino-foreign joint ventures toward changing management practices elsewhere in the PRC and particularly in state-owned enterprises (SOEs). Paradoxically this was one of the primary justifications given for inviting foreign firms to establish joint ventures in the first place but little seems to have been published concerning the foreign joint venture's impact on Chinese partners' management styles, still less on the trickle-down effects among enterprises that have no direct relationship to foreign management.

Advances in Chinese Industrial Studies, Volume 5, pages 365-368.

ISBN: 1-55938-961-3

A second aspect that might repay detailed investigation concerns the actual profitability of the joint ventures. While the Chinese statistical evidence of tax collected from them suggests that many are making at least sufficient profit to justify continuation of the operation, actual earnings are rarely revealed to researchers. Companies are more likely to be prepared to discuss systems, organization, and cross-cultural problems than balance sheets. Anecdotal evidence, however, indicates that for many operations a break-even performance is acceptable, since the foreign partner is content to be establishing a position for the long term while the Chinese partner's aim is to acquire management, technical, and business skills. Nevertheless it is important to discover the extent to which foreign partners are holding on in the hope or expectation of long-term profit, rather than because they are making a reasonable profit now.

Further anecdotal evidence about Asian investment in joint ventures or wholly owned foreign enterprises in Europe suggests that there, too, it is frequently faith in the long term, rather than immediate prospects of profit, which keeps the Asian investor involved in manufacturing enterprises in Europe.

John Child's work, directed from Cambridge and part of the continuing research efforts which he has applied to this topic since the beginning of the PRC's open-door policy, is an excellent example of the need for scrupulous reexamination of the developing picture. The large sample used by Child and his colleagues provides a wider base for research than most academics have been able to create. The continuity of such research is valuable, since it enables the observer to take an overview of the emerging trends in the Chinese business environment.

Once again in this collection of disparate papers there are commentaries by Chinese writers based in China. Useful as they are in offering some PRC perspectives, they tend, however, to approach the subject from the outside, using official statistics, policy statements, and conclusions about the macroeconomic situation. The shortcomings of intercultural management in joint ventures (JVs) are by now quite familiar. Although Western academics have identified problems and analyzed solutions with their Chinese colleagues, such analysis has been from the Western academic base. There continues to be disappointingly little input from Chinese academic researchers within the PRC on the topic.

China-based research that goes further than overviews of the historical development of JVs and their impact on the PRC economy as reflected in statistics on output, tax revenue, exports, and employment is urgently required. For example, the Chinese view on management styles and cross-cultural problems within JVs, derived from detailed enquiry, engaging managers and indeed workers in discussions on their experiences, would be significant. Furthermore we note the complete absence, other than anecdotal evidence, of any Chinese material on the indirect impact, if any, of the JV on Chinese management and business practices.

One major area requiring attention is a study of the academic literature written in the Chinese language. Here there is a quarry of unknown size and content which can only be tackled by those with Chinese reading skills. Western management academics are not usually from sinologue backgrounds. Thus literature surveys of Chinese language publications would provide the world with a fresh perspective on the JV in China.

Another research topic connected with language is the problem of language itself within the management of joint ventures. Many writers on JVs have noted that the Chinese side may have enough English for practical business affairs, but not enough for full exchanges with foreign managers or full participation in overseas meetings. In contrast, the foreign side is very unlikely to have sufficient Chinese to conduct even limited business conversations. Is the linguistic barrier causing serious trouble? What can and should be done to overcome the barrier: does language matter and, if so, what prophylactic action needs to be taken to improve English language skills among Chinese managers, and to provide Chinese language skills for foreign managers? This is a major human resource question, seldom addressed even in the most general terms; there is no easy answer but it would be useful at least to know the extent to which the language barrier is adversely affecting the work of JVs.

The present collection of papers mentions changes in the Chinese tax environment and here we have a field where little seems to have been published. Is it true that the removal of tax concessions will have no significant impact on foreign investors, since their central objective is not minimizing costs but penetrating the Chinese market? This is the assumption clearly of the Chinese policymakers, but the reactions of foreign investors do not seem to have been recorded.

Little work has been included in this volume based on what might be called a Marxist approach. There are great possibilities for studies on such topics as whether we are seeing the evolution of a "labor aristocracy" and, if so, what form can it take without the traditional underpinnings of a predominantly nonconformist Christian culture and view of self-improvement? To what extent is it possible to separate a reaction to the foreign from a reaction to the capitalist in contemporary Chinese thinking about labor law and issues and how are modern enterprises like JVs perceived in the broader form of Chinese art and literature? To what extent is the language of human rights, gender, or objective morality, applicable to workers' protests against foreign influenced enterprises? Even more challenging might be an attempt to discover to what extent the Cultural Revolution actually suppressed the influence of earlier Chinese management techniques and created the vacuum now being to some degree filled by foreign methods.

Sino-foreign joint ventures continue to present socioeconomic and legal problems for management theorists and practitioners. This volume provides the framework to put problems into the wider context and emphasizes the essential fluidity of the terms of reference for management.

BIOGRAPHICAL SKETCHES OF THE CONTRIBUTORS

Ingmar Bjorkman is an Associate Professor at the Swedish School of Economics, Helsinki. He has been a Visiting Professor at the School of Business, University of Hong Kong. His current research is in the operations of Western companies in China and international human resource management.

Erik Joost de Bruijn is a Professor in the Technology and Development Group of the University of Twente's School of Management Studies, the Netherlands. He holds a M.Sc. in industrial engineering and operations research, and a Ph.D. in engineering, and has worked as a project coordinator in developing countries.

Anne Carver is an Associate Professor in the Faculty of Law at the University of Hong Kong. She graduated from the University of Cambridge and has practiced as a solicitor in England, Africa, and Hong Kong.

Chen Lingzhu graduated from the Department of Electrical Engineering, Shanghai Jiaotong University. She has worked in the Institute of Aviation Technology of the Chinese Ministry of Aviation Industry and has been the Executive Director of the International Technology and Economy Institute since 1985. Her main areas of research are international technology and economic macro-strategy.

John Child is the Guinness Professor of Management Studies at the Judge Institute of Management Studies at the University of Cambridge. He is the author of *Management in China during the Age of Reform* (Cambridge University Press, 1994).

Yu-min Chou is currently a Professor of Finance and Business Economics at the University of Michigan at Dearborn. He obtained his B.A. in political science, M.A. in economics, and Ph.D. in economics from the University of Illinois at Urbana-Champaign. He has taught in Japan and given lectures in China on the industrialization strategies of the East and Southeast Asian countries. His research focus is on market force-driven economic integration and on international comparison of conglomeration of enterprises in China, Japan, and the United States.

Clement Chow is a University Lecturer in the Department of Marketing and International Business, Lingnan College, Hong Kong. He received his Ph.D. from the University of Western Ontario and has conducted research in a variety of areas including pricing issues, productivity, and efficiency issues in Chinese industries, foreign direct investment, small business, and entrepreneurship in China.

Liping Deng is an Assistant Professor in the Department of Economics, Mount Allison University, Canada. He is also a Professor in the Department of International Economics, Xiamen University, China. He received his Ph.D. from Dalhousie University, Canada. He has authored (or co-authored) five books on economics and management and a number of papers on the Chinese economy.

Michael Fung is an Associate Professor of Managerial Economics in the Faculty of Business Administration, Chinese University of Hong Kong. He received his Ph.D. from the University of Western Ontario and his research interests focus on international trade, foreign investment, productivity, industrial reforms, small business, and entrepreneurship in China.

Judith Hollows gained both her M.Phil. and Ph.D. degrees from the University of Hong Kong. Her master's dissertation investigated the Japanese influence on the Shanghainese cotton spinning industry, and her doctoral thesis examined the development of cotton spinning firms in Hong Kong, Japan, and South Korea. She is currently an Assistant Professor in the Department of Management at the Hong Kong Polytechnic University.

Xianfeng Jia is currently a researcher in the School of Management Studies, University of Twente. He has an M.B.A. and Ph.D. in business management, and is a director of the China-Europe Trade Investment Consultancy in the Netherlands.

Ina Konterman is a researcher in the Technology and Development Group of the University of Twente's School of Management Studies. She holds an M.B.A.

Orlan Lee teaches business and capital markets law in the School of Business and Management of the Hong Kong University of Science and Technology. He gained his Ph.D. from the University of Freiburg (Germany), and holds law degrees from the University of Pennsylvania and the University of Virginia. He has published variously on the comparative development of legal and political institutions, and on topics in international and financial law.

Elizabeth Li worked for more than 10 years in industry before becoming a management consultant and is also a part-time Lecturer in International Business and Strategic Management in the School of Business at the University of Hong Kong. She has an M.S. in organization development from Pepperdine University. Her work focuses on the absorption of Western concepts within the PRC, where she has traveled regularly for many years.

Peter Ping Li is an Assistant Professor of Management at California State University at Stanislaus. He received his Ph.D. in International Business from George Washington University. His research interests lie in the area of the comparative study of strategic management of multinational enterprises, particularly the contrast in managerial culture between the West and the East. Current research projects include a conceptual study on organizational form, especially network organization from the Asian perspective, an empirical study on American, Japanese, and Chinese types of network organization, and two empirical studies on strategic style of American and Japanese multinationals in Taiwan and Singapore.

Lin Danming is a Lecturer in the Department of Economics at Shantou University, Guangdong, PRC. He received his Ph.D. from the Department of Management Studies at the University of Hong Kong. His research interests include the management of Sino-foreign joint ventures and the overseas operations of mainland Chinese firms.

Niklas Lindholm is a Doctoral Candidate at the Swedish School of Economics and Business Administration (SSEBA) in Helsinki, Finland. He is a co-founder of the Institute for Corporate Competence Development associated with SSEBA. His doctoral research deals with learning and change processes in international joint ventures in China. He has been doing research and consulting in a European multinational's joint venture operations in Beijing since 1995.

Yuan Lu is currently a Visiting Lecturer in the Department of Management Studies at the Chinese University of Hong Kong. Prior to going to Hong Kong, he was the Rothmans Research Fellow in International Management at the Judge Institute of Management Studies, University of Cambridge. He is the author of *Management Decision Making in Chinese Enterprises* (Macmillan, 1996).

Ng Sek-Hong graduated from the University of Hong Kong, and studied for his Ph.D. at the London School of Economics and Political Science. He is a Reader in the School of Business at the University of Hong Kong and has published extensively on industrial relations and labor law.

Sally Stewart is a Senior Lecturer in the School of Business at the University of Hong Kong. She holds her degrees from Oxford University and taught previously at the University of Malaya. She has been studying joint ventures in the PRC since 1982 and was the editor of Volume 4 of *Advances in Chinese Industrial Studies.*

C.S. Tseng is an Associate Professor in International Business in the Department of Business and Management, City University of Hong Kong. He has worked as a senior manager and general manager for multinational corporations in Singapore, Brunei, Hong Kong, and China. His main interest is in FDI in China and he is currently consultant to a number of Singaporean and European multinationals, and senior researcher on multinational corporations at Shanghai University of Economics and Finance.

Piet Vanden Abeele is Full Professor of Marketing and Chairman, Department of Applied Economic Sciences, Catholic University of Leuven, Belgium. Trained as an economist, a psychologist, and a statistician, Dr. Vanden Abeele is currently interested in problems of marketing strategy and of international marketing. He is an academic trustee of the Market Science Institute.

Yanni Yan is an ESCR Research Fellow at the Judge Institute of Management Studies, University of Cambridge. She is completing her Ph.D. at the University of Cambridge on ownership and control in international joint ventures.

Zhang Shiquan is a graduate of Capital Normal University where he also attained a masters degree in Economics. He is currently an Associate Researcher at the International Technology and Economy Institute, Beijing. His main area of research is world technology and economic relations.

Fan Zheng is Associate Professor and Chairman, Department of International Business Administration, Shanghai International Studies University. He holds an M.B.A. degree from the Management School, Shanghai Jiaotong University and is currently in Belgium as a Visiting Professor at the Catholic University of Leuven. His research interests are in cross-cultural management, European Union business, international business administration, and corporate image studies.

International Research in the Business Disciplines

Senior Editor: **Carl L. Swanson**, *Department of Management, University of North Texas*

Series Editors: **Abbass Alkhafaji,** *Department of Marketing and Management, Slippery Rock University* and **Mike H. Ryan,** *University of North Texas*

Volume 2, 1995, 235 pp. $73.25
ISBN 1-55938-622-3

CONTENTS: Introduction to Volume 2. PART I. REVISITING SOME RESEARCH MODELS. World Bank Compliance with Adelman Prescriptions Revisited: Has LDC Growth Been Improved?, *Conway L. Lackman and Eleanor M. Lackman.* Managerial Motivation: A Cross-Cultural Validation Study of Miner Sentence Completion Scale (MSCS), *Bahman Ebrahimia and Sandra A. Young.* PART II: ANALYZING SOME SELECTED MANAGERIAL BEHAVIORS. The Manager and His Personal Value Systems: An International Perspective, *Abdalla F. Hayajneh and Carl L. Swanson.* Effects of Time and Task Difficulty: A Study of Eastern European Managers, *Stephanie E. Newell, Dianna L. Stone, Rein Peterson, and Robert S. Goodman.* Time Management and Reporting Behaviors in Accounting Firms, *Mohammed E. Ibrahimia and Jeong B. Kim.* PART III: CONSUMERISM IN THE GLOBAL MARKETPLACE. U.S. Consumers' Willingness to Buy Foreign-Made Products: Country-of-Origin Attitude Changes from 1982 to 1990, *James R. Lumpkin, Charles Madden and Sheb L. True.* The Impact of Consumer Modernism on Mexican Consumers of Technologically Novel Durable Products, *Pavlos Michaels and Jose F. Medina.* PART IV: SOME MORE EXPLORATION OF JAPANESE BUSINESS PRACTICES. World Class Manufacturing Practices of Japanese Manufacturing Organizations in the U.S.: An Exploratory Empirical Study, *Jaideep G. Motwani.* Japanese Banks in America and American Banks in Japan: Their Performance and Problems, *Mrigen Bose.* PART V: ENLARGING THE EUROPEAN PERSPECTIVE. European Integration and the Potential of Banking in Greece, *Ioannis N. Kallianiotis.* Post-Cold War Eastern Europe: Marketing Strategy Implications, *Jamal Al-Khatib and Bruce Keillor.* PART VI: APPLYING MILITARY CONCEPTS TO CORPORATE STRATEGY. 'Blood and Guts" Strategy: Military and Corporate Strategic Theory, *Craig S. Galbraith, Curt Stiles and Oliver Galbraith, III.*

Also Available:
Volume 1 (1993) $73.25